THE BLOOD
OF ISRAEL

THE BLOOD OF ISRAEL

The Massacre of the Israeli Athletes The Olympics, 1972

by Serge Groussard

*Translated from the French
by Harold J. Salemson*

WILLIAM MORROW & COMPANY, INC., NEW YORK   1975

Originally published in French by Editions
Denöel under the title LA MEDAILLE
DE SANG copyright © 1973 by Editions
Denöel, Paris.

Printed in the United States of America.

1 2 3 4 5   79 78 77 76 75

Library of Congress Cataloging in Publication Data

Groussard, Serge (date)
  The blood of Israel.

  Translation of La médaille de sang.
  1. Olympic Games, Munich, 1972. 2. Athletes—
Israel. I. Title.
GV722 1972.G7613   796.4′8   74-28494
ISBN 0-688-02910-8

Book design by Helen Roberts

PLAN OF THE OLYMPIC VILLAGE

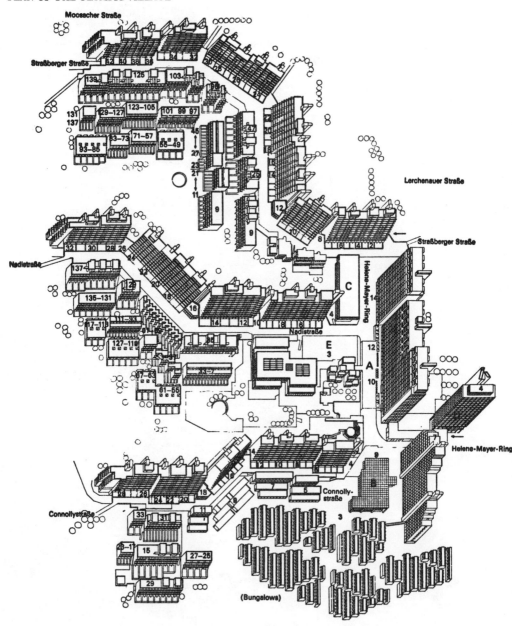

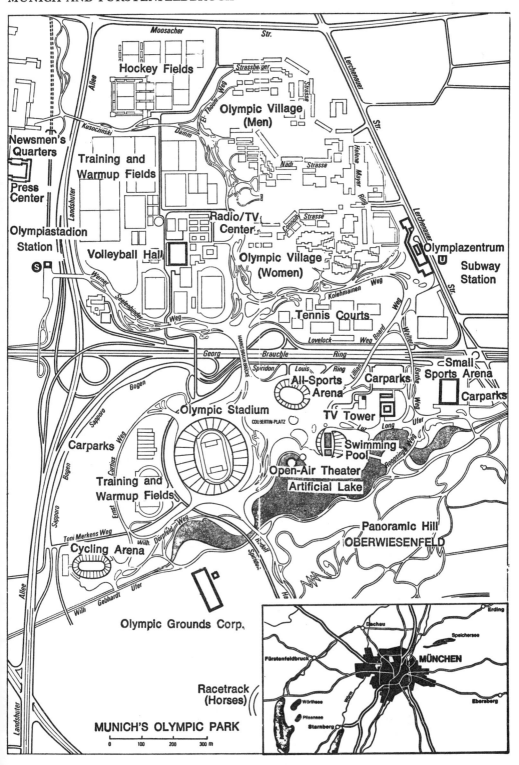

MUNICH'S OLYMPIC PARK

On pages 459–462 appears a Cast of Characters

Contents

Contents

Foreword

This is a true story: a horror, in the bright sun of the Olympics and the dark of night. But from end to end it is infused with nobility. I lived it as a witness, from the first negotiations in front of Building 31 on Connollystrasse to the final shots at the military air base of Fürstenfeldbruck, its few lights still clouded with the smoke of the crematory helicopter.

After that, I had to find out how it could have happened.

Step by step, I tried to re-create the story. This proved as fascinating as it was difficult, for the responsible authorities immediately threw up a wall around the events of September 5–6, 1972.

My stubbornness won out: Totally unexpected elements hove into view. Twenty-one fantastic hours took shape. The horrors and the courage, the mistakes and trickery—nothing herein but has been corroborated by facts, trustworthy statements, and personal investigation.

We were in Munich because of the Games of the XXth Olympiad. That great fiesta of world athletic youth was a colossal success. And by the same token an ideal springboard for an attack by Black September.

Why the bloodshed? In the course of the tale, the Palestinian question, we hope, will find its place within a new and proper perspective.

Yet—how to know that, in Germany, at the start of a radiant day in the Olympic Village, there would once more be the blood of Israel? . . .

THE BLOOD
OF ISRAEL

I
SAKANAH!

One calleth me out of Seir:
'Watchman, what of the night?
Watchman, what of the night?'
The watchman said:
'The morning cometh, and also the night—'
Isaiah 21:11,12

4:00 AM, SEPTEMBER 5, 1972: DAWN WAS NEAR. THE ELEVENTH DAY of the The Games of Joy promised to be a fine one. A telephone lineman and a mailman were walking along Kusoczinskidamm, beside the wire fence, two meters high, enclosing Olympic Village.

They suddenly stopped and nudged each other: four young men, outside the fence, were throwing into the Village heavy sports bags and some long things wrapped in canvas. They were as careful about it as old men. On the other side, two of their friends were catching the packages they threw. All were dressed in a variety of sweat suits, of different colors.

The two Bavarian civil servants have refused to be identified. I've read the postman's deposition. He was walking his friend back a short way before going to the *Sonderpostamt* (Temporary P.O.), in the Village Plaza, near the Recreation Center. He said the outfits the six men wore belonged to several Moslem nations taking part in the Games. Their shirts had the names of at least three countries, in two languages: Arabic, and English or French. *Liban, Libya, Saudi Arabia* . . . But nothing would be easier than to get hold of outfits like that. At Munich, as at any big sports meet, barter and swapping were S.O.P.

"Look at them!" the phone man said. "Their events may not even be over yet, and they're painting the town already."

"Funny, those big sacks they're bringing back. I wonder what's in them."

"Things they bought. I don't know. Maybe fishpoles!"

The boys who had tossed the bags over saw the two men walking up in the large-pocketed mouse-gray outfits of Organizing Committee technicians. One of the nightlifers waved and smiled knowingly to the two who had stopped about ten meters away, near a plane tree. Then they started to shinny over the fence: child's play, as I myself checked out. There is easy footing in the spaces of the wire netting. The top of the fence had little rounded cones; no barbed wire: that would have gone against the smiling, brotherly spirit of the Games.

The two Bavarians were not surprised that these fellows had not used Gate 25A, nearby. It closed at midnight, and was padlocked; the sentry box beside it was empty. Every night, hundreds of athletes jumped the fence this way to get back in after hours.

"Those long narrow things must be guns," the postman said, as they walked on, the boys now quietly inside the Olympic sanctuary.

"Could be. The rifle events are over. They're turning in the equipment."

The two workers had seen too much since the beginning of the Games to be surprised at anything. Anyway, these young athletes from around the world were nice, colorful people, and they had created a happy, brotherly atmosphere, without regard to race, color, or creed.

The Israelis were billeted at 31 Connollystrasse. The street was named after an American, James B. Connolly, gold-medal winner in the running hop, step, and jump, with 45 feet in 1896, at the Athens Olympics, first of the modern Games, then silver medalist at St. Louis in 1904.

The building stands three stories, with a little penthouse at each end of the roof.

It was about 50 meters from where the nightwalkers had jumped the fence to the Israeli quarters. No more, despite some official estimates given later. And no less—whatever the more sensational reports may have claimed.

Block 31, as the Germans called it, had the same standardized lines and functional perfection as the rest of the Village. It was an oblong building painted in bright colors, largely white, sky-blue, and orange. The balconies climbing obliquely across its facade faced due south. For the duration of the Games, such buildings were called the bungalows.

Once inside the Village, the six figures crouched at the foot of a grassy knoll, between the fence and the last house on Connollystrasse, 33. Or that at least is the most widely accepted official version.

They took off their sweat suits (never seen again), and put on the outfits 900,000,000 televiewers would see. They adopted a variety of disguises, including masks, skin coloration, and clever makeup. They took some of the weapons out of the bags, checked them, and got up again.

Connollystrasse was a broad pedestrian mall, like all the Village streets; at the place where 31 was, it had a sharp north-south slant, so the street had two levels. This was one of the three main streets that ran from the east end of the Village toward the west in all kinds of zigzags: all three were broken up into various separate branches. Alongside the main mall, there were the satellite byways or service roads, going off into the greenery before the buildings. So it often was a real puzzle to locate a building number on those offshoots.

At the end of the Games, the Village went back to being a Munich sleeping suburb: I am sure the people who live there have insisted that different names be given the sidepaths of those three main malls (Connolly, Nadi, and Strasseberger).

Wherever the six terrorists may actually have come from, after jumping the fence they split into two groups of three. The first went up main Connollystrasse, at the north facade, toward the front door of 31. The others took an offshoot around the south, or back of the building.

Block 31, at this point, contained twenty-four lodgings. . . . Except for two studio apartments, all the lodgings ran the full width of the building, with openings facing front and rear, or, in Olympic parlance, facing both Connollystrasse and the "garden side."

Eleven of the twenty-four apartments were duplexes, with a spiral staircase going up from the ground floor. They were one next to the other and numbered 1 to 11 along Connollystrasse, meaning that Apt. 1 was farthest from the fence.

Block 31 was occupied not only by Israel, but also by Uruguay and Hong Kong. The Israelis were in duplexes 1 to 6.

Uruguay, with ten athletes and thirteen officials, had duplexes 7 to 10, between the Israelis' and the fence; and they also occupied apartments 17 to 21, on the third floor.

Hong Kong had fourteen officials for only six contestants, and occupied apartments 12 to 16 on the third floor, upstairs of the Israeli duplexes. They also had the two penthouses.

The building had a concierge and a steward. The concierge did the usual janitorial tasks: maintenance, tidying up, mail, policing, and so on. The steward, an Olympic innovation, was in charge of amenities for the delegations, as well as general supervision of the building; thefts were to be avoided. It so happens that during the events in question the steward was simply not seen; but, since he was a student, we can hardly fault him for thinking it was all right to be asleep between 4:00 and 5:00 AM.

The steward and concierge were housed at the west end of the building, as far as possible from the Israelis and closest to the fence. The steward had the last third-floor apartment, studio 22; the concierge and his family had the last duplex, 11.

He is still working there; I met him, a very nice man. He says he was first to go to the Israelis' first three apartments when the attack took place, and gave some very interesting details on what happened. Thirtyish, stocky and tough, with mobile features and a small brown mustache; as far as I could see, he let his wife watch their two kids, for whom the wide mall, the tricky stairs and grassy knolls, and the luxury of the building, were heaven on earth.

When the terrorists came in from the fence at the end of Connollystrasse, they followed the numbers in decreasing order, 11, 10, 9, and so on.

In the ground floor of 8, the Uruguayan hammerthrower, Darwin Pineyrua, twenty-seven, 6 ft. 2, 220 lbs., could not sleep; he was on edge. At the end of the previous morning, he had appeared in the only event he came for, and he had been eliminated in the qualifying round. He sent his ball and chain out 59 meters 84, or 3 meters short of his own record. Had he made his best throw

4

(which rarely happens in these cases), he would have been 27th. So, no great tragedy, and his officials had not expected any miracle; he had been entered only as a reward for his fine national showing. These days, when sport like everything else is being buried in gigantism, he was 20-odd pounds too light to be internationally competitive, as the phrase goes.

Still the champ from Montevideo was disappointed, and he had just gone for a glass of water. Before going back to bed, he looked out the bay window on the garden side. In the gray dawn he saw three strange individuals on the quiet deserted path. They were built like Olympic athletes, but their faces were hidden behind scarves or hoods. The one at the head had on a white beach hat. The Uruguayan blinked: they were all armed, two with machine pistols, the last one with a rifle. Then he lost sight of them, as they headed toward the end of the building and the eastern part of the Village.

Pineyrua never thought of terrorists. The Village had a very youthful population: the masks and guns looked like some practical joke. He might, just for a second, have thought of robbers, because there had been lots of thefts: someone had broken into a TV demonstration and sales place, and made off with all the sets. That must have taken quite a few trips, with quite a few sacks— and these guys were carrying sacks. But, anyway, the Village had its own security service: that was their business. . . .

Some of the Germans said Pineyrua ought to have done something. But what? Even if he had wanted to? He would first have had to alert the mission head, who was asleep upstairs in Apt. 9 or 10. When he woke him, and got him to listen, maybe he would decide to phone the police, find the number in the little Olympic Directory, or ask the switchboard for it. Then a cop would come with a walkie-talkie, or less likely a foursome with the 7.62s carried by the night patrols. By the time they got there, it would take at least five minutes. Anything could happen by then.

What time did Pineyrua actually see the trio? That is one of those strange contradictions in which September 5–6, 1972, abounds. The two Munich employees say it was only 4:00 AM when they saw the six Arab "athletes" jumping the fence.

4:20 AM: This seems to be when Pineyrua saw them.

5

4:25 AM: They arrived outside Apt. 1.

One of the terrorists temporarily in custody after the Fürsten-feldbruck butchery insisted the six of them, out in the open from the fence to the Israelis, had moved with extreme caution and slowness. They thought they heard suspicious noises as they edged along the two faces of Block 31. Their two columns of three fedayeen each stopped, hiding in the flowered parterres, in the large tubs of sand.

Even though one of the best-informed of the Bavarian officials involved alleges the fedayeen lied continuously and outrageously during their interrogation, what if this statement were true?

Twenty-five minutes for getting on a war footing and crossing half-a-hundred yards seems quite a lot. Besides, changing as they did out in the open, and taking their weapons, why did they not worry about being seen?

What if they went inside somewhere—to accomplices on some Olympic team, billeted not too far from 31? That would make more sense, and explain the missing half hour or so.

There is a chart of team lodgings as an appendix, which may be consulted. The author points no fingers. Nothing (as we see it) proves any such complicity. Despite the very persistent rumors, we make no accusations. But . . .

Olympic Village was a super-modern, compact sleeping-city. Concrete and metal were molded into it like clay.

The women's section, off limits to males, was a series of narrow low buildings, rather ugly and looking like a bunch of livid warts. The men's section, on the other hand, was a frenzy of compacted color and variety. Proud buildings, suggestive of pyramids, stuck up from it. Some were twenty stories high; and between their solid masses, the smaller "intimate" bungalows.

Throughout the human beehives set deeply into cellars were many measured staircases.

Inside the Village, all roofless streets were pedestrian malls: but vehicles got about wondrously, along an impressive network of underground roads underpinning all of the busily shimmering surface of it.[1]

[1] Reminiscent, one might think, of Fritz Lang's *Metropolis*, filmed a half-century earlier. (Tr. Note)

Sakanah!

In this truly impressive Village, the concrete walls were so vari-colored that each street was alive with bright attractiveness. They were on variegated levels, with Japanese gardens and greenswards, play areas, pop sculptures and thousands of transplanted linden trees and silvery poplars.

Water was everywhere, in small cascades, fountains, and vari-colored pipes. The pavements of these yellow-brick roads included natural brick and stone as well as plastics, endlessly mixing up reds, blues, grays, and purples, with the yellows.

Up above, sometimes 10 meters up, sometimes 20, on occasion at ground level, water pipes displayed their splashes of exciting colors—colors so bright that, if you turned around, you felt you were somewhere else. Normally, pipes get hidden, but here they were featured, shining and daring even in the dark. There were all kinds: from fat sausages down to thin flutes, straight or twisted, some with branches that spouted jets of shimmeringly colored water.

What did the innards of these spectacular conduits hold? The big thick reinforced concrete ones, of course, carried cables: electrical, telephonic, telegraphic, with little brothers to service video-cassettes, and anything else you can imagine. But there was also piped music, to be heard mutedly on the Plaza, in the shops, and water, the technicolor water that was the living lacework of Olympic Park.

Israel's delegation officially had twenty-eight members: fifteen athletes and thirteen officials. Three were at Kiel for the yachting: competitors Yaïr Michaeli and Yitzhak Nir, with one official, Elie Friedlander. Two were women: Shlomit Nir, a swimmer (100- and 200-meter breaststroke), and Esther Shahamorov (100-meter hurdles). They, of course, were in the women's section—and chaperoned by a young lady with long dark hair who did not take part in the opening parade, and of whom I know nothing else.

Two members of the Hebrew group, and not the least, lived at the Sheraton Munich: Josef Inbar, President of the Olympic Committee of Israel (headquartered at 6 Ha'arbaa St., Tel Aviv), and Chaim Glovinsky, Secretary-General of that Committee. . . .

The other "registered" representatives—men, of course—were in

7

the *Olympisches Dorf Männer* (Men's Section of the Village). These twenty-one athletes and officials were in six apartments, numbered 1 to 6, in 31 Connollystrasse, as follows:

Apt. 1 (7 occupants):

Yossef Gutfreund	wrestling judge
Amitzur Shapira	track coach
Kehat Shorr	rifle coach
Tuvia Sokolovsky (called Sokolsky)	weight-lifting coach
Andrei Spitzer	fencing master
Yacov Springer	weight-lifting judge
Moshe Weinberger (called Weinberg)	wrestling coach

Apt. 2 (5 occupants):

Dan Alon	fencer
Henry Hershkowitz	rifle shot
Zelig Shtroch	rifle shot
Shaul Ladani	walker
Moshe Yehuda Weisenstein (called Weinstain)	fencer

Apt. 3 (6 occupants):

David Marc Berger	weight lifter
Zeev Friedman	weight lifter
Yossef Romano	weight lifter
Eliezer Halfin	wrestler
Mark Slavin	wrestler
Gad Tsobari	wrestler

Apt. 4 (2 occupants):

Dr. Mattityahu Kranz	medical officer
Dr. Kurt Weigel	medical officer

Apt. 5 (1 occupant):

Shmuel Lalkin	delegation head
Office and Meeting Room	

In Apt. 6, there was no name on the door, either before or after September 5.

Sakanah!

On the face of it, that should be that. We have accounted for the twenty-eight members, the number supplied August 26 and then September 8 by the Committee, and indicated in the computer that answered all questions concerning the Olympics.

Yet, during the opening parade, it had happened I counted the size of the Israeli delegation: and it included twenty-nine people, not twenty-eight.

Naturally, there were last-minute discrepancies between the official lists furnished and the number of people who arrived, at Munich as at any other such event. There were three other names on the so-called final official Israeli list, but they just plain disappeared: Zvi Finkelstein, Yitzhak Fouks, and Yitzhak Kaspi.

One more thing: there were officially twenty-one Israeli occupants at 31 Connollystrasse, but the day after the attack I went through those apartments. In four, there were the right numbers of beds, corresponding to the occupants listed. But duplex 5, supposed to be Lalkin's, had no bed in it at all; while 6, which had no occupants listed, held four beds. Perhaps Lalkin's had been moved in there (they were light camp-beds), but this still made a total of twenty-four beds, not twenty-one.

I have every reason to believe—and well-informed persons agree—that the Jerusalem delegation included at least two and perhaps three security men; that is a custom that is spreading everywhere. At Munich, each Arab delegation, bar none, had numerous bodyguards, to say nothing of the well-guarded larger nations.

The two or three Israeli security men certainly played no part on September 5. Perhaps they were in the building, and if they were must obviously have been billeted in Apt. 6, isolated at the end of the section reserved to their team, and thus automatically out of the action in case of an emergency.

But were they in, that dawn? They were guarding not only the twenty-eight team members, but also the Israeli notables who were at Munich, usually about twenty (politicians, musicians, artists, and so on). Theoretically the German police guarded all VIPs, but in practice that was not always the case.

Apt. 1 is rather isolated: it is at the east corner of the building, and for half its width it is separated from the other duplexes by the building lobby on the Connollystrasse side.

9

There are an elevator and cement stairway in the lobby. The elevator goes from the basement to the third floor, as do the stairs, although they also lead to one of the penthouses. So the Hong Kong Chinese and Uruguayans had to use the lobby constantly, and all three delegations most often went out through it to take their buses.

Apt. 1 is not entered from the street as are the other duplexes; its door opens on to the lobby, which in theory was not accessible to outsiders. An intercom, near the street door, let visitors phone the duplexes. At the other end of the building, near an exterior stairway that went up to the roof, there was another intercom for calling the third-floor tenants.

Actually, while each of the three delegations had two sets of keys, the outer lobby door was never locked. "That would really have made them squawk," as the Israeli newspaperman Amiel Slavik told me.

So, it was a fine meeting point for the aggressors.

Six of the seven occupants of Apt. 1 were sound asleep. On the ground floor, Moshe Weinberg's bed was empty, but all the others had come home together at about half past twelve.

They had been to the Deutsches Theater in Schwanthalerstrasse, to see *Anatevka,* the German version of *Fiddler on the Roof.* On Monday night, September 4, the whole team had been invited to the show by Shmuel Rodensky, who was Tevya, the pious milkman.

Apt. 1 was playfully referred to as "Big Wheels Inn." It was occupied by the five coaches and the two judge-referees whom their respective international federations had designated.

Yossef Gutfreund, the wrestling referee, slept on the ground floor: he weighed 275 lbs., and stood 6 ft. 2 plus. A tinkling, a noise of a key in a lock that didn't want to open, even when shaken, woke him up.

He got up immediately, without disturbing his roommate, the weight-lifting coach, Tuvia Sokolovsky. With his huge bulk, heavily padded from cheeks to calves, and his crushing packets of muscle, Gutfreund was more careful than others about not disturbing anyone else. He got to the door in silence.

His first idea must have been that this was Moshe Weinberg,

who had been given the second key, because this night he was to be the last one in. Moshe obviously couldn't get it open . . . The Village was brand-new, and its tenants had all the problems that first tenants in new buildings face. Several times, the men in Apt. 1 had had to call the concierge because the bolt, a little too wide, stuck in the lock.

Then Gutfreund heard voices. The key started to turn again. He must have guessed—but he never could have imagined the scope and preparation of the attack they were about to face.

There were eight men the other side of the brown wooden door. Two accomplices, come up out of the underground, had joined the six who had vaulted the fence.

For that underground was the hidden face of Olympic Village. Housing garages, cellars, avenues, galleries lined by rough pillars, many openings, huge gaping mouths toward the sky, it was the lungs of this new suburban neighborhood, created to take care of 12,000 inhabitants. It was more closely supervised than were the open-air areas. But the last two aggressors did not care, for they had all the requisite passes: they were quite legal denizens of the Village.

One—who will often be referred to by his *nom de guerre:* Tony —was a cook in the athletes' huge restaurant. The other, known to the guerrillas as Abu Halla, was a greenskeeper in the Park, often circulating in one of the electric carts.

The terrorists had a third worker inside the Village: their head-man. The two scouts who came up from underground had simply brought their weapons with them.

To get from the underground into a building, there is a metal door that opens on to the area facing the elevator and stairs. It also should have been locked—but it never was until the bloody dawn of September 5. Of course, if it had been, all the guerrillas would have had to do was place one more order with their Munich craftsman.

Big Tony was the one who handed their leader the copied key to Apt. 1. The locksmith had done a good job, unable to foresee that the bolt might stick. The cook, who had taken the impression of the lock himself, said, "I'm sure that key fits, Issa."

Issa was the name the other seven called their leader, as the

Israelis, the long day's negotiators, and the interpreter would discover time and again. Issa had the kind of cruel smile that does not go beyond the mouth. He was the one wearing the little white beach hat, set straight on his head, above his charcoal-darkened face. Big round glasses with very dark lenses hid his eyes. He was rather small, in a very soft blue-gray safari outfit, accentuating his slimness. He whispered, "Any more problem, we blow it out and charge."

Putting the key in once more, and giving his gun to his neighbor, he grasped it in both hands and twisted to the left, grunting with effort. The lug moved. The door was ajar.

At that point, Yossef Gutfreund caught on. As the door began to open, he saw guns in the shadows, heavy bulging bags, and masked faces. The unarmed Issa could now see the huge coach, with his hairy chest, his broad full face, and clear eyes.

"Don't shoot!" Issa hissed.

They knew the Israelis were spread through several apartments. One shot might alert them all. Besides, from the start, they had hoped to take the whole Israeli delegation alive, and thus appear to world opinion as warriors devoid of cruelty, in full control of the situation. They wanted to be able to say, "We shed no blood as long as possible. You made us kill."

An eight-headed battering ram, they hit the door, shoving with shoulders, arms, and guns. Gutfreund pushed back, with all his power, all his being. An amazing struggle, it lasted some twenty seconds. They slipped two rifles into the opening, as would be evidenced by the guns and the doorjambs. Gutfreund's 275 pounds of desperation crushed against the door that shivered like a living thing and would have to be replaced after the attack, because its hinges were twisted and it was full of dents and slits.

As his efforts began to wane, Gutfreund yelled as loud as he could, in his baritone voice: *"Terroristen! Hevreh, sakanah!"* (Terrorists! You guys, danger!)

His voice rolled up toward the second floor, and could not fail to reach the sleepers up there, despite their closed doors.

Were they really so sound asleep? Apparently. Yet, in Apt. 2, Shaul Ladani heard Gutfreund's shouted warning. And he was five times farther away. And two of the Hong Kong men, another

floor higher, heard in what they thought was some unclear nightmare:

"Harbiya! Terroristen! Haverim, lehu maher!" (Arabs! Terrorists! Comrades, get out fast!)

The attackers butted harder. Gutfreund still held the shaking
door. Just as his voice broke, the Israeli fell before a new assault.
The Arabs stumbled in over the referee's thick legs, amazed to
find that he alone had held out against them all.

They were now in the apartment's vestibule.

Before them, the kitchen, with its sliding door. To the left, the
deep vestibule, where a dining room later would be, between the
kitchen and the Connollystrasse wall, lighted at full length by a
large three-framed casement. (At this early stage the partition was
only half completed.)

Against the whitewashed outer wall at the east, a high metal-
framed bed, one of the thousands that, after the Games, would be
turned over to new public institutions in Munich. That was Moshe
Weinberger's bed. Briefly, the terrorists took it for Gutfreund's,
until they saw it had not been slept in.

To the right, the stairs to the upper floor, between kitchen and
garden-side bedroom from which Gutfreund had come. Its door
was ajar: Tony leapt silently to it, kicking it open.

Loud explosion of breaking glass.

That was Tuvia Sokolovsky, the stocky little weight-lifting coach,
with his mobile triangular face, great punster and good-natured
taskmaster to his charges, who adored him. When the first noise
of keys was heard, Tuvia was literally buried beneath a featherbed:
that was how he slept, to keep sounds out. His head was not visible,
just the featherbed rhythmically rising and falling. He dreamt a
lot. And this dawn he was still in Anatevka, though not consorting
with the milkman's five dark- or redheaded daughters. The staid
married man was busy dreaming of Tevya, his perpetually lame
mare, and the enchanting songs inspired by three thousand years
of brilliance and exile, exterminations and hopes.

Then the dream turned nightmare, as in the show: cossacks and
muzhiks broke in to the wedding of sweet Tzeitel and Motel the
tailor, knocked over and broke gifts, banquet tables, Tevya's and
Golda's furniture, beating and yelling all the while . . .

"Harbiya! Lehu maher!"

How that soft German eiderdown suddenly flew off!

A few hours later, I saw Sokolovsky, being interviewed by a crew from the *Deutsches Olympia Zentrum* (generally known as DOZ): this was the pool of the two West German TV networks for exclusive world coverage of all the events of the Games. But for hard news, not sports, the exclusive was off. So that, on that bloody Tuesday, September 5, all the telecasters present fought in merciless competition.

At 2:30 PM, DOZ's well-dressed interviewer would be talking to Sokolovsky as he came out of the Village's offices. Beneath his tan, the coach was frighteningly pale, like a patient coming out of a major operation, still anesthetized enough to feel no pain. Later in the evening, he would collapse, but for now, he was in good shape, despite his deeply circled eyes and wild look. He was surrounded by three plainclothesmen, who visibly would have preferred to have him locked away somewhere.

I had met Sokolovsky twice at the swimming pool, and had sat next to him: he speaks English. He was absolutely certain Mark Spitz would make good on his bet to get seven gold medals. That was his only sign of ethnic bias, and it entailed no antagonism toward Mark's opponents. Now I saw him again, and motioned to him.

I shouted in Hebrew (I have a few words of it): "Hi, Tuvia! Keep your chin up! Have hope!"

He responded with a tight smile, waving at me, and in a hoarse, hesitant voice, told his short, awful story of that 4:30 AM, as dawn was breaking in Munich:

"When I heard Gutfreund yell, it was like an electric shock. First I went to the door; Yossef had left it open. I took one step into the hall. I understood the warning; it was terrifyingly obvious. But there was nothing else I could do: I had to watch. Yes, there was light enough already, a dull light . . . In his underbriefs, Yossef's bull-like mass was holding back the door, and he was yelling, *'Lehu maher!'* His knees were bending—and then the door swung open, slowly. Gunbarrels and stocks flashed, and that face appeared in the opening, in its black mask . . . The man aimed a pistol at me, and I was no longer paralyzed. I did what Gutfreund was yelling:

14

Sakanah!

I ran into the room, and grabbed a chair. Our French window had been hard to open; the latch stuck. So I smashed the glass with the chair, and out I jumped. All I had on was pajama pants: that's how I sleep. I was barefooted. But I didn't even get a scratch from all that broken glass. I landed on a cement walk behind the building, among all the grass and flowers.

"When my foot hit the ground I heard the shots. All around! They must have come within a centimeter of me on all sides: I'll never know. I did a quick rollover and ended up on the grass. The shots kept coming. I turned right, toward the fence—where they had come in. I got to about the door of Number Eight or Number Nine, I can't remember. It was still Building Thirty-one, but these were the Uruguayans' quarters. I knocked on their window—like a crazy man. They didn't open. I didn't see a soul; maybe they never heard me. I thought: 'Those Arabs'll be coming after me. They'll shoot me down.' But they didn't. I was hidden by the jutting-out of the concrete pillar, and I guess they thought I was long gone. I crossed the path: that was where they could have got me. But I was running blindly, and ended up at the Koreans'. They're in Building Fifteen, right behind ours. The Koreans let me in right away."

They were South Koreans. The firing had awakened them. North Korea was represented at the Games, too, as the Democratic People's Republic of Korea. It was billeted at the other end of the Village, at 125 Strasseberger Strasse. Care had been taken to keep the two Koreas apart.

The offshoot of Connollystrasse that Sokolovsky crossed to get to the South Koreans was quiet and rustic: in the middle of the road great cement cubes filled with earth, huge flowerpots, full-grown bushes, cut it into two broad walks. And there were swings—for the children.

Maybe the bullets around Sokolovsky, who until that dawn had radiated life, were less numerous than he thought. But several bursts did come dangerously near him. At least four of the South Koreans heard them clearly. At first they wondered: Was it a joke? A night patrol chasing robbers? An attack on them? Or on someone else?

In a moment, their whole group was up, but there was nothing

15

to see down the green, flowered road past Blocks 31 and 15. All quiet.

Sokolovsky had shortened events as he told them. He had actually lain more than ten minutes flat in a flowerbed in the middle of the road.

4:40 AM was when he must have entered the Koreans', after a second single shot rang out on Connollystrasse. At this report, the people from the Land of Morning Calm were sure something terrible was going on, probably at the Israelis'. When the half-naked coach came to their door, like an apparition, the Koreans were all on a war footing, and Sokolovsky did not need to explain anything for them to open to him.

Did the Seoul officials phone the police? Apparently not. If they did, it was to no avail. They were sure the Village authorities had known immediately of what was taking place and gone into action. But Sokolovsky asked to use the phone. He got the switchboard rather promptly, but being extremely nervous, he had a hard time making that operator, and several others, understand him. When he finally did get through to the police, the officers (finally) were already aware of the situation.

What about neighboring delegations? Close by, facing the rear of Building 31, Mali was in Block 17, next door west of the Koreans' Building 15. On the other side of 15, 27–25 housed Trinidad, Ceylon, Cambodia, and a small part of the Canadian team. I talked to a lot of the athletes. Except for the Canadians, everyone slept very soundly that day: none heard anything, sensed anything. Half-a-dozen of the Canadians, on the other hand, were jolted awake by the first shots. They bolted to their windows, but seeing nothing but peaceful flowers went back to bed. Yet, in their east wing of the building, they were the ones farthest away from Block 31!

Back now to the eight fedayeen, who had just swarmed into Apt. 1. While two of them were shooting at Sokolovsky, a third was guarding Gutfreund, and a fourth watching the lobby. The four others were going up the spiral staircase. Issa was furious that the coach had gotten away. He figured that meant, logically, that in a few minutes the police would pounce on them.

There are two rooms upstairs in Apt. 1. In the first, on the

16

Sakanah!

Connollystrasse side, fencing master Andrei Spitzer and rifle coach Kehat Shorr were sleeping; on the garden side, in the other, weight-lifting referee Yacov Springer and track coach Amitzur Shapira. All four were collared just as they woke up. The terrorists caught— or rather, borrowed by West Germany—when the shooting was over, perhaps stopped lying for a moment when they said, of these four hostages, "They were all still in bed, their eyes puffed up with sleep. But they didn't even seem surprised."

Right. Gutfreund's desperate warnings must have merged in their sleep with the tragic events embedded in their lives, for even the *sabra* (native Israeli) Shapira and young Spitzer had a gut understanding of anti-Semitism. Pogroms. Rapine. Screams. *Sakanah, hevreh!*

And now, these killers in grotesque disguises, waving weapons as they burst into the room: *"Hände hoch!* Hands up!"

4:30 AM: It took a minute to get the four upstairs prisoners together in Shorr's and Spitzer's room. They were tied at wrists and ankles with ropes as thick as a finger, carried in in one of those bulky sacks. Gutfreund was immediately brought in to them, tied up like a mummy, from the shoulders down, arms tight against his torso, legs together. In reprisal! He was tied so tight that the autopsy doctors were to be struck by the cuts the ropes made, biting into his flesh.

Issa, the nasal-voiced leader, violently grabbed each of the four prisoners by the arm, and each one fell as he was yanked. Roughly, they were picked up. Issa and an accomplice then led, or rather dragged, each captive to the stair landing, between the bedrooms. He spoke to each in German, English, or Arabic, according to his preference, saying first: "None of your friends can hear you," and then asking where the rest of the Israeli delegation was housed. He offered instant freedom if the captive would guide the fedayeen there and, by identifying himself, get the doors opened for them.

Not one of them replied.

Each Israeli was beaten. "Slaps, nothing more," the Black Septembrists would later claim. But only for starters.

Issa did not even try to question Gutfreund.

The five prisoners from No. 1 were then soon together again

17

in the second-floor bedroom with the three-paned bay window facing Connollystrasse. Their ropes were bound tighter. They were gagged with rags found in a kitchen closet.

So the terrorists were not really sure where all the Israelis were lodged. For "pros" (as the Munich Police Commissioner, Dr. Manfred Schreiber, would call them), this was a poor showing, especially since three of them lived within the Village and had free access to virtually all of it.

Charts and lists giving detailed occupancy of every billet were everywhere. Each building had big panels in front of it, mounted on tripods, with white-on-blue lettering telling who was in which apartment, and the room numbers for mission heads, athletes, doctors, and so on. Small-time gangsters would have had no trouble making do with the kind of conditions these Arabs faced: weapons galore, unarmed opponents, no real surveillance to speak of, three scouts already inside the joint, an isolated building, near the fence, and their own number: eight men to do the job! To say nothing of inside accomplices, that seem inevitably to have existed . . .

Luis Wolfgang Friedmann, one of the Uruguayan officials, was beside himself that bloody Tuesday: he was sure the terrorists had had vast unreported support. Pacing the Plaza he reiterated: "Sure, I heard someone knocking at my bedroom window. My roommate didn't even wake up. The curtains were drawn. We didn't hear the first shots; after all, we had not been to the theater, and we get up very early. But when Sokolovsky knocked, yes, indeed! I thought it was some nightlifer. We've been awakened twenty times by passing pranksters, meaningless phone calls, and the like. So I went back to sleep. But a quarter of an hour later, about four forty-five, there was that *tiroteo* in which you could recognize the kind of weapons used: it would have wakened the dead . . ."

Later, on several occasions, Friedmann also reported this: "Yesterday morning, Monday, September 4, just before eight o'clock, I went into the room used by our service people. I usually prepare instructions for the athletes before anyone gets there. The personnel arrive after breakfast, about eight fifteen. But this time I found a young fellow in a sweat suit, obviously an Arab.

Seeing me, he was taken aback. I was, too. I asked him in English how he had gotten in. He answered in German: 'It was open. And—I know someone who lives around here. I don't know his name, but he gives me fruit—good fruit, the kind they distribbute to the athletes. But I don't get them, because I'm only a worker . . .' He seemed so shy, so nice. I went to one of the crates of apples and pears and gave him all the fruit he could handle. He couldn't thank me enough. And then, now, through the glasses looking at the balconies over there, and on TV, there he was. He's one of the Arab attackers. The tall stooped one. The one with the tropical hat and the yellow sweater. Yesterday, he was casing the place."

That was Issa's assistant, Tony, who liked to be called Guevara.

Inside No. 1, the attackers had organized under Issa's command. Three of the fedayeen—we'll call them by this Arab name, which means "fighters for the faith," since even Israelis use it on occasion, and it is both handy and colorful—were upstairs. Two of these were guarding the five hostages in the bedroom on the Connollystrasse side. The third was posted on the balcony of the room in which Springer and Shapira had been caught. . . . Issa quickly began his interrogation.

That left five other terrorists, one on sentry duty in the lobby, before the apartment door, and the four others temporarily staying with him. But then they split into two pairs, under Tony's direction.

The first pair looked carefully into Connollystrasse through the outer door that was ajar, then jumped out catlike. They ran to a hiding place behind the tripodded panel, on the sidewalk outside Apt. No. 6, listing the Israelis' quarters.

A little farther, two meters beyond the panel, during the Games, there was a sort of temporary low wall, made of bricks set in concrete, and daubed with Olympic colors to match the rest. . . . With one scout staying at the panel, the other went to kneel by that low wall. So the two men, backs to each other, had an eye on Connollystrasse in both directions, up to its curves. And at the same time they could cover their two accomplices while the latter tried to open the next door.

As soon as these two were set, the other pair, the last of the

19

eight fedayeen, went out. They walked single file toward Apt. No. 2, whose turquoise-blue door was four meters away.

All of them had spectacular weaponry, most of it quite clearly "Made in USSR," Kalachnikov AK-10 assault rifles, Tokarev 7.62 assault rifles, or Kalachnikov AK-47 submachine guns. There was also a very compact and excellent Czech automatic carbine, the SKS. And each carried a pistol besides. Tony had two grenades at his belt, and the others probably had some in their pockets.

A quick step was suddenly heard on the varicolored pavement of Connollystrasse.

II
WEINBERG'S BET

For they sow the wind, and
they shall reap the whirlwind . . .
                    Hosea 8:7

THAT WAS MOSHE WEINBERG. HE HAD BEEN TO SEE *Anatevka* WITH
the *haverim*. Then the star, his friend Shmuel Rodensky—that
barrel-voiced Tevya—had asked him out to supper with some
other Israelis. They had been to Schwabing, Munich's Mont-
parnasse, spending a lot of time at the Shalom, the currently
popular discothèque. Weinberg and Rodensky, hardiest of the
lot, had ended the night walking each other up and down Leo-
poldstrasse, Schwabing's main thoroughfare, bright and noisy
with its nightclubs, café terraces, and swarms of hippies.

With chest expanded, light of foot, well-built and solid, muscles
bulging à la Charles Atlas, Moshe was probably whistling softly
as usual. He too had jumped the metal fence, lithe as a big jungle
cat.

He was wearing the Israeli dress uniform, the same as in the
opening ceremonies: royal-blue jacket with the shield of Israel,
wine-colored tie on white shirt, and light beige trousers.

He was surely smiling his crescent smile, smiling at life, at the
good sleepless night he had just spent, the bit of sleep he would
snatch before going out to supervise the matches of "little" Mark
Slavin, his most gifted entrant, a real hope in Greco-Roman
wrestling, and perhaps also in freestyle.

Weinberg was walking on the opposite side of the street from
31, outside the pyramidal mastodon housing the huge delegation
of the German Democratic Republic, West Germany's tough

Communist neighbor. As he reached the level of Apt. 4 in Block 31, he hurried down the stairs and started to cross the double-leveled pavement. The two scouts were already at their posts, against the panel and the low wall.

They saw the Israeli coach as he drew even with the East German tower. It was easy for them to slide around so he could not see them. And the last two fedayeen, who were going toward Apt. 2, had also caught sight of Weinberg, when he swung right in his happy euphoria. They had just come out of the foyer of Apt. 1, so he had not noticed them. . . . But the four had no trouble in identifying him as an Israeli, from his uniform: he was their prey, not to be allowed to escape.

The pair near Apt. 2 veered about, showing him only their backs, and hiding their weapons on their chests under their folded arms. And they headed back toward No. 1, which, unbeknownst to them, was where he was headed, too.

The coach must have seen them just as, near a waterspout, he was stepping over a large tub of nasturtiums in the middle of Connollystrasse. And they must somehow have bothered him, for he suddenly slowed down. But not seeing that they were armed and that their faces were disguised, he continued on. They had rubbed the same makeup on the backs of their necks as they had on their faces and hands, so he must have taken them for a couple of black Africans out for a walk. Not necessarily athletes. They were rather dressed as tourists. Weinberg may have thought, as the Uruguayan had, that they were thieves. Anyway, he had an eye on them, so he'd be able to decide what to do, if they should turn on him.

He got to the sidewalk, in front of No. 4. Still watching them, he wondered now why one had such a dark hood that came down over his ears. But he went on. Taking it easy, he got up to No. 3. He was doubtless wondering at their own slow pace, their stance and twisted posture, as they went by the door to No. 1.

"Hands up!" the two hidden scouts shouted in English as they jumped out. Weinberg realized the scope of the trap, at the same time that he felt the muzzle of the machine pistol dig into his ribs. Without a sound, he swung around on one foot, sent the pistol flying by kneeing the forearm that held it, and got all his weight into a right jab to the fedayee's eye. Weinberg stooped, picked up the pistol, and vaulted over his spread-eagled opponent. His finger was already on the trigger. Visualizing the setup, he jumped sideways, probably seeking shelter behind a fountain or hydrant.

Weinberg had glimpsed the other terrorist, behind the one he hit. He aimed at him, while attempting his escape. Now he surely guessed the first two he had seen were not just standing by. In those four seconds, he had no choice: he yelled, or started to yell, "Help!"

Two meters away one of the fedayeen heading toward No. 2 aimed his Tokarev, with its removable stock and big ammunition wheel, at Weinberg, who was sideways to him, and looking away. The man fired.

Weinberg's yell was cut short. The bullet hit his cheek just over the right corner of the mouth, and came out at the jaw joint, missing teeth and bone but tearing out a big hunk of flesh. The Israeli had a gaping hole the size of a matchbox. Blood squirted from it.

Weinberg groaned hoarsely and stumbled, stunned. The three terrorists rushed at him, shoving their weapons into him. The one he had knocked out came to, and started to get up: little Abu Halla, moving with the slitheriness of a skinny cat. He worked as a gardener in the Village. Now, his right eye was puffed shut, the flesh above it opened, and blood oozed on to his face.

4:35 AM: This was right under the windows of the East German building. And there were people in 31 too. Did really no one —except the Jews—hear or see a thing? Not a soul look out a window? If they had, they would have seen three weirdly disguised characters, armed to the teeth, and a fourth getting painfully up, all belaboring a man who should have been plainly visible, from above: a huge stevedore type, in Israeli dress uniform, bleeding like a pig, as the gunbutts beat down on his neck and sides.

A shot. A deep groan. A wounded man. His attackers deploying a veritable arsenal. Right on Connollystrasse. And no one to witness it except the Israelis?

To the right (or west) of the East German tower, there is another big building, called 26–28. It is the last one on the street,

THE BLOOD OF ISRAEL

before the fence, so it is close enough to 31. The teams in the side of it closest to the Israelis were Libya, Togo, and Tunisia. None of them, they told me, noticed a thing. Yet, on the far side of 26–28, away from Block 31, many of the Argentinians were awakened by the shot; their officials were among the first to call the police.

On either side of Building 31, Zambia was in 33 toward the fence, and Bolivia in 11 on the Village side, but a good fifteen meters from the Israelis. Some of the Bolivians heard the shooting.

What about the East Germans? Their huge building was squarely opposite Israel's, dwarfing 31 by its size. Did they really observe nothing from this ideal vantage point?

On the afternoon of September 5, most of the Olympic athletes, of whatever persuasion, were heartsick at the turn of events. Two East Germans told all and sundry on the Plaza of the *Olympisches Dorf* (Olympic Village) that they had indeed seen one hell of a sight. Jarred out of their sleep, they had thought they heard automatic fire. So, even though it seemed unlikely, they got up and went out on their balcony, overlooking Connollystrasse. From there, as they told it, they watched all the bloody capture of Weinberg. When the gruesome thing was over, one of them dressed in haste to go and inform their track official. This man was hardly awake when his phone rang. The head of their delegation, Herr Manfred Ewald (actually Minister of Sports of the German Democratic Republic), was calling to convene an immediate meeting of all their officials: something serious was going on across at the Israelis'.

The amazing part was that the fedayeen apparently did not even take the precaution of trying to move Weinberg toward Apt. 1. They dragged him stumblingly by his jacket to the door of No. 2. . . . The street doors of these duplexes come in twos, so 2 and 3 are side by side, separated only by the partition between the two apartments, as are 4 and 5, 6 and 7, and so on.

(This should be in the past tense, for the apartment numbers in Block 31 have been changed: 2 and 3 now are 3 and 4.)

"Any Israelis in there?" one of the terrorists (anguished-looking Tony) demanded of Weinberg, as his pistol rubbed near the wound

24

that was now a mass of blood, beginning to coagulate, while red streams still flowed down on to his neck and clothes.

If all the evidence did not corroborate this question, we would not believe it had been asked: for all the fedayeen had been engineers, students, or technicians of good education. All had good fluency in English or German. And right over the door, in Hebrew as well as Roman lettering, the names of the five Israeli occupants were carefully printed. Even if the terrorists had some doubts, the panel would have told them Apt. 2 was occupied by the Jerusalem delegation.

So, that becomes one more mystery of the day . . .

The fedayeen never expected the Israelis to be so fatalistic in their approach to security, nor the Germans so much more flighty in their concern for it. The Arabs expected tricks, fake addresses, last-minute switches. They knew the Israelis were only one of three teams housed in 31. To seize non-Jewish athletes would have been the most frightful of boomerangs, especially if blood were spilled—always a danger where athletes were involved.

They were still shaken up by their invasion of Apt. 1 and their encounter with Weinberg. And leery. They did not want to spoil an operation that had gone so well so far. But still—for four people to walk about, guns in hand, with a gapingly wounded hostage, in the middle of the street at dawn, takes (at the least) a certain amount of nerve.

Moshe Weinberg answered with a shake of the head: No, no Israelis in there.

"Then who?"

"Uruguay."

Why did the wounded coach say that?

The ones in Apt. 2 were what the Israelis among themselves called "the quiet ones": two fencers, Weinstain and Alon, two riflemen, Hershkowitz and Shtroch, and the heel-and-toe artist, Ladani. Not a fighter among them! Not even a fencing foil for a weapon! Bare-handed, they would be helpless.

The terrorists believed him.

They grabbed him, and the tall fellow with the gray-green tropical hat and yellow sweater, who today was answering to the

25

name of Tony, Issa's second-in-command, decided on a precaution that would make the awful adventure seem even more unreal. He took out of his pocket a big checkered red-and-white scarf that he had planned to use later to change his disguise. Now he folded it, to gag Weinberg with. In doing so, he compressed the wound right under it. With the bottom of his face hidden, no one could tell that the Israeli coach, bloody or not, was not just masked like the others.

They were now in front of No. 3. Tony may have asked Weinberg again to tell by sign whether there were Israelis in there. We will never know.

At any rate, one of the fedayeen took out a ring of hooks and skeleton keys and went at the lock. They are supposed to have rung the bell: that is incorrect. It would have been stupid. They had other duplicates besides the key to Apt. 1. Whether or not they had one for Apt. 3, they had a fine assortment of passkeys and burglar tools.

4:40 AM, less a bit: The door to No. 3 opened after a minute, and the fedayeen did not seem the least impatient. They probably figured if they were caught and threatened, they could just point to their weapons stuck into Weinberg's body.

In the moments following the opening of that door the wrestling coach had the worst disappointment of his life, because he loved his boys so, and knew they could be counted on!

In No. 3, as in the other duplexes, there were three bedrooms: one downstairs, and two upstairs. On the main floor, the two weight lifters, Zeev Friedman and Yossef Romano, were asleep. Upstairs, on the street side, the wrestlers, Eliezer Halfin and Mark Slavin; and, garden side, David Marc Berger, weight lifter, and Gad Tsobari, wrestler.

Weinberg, at thirty-three, was an elder to them, even though he was only a couple of years older than Romano. The spread over the others was much greater. As a national coach, he was also one of the directors of the Wingate Institute, and as such had handled all of Israel's international competitors. So he knew these six and, from Romano to Tsobari, he could vouch for it: they were fighters.

At Athens, earlier in the year, he and five of the others (only Slavin was not along, not having gotten to the Promised Land yet) had been challenged one evening by a group twice their number, at a café-dance hall, in the Palaio Faliron, a pink seaside suburb. That time, too, it was because they were wearing the fine sky-blue-and-white Israeli emblem: the Menorah. These Arab sailors had come toward their table, picked up their mugs of wine, and flung the contents in their faces. Ten minutes later, the six Israelis, Weinberg at their head, had the whole room at bay. Half of the dozen Lebanese and Syrians were lying on the floor; the others had run out. And there was plenty of work for the Athens hospital emergency-rooms that night. What's more, the Israelis had been able to duck out just before the cops arrived.

The lock opened all too quickly and quietly.

The next day, September 6, coming back from the memorial ceremony at the *Olympiastadion,* Shmuel Lalkin, the head of the Israeli delegation, said: "They never could have gotten in without a key. Not into Apartment One or Apartment Three. They had to have complicity. Serious complicity!"

Scores of important people and newspapermen heard him say that, just as I did.

The fedayeen came into the vestibule in silence; Weinberg was helpless with his bloody gag.

They turned the knob of the door behind which Friedman and Romano slept dead to the world. The fedayeen went up to them and put the muzzle of a gun upon each of the weight lifters' throats. The black steel twisted silently, like a screw.

Everyone in No. 3 was asleep. Twice I heard the sole survivor among those six tell the horror of it, tripping over his words. First at noon that day, September 5, when hope was still in the air.

His name was Gad Tsobari (the *Ts,* I find, renders it better than the more common *Z*).

"I figured I was dead, once those guys had us," he said.

Tautened like a frightened animal, under the glare of the floodlights he blinked his big black eyes deep-purple-circled under their large lids. He was on the small side, as were many in the Israeli delegation. He only stood 5 ft. 4, slim, flexible, all shoulders and thighs, with a long open face. His nose was broad and lumpy, his chin prominent, making him look both determined and shy.

I saw him again the next evening, in the stupor of the epilogue.

By then he was already a new man, full of unanswered questions about the mystery of it all, about himself, almost ashamed to be alive. He answered me in a dreamy calm, reflecting an immeasurable sense of being overwhelmed. He was dressed in the Israeli dress uniform. Time was dragging, before the departure for home, in a mixture of impatience and fear at the idea of seeing his family again, hearing their questions, their judgments.

"I think I was dreaming about that wonderful musical show we had seen on Monday evening—the day before yesterday, if you can picture it. Only the day before yesterday . . ."

He was speaking in Hebrew, in his jerky delivery. His voice was rather deep, thoughtful and muted. My friend Amiel Slavik translated.

"It was *Anatevka*. We had gone there in a minibus, all piled in together. I was crushed between Gutfreund and Berger. Those two big lumps, and me between . . ."

Gad Tsobari roomed upstairs, with the weight lifter David Berger. By September 5, Tsobari's events were all finished. He had come in 12th in freestyle wrestling, 48 kg. (105.5 lbs.) category. He was a little bit of a sandy-colored thing.

A shot broke his dream off abruptly. He sat bolt upright on the hard-mattressed narrow bed. He was conscious at once, sure he was not mistaken. Instinct, subconscious came alert within a thousandth of a second of the shot sounding. Tsobari was under fire in the Six Days' War, and then fought the fedayeen on the West Bank. He was a sabra, his parents having come from Yemen.

He called to his roomie, "David, did you hear that?"

In Hebrew, naturally, addressing young Berger, the lawyer who had come from Cleveland's fancy Shaker Heights to be a full-fledged Israeli. Tsobari really liked him. From a well-to-do very middle-class family, "the American" was wholly unpretentious and tactful. Tsobari appreciated this, coming as he did from a very poor background, out of a large family, having to work at two jobs to subsist, a linotype-operator at night, a messenger afternoons.

Berger got up on one elbow. As usual, they had hastily closed the curtains, without bothering to shut them completely. The light of day was softly breaking in to the room. Tsobari saw his roomie rub his eyes, and ask, "What?"

Weinberg's Bet

That was when the loud knocking on the door came. Three or four quick, panicky knocks. Tsobari will never forgive himself for not knowing, or rather not understanding, that that moment's respite, that warning, had it been heeded, would have been enough. But even Berger, who perhaps should have been more alert to the danger, did not have the one and only salutary reaction.

Tsobari jumped out of bed, and into a pair of pants: he slept naked, it being a warm summer and German covers so thick. Berger sat at the edge of his bed, yawning. Tsobari opened the door.

In the hallway, outside the bathroom, stood a man with his back to their room. The other bedroom, facing Connollystrasse, housed the wrestlers Halfin and Slavin. Between it and Tsobari's, there were in turn a toilet, a bathroom, and the stair landing.

To the right of that unknown man was Eliezer Halfin. He was near the door Tsobari had just opened; so near, in fact, that the latter almost touched him. At the other end of the long corridor, the bedroom door was wide open: a dazed-looking Mark Slavin stood there, back a bit, one shoulder against the wall.

It took one second for Tsobari's eyes to perceive that Slavin had his hands up, and almost at the same moment that Halfin did too. He understood, but all he could feel was a pressure on his chest.

The stranger turned around at hearing the door open, and aimed his submachine gun at Tsobari. With his left hand, he indicated, "Hands up." The pocket wrestler obeyed, and then saw, in the doorway facing, the muzzle of an automatic carbine, and tanned hands tensed on the steel. The closest terrorist, with the end of his weapon, pushed Tsobari against the wall.

Tsobari's eyes met Halfin's. From the look on his face, Tsobari knew it was Halfin who had knocked: not with his fist, probably with his heel, while for one second the two attackers were distracted by other noises, for the fact is they did not open the door, but Tsobari did himself. They would have, no doubt, but only after a moment. The interval might have been time enough for the two Jewish athletes to open the window and jump off the balcony. In truth, Tsobari will never really be sure that it was Halfin; there was just that look between them. Anyway, it was all over now.

29

"Mark [Slavin] was still asleep, face dull, hair tousled. He only had briefs on, the same as Halfin. The Arab guarding us was watching me. He was the one who had pushed my cheekbone with his submachine gun. He was very tall, skinny, slouched over, you see? Neck forward. He had no mask on, no disguise, nothing. Really a big head. Bony, very long, wide, with kinky hair. He wore base makeup, making him look like a Red Indian. And a yellow jersey sweater, shiny black pants, tight-fitting, with bell bottoms. He was the leader. He made all the decisions. He rushed into our room. And saw David [Berger] . . ."

The young lawyer had had time to get up and go to the French window. He was looking at the fedayeen leader, saying nothing. Tsobari noticed that when the terrorist (Tony) arrived Berger's hand was on the French-window knob, as if he . . .

"David [Berger] was calm. Eyes hard. I knew him well. He raised his hands, but not all the way, not the way we did. The leader realized that. He put the muzzle of his gun to his throat, with a wave of the chin that seemed to say: I know what you're up to . . ."

Tsobari felt a light gunstock blow on his shoulder blade and saw an index finger wave under his nose, pointing to the stairs. A sharp voice said: *"Lumahtah!"* (Downstairs!)

"Yes, it was their leader, talking Hebrew to us. Can you picture that? He was talking Hebrew!"

Tsobari went down: behind him, Slavin, Halfin, Berger, with the two terrorists bringing up the rear.

"I hurried; I felt like running. The stairs were in a spiral, and I knew they were both up at the top, last in line, so they wouldn't even have been able to shoot. And then I saw the third Arab. Yes, that's right! I think they were all Arabs. This one was standing with his legs spread, at the foot of the steps, covering me with his Kalachnikov. Get the picture?"

Poor little Gad Tsobari, caught in a cataclysm that befell him on the most beautiful days of his life. He will probably keep asking himself questions about those nameless minutes till the day he dies.

"I took one step, my hands up on my head. And then another shock to the heart. There were Zeev Friedman and Yossef Romano, both half naked, arms raised like candelabra. To be expected. We were trapped like rats, all six of us. But then, what did I see next to them? And in what shape? Moshe Weinberg! All dressed, in our fine dress uniform, you see? Wine-colored tie, impeccable creased slacks, high shine on his moccasins, the way he liked them. He had his right forearm up, like the others, but with the left he was wiping the blood, because he was all bloody: it started under his right cheekbone and ran down his cheeks, his lips, his mouth, running over the jaws on to his neck, on the fine blue jacket, the slacks. He was stronger than any of us, Moshe Weinberg, a real hulk of a guy. And the blood was running just as strong as he was."

They had apparently taken Weinberg's gag off. Indeed, it no longer served any purpose.

"He had put some kind of scarf around the lower part of his face, and it was soaked. He held it with his left hand, and you could see the blood running on to his fingers. Why was he there? Why had they wounded him? I went near him. As far as the Arabs were concerned, as long as we were all together, with our hands up, it made no difference. I whispered, 'Moshe, what happened?' He answered, 'A bullet. They shot at me.' Then the leader gave him a sharp blow on the side, with the back of his gun. Another Arab hit me, too, but not so hard. Just as a warning. And the leader said, 'Silence! Understand?' still in Hebrew. He had an Arab accent, but spoke real fluently. With a kind of involuntary hiss to his words. Like a cobra."

It was almost three-quarters of an hour since the guerrilla terrorists had started work in the Village: they had taken twelve hostages and two apartments. While Tony, at this early point, looked fully self-confident, the other two who had gone into Apt. 3 with him looked just as unsure of themselves and nervous. They jumped at the least noise. They expected police reaction at the first shots fired.

Neither of them was masked, nor was their leader. Both wore long-sleeved black shirts. The smaller one, slight and strangely blond, started to threaten Weinberg by putting the muzzle of his rifle to his forehead because the coach kept wiping his wound. That little blond was a real Palestinian Moslem, from Jerusalem. His name on his fake papers was Abdullah Mohamed Talifik, but his buddies called him Samir. As Weinberg continued to wipe his wound, Samir slapped him on the unhurt cheek. The coach let out a stifled groan.

The other black-shirted fedayee got after Berger, who had dropped one of his arms, and started to shake him. Tony spit three or four Arabic words to the two men, in a tone that sounded like a whiplash. Then he turned to Berger. As Tsobari told it: "That Arab was half-smiling, and it was easy to see he meant, 'I got the best of you guys, but you won't get me.' All six of us from Apartment Three were barefooted, except Romano. He had bedroom slippers on; he never liked to walk around barefoot indoors. I had pants on. The other five had only briefs. Some probably put them on after the Arabs got there, but Berger slept in his. Bright-colored shorts he had brought back from the States. The pair he had worn this night were all red. Poppy red. They shone in that vestibule. But we were all barechested. Standing there, at that hour, it wasn't so warm.

"The stories of executions of hostages, the butchery at the Lod Airport, the Kalachnikovs and grenades dangling from the terrorists' belts, the sneering look of their leader painted like a Redskin were all swimming in my head, and beside me was Weinberg breathing hard, regularly but hard, understand? The way we wrestlers do between rounds. I kept telling myself: This is it, it's all over. But I didn't really believe it."

The ten of them—seven Hebrews and three Arabs—stayed that way for about five minutes on the ground floor of Apt. 3. Tony sent a man upstairs, probably to make sure there was no one in hiding there. Furniture was moved around, doors slammed. The same inspection was taking place downstairs. One of the fedayeen went and opened the Connollystrasse door slightly, carefully, then closed it again.

"Weinberg's eyes met mine. I could read a smile through the smear of his blood; there was light in his eyes. I did not hear him groan, or sigh, or anything. What dignity! He cleaned his wound, rolled the scarf up and squeezed it. The blood ran out on the floor. He managed to unfold the scarf with one hand (because the other had to stay up above his head) and put the scarf back. I could tell there was a big piece of his right cheek torn away. But it was hard to see, because I was on his left, see?

"Suddenly, the big skinny leader walked right up to him and demanded to know: 'Where are the other Israelis? Where is the head of your delegation?' in English and Hebrew. Not that he could speak both of them well, but he could make out. Moshe looked him right in the eye, with amazing strength and pride. We held our breaths as we watched. The leader curled his lip. He had buck teeth. He half-smiled again. He waited. Moshe went right on wiping up the blood, squeezing the rag, without turning his head. Then the chief walked away toward the garden.

"David [Berger] jumped at the chance. He said, in Hebrew of course, in a whisper, but he had a deep voice: '*Hevreh,* they're out to take the whole Israeli team. Let's jump them! We've got nothing to lose. We're lost anyway.' He said it real fast. By the time the two young blackshirts could start to complain because they were vaguely aware he was talking, the leader swung around, and lunged at Berger on his long legs. Holding his Kalachnikov by the barrel, he hit David a solid pistolwhip on the head. Then he ordered me to move. I was between David and Moshe, can you see?"

Since being captured the occupants of Apt. 3 had heard nothing from the outside. Nor had any of them heard the shooting which punctuated Tuvia Sokolovsky's escape from No. 1, before the Arabs broke in to No. 3. Apart from that firing, there had also been the single shot fired at Weinberg, and the shouts, the unforgettable calls from Yossef Gutfreund, in his titanic struggle.

Between the shots fired at Sokolovsky and the time the six prisoners from Apt. 3 were taken outside, a quarter of an hour went by. Absolutely no one interfered with the terrorists. The police were not on the scene: they would not become aware of anything for another twenty minutes. Where could the night patrols of Olympic Village have been patrolling? How could it be that no one at all around the Israelis, in Block 31 itself or the neighboring buildings, noticed anything at all?

All that deafness, all that blindness seem to form a terrible congeries of circumstances, compounded perhaps by the fear and selfishness of our times. No one wants to get involved.

33

To get Tsobari away from Berger, the leader had had him cross in front of Weinberg. The fedayeen made the hostages turn toward the south, that is toward the garden, and lined them up in that direction. Tsobari noticed the French window was wide open: outside, the dawn was white and pink. All seven Israelis in the corridor were taking it in.

Tsobari could now see he was the closest of the captives to the window. The leader came abreast of him and with a wave of his arm ordered them all out. A blackshirt was alongside the lino-typist; Tony, the leader, was halfway down the line; the blond Samir guarded the rear.

They marched out through the French window, the fedayee alongside him touched Tsobari's shoulder with his weapon to get him to veer left, and now the seven of them were out in the open. The side street of Connollystrasse before them was much quieter than the main stem, and narrower. Before the buildings on it, there were grassy plots that did seem like gardens with their seasonal flowers that ran out from the bay windows. Facing, there was no tower building, as there was on the main avenue, but a building not unlike Block 31: South Korea, as we know, was housed there, and Sokolovsky had already found a haven in it.

But the seven Jewish hostages had no idea where they were going. Only Weinberg perhaps suspected it was simply and ter-ribly the rear of Apt. 1.

4:45 AM: All the duplex apartments of Block 31 had several steps outside their French windows, on the south, by which you went down to a walk that ran along grassy rectangles with bushes and flowers. The cement walks were at the base of the second floor. The path between these miniature gardens led to the off-shoot of Connollystrasse.

The entire distance between the French windows of Apts. 3 and 1, shaped like a Greek letter pi (π), was 25 meters at the out-side. That does not give much room for escape.

"It was very bright out, a blue morning like back home," Tso-bari went on. "I looked over at the Koreans' windows: no one there. Were they asleep? All you could hear was the sparrows chirping. I thought: Somebody has just *got* to see us. The Ko-

34

reans, the Canadians who were close by, the street cleaners, a guard, somebody . . .

"Picture it: the three Arabs covering us with their submachine guns and rifles, the grenades bulging on them, Moshe Weinberg with his cheek torn away, his blood gushing out, the shiny soaked scarf—and us with our hands on our heads, barefooted, barechested, me in pants, the others in their tiny black or white shorts, Berger in his red briefs. I thought if anybody saw this even at a distance, he'd get the idea, wouldn't he? I walked slow. The blackshirt next to me urged me along with 'Go! Go!' in English. I pretended not to understand. I had no special plan at the time. I guess deep inside me I felt the one chance there would be was right then and there. But it never became a real thought, you understand?

"We were passing Apartment Two, where the fencers and shooters stayed. We reached the tip of one of those cement projections that separate the gardens from each other.

"Just then I bumped into someone. Oh, I barely touched him. I hadn't seen him because my eyes were on the Koreans' windows. My shoulder bumped him; I turned my head: it was an Arab, the fourth one. He had a hood, or some kind of sack, on his head, covering everything except for the two eyeholes. It was blue, a blue mask, with those black, wet eyes in it, bloodshot in the whites. I noticed it clearly because I was so surprised to see him. I stopped. He didn't say anything. His big eyes just looked into mine. Behind me, Moshe Weinberg—it had to be—was taken aback by my stopping. I felt him striking my back: one, two, three. Wasn't he telling me this was the time to bolt?

"The masked Arab had a Kalachnikov. He pointed it at Apartment One and moved it to show me the door, which in fact was a French window, like they all have on the south side. They can only be opened from the inside: it was open, so I understood they meant to lock us in there, and that all the guys from Apartment One had been captured just as we had. Meanwhile, the young blackshirt who had been next to me since we left Number Three was getting jumpy, pushing my shoulder, and saying, 'Go! Go!'

"I took a step forward. And then I started to run. To be honest,

I hadn't thought about it. My body, my insides, just exploded and took off. I remember: I jumped as if I were going over a hurdle and ran away. I was past the corner of the building. I wanted to go around it to get on to Connollystrasse, but I thought I saw someone. Maybe I did, maybe not. You understand? I had started running at most five meters from the corner of the building, and now I was just past that corner. It had taken half a second. Then I jumped to the right, coming back on the garden side, and took off as fast as I could, zigging and zagging, because they were shooting at me. I did not worry about their catching up to me. I couldn't think straight right then, but instinctively I felt they were too careful to show themselves out in the open.

"I heard the salvos. The bullets whistled all around me, and I ran as I never had before, hooking to the right, and to the left. How far? Maybe forty meters, when I came to a fence.[1] It was above my head, because I'm not very tall. But I scaled up and over it, I can't remember how. I landed on my knees on the other side, just in front of a Village Police sentry box. It was empty. I started to run again.

"There was an apartment open, I don't know where, somewhere farther on, in a white house. I went in, and I could smell coffee brewing. I yelled in English: 'Four Arabs want to kill Israelis!'

"The people there were police. Can you imagine, such luck? I was with the police. But it was a long, slow business, trying to make them understand!"

Hard as it is to imagine, Tsobari was later attacked in the Israeli press. "A few journalists," as he put it, wrote that he should have stayed with his comrades, and that he had shown a nasty streak of selfishness by leaving them. They claimed that in doing this he made the terrorists more vigilant . . . Poor Tsobari!

---

[1] The fence to the women's section of the Village; the terrain covered by Tsobari here, fortunately for him, was very uneven.

III
THE KNIVES

. . . say unto them:
Thus saith the Lord GOD: Behold,
I will open your graves, and
cause you to come up out of your graves,
O My people; and I will bring you
into the land of Israel.
Ezekiel 37:12

THIS WAS WHEN MOSHE WEINBERG, WHO HAD TURNED HIS BACK ON the wisdom of mortals, committed the most brilliant madness of his short happy life.

Tsobari was running in zigzags, with the three raging fedayeen shooting at him. Weinberg, now at the head of the line, threw himself at the young blackshirt nearest him, who was not shooting, because he was supposed to be guarding the six prisoners.

A tall, well-built and olive-colored fedayee, he called himself Ibrahim Messaud Badran (Badran to his friends). He was nineteen, the baby of the group. Weinberg's fist caught his lower jaw, splitting the skin on the left side, knocking out three teeth and fracturing the bone. Pictures taken when the massacre at Fürstenfeldbruck was over show Badran's lower cheek puffed up and swollen. He rolled down on the yellow pavement—knocked out.

Like the wrestler he was, Weinberg in normal shape would have grabbed the man, twisted his arm behind him, and used him as a shield. But he was terribly weakened: he had lost so much blood! And was still bleeding, his strength ebbing away, to say nothing of the pain he must have been suffering from that wounded jaw.

"Let's go, *haverim!*" (comrades!), yelled that fine colossus—for Moshe passionately loved life and felt no worry before death, the unknown.

In those few seconds, he knew he was sealing his sacrifice. Hav-

THE BLOOD OF ISRAEL

ing brought down the closest opponent, what other reasonable thing could he do? The three fedayeen (Tony, Samir, and the masked one) who were shooting at Tsobari would turn their fire on the wounded tiger who was counterattacking again and shouting rebellion. A fourth terrorist, watching from the upstairs balcony of Apt. 1, aimed at him, but Weinberg was not trying to be reasonable. He picked up Badran's rifle, and just had time to get erect before the strands of bullets started hitting: when Tony fired the last burst Weinberg's lungs were already punctured.

"Romano," Badran would say later, "kept looking every which way while we were moving them. He was limping, and seemed to be doing it on purpose."

Unfortunately, he was not limping deliberately. Otherwise . . .

At Munich, training too vigorously just before the middle-weight events, solid Yossef Romano had aggravated a ruptured knee disc that had been bothering him for a year. During the actual event, he had had to drop out after the clean-and-jerk. He sobbed over it for hours. Israel's athletes, necessarily, operate on minimum allowances and Romano, having exhausted his funds, was to leave Munich on the morning of September 6. Sokolovsky had made arrangements for his ward to have an emergency operation in Tel Aviv, and on the 7th Romano was due to go into the hospital to get cured of this bum knee.

Seven hostages had left No. 3, but only five were going into No. 1, through the window Sokolovsky had broken as he escaped. Only two fedayeen were with them. The third (Samir) was picking up Badran's fallen weapon and trying to revive his still-unconscious fellow-terrorist. All of this, right out in the open, on the path across from the big buildings facing them. How many people must have watched from the balconies and open windows, heard the bullets showering, and then just waited. . . .

Romano and Berger must have been heartbroken at not being able to heed Weinberg's call to fight. Just as they too were about to go at the terrorists, they saw them stop shooting at Tsobari and turn their guns back at them.

What the Arabs wanted was clear: to get all their hostages back together again. From this point on, they must have realized they could no longer go for the greatest possible number of Israelis. If

38

the ones they had had not resisted so, they would have had plenty of time to go through the rest of Block 31, and pick up some twenty-three or twenty-four Jews.

Six of the eight fedayeen were now together in Apt. 1. Only Badran was missing, with the one trying to shake him back to consciousness. As for Abu Halla (whose eye Weinberg had closed when he was first taken), he had come quietly around by way of Connollystrasse from Apt. 3 where he had stood guard till the captives were moved.

The Israelis were walking through the room in which Gutfreund and Sokolovsky had slept. Walking single file: Romano, followed by Berger, Halfin, Slavin, Friedman. Issa, come down from upstairs, motioned to them to watch out for broken glass with their bare feet. He didn't want them cut up for nothing.

At that point, Romano's limp got worse. He alone, as we know, had slippers on. He kicked them off and leapt up as if his stocky legs had been springs, despite his painful knee. Berger did likewise. They took off in the middle of the room.

Their aim, obviously, was to get into Connollystrasse. In three bounds, they were in the foyer of the apartment. Romano swept back the half-open door that led into the lobby, the very door that Gutfreund had made such a stand at. Three shots rang out. There was a fedayee guarding the other side of the door. The two Israelis turned back.

"Out the garden!" Romano yelled.

But at the threshold of the bedroom they had to go through stood Tony, who fired several shots. Berger was wounded in the left shoulder. Issa, who was at the foot of the stairway, hit him in the shins with his riflebutt. The lawyer fell.

"Don't kill him! Tie him up!" Issa ordered.

Halfin, Friedman, and Slavin, foreheads against the wall of the room from which their two comrades had sprung, had their hands behind their backs under the watchful eye of a terrorist. Samir ran in to reinforce him. Badran had finally come to: he also stumbled in.

Romano was turning in circles. There was only one other way out: the kitchen. There was a window in it, in the east wall of the building. Unfortunately, it was closed and hard to open because the new paint made the latch stick. Romano pushed the sliding door open, ran into the kitchen, grabbed the window knob and started to shake it hard. This room still had no partition up on its north side. One of the Arabs came in through there and shot at the weight lifter. How could he have missed him? There was another terrorist standing in the doorway. Romano slipped to the floor, grabbing a long kitchen knife off the sink on his way, and rushing at the man in the sliding door. The Arab let go a wild shot, as he dodged, missing by a hair being cut by the knife. But Romano was no sooner in the corridor than another shot was fired at him.

Yet, the miracle went on. The Israeli was not hit. He did not give up. Last hope: the upper floor, from which he might jump through a window.

How did the bullets all around him miss him? How did the terrorists ever let him get up those stairs?

There were three on guard up above.

Romano dashed first toward the bedroom on Connollystrasse. He had no way of knowing that in there he would find the five Israelis captured in Apt. 1: Shapira, Shorr, Spitzer, Springer, and the unforgettable Gutfreund. Tightly tied up, they were being guarded by two men who were alerted by the commotion. One of them had stepped into the doorway: he fired as soon as Romano appeared in the corridor.

The little weight lifter fell to the ground, against the bathroom partition. Missed again! He swung around and headed for the last chance: the bedroom with the balcony, facing the one the prisoners were in. Open the French window, or break through the glass if the knob sticks, and then jump . . .

The French window happened to be wide open—because one of the sentries was there. His name: Paulo. Later, in the hope of confusing matters, the surviving terrorist claimed his name was Saïd. That is not so.

Paulo was the one whose shot, just now, had been first to hit Weinberg after the wrestling coach knocked out Badran. Romano swung the door back, leapt into the room, and the terrorist who had come in from the balcony and was standing in the open window emptied part of his clip into the Israeli.

The Knives

This time, Romano was shot, probably already fatally. But he kept coming on toward the fedayee. Leaping like a jaguar, the kitchen knife upraised, he was in the air when a second burst went through his neck or chest: he fell to his knees, without dropping the knife.

Paulo was the most athletic of the Arabs. He was wearing a purple hood. Panting, he eyed the little bullet-riddled Jew. Romano succeeded in coming suddenly up and sinking his blade right between the fedayee's eyes, as the latter screamed. The steel went deep into the base of his nose. The wound would show up sharply in later pictures of him. Fear and pain stopped Paulo from firing any more. Romano, grunting with exhaustion and suffering, wrenched his knife free, and the Arab jumped back.

One of the men guarding the prisoners ran in. He sent an endless burst of automatic fire into Romano's back, swinging from one side to the other. So that later, at 11:00 PM that night, when the stretcher-bearers tried to pick Romano's body up to carry it away, it split in two at the waist, to their amazement.

The next day, September 6, I was able to go into Apt. 1 and see where the bullets had hit, the holes in the furniture, the singed mattresses, the intimate personal belongings ravaged by the terrorists.

In the bedroom where Yossef Romano fell, the walls were spattered with matter: some of the spots were sticky, yellow or gray. The weight lifter's innards had been splattered on to them under the mad point-blank fire. The ceiling was veined with blood spots, some of them very big. It was viscous blood, full of other matter, or else it would not have stayed stuck up there.

Now comes a confusing episode.

Weinberg was not yet dead, even though he had a dozen bullets in his body.

He still had the strength to get up from the ground, and instead of trying to crawl away from Apt. 1, he went toward it. He went in, bent in two, through the window Sokolovsky had smashed. Romano had just died, with his weapon still clutched in his hand.

The fedayee on duty in the doorway saw the terrifying colossus come in: a bloody mess, stumbling along. He called to his

41

leaders, but, paralyzed with horror, did not fire. Weinberg did not seem to notice him, but stumbled on, gushing blood as if he had not already lost so much, toward the kitchen. Issa uttered an order to tie him up: probably thinking that that way they could get a doctor to look at him.

But Weinberg moved too fast for them. He karate-chopped the fedayee who had grabbed his jacket, and got into the kitchen—as far as the sink. There were two knives on the counter, when Romano took his; now Weinberg took the other, so both served a purpose. Three fedayeen burst in, and rushed at the coach. He raised his long knife and struck. The one he was aiming at got away by swinging around, but not without getting a deep cut above the elbow: this happened to be Abu Halla, the one Weinberg had already done in before on Connollystrasse. The little fedayee with the long narrow face jumped back, pulled out his pistol, and furiously fired at Weinberg, blowing his skull off.

Weinberg collapsed, his head a pulp: that square head with the brilliant smile, set on the hefty neck, the T-squared shoulders, and the King Kong torso. Even in death, he was in the way of the terrorists: his body was a huge, gigantic ball in the doorway of the kitchen, with blood running out of it as if it would never stop.

4:50 AM, the clocks now read.

There had been Moshe Weinberg.

He was a sabra, a native Israeli, born in Haifa in 1939. He had graduated as a phys. ed. teacher, while becoming one of his country's popular champions. He had long held the national middleweight titles in both Greco-Roman and freestyle wrestling, and been brilliant in many international events. His finest accomplishment: the gold medal for freestyle wrestling at the 7th Maccabean Games in 1965 (the quadrennial Jewish Olympics).

An explosive force with a triumphant smile, Weinberg burst with the joy of living. He had often defied death. Some said he headed the secret security force of the Israel delegation. That is a myth. He had more than enough to do with his three boys, the wrestlers Eliezer Halfin, Mark Slavin, and Gad Tsobari. To say nothing of all the people he knew in Munich, for he was a man of many parts. His mother, widowed early and remarried, lived near Munich, and as soon as he could Weinberg would rush to see her: she was a very refined lady, with great class, tall and slender and elegantly attired. On the morning of September 6, a billion televiewers who saw her in black on the official stand could judge how the mother of a young murder victim controlled her sorrow.

There was one bit of truth supporting the lie about Moshe's position: when doing his military service, he had been in the special commando forces of Israel's Defense. He was too huge to act as a secret agent. But he had a gift for lightning attack, a feel for terrain, and the shrewdness of a beast of prey. What military operations he may have been involved in between 1959 and 1970 still remain secret; some were those heard around the world, the daring strikes that were so fabulously successful. The men under him attest that this fantastic scrapper who always hit his target unexpectedly never killed for the sake of killing, and never authorized the slightest cruelty.

He was a scuba adept, and trained frogmen. He was a promoter and organizer. He was not yet thirty when he was made national wrestling coach. Then he became one of the directors of the Orde Wingate Physical Culture Institute, Israel's national training center. It is a magnificent setup among the dunes near the sea north of Tel Aviv, in the Plain of Sharon. A few miles beyond, to the north, is Natanya, the finest of beach resorts and a mushrooming town.

British Captain Orde Wingate had nothing Jewish about him. In 1937 as an intelligence officer, he was sent to Palestine, under British mandate since 1922, and became incensed at London's anti-Zionist policy. The Moslem chief Fawzi el Kaukji was at the time attacking Jewish farm settlements with his armed gangs, and the British were obligingly "neutral." Orde Wingate, with the help of the Haganah (Hebrew word for "Defense": the underground Palestinian Jewish army that later became the Army of Israel), organized counterguerrilla groups. These were the "midnight commandos," in which Moshe Dayan, Yigal Allon, and others learned how to fight.

In 1944, the Allies finally agreed to set up a corps called the

43

Jewish Brigade, comprising a very limited number of the more than fifty thousand Jewish volunteers from Palestine (or planning to settle there) who were dispersed among the various anti-Nazi forces. Wingate's shock troops were the ones in this Brigade who became the famous "night wolves," darting into enemy territory for effective raids. Wingate himself, now a general, succeeded in putting Haile Selassie back on the throne of Ethiopia, set up the Chindits in Burma to war against the occupying Japanese, and was lost in a plane accident in 1944, only to live on in legend.

"They say we Israelis are chauvinists," Weinberg would say, "but tell me: Do you know of another country in which the great national sports center is named for a foreigner?"

Weinberg was fully happy among its white walls and young pines, its sands and hopes.

The French wrestler Daniel Robin, a former world's champion, two-time silver medalist at the Mexico City Olympics, had been to Tel Aviv at the beginning of August 1972, to test the Israeli wrestlers and see who ought to be sent to Munich. Moshe Weinberg, who had married for the third time at the beginning of the fall of 1971, invited the Grenoble wrestler to stay at his house. Miriam, the young Mrs. Weinberg, the very day after Robin got there, on August 3, gave birth to a boy, named Gur.

"Moshe was beside himself with joy," Robin told me. "He overflowed with vitality and kindness. But, during that evening, I noticed him with a faraway, almost sad, look. I wondered aloud whether anything was wrong, and he forced himself to laugh, and said, 'Nothing at all! It was just, you see, that I was wondering whether my son, Gur, one day, would get to know what peace is.' "

That was Moshe Weinberg, with his rolling laughter, his eager white teeth, warm velvety eyes, and the wartime feats that only a few might tell of, but which surrounded the dynamic coach with a kind of mysterious aura. Now, finally, his life ending, as it had been lived, like an arrow.

So, Moshe Weinberg had saved the lives of the occupants of Apt. 2. Temporarily, or not? The terrorists had taken No. 1 and No. 3. The uneasy peace that, as 5:00 AM approached, still bathed

The Knives

No. 2, caught between the two captures, was strange—and fraught with anxiety. With each passing instant, the danger increased.

For one of the five Israelis in No. 2, the wait at the gates of hell was over. He was Shaul Paul Ladani, doctor of laws, professor of economics at Tel Aviv, thirty-six, walker, champion of Israel.

I met him at least ten times during that day of September 5.

On September 3, he had taken part in the 50-kilometer walk and come in 19th out of 36; he had been shown in closeups on TV—not because of placing 19th (although there is nothing shameful in that), nor because of his style or looks. He is a short man, whose slightly bowed legs are inordinately stocky and ill-proportioned. His thick myopic glasses kept sliding down his nose. Half bald, he had shaved off the remainder of his hair. As his arms worked frenetically, his shoulders heaved, and his hips swiveled in the intensity of the heel-and-toe event, he looked as though he were in torture—which was absolutely not true.

No, Shaul Ladani was on TV because he had been born in Germany, at seven had been arrested with his parents and sent to the extermination camp of Bergen-Belsen. In 1945, a miracle happened: he was included in a batch of children and old people an American organization was able to ransom from the Third Reich for a fortune in cash. His whole family had perished. He himself had typhus. Born April 2, 1936, he was going on the age of nine.

He had escaped from Apt. 2 at about 4:30 AM, just after the terrorists broke into No. 1, while Gutfreund shouted the alarm.

"Everything took place so fast, that I acted instinctively, without a chance to think," he told me in a muffled even voice that was beyond pathos.

I could see his dark eyes, behind the imitation-shell glasses. They dwelt on mine, but did not see me. He is solidly built, his thighs seem to be of steel; on the top of his head, the sparse hair was growing back, graying.

"I was sleeping upstairs, on the garden side, alone," he said. "It had just worked out that way. Strange voices jolted me awake. I had the feeling someone had called me, from downstairs. I went down the stairs. The calls came again, from outside, somewhere close by. The whole place was totally, strangely silent. I did not

45

really know what it was, but it gave me the shivers. I went into the kitchen, because it seemed to me the shouts had come from the building lobby, which is alongside half our ground floor, from the kitchen to the wall on Connollystrasse.

"Then I heard Gutfreund's voice, dimmed, but so recognizable, *'Sakanah! Harbiya!'* I understood, I thought—well, I don't know what. I had the absurd feeling that everyone had run away, and I was left alone, and the Arabs were coming. I ran up to my room. I must have waited there a few seconds. I didn't dare move.

"And then the shots rang out. Ever since Bergen-Belsen, I recognize *them* right off. It was Sokolovsky running out through the back of the Block on what we call the 'garden path.' I was sure it was from the main floor of our own apartment that the shots were raining. I opened the French window, and went out on the balcony. I looked at the distance to the ground—five or six meters. I jumped. I skinned my knees pretty badly but didn't feel it at all. I got up and ran, and ran. Finally, I went into a building. Italians . . . Time to explain to them, and to call the police. The Germans had just heard about the attack. . . ."

He stopped, and cracked his knuckles. He answered my question forthrightly: "Did I think of the others? Sure. I felt terribly sorry to leave Gutfreund and the other guys, but it wouldn't have done them any good at all, for me to be just another hostage."

Doing what he did, Ladani brushed up against death. He appeared in the fedayeen's view just as they finished shooting at Sokolovsky, now out of their sight. They were too surprised to fire at this man who appeared from nowhere, in white undershirt and shorts, running barefoot with his glasses slipping down his nose. He got to the main part of Connollystrasse, by going around the Bolivians' building. After that, he went forward in leaps and bounds, hiding in between walls or hydrants. He reached the Italians' quarters (the tower called 8–12 Connollystrasse) at only about 4:45 AM.

4:30 AM: (But the flagbearer of the Israel delegation, Henry Hershkowitz, would never be sure of the time, nor would his roomie, Zelig Shtroch, upstairs in Apt. 2 of Block 31.)

"Did you hear?"

The Knives

"Yes, did you?"

No need to wonder what those two, three reports that woke them were; the age-old terror of Israel told them. Like falling out of a dream of liberty, back into nightmare, they leapt toward the window.

They were on the street side, across from Ladani's room. They leaned out, scrutinizing Connollystrasse first down toward the nearby fence, then the other way toward the turn in the street as it comes into Olympic Village. Nothing: deserted; silence.

"No question about it, those were shots," said Hershkowitz.

"Sure enough," his roommate said, shrugging.

They knew what they were talking about. They were the two amateur shooting champions of Israel. They did very well in their two events: small-bore rifle prone, and small-bore rifle three positions. Many felt Hershkowitz, at forty-five, was too old. Yet he finished 23rd out of 101 in prone, with a weapon that was out of date compared to those of his competitors, and 46th in the three positions, despite having his share of technical mishaps.

Shtroch, at twenty-six, represented a hope: he finished 57th, but learned a lot, that he aimed to use at Montreal, in the XXIst Olympic Games.

Hershkowitz smoothed his pirate's mustache. "Some Olympic Village! Every night, there's that kind of racket!"

About 1:00 AM on Sunday, September 3, the Israelis, more than others, had been disturbed by a hail of fire: a big group of shooting contestants had been celebrating the conclusion of their events. With breaks, the outburst lasted well over two minutes, accompanied by cheering and yelling. And at other times, there had been firecrackers, snake dances, guitar serenading, ignoring the cussing of those who had to compete the next day. They never lasted long—just long enough to break up a night's sleep.

So, they went back to bed. Shtroch fell asleep immediately. Not Hershkowitz.

"I was uncomfortable," he was to tell me. "A weight on my chest. I was impatient for the night to end. That firing just didn't seem normal. I know what war is. I thought: Funny, you're as tense as if there were some awful threat. If there were terrorists, you'd know it by now. I closed my eyes, but I had recognized that

47

machine-fire sound. It was more than strange. And it didn't seem so far away. I tried to reassure myself again, when—"

One of the other men in the apartment, the fencer Dan Alon, ran into the bedroom, shouting abruptly, "Has Shaul Ladani lost his marbles or what? He just suddenly disappeared, you should see how. Yehuda [Weinstain, also a fencer] and I heard some noise outside the window. I went to look, and Shaul was getting up. He had fallen, or jumped, from the second-story balcony. I yelled, 'Shaul!' but he didn't even make a sign. He looked like one possessed. He probably didn't hear me: his knees were bleeding. He started to run as hard as he could toward the Girls' Village. In his underbriefs, can you imagine? Yehuda didn't want to wake you, but I thought—"

Dan Alon and Weinstain, of course, were the ground-floor, garden-side tenants.

When they sat up in bed, they realized both had thought shots had been fired. Where? By someone celebrating? Little by little, they were reassured as the calm and silence returned.

Shtroch was fully awake by now. The two fencers left. Hershkowitz was turning and twisting in his bed. He decided to phone Lalkin, the head of the delegation, who was alone in Apt. 5. Just as his foot hit the floor, it started in again.

Bang-bang, bang-bang . . . Bang-bang . . . 9-mm submachine guns, 7.62 pistol, SKS automatic carbine with its characteristic hissings.

The two of them were at the window again. Dawn was coming up rosy by now.

Some 10 meters off, toward the end of the street and the metal fence, there was another Israeli: he too was at his three-paned bay window for the second time. This was Shmuel Lalkin, head of the delegation, and also President of the Israel Sports Federation. In that position, he was in a way boss of all Israeli sports, except that his authority was almost purely moral, the financial subsidies awarded by the Government being minimal.

Lalkin's long rectangular face stood out against the window like a target. His deep eyes searched the street on two levels. The little acacias were full of sparrows.

4:47 AM: "Lalkin, what's going on?"

48

The Knives

The chief turned to the right and saw his two riflemen. He answered, in a voice that suddenly struck him as being much too loud: "Damned if I know!"

"There were some before, too," Hershkowitz said. "They're coming from around here."

Lalkin shook his head. Sure, something was going on. But where? Hershkowitz added, "Ladani beat it. Without a word. All alone. He went that way—"

And he pointed east, toward the wide part of Connollystrasse, the tall lacework of the towers. Lalkin nodded understanding.

Lalkin, who was billeted alone in No. 5, was on the same level as the rifle contestants. There were two apartments separating them: No. 3, with the weight lifters and wrestlers, and No. 4, belonging to the two physicians, who also treated any other Israelis present at Munich.

Lalkin signaled his friends to listen to the dawn, and not talk too much. They were on the alert for any sign, any sound. Another burst of fire. Then quiet again.

The mission head was able to make out slight noises in the silence: a muffled conversation coming from the belly of the building. A piece of furniture being moved, or something else very heavy, scraping the floor. And then—especially—something that sounded like a groan. Maybe a cat meowing? But then, the end of the meow was stifled, as if a pillow had been put over the cat's head, or the fur of another animal in heat had covered its mouth. After a bit, Lalkin asked, hardly above a whisper: "See anything? Hear anything?"

Hershkowitz and his friend shook their heads.

Suddenly, among the tweeting of birds in the branches, there was the unmistakable slap of soles running on the pavement. It was coming from the bend of the street, coming into sight. There! A Village security officer, in the turquoise-blue uniform with the four flap-pockets and white shirt with two-toned tie. He was on duty this night. In his hand he had a little walkie-talkie. Craning his neck up toward the three Israelis in Block 31, he stopped and yelled in English, "What happens?"

The three men responded with the almost identical gesture of palms powerlessly outstretched before them in ignorance and fear

49

of catastrophe. The security man said a couple of words into his set, pressed a button, a hiss was heard, and someone was answering.

The young Olympic policeman ("All pink and gold, with a neck full of curls," Lalkin described him) still had time to yell, "What did you see? Nothing?" in irritation, as if he thought he might have been called out for nothing—or, rather, that he had been called out because some old woman got scared by a few firecrackers . . . For at

4:50 AM: A cleaning-woman had phoned the office of the *Ordnungsdienst* (Security Service) of the Village to say there was "shooting, around 31 Connollystrasse." He had been sent out.

4:55 AM: The cop had been on the sidewalk there for two or three minutes. He had had enough. He said in his schoolboy English: "Okay! I'm leaving. If anything really happens, just phone. Did you in fact hear any shooting?"

Lalkin told him of the bursts. He suggested the cop wait down below; he wanted the German to make the rounds with him through the building lobby and the Israeli lodgings.

Lalkin was about to leave his window when two new noises were heard. A window opening with a squeak, and a door being opened. It was the door to Apt. 3. It had the sustained blue color of happy Bavaria against a background of very dark blue. Other buildings featured red or green.

The delegation head jumped back. His two fellow countrymen, the other side of the door to No. 3, with equal view of it in diagonal, reacted the same way. And the three Israelis, holding their breaths and bending back so as not to be seen, watched.

An Arab.

Lalkin, first seeing his back, identified him instinctively, perhaps by the wrist, the back of the neck tapering off, or the way the left hand lightly grazed the somewhat arched leg, in its shiny black trousers. Lalkin told me: "He was wearing a sports outfit, the kind they make now, half sweat suit and half street dress. He turned around in one movement. I was even faster flattening against the wall. He was holding a submachine gun, with his finger on the trigger. His face was hidden by a blue-black cotton hood, with two holes for the eyes. And over it, a kind of tropical hat.

The Knives

He was thin. I swear: I wasn't surprised. I just thought: Well, this is it."

It was Tony. He had put a black gabardine jacket on over his goldenrod polo shirt. At first he seemed not to notice the policeman. The officer had stepped back a few meters when he saw the terrorist, then he stopped short, and started to talk into his walkie-talkie again without taking his eyes off that apparition out of Dante. The man in the hood had quietly taken a step out into the street. He was looking over the facade of 31, pointing the muzzle of his weapon at it, with no concern for the policeman.

Suddenly, the Arab turned, facing the street again. Behind him, the door was still ajar. The policeman, now fully in control, called to the hooded character: *"Was soll das heissen?"* (What's the meaning of this?)

He repeated the question in English, carefully pronouncing each syllable, loudly, but not yelling, without any trace of anger.

Did the terrorist understand what he said? As if not hearing him, he disappeared.

Immediately, Lalkin called to his associates: "Henry! Zelig!"

"Ken, Shmuel?" (Yes, Shmuel), Hershkowitz answered, barely above a whisper.

"Alert all the men in Number Two! Make sure there's nobody in the street watching you, and all come here. Quick!"

Lalkin could barely make out Hershkowitz' *"B'seder"* (Agreed).

Lalkin flew down the stairs. He made three phone calls. He was taking full advantage of these instants in which every move, every second counted—or should have counted, were it not for bad luck, and in the last analysis general mass indifference to the troubles of a small distant community. Lalkin would be able to say that, for his part, he did not miss the shadow of a chance, never lost control in any way.

As soon as they got to the Village, he had written down all the vital numbers on the tablet between the two phones he was entitled to as a delegation head: a black one for local Munich calls, and a red one for long distance. His first call was to Apt. 4. Why had Drs. Kranz and Weigel not also gone to their windows? The mission chief feared the worst, especially after the ringing con-

51

tinued—loud in the rising sun that made the limpid air shimmer. The fedayeen—there had to be more than one—were surely listening to it.

Lalkin was getting ready to put the phone down and risk going around by the rear of the building, when finally there was an answer. But no voice: just breathing.

"Hello," said Lalkin—who had guessed what the breathing meant—for it can express an infinity of suffering, appeal, fear.

He spoke his name. He called the two doctors by name in turn. Dr. Kranz, relieved, started to say hurriedly that Arab terrorists were . . . But Lalkin cut him off, ordering him and Weigel to come, right now, to No. 5.

"But—" Kranz retorted.

"You heard me: right now. If there's an Arab at the door, go out the back way. If you've lost the key to the French door, smash the glass."

One problem was haunting Lalkin: What had happened to the six boys from Apt. 3? Could they have been killed? The man in the hood seemed so satisfied!

Later, his face drawn by the ordeal, he told me: "There was no use phoning Number Three. But what about Number One? I was sure—you hear?—that the fedayeen had hit Number One first. I had already told my people that in case of attack—for, don't you think I had thought about an attack?—that was the most vulnerable of the lodgings. That was why I had put the solidest, most mature elements there, the coaches, the referees. Look at that corner apartment, with the lobby, the elevator, the building stairway. Impossible to lock the metal door closing the building off from the public cellar because everybody in the building uses it all the time. Some chance for attackers. What I didn't understand was why the fedayeen had hit Number Three but not Number Two."

Lalkin's second and third calls were to Israeli newspapermen at the Press Center. He knew they would spread an immediate alarm. He reminded them that 1500 Israelis had come to the Olympics in organized tours, and that almost a third of those were children and teenagers in the International Youth Camp. That shining camp, with its impeccable organization, its ideal atmosphere, was right near the Riem airport. The long tents, in the happy colors of the Games, were laid out, to form the five intertwined Olympic rings. It was a grandiose vision, the first that arriving passengers saw, as the planes came down.

5:10 AM: The delegation head had just hung up.

One of the newspapermen was named Aaron Lahan. He immediately informed the central police commissariat of Munich, as well as the Village police. He got the feeling, in both cases, that they already knew all about it. They were deliberate. No problem, sir; the German authorities are right on top of the matter.

Without shaving, Lahan ran out toward Gate 25A, the one he had so often gone through when visiting his compatriots in Block 31. The Village security had already started locking up the west end of the Village. But Lahan was determined to get on the scene: he proved his nationality and got a guard to let him through.

In Apt. No. 2, Hershkowitz was the senior man, the guide. He felt very sure of himself, and knew Lalkin was right; yet his instinct told him to stay put. He explained to the others: "Ladani, running away by jumping like a goat, made the Arabs realize they were far from capturing the whole team. Anyway, they must have been at the Opening Ceremony, and they can count. They know that to get in here, they have to break the door down. They can see that won't be easy, because we could barricade it with furniture. By the presence of the security men they now know the police have been alerted. They must be afraid that if they try to storm our lodging Germans will shoot at them from the rear. So they're waiting for us to walk into the trap. They want us to do like Ladani, so they can shoot us down like rabbits."

The others were thinking. Zelig Shtroch put it: "Maybe one of our guys they took told them Number Two has Uruguayans or the guys from Hong Kong in it. They never did get Ladani, so they may be thinking he was just a South American who got scared."

Racking your brain that way, you sometimes come up with the truth. But you also sometimes drop it for some other idea, more attractive, but untrue.

Dan Alon, the fencer who looked like an Aztec, was sure that there were already fatalities among the captured comrades. Besides, by now they could hear groans, from time to time. (It was probably Berger, who was terribly beaten up several times during the course of the morning.) Hershkowitz and the others could not help thinking those awful sounds came from the occupants of Apts. 1 and 3, and wondering who . . . Shtroch was afraid that the fedayeen were torturing one of the Israelis, to find out who was in each of the other lodgings.

The one who broke out was Yehuda Weinstain, the youngest member, seventeen. He was rather tall, lithe, nervous, a thoroughbred of the sandy land. He was also the youngest foils contestant, and had handled himself very well, getting to the round of 16 in his first international competition. He wanted out. What did running 20 meters or so mean? "The German police'll surely shoot at them to cover me, if need be."

Hershkowitz, who belonged to the war generation, sneered painfully: "Germans, to cover a Jew trying to save his neck? What gives you the idea their police are deployed for fire? Did you see any of them out the windows, fellows? Listen. Let's admit you make it. OK. Maybe a second guy will, too. But there are four of us. They'd have to be blind to miss the third one."

"I'm willing to go last."

"That's not the point. You or another. We're all Israel."

"Then let me go alone."

Weinstain had hardly uttered those words when he thought better of his idea—for fear this second escape by someone from No. 2 might seal the doom of the three left behind. . . .

I was able, in preparing this book, to see very large extracts of the reports collected by the prosecutor's office of Munich I *(Staatsanwaltschaft beim Landgericht München I)*, which, under the direction of Herr Otto Heindl, opened its investigation into the tragic events of September 5–6, in response to some fifteen plaintiffs. I was allowed to see almost all of the final overall conclusions reached by Herr Heindl. Everything in it, of course, does not agree with our view, many facts being absent from the whereases which resulted in the decision of non-actionability. Nevertheless, these were official findings and did prove useful.

The Knives

I will also have occasion to come back to a document drawn up by West German authorities to relate the "events of Munich." It is made up of three mimeographed clips numbered Pages 1 to 71 and generally referred to as the *Dokumentation*.

To begin with, its aim is self-serving. On September 20, 1972, it was distributed in Bonn by the Federal Government's information and press service and in Munich by the press service of the Government of the State of Bavaria, under joint sponsorship of the Chancellor of the Federal Republic and the Minister-President of the State of Bavaria.

How many fulltime employees did Herr Manfred Schreiber, the ultimate security official for the Olympic Games, have at his disposal?

Herren Brandt and Goppel's *Dokumentation* covers that on page 7. It says, in part: "Apart from the police personnel of the City of Munich and the district of Upper Bavaria," other personnel "recruited from all the police services of the Federal Republic and the *Länder* [States]" were also put at Bavaria's disposal for the Games. These "outside" reinforcements numbered 7,643 people. To which figure, of course, must be added the Munich and Bavarian officers assigned exclusively to the Games.

In all, according to the Organizing Committee and Herr Schreiber—who showed some inconsistency in his various estimates—there were 12,000 to 13,000 police officers concentrated on the Games.

The equipment they had was remarkable. Just two items in the impressive catalogue: twenty helicopters of the *Bundesgrenzschutzpolizei* (Federal Frontier Police) and four whirlybirds of the Bavarian police.

Bonn had also assigned 12,000 men of all branches of its *Bundeswehr* (armed services) to the Organizing Committee for the Olympic Games, as well as some 100 counterintelligence agents.

In all, then, a security force of close to 25,000 was watching over the Munich Games.

Now who was the No. 1 terrorist, skinny little Issa?

He knew West Germany well: he had been graduated there as a civil engineer. West German authorities, police as well as academic, gave no information about him. One thing, however, is certain: Issa traveled in the German Federal Republic with a Lebanese passport in the name of Mohammed Mahmud Essafadi. It seems quite probable, according to several witnesses, that where he studied was the University of Frankfort.

Palestinian circles alleged that that name of Mohammed Mahmud Essafadi was the name of another of the eight fedayeen, the one who said his name was Abdelkader el Denawi. "A brother of the fake Denawi recognized him on a picture!" the El Fatah people claimed. But Issa had left too many reminders of his being Essafadi, in fact or in fake, for the Fatah canard to stay afloat very long.

IV

MIRACULOUS ESCAPE

I went down to the bottoms of
the mountains;
The earth with her bars closed
upon me forever;
Yet hast Thou brought up my
life from the pit,
O LORD my God.
        Jonah 2:7

5:05 AM: *Polizeioberwachtmeister* (POLICE BRIGADIER) WOLFGANG X,
night commander in the Olympic Village security office, looked at
the clock and sighed. The business at 31 Connollystrasse was becoming really serious. As far as he was concerned, he had done
all he could. Now he had to put it all into the kind of report his
superiors liked: succinct, but "catchall."

Wolfgang's office was on the ground floor of the main administrative building, G-1, the nerve center of the Village, housing "City
Hall" and all the vital services. This Bavarian police administrator,
along with two thousand of his fellows, had been detached for a
month's time to the Olympic Village security force. For that
period, they all wore the turquoise-blue uniform that was their
summer outfit, all charm and smiles.

This security force was not a public police, but a private one,
made up of both outside elements and members of various secret
services of the Federal Republic. This was the formula that had
been adopted to give a special, relaxed and friendly, character to
the *Ordnungsdienst,* and be able to add to it on a moment's notice
any new recruit required, without formality.

The *Polizeioberwachtmeister* started his report:

4:47 AM: Frau Gertrud Z, temporary charwoman of the Olympic Village, officially employed by the City of Munich police department, on her way to her daily assignment, located at 20
Connollystrasse with the delegation of the German Democratic

Republic, hears shots and shouts as she goes by 31 Connollystrasse. She turns back in order to reach a telephone.

4:50: Brigadier-chief Wolfgang X, night charge of quarters, having received Frau Gertrud Z's message, sends Officer Y to investigate.

4:51: The Italian delegation phones night headquarters that an Israeli athlete has taken refuge with it, claiming to have escaped and that Arabs have invaded Block 31 and fired shots.

Simultaneously, a similar message comes from another Israeli athlete who has taken refuge with South Korea.

4:52: Brigadier X reports to the Praesidium of the Munich police.

4:55: Officer Y sees a man (apparently Arab) with a submachine gun in the doorway of Apt. 3 in Block 31. He advises his superior. At the same moment, the Arab, seeing him, signals him to stop talking into his walkie-talkie.

4:57: Brigadier-chief Wolfgang X sends two more officers to Block 31, keeping in touch with them and reporting to the Praesidium.

4:57: A member of the Israeli delegation, named Gad Tsobari, sends a phone message to headquarters to state that terrorist guerrillas have invaded Apts. 1 and 3 at 31 Connollystrasse. Herr Tsobari has escaped and taken refuge in a box of the *Ordnungsdienst* situated near Bungalow 20 in the Women's Village.

5:00: Officer Y, back at headquarters, states the Arab's face is covered by a hood. Two other characters, one masking himself with a scarf, were seen by Officer Y at the windows of Apt. 1.

Henry Hershkowitz and his three comrades were waiting—and watching. They were ready to make a fight for it, even though they were unarmed, except for kitchen knives. They had moved the furniture. The Arabs would not find it easy to open the outer doors.

"How come no police have come to help us yet?" Weinstain was angrily demanding.

Hershkowitz answered, "I don't think they'll ever come, for fear of seeming to attack or provoke the terrorists. They're just going to forget about us."

In the ensuing silence, everyone had to agree it was logical. It was also correct.

Miraculous Escape

One of the first of the terrorists' demands was that no one, except the official negotiators, come near Block 31. But this ban had not yet been voiced when Hershkowitz reached his pessimistic opinion.

Several times the fedayeen would threaten during that somber day to kill a hostage if the sharpshooters—whom they often had no trouble spotting—did not go away. Among the hindsight decisions, always easy to make, this one should have occurred: *Immediately,* in the heat of things, the highest German authorities involved should have informed the terrorists that they were not going to try to free the hostages by force, but that within the next two minutes an armed squad would come to escort out of Block 31 all the persons still in apartments other than Nos. 1 and 3. For want of that, there was almost a much greater tragedy than the one that actually occurred.

Through Shmuel Lalkin's calls, the police had been precisely informed of the identities and locations of the members of the Israeli delegation not yet in fedayeen hands, but trapped in Building 31. Professor Shaul Ladani had confirmed what Lalkin said. But, in their overwhelming desire to save the hostages while sparing the blood of any German police, the Munich authorities succeeded in tying their own hands.

The four occupants in Apt. 2 were taking turns upstairs in the duplex: they were not going to allow a surprise attack via the south balcony. Many of the Israelis had previously pulled the trick of going the whole length of the garden side of the second floor, hopping from balcony to balcony. Naturally, now, they had barricaded the French door leading in from it.

5:05 AM: It was Shtroch's and Alon's turn to go upstairs. Below, Hershkowitz and Weinstain kept watch on Connollystrasse through the curtain of the wide window.

They went pale.

An Arab in a gray-green waterproofed tropical hat, with his face painted red, was standing guard in front of the main door to the building, in front of the lobby leading to Apt. 1.

"Henry," Weinstain asked, "Henry, why are we hounded like this? They've captured Apartment One."

Appalled, Hershkowitz started to reel off the names of the occupants: "Moshe . . . Andrei . . . Kehat . . . Tuvia . . ." And Weinstain chimed in, as if continuing the prayer, "Yacov . . . Amitzur . . . Yossef . . ."

The Arab with the big slouching body was moving from one foot to the other; there were cigarette ashes on the yellow turtle-neck that covered his thin, hollow chest. It was Tony, whom Issa had sent to lead the attack on Apt. 3. It must be noted that when the first police officer showed up ten minutes earlier (4:55), Tony was in the doorway of Apt. 3, which was strange, since the hostages taken there had been moved out at 4:45 to Apt. 1, not without having put up a hefty resistance.

The reason that Tony was in front of that empty lodging at the time was that he and Samir were studying it to see how best to go at Apt. 2. Several indications on this score corroborate what the surviving terrorists said, such as the moments Tony and Samir spent hugging the partition separating the balconies of No. 3 and No. 2. Issa, who was cautious, finally decided there were too many imponderables to warrant the attack: that was why Tony was now back at No. 1, turned into the Arabs' redoubt.

On his hip, he had his Soviet Kalachnikov AK-47 submachine gun. He was aiming it at the same turquoise-blue officer as before. The officer had come back alone. The Arab started to address him in German, in a shrill and bitter tone that reflected his nervousness. The Israelis in Apts. 2, 4, and 5 ran to their windows.

"We won't say anything to you," Tony was shouting. "We want to deal with a responsible intermediary. You have no authority. You're a simple police officer."

Calmly, the handsome blond repeated each word into his transmitter. "Your message has been relayed," he told the terrorist, and left.

Shmuel Lalkin, after his phone calls, had returned to the upper floor of No. 5, and was watching out of the corner of the window, horrified at the idea that the four occupants of No. 2 might choose this moment and this side of the building to come out.

The two doctors in No. 4 were also watching the terrorist. These Israelis, trapped and hidden a step away from the guerrillas, were fascinated by this display in which their lives hung in the balance.

Miraculous Escape

5:08 AM: They saw another officer of the Olympic security force in the Courrèges uniform appear before the building. This one, it would turn out, was an actual police officer. The tropical-hatted fedayee was gone. The officer was unarmed and had his hands free, but looked tense beneath the waterproof linen cap with the tiny visor, sitting square on his head. He was careful to walk in the middle of Connollystrasse, in between the containers of greenery and flowers. He stopped and looked up at the three-story building. Toward the bay windows of which the raw-silk curtains were drawn, he waved what seemed like a cordial welcome.

A window opened: a hand slipped out, and let a sheet of paper drop. The policeman picked it up and started off into the empty street. The pearly dawn was turning blue, and it was a bit chilly, but one could sense it would be a fine, hot day.

The officer had gone only some 10 meters, toward the east, when an order rang out: *"Warten Sie!"* (Wait!).

He turned around. On the second floor of Apt. 1, in the open window, he could see a white beach hat. Under it, big black glasses and a charcoal-covered face. The head disappeared, as if into a trap, and in its place appeared a hand that looked covered with soot: it dropped two more sheets of paper, held together by a clip but then partly blown apart by a sudden gust. The officer caught the sheets just as they were coming down on the gurgling water pipe. No, not a pipe really, but a canal open to the Bavarian sky, a mini-canal, concave and painted in the colors of the Munich Games: prairie green, purple, turquoise blue, apple green, yellow, orange, in successive layers from top to bottom. The policeman took the sheets with utmost care, without folding them, and turned back toward the invested building: no one was to be seen. It seemed to be asleep. The officer left.

What he had just picked up was the text of the ultimatum.

West German authorities refused to release the full text of that first terrorist message. On this, as on many other details of the twenty bloody hours, I was able to get precise tips from some friends well-connected in Bonn.

What the 5:08 message essentially said was: "The revolutionary organization *Black September* demands that by 9:00 AM the Israeli military regime free the 236 revolutionary prisoners whose names are listed herewith . . ." The list covered the two clipped sheets.

First it listed the 234 political prisoners of the Jewish State. Among these were the kamikaze Kozo Okamoto, sole survivor of the three Japanese terrorists responsible for the awful massacre at Lod Airport on May 30, 1972; the four French young women who had carried the explosives in the "Easter Commando" of April 19, 1971, Evelyne Barge, Marlene and Nadia Bradlybardali, sisters, and Edith Burghalter; the two survivors of the group of four terrorists who skyjacked the Sabena Boeing 707 at Lod, May 8–9, 1972: Thérèse Halasseh and Rima Tannus.

Two other names that at first glance had nothing to do with Jews and Arabs appeared on the typed list (it would be found later that the terrorists had several photocopies of the list with them): Ulrike Meinhof and Andreas Baader. These two, with a lawyer named Horst Mahler and a few others, in August 1970 had started an extreme-left terrorist gang. They had carried off some eight well-organized bank robberies, and planted time bombs in the U.S. Army camps in West Germany under the terms of NATO, killing four American soldiers, among others. Elsewhere, they killed three police officers and committed numerous other depredations, until their arrest in June 1972.

Specialists in the matter were surprised that, if Meinhof and Baader were included, the verbose, bearded Mahler had been left off the list, for until his arrest he had been the kingpin of the gang (many of whose members had made long stays in Lebanon and Libya, and had sustained contacts with El Fatah).

For reasons best known to them, the Germans would not even release the full list of prisoners whose liberty the terrorists demanded. (A year later, there were some 1600 prisoners in Israel convicted of endangering the State.)

The 5:08 message went on to say that, once all these persons were let out, the group in Connollystrasse demanded the right to leave freely with their hostages for a country of their choice, where the Israeli athletes would be exchanged for the 236 freed. The text read:

> Transportation of the fedayeen of Black September and their Zionist hostages will be in three long-distance planes put at the commando's disposal by the Federal Government. There will be

three successive departures. When the first plane with its group of fedayeen and hostages has arrived safely at its destination, the second plane will leave, and the same will apply for the third.

The deadline of our ultimatum expires at 9:00 AM [the time written in with a ballpoint pen]. Any attempt to interfere with the carrying out of our mission will bring about the immediate liquidation of all the Israeli prisoners, either one at a time, or all at once. If the deadline is not met, the Zionist prisoners will be executed forthwith.

This whole document was typed in English.

5:15 AM: The Police Commissioner of the City of Munich, Dr. Manfred Schreiber, alerted at 5:04, ordered all access routes to Building 31 to be sealed off, with the building to be surrounded as closely as possible without the terrorists seeing it. Herr Schreiber instructed the Bavarian police to seek out their best available sharpshooters and send them to the Village. As head of the security forces of the Organizing Committee for the Games, Dr. Schreiber had full authority over all security for the village.

Squat as a stevedore, short but solid in his well-cut suit, with his imperious chin and Aryan profile, Dr. Manfred Schreiber was to be the main operating executive of the whole affair, both in the Village and at Fürstenfeldbruck.

He was a pure Bavarian, born at Hof, near the Czech border. He was forty-six in September 1972. Which means he started his adult life during the war: drafted into the Wehrmacht in 1944, he was very seriously wounded in the abdomen and spent two years in a wheelchair. This did not keep him from studying law at the University of Munich. He presented his doctoral thesis in 1952, and then joined the bureaucracy of the *Land* of Bavaria, specializing in law and order and security services. He soon entered the Munich city service, becoming successively head of personnel for the emergency police, and then, in 1960, head of the criminal division.

Herr Vogel, then *Bürgermeister* (Mayor) of Munich, in 1963 named him *Polizeipräsident* of the Bavarian capital, or Police Commissioner. He proved receptive to modern work methods, hiring a psychologist as well as qualified technicians, and seeking out first-rank personnel. In 1966, he was designated to be head of security for the Games, a position which in fact duplicated his functions in the Munich city government.

Herr Schreiber has always known how to be both responsible and cautious. During the twenty-one hours of the Black September affair, every one of his important decisions was submitted in writing for the approval of Herr Bruno Merk.

He was also something to watch at the stormy, fantastic press conference held by the Germans principally responsible for the operations of September 5–6, at Munich's City Hall on the afternoon of Thursday, September 7, for over four hours. How proudly and cleverly he parried! How quick he was to help Herren Genscher and Merk, and prompt them with the right answers!

Those who know him well insist his dominant qualities are his capacity for work, gift of command, sense of organization, and relentless discipline for his men as well as himself, along with unflinching faithfulness to both his subordinates and his superiors.

He has flash. On some breakneck subjects, his frankness is the delight of the Bavarian press. Such as this proclamation that electrified the *Pressezentrum:* "I am all for bordellos, but against prostitution with pimps."

He is unquestionably very popular within the Munich police. One reason: he always seeks maximum security for his men. He never forgets he is there to protect the people of Munich and law and order. And he does it well, since in 1971 Munich had the lowest crime rate among West Germany's big cities. In his own terms, his motto seems to be, "Let the bastards have it" (or, as we might say, "Shoot first and ask questions later"). One typical case cited happened on August 4, 1971.

That day, two bandits held up a Munich branch of the Deutschen Bank in Prinzregentenstrasse. They took four hostages (three women and a man) and collected two million marks (or close to $600,000). They demanded a car. When it was parked outside, the leader, an ex-convict named Hans-Georg Rammelmeir, got in with one of the women hostages, a very young cashier, Fräulein Ingrid Reppel. "Hundreds of people were massed near the bank, pushing against the police barricades, and EXTRA papers were being hawked twenty paces away from where the holdup was going on.

A real circus!" a French diplomat then serving in Munich told me. Herr Schreiber was on hand to direct matters personally. The police opened fire the second Rammelmeir sat down next to the girl; both of them were killed on the spot.

Fräulein Reppel's parents sued for deliberate homicide. There were loud protests. An autopsy was held, naturally. And, to the cynical sneers of most observers, the bullet fragments taken from her body "proved" that Fräulein Reppel had been shot by Rammelmeir.

Schreiber had not for an instant given in to his critics. As far as he was concerned, that autopsy report "cleared" him.

There would be autopsies after Fürstenfeldbruck, too. Straight as an oak, eye sharp, voice crackling, Dr. Manfred Schreiber this time would come out smelling like roses. No one in Munich doubted that he had done what was best. Everyone was grateful that, from beginning to end, he had exposed his men to as little danger as possible.

This Munich police chief is said to have political ambitions. A member of the SPD (Social Democratic Party) for a quarter of a century, he has solid support in it. But that is another story. . . .

5:20 AM: The policeman in the *Ordnungsdienst* uniform came back, strong, built like a basketball player, round-cheeked, with heavy brown sideburns, looking concerned and tough. The beach-hatted fedayee, now carrying a pistol, came out in front of the lobby and signaled the German to come over. They argued for two or three minutes, close enough to touch each other. The terrorist knew how to dress: very light blue-gray safari outfit, with a sheen; white sweater with round neck; good shoes with elevator heels. That was Issa, quickly emerging as the leader. The officer noted that he spoke perfect German.

The charcoal daubings on face, neck, wrists, and hands, seemed childish—but children do not kill. Suddenly, the fedayee lost his temper, and his words could be overheard: "If you don't believe us, we'll show you we're not talking to hear ourselves talk!" he yelled.

Was he pretending anger? Apparently not. His thighs could be seen quivering inside the high-style tight-fitting trousers.

"We'll show you a corpse!"

He raised his left arm, snapped his fingers. The other hand kept the pistol pointed at the policeman. He was in the corner of the glass-paned door, wide open inward behind him.

A body came flying through the opening: it sailed straight and then smashed down on the pavement, head first. There, on its back, it lay quiet, in the stillness of death. He was wearing the dress uniform, as if he had gotten dressed up to die. His outfit was soaked with fresh blood and darker spots where it was mixed with bits of bone, brain, or body matter. The head was horrifyingly mutilated, half the forehead shot away, one eyesocket empty. Yes, there was Moshe Weinberg with his tiger's strength and reflexes, "Moshe, the well of joy," as Josef Inbar, the President of the Israeli Olympic Committee, used to call him.

Shmuel Lalkin more than anyone else, who had been under fire in the wars of 1948, 1956, and 1967, who knew of Weinberg's exploits, and had always seen him victoriously overcome the worries of everyday life, looked at those powerful remains with a kind of disbelief. He thought he saw the chest heave, but then realized it was crushed, smashed, so badly that you could see the inside of the lungs, like magma, through a tear in the shirt. There was also one particularly horrifying mutilation, and Lalkin remained transfixed for minutes on end looking at his young friend thrown on the sidewalk like a bunch of rags, in the dawning, radiant day, with the sky turning blue. He was to say to me later: "You know what I kept repeating all of that Tuesday morning, while we were wringing our hands as we waited? If they don't attack those gangsters, they'll kill us all. Maybe one by one, maybe together. It'll last a day, maybe a little less, maybe a little more. But none of us will be saved."

The seven Israelis, haunted by the idea of escaping from the building, had seen people as early as five o'clock on the East German balconies: athletes in navy-blue sweat suits, and officials in garnet blazers. Some said, "They must be cops in mufti," but others, with binoculars, recognized some of the athletes, and knew that was not so.

5:30 AM: A khaki ambulance with a red cross on it came through the underground to the entrance of the big white East German building. Two men in white smocks, a minute later, came out of the building on to Connollystrasse, facing 31. They were carrying a litter with satchels and all the heavy first-aid needs on it. They came down the steps between the bushes, and began to cross the street. Big Tony with the neck that bent forward appeared near Weinberg's body. He aimed his submachine gun at the two men. Two rifles also stuck out the corners of the window, upstairs in Apt. 1.

The white-clad men—two German physicians serving as volunteers at the Village—paid no attention to the terrorist in his tropical hat.

They stepped right on up to Weinberg. With very fine careful motions they moved him to the stretcher, and knelt. One took his pulse, the other put a stethoscope to the crushed chest. It was so obvious he was dead! But that was what they did.

They softly raised the martyred face. They looked at it, and you had the unreal feeling they wanted to say something to him. They set him down again. One of the doctors shrugged. The other stood up and, in a motion that Shmuel Lalkin and the other survivors who saw him will remember to the end of their days, this rather elderly man, heavy in his white smock, slowly raised his two arms toward the sky, shaking his fists as his overwhelmed face peered up at the windows of Block 31. Then, all at once, he let his arms fall to his sides like two dead sticks.

They raised the stretcher, no longer in any hurry, and left.

During this time, the tall sideburned policeman remained in the middle of the street, near the gurgling water conduits that fed the pretty fountains a few meters away. The fedayee in the safari outfit was yelling at him, in his shrillest twang: *"Verstehen Sie mich?"* (Understand?). "We'll kill them all, starting at nine o'clock. One each hour. And we'll throw their bodies into the street!"

The Olympic security-service man said nothing. He went away.

5:35 AM: He came back, with another officer in a brown-and-green uniform and an expressionless face under a long-billed cap. The fedayee in the beach hat yelled something at them again, but this time went on in without waiting for an answer.

5:40 AM: A young blonde, with rose-colored glasses, was walking most naturally toward Block 31. She was alone. She wore the regulation turquoise-blue suit uniform, simple but attractive, of the women's Olympic security service. It just happened on her it looked good.

An attacker wearing a red woolen hood (probably pretty hot by now already) kept his eye and his gun on her from the window of No. 1.

Just before reaching the doorway to the lobby, she raised her left hand, the right holding the strap to her purse. In her left hand she had the ubiquitous walkie-talkie. She addressed the masked fedayee in Arabic. The safari outfit came down, stood on the threshold of the street door, and talked to her. Calmly.

This cute, if plump, young woman, with the shapely legs, was in fact an officer in the Munich criminal division. She had been called in less than half an hour before; until then she had not been assigned to the Games. She would soon be identified as Fräulein Echler—although the March 1973 public prosecutor's report signed by Presiding Judge Otto Heindl was to call her Fräulein Graes.

Whatever her name, she was at ease and had know-how. She did not put on any airs.

Lalkin as well as Hershkowitz, Ladani as well as Tsobari, all of the Israelis who were not, or no longer were, in the hands of the terrorists, knew that, under no circumstances, not even if in front of the TV cameras of every network in the world the Black September fedayeen killed all of their hostages one by one, except the last one, warning viewers that if their demands were not met within the hour, they would kill this last one, too, not even then would the Israel Government yield to blackmail.

Not ever.

That is one of the characteristics of Jews. They can, as much as and sometimes more than others, weigh pros and cons, split hairs, listen with impartiality to two sides of a question. So that, as long as they have not reached a final conclusion, it is often tempting to accuse them of indecision, weakness, even fear. But once they have made their choice among the essential circumstances of life their determination becomes irrevocable, unshakable. That is the Rock of Israel.

The hostages, the nine survivors, who had been penned up on

the second floor of Apt. 1 by the terrorists, knew that, too. The bedroom they were in was not the one facing Connollystrasse, but the other, in back, on the garden side, with the flowered balcony.

Since 5:30, the nine captives had been in the bedroom in which Yossef Romano had made his glorious last stand. The terrorists had felt it was risky to leave their prey too near the street where the negotiations would take place.

In this balconied bedroom, nothing had been removed or cleaned since one of the fedayeen, emptying his clip, had cut the body of the Israeli weight lifter in half. The pools of blood, pieces of skull, bits of lymph, bone fragments, and the remains themselves were all still where they were. The fedayeen had had the hostages sit down at the foot of the two beds. They had bound their wrists and ankles, and then tied them to each other with the rope thick as a finger that they had brought in with them. The hostages had not been able to clean the spots where they had to sit; they had to walk straight forward with arms in the air, when they asked permission, under guard, to go to the toilet. That is why all of their clothes, to a greater or lesser extent, were soiled with Romano's blood and the matter from his body.

They spent seventeen and a half hours cooped up that way.

And all of them, even if not admitting it to themselves, knew that Israel would not give in. All, that is, perhaps except Mark Slavin, the handsome eighteen-year-old who had been living in Israel for only three months and to whom, since his arrival from Minsk, it had been an unknown world, one of radiance, splendor, brotherhood, all shiny and bright. The Promised Land.

But eight of them knew too much of the Arab soul and the reactions of fedayeen not to understand two other things.

First: An enemy who is down awakens no pity generally in an Arab, for if that is his fate, it is because Allah willed it so. Therefore, to rejoice. How much more deserving, too, of punishment if the loser be an infidel and especially a Jew!

Second: When fedayeen have hostages at their mercy, they kill them if negotiations don't turn out right, and unless doing so means certain death for them.

So we may be sure the hostages of September 5 had no illusions about their situation. That did not keep them from having hope, for no people has practiced and professed hope more than Israel during its supernatural history. Oh, the constant hope for miracle, the incessant defiance of future logic and present reality, that demented hope that so often the Finger of the Lord God has made come true!

Alone in No. 5, Shmuel Lalkin refused to leave. None more than he knew what danger he was in.

I had met him prior to this horrible day, in Ladenstrasse, the business street of Olympic Village. A whole bunch of us were seated at a café terrace, a soft-drink café with tables made of fake marble, but with a real August 24 sun outside. The head of the Israeli delegation was as joyful, as joking as anyone else. Despite his cordiality, you could feel he was on guard, not toward us specifically, of course, but in general. The way he kept looking around, keeping an eye on certain people who walked about looking for an acquaintance or a place to sit down. I can confirm that he was speaking the strictest truth, when he later mentioned the worries that had kept at him, his feelings that danger was lurking around his team. Strong, sturdy, compact, with a vigorous handclasp, he became warmly effusive once confidence set in.

He was forty-seven on the day of the attack, having fought in young Israel's three wars. In that small country where being under fire is a natural thing, and the state of war is everyday reality, where decorations are scorned, Lalkin had had no visible honors for his actions under arms. But his qualities of courage and command had helped to advance his professional career.

Those who saw the head of the Israeli delegation the next afternoon, September 6, will remember his dignity, which overpowered his exhaustion: it seemed as if Lalkin's hair had turned much whiter in a few hours. It was not so, but the drawn lines of the face, the paleness underlined the suffering in his eyes and the graying growth of beard that was forty-eight hours old. He neither wept nor moaned. The arch of his nose seemed sharper, there were wrinkles on either side of his mouth alongside the bushy mustache, and he hunched his head into his broad shoulders, like a groggy boxer trying to force himself to hold on.

The escapee from Apt. 3, Gad Tsobari, before getting away,

had heard Tony mention Lalkin several times. They surely put a big value on the mission head. Had they gotten him, they would not have cared that they had captured only a minority of the Israeli delegation. That was why Lalkin was running the greatest risk by staying in No. 5. But he would not leave for anything in the world before the occupants of No. 2 got there, after he had instructed them to join him.

Now that Moshe Weinberg's body had been taken away, and no terrorist was in the doorway of No. 3, Lalkin could not understand what Hershkowitz and the three with him were waiting for. They had lost an hour already. He was afraid they might decide to try to make it out through the garden. He, too, was distrustful of the balconies, and preferred not to open the French windows of the main or upper floors.

5:30 AM: The Mayor of Olympic Village, Herr Walter Tröger, came to the administrative offices. Only till the end of the Games was the Village to be independent administratively. After that, the whole area would go back under the Munich municipality. The Minister-President of the *Freistaat Bayern* (Free State of Bavaria), Dr. Alfons Goppel, was constitutionally responsible for all purely Bavarian matters. Federal authorities had to go through his State Government. So *Polizeichef* Schreiber first advised the Bavarian Minister of the Interior, Dr. Bruno Merk, who of course was in Munich. And at 5:10 Herr Merk had called his Federal opposite-number, Minister of the Interior Hans-Dietrich Genscher, who was in Munich, too, at the Hotel Continental.

Herr Genscher immediately phoned Chancellor Willy Brandt and Foreign Minister Walter Scheel. The latter immediately instructed one of the State secretaries (in West Germany, these are not appointed under-secretaries, but the highest rank of permanent civil servant), Herr Paul Frank, to advise the ambassador of Israel at Bonn, H. E. Eliashiv Ben Horin. At 5:30, Ambassador Ben Horin was able to talk to Jerusalem: they had come full circle.

Lerchenauerstrasse is a royal road that goes along the Olympic Village on its eastern flank. Now it was closed to automobile traffic, between Petuelring at the southeast, and Moosacherstrasse at

71

the northeast, or over the whole extent of its contiguity to the Village. Pedestrians could still use it, subject to many identity checks and roadblocks.

Connollystrasse crosses the Village from east to west; Block 31, at the end of it, is therefore at the other extremity from Lerchenauerstrasse, the west end.

The *Olympiazentrum* Station of the *U-Bahn* (subway) was located on Lerchenauerstrasse, and there was a lot of activity there. This was also the way most motorists—if they had passes—drove into the Olympic Village.

5:35 AM: The terrorists made their first phone call. They asked to be connected with a number in Beirut; if they did not get it, it was not the switchboard's fault, but because there was no answer. Herr Schreiber felt correctly that that call might have given some useful information. To date, it has never been revealed whom they were calling.

Mr. Ramon Young, head of the Hong Kong delegation, was housed in Apt. 12, on the third floor, just over duplex No. 1. On that floor, on the north or Connollystrasse side, there was a covered gallery that ran the whole length of the building, and the doors to the apartments opened off of that gallery. On the south, like the other apartments, these had their private balconies with guaranteed sun exposure.

Mr. Young was rudely awakened by a series of chilling noises: bursts of gunfire, screams, breakages, and falls. He jumped out of bed. And that afternoon, September 5, in the huge air-conditioned lobby of the *Pressezentrum*, he told me: "In cases like that, you think fast. I immediately realized what was happening. I had recognized good old Gutfreund's voice, as powerful as he himself was; I had known him for years, for he had been to other Olympic Games before.

"I went out into the gallery and went from room to room to tell all of my men to lock themselves in. Some had to be awakened by repeated knocking. It took a little time. When I was finished, I went toward the steps that lead to the main floor, down in the lobby of the building. I was hesitant. Should I go down? Or wait? Then the firing started again. This time, it lasted longer, with

72

breaks in between. There were guttural calls, shouts, a groan, long bursts of fire, and it all echoed in the stairwell. I was surrounded by the noises."

Young finally decided to go down. At the last turn, he leaned over. In the lobby, near the glass door opening on the street, there was a dead body, of a still-young man, in Israeli dress uniform. A dark and large body, muscular, and giving off an extraordinary feeling of broken strength. It had been horribly mutilated. As for the head, "It was like a reddish mushroom."

The delegation head pursed his lips so as not to feel faint. From the silhouette, the size, the powerful well-cared-for hands, he had just recognized smiling Moshe Weinberg, with whom he had exchanged hellos and daily pleasantries.

Young went back up. He was barely up to his floor when he thought someone was carefully coming up behind him.

"I said to myself: 'Better stay on the landing. Otherwise . . .' A little fellow, skinny as a gutter cat, nervous, with a crane's neck over his black shirt, popped up."

That, of course, described the fedayee we have not yet mentioned: Salah, also known as Atif.

"As soon as he saw me, he aimed the submachine gun at me, telling me to raise my hands, which I did. He looked like an Arab. I softly said to him that this floor had only the Hong Kong and Uruguay teams. I spoke English. He seemed to understand. He motioned to me not to move, and went back down. After a bit, another terrorist came up, the one with the white beach hat. He understands English very well. He saw me to my apartment, told me it was forbidden to leave it, and then said that if anyone at all tried to get down, either by the stairs or by the lift, they might be shot down. He waved his pistol as he spoke, and then left without waiting for me to answer. I went to the balcony on the garden side, and that was when I saw that policemen both in civvies and in the turquoise-blue uniform were surrounding the building, taking up positions where they were hidden behind corners of the building opposite. There were also some flat on their stomachs on the roof, behind any coverings: pillars, TV aerials, domes, and so on. It was not yet five-thirty."

5:50 AM: The policewoman-interpreter was back, calm, in front of the lobby of Block 31. She spoke civilly with Issa, having been told by the German authorities to inform him that:

"We can do nothing about freeing all those political prisoners you want from Israel. We can only transmit your terms. Why not give us conditions which it is possible for us to meet?"

She spoke in Palestinian dialectal Arabic, which experts say was impeccable. Issa for the first time smiled thinly with his mouth alone, the rest of his face staying put. He said: "Free all those prisoners or all the hostages will die."

The young blonde woman smiled, too. What could her smile have meant? She said she would tell them. And she left.

5:55 AM: Hershkowitz and his three companions noted a basic change on the face of Apt. 3: the curtains had been closed upstairs as well as on the ground floor.

The reason (impossible to know for sure at the time) was that the fedayeen, having moved all their prisoners into Apt. 1, had decided all to hole up in it, too, but they wanted to go as long as possible without showing they had left No. 3.

The four Israelis in No. 2 quickly agreed that it was now or never. At worst, the curtains would impede any firing the Arabs might do. They went down to the main floor, quickly opened the door, and took off.

Shmuel Lalkin was watching Connollystrasse when he finally saw Hershkowitz, Shtroch, Alon, and Weinstain on the sidewalk. They were single file, running like arrows, backs bent. They dashed into No. 5. Lalkin muttered: "Go on back right out through the garden. Head for the fence."

They all followed his orders, and he closed the door behind them.

As head of the delegation, he still had a problem: the two medics in No. 4. Why did they not give a sign? Their apartment was right next to 5, so that, by knocking on the wall between at either floor, Lalkin could have been heard in No. 4. But how did he know there were no terrorists in there by now?

He waited. He knew that if no one phoned him, it was because they were afraid. Either of hearing an Arab answer, or of having the ring alert the nearby terrorists to think: "Why shouldn't we go into Number Five? Either there's nobody there, or there's an Israeli who doesn't dare answer."

He decided to dial the doctors. The phone rang three times; no answer. He hung up. After all, they could possibly have gotten away without his seeing them. He had done his best.

The two doctors, as he had feared, were still there, chewing their nails. They had looked at the phone, while it rang, without moving, for fear that this time it might be the fedayeen. . . .

V
BUNDLES OF NEGLECT

Woe to him that buildeth a town
with blood,
And establisheth a city by iniquity!
Habakkuk 2:12

6:00 AM: THERE WAS NO GENERAL ALARM AS YET. THE POLICE HAD closed Connollystrasse from No. 11 to the fence, stopping anyone whosoever not only from entering but also from leaving the guarded zone without well-established justification. The protests by Herr Ewald, head of the East German delegation, for the time being were of no avail. For reasons of their own, which after the fact we cannot approve of, the responsible authorities had decided to keep the affair secret as long as possible. They knew that, while having no specifics, many of the East German, South Korean, and other athletes from teams lodged near the attack had some suspicions of what it was all about.

Most competitors with events still to come were up very early, to train, or warm up if they were scheduled that morning. They by and large suspected nothing, but were beginning to be puzzled: today things did not seem quite normal. For the first time in the history of the Games, there were patrols of armed officers where the athletes were assembling.

The Italians were saying that Arabs had attacked the Israelis and one Jew had taken shelter with them. Throughout the Village now, military uniforms were seen among the smart security-service outfits, which were light and elegant as the smiling sky itself. These were the Games of Joy; they had been a brilliant, ideal fortnight, replete with fine performances and brotherhood, as now we realize.

76

6:30 AM: Shmuel Lalkin ran out of Apt. 5. The surviving fedayeen said that before the job they had studied pictures of the
Israeli delegation head—they were obviously bent on catching
him. Had they seen him in time, they would certainly have shot
at him. But, as he told me, "I went out the back way. I ran better
than I did when I was twenty. I was scared. But mostly my heart
was broken at the idea that twelve of my boys had been taken by
the terrorists. I thought there were twelve, because I did not know
that Sokolovsky and Tsobari had gotten away, nor that Romano
was dead. I could still see Weinberg's corpse, and wondered
whether the two medics had been able to escape. Ideas tumbled
through my mind the way they must when your parachute crum-
ples or your car starts rolling over."

At about the same moment, the Israeli newsman Aaron Lahan
saw the horribly mutilated corpse of Moshe Weinberg. They were
getting ready to move it to the basement of administrative tower
G-1: there was no morgue in the Olympic Village yet.

7:15 AM: A meeting was opening in G-1, presided over by the
Innenminister (Minister of the Interior) of Bavaria, Herr Bruno
Merk, and including Herr Genscher, Federal Minister of the In-
terior, Dr. Schreiber of the Munich police, Willi Daume, head
of the Organizing Committee and President of the *Nationales
Olympisches Komitee für Deutschland*, Walter Tröger, Mayor of
Olympic Village and Secretary-General of the German National
Olympic Committe, Hans-Jochen Vogel, Vice-President of the
Organizing Committee and former Mayor of Munich, and Avery
Brundage (U.S.A.), outgoing President of the International Olym-
pic Committee.

Those attending decided unanimously that every effort must
be made to negotiate with the fedayeen. Use of force to free the
hostages was to be countenanced only as a last resort, and only if
it seemed in case of nonintervention the hostages would be killed.
They decided to set up an emergency executive or crisis staff
(*Krisenstab*) headed by Herr Merk. It was given full powers to
resolve the current problem, and could assume all responsibility.
It would headquarter in Herr Tröger's office on the third floor.

Meantime, the report, starting as a whisper, had become a roar;
it was spreading throughout the Village, through Munich, through

77

Israel: Palestinian terrorists had attacked the Israeli Olympic delegation.

At the Press Center, nervousness had been waxing since 7:00 AM. Italian and Japanese (why Japanese?) reporters were giving details that seemed unbelievable. Where were the Israeli newsmen? Their absence was strange, to say the least, and added to the growing fears.

7:35 AM: The first wire-service bulletins, reporting the attack guardedly, were off the tickers.

7:45 AM: The meeting at G-1 adjourned.

7:52 AM: At the insistence of phone calls from every continent, the Munich police confirmed that an attack had been made on the Israeli team, in its billet at 31 Connollystrasse, at the southwest corner of *Olympisches Dorf*. What is most striking in these first statements, is their misinformation:

> The affair started at 5:20 AM. There are five attackers. They got into the Village over a fence. They broke into the Israeli billet as the delegation was getting up. The police were immediately alerted, and sealed off that section of the Village. Negotiations have already begun with the aggressors, who claim to belong to Palestinian guerrilla movements. The exact number of hostages is not known. There seem to be at least thirteen. The Israelis tried to resist the "Palestinians," and one Israeli was fatally wounded.

Thus started a whole series of false or distorted reports, put out by the most important personages involved. From the very start, word would get out only bit by bit, both on the overall picture and the dramatic turns of events throughout bloody Tuesday and Wednesday. From one end to the other, the fantastic media mobilized will only further emphasize the thinness of the information allowed to filter out by the authorities.

The film files of the TV networks seem unbelievable when you go back to them. The cameras show us where the action was taking place, bringing in some of the participants, those who escaped, their weeping friends, the mobs that it is easy to consider conscienceless, and the delayed competitions. The color coverage brings the suspense to life: the trembling questions of an Israeli swimmer, the tight lips of Dr. Schreiber, the mysterious comings and goings of two Volkswagen minibuses. And a quartet of fake athletes in bright blue, orange, or red sweat suits, each having a rifle with telescopic sight slung about him, helping each other up as they climb to a balcony out of the attackers' range in a building very close to the hostages' apartment.

Then, blackout! The whole day of September 5, no word of what really happened, what was planned, or how things were inside Block 31 where the victims and their executioners were waiting. Nor on what the West German authorities wanted or didn't want. Obviously those closest to the hostages, their teammates, a wife, a mother, knew no more than outsiders.

Less to kill time than to establish a sort of obbligato to the devilish concert, TV played and replayed the entrance of the Israeli team to the Olympic Stadium during the Inaugural Ceremonies, August 26, and its parade behind the blue-and-white flag with the Shield of David on it. Friendly applause, neither too restrained nor exuberant, off and on greeted the Jewish representatives, and swelled for a moment when the two women and twenty-seven men doffed their hats and turned eyes right to salute Herr Gustav Heinemann, the President of the G.F.R.

8:15 AM: "They've mounted a machine gun in the Tower's control-block!" Word was getting around like wildfire, and it was true: the Munich police had a 12.7 set up there.

The TV tower (*Fernsehturm*), naturally also referred to as the *Olympiaturm*, was the most spectacular height of the Gamesite. It lorded it over Munich like a wild pale-concrete lightpole: it stood 292 meters (322 yards) high, and the five rings interlaced near the top made it look like a space rocket for the year 2000. At night, the thin uprights, now black, became festooned with red, gold, and yellow brilliancies: the lighthouse beam blinking at the top, the revolving restaurant below it, and the lights strung along the stem.

Two elevators went up to it at 7 meters per second—a world speed record, it was reported. You went up to the highest of the platforms, 192 meters (212 yds.) up; it had a simple grillwork around it, so you got the fresh air and fragrances of the winds. To the north, the Bavarian plateau slanted gradually down toward the Danube, dotted with agriculture and cities with proud pasts. To the south, beneath the faithful sun of the '72 Olympics, a garland of lakes and forests, and beyond them, shining Alps, from the Algäu down to the Tyrol.

8:30 AM *(Diary):* "Listen! They're barking, the way they used to under Hitler!" That's Daniel Rocher, head of sports for Agence France-Presse, and he is right: two officers of the *München Stadt-polizei* (City Police of Munich) are storming around waving their submachine guns as if they were canes, because a reporter from the *Daily Express* is trying to scale the metal fence.

Rocher, a gold medalist in sports reporting, was first to note the (*kolossal*) move to seal off the Village. As an experienced newsman, he predicts, "It'll be one hell of a day . . ."

Around the barriers of what is now an armed camp, there is a constant stream from the *Pressezentrum*. The very best in TV cameras, microphones, and photographic equipment, as well as the binoculars of the written press, are deployed around the gates, knocking at them. The least hump in the ground is a prize observation post. Technicians set up their cameras to get the best angles from it. Every language of Babel is used to curse the interfering security service. The passes issued yesterday for today, previously unimportant to the accredited press, because there was no problem in getting into the Village, now are no longer good for anything at all.

Newspapermen are using every trick in the book to try to get their stories. The luckiest ones have been able to get hold of coaches', referees', and even delegation heads' identification—the only way to go, if you can find a willing team member, for even the *Krisenstab* can't keep the tenants of the *Dorf* from getting to their apartments. But there are now only two gates open. There are long lines at both, and the happy-go-lucky security service seems suddenly to have turned into the *Feldgendarmerie* of late, unlamented thoroughness. Some of the cops, fortunately, can't tell an I.D. picture that doesn't really look like the bearer—and there's always a chance of slipping in as an extra member of a volleyball, handball, football, or hockey team going through on the double without time to waste.

"*Madonna!*" says Cino Lozzati. "You know fat Gionatto? He

80

tried to jump the fence near the hockey field, and fell and broke a leg. Didn't even come down on the right side!" / [1]

Lalkin knew what it was to be powerless: he had spent two years in prison under the British mandate, for sabotage and acts of war. He belonged to the Wingate commandos. But never had he felt as totally and insanely powerless as on September 5 when, as he saw it, had they listened to him, there would have been at least a ghost of a chance.

Some of Lalkin's statements sound quite serious, today. He reiterated them to those who later came to visit him in the sunny garden of his white home at Tel Aviv:

"In June 1972, as future head of our delegation at the Games, I was sent to Munich. I was in charge of a lot of things, but not security. However, I felt responsible for those boys and girls. I explained to the Organizing Committee that I was concerned about their security. Despite their assurances, I wanted to meet with a qualified authority to discuss the matter in person. Through Mr. Daume's office it was arranged for me to see a very important character in the West German secret service. I cannot be any more specific.

"I said: 'I visited the Village, and have heard about all the precautions that are planned. But I have lots of doubts. You see, we understand very well that you neither can nor want to turn the Village into an armed camp. We too want to see a spirit of joy, freedom, and brotherhood. But I most energetically stress to you that we are sure we will be running serious risks by coming to the Games. We ask that you help us reduce these to a minimum. We are especially apprehensive of armed attacks by Arabs. There are tens of thousands of Arabs in your Federal Republic. I have not been able to get any idea of the arrangements made to defend us against possible attacks. I don't want to know the details, which must obviously be secret, but would like to know about them in general lines.'

"This important person smiled indulgently, and told me I had no reason for alarm. He added heatedly: 'Do you know how many officers will police the Games full time? Thirteen thousand! In the

[1] This slash sign (/) indicates the end of each Diary extract.

Olympic Village alone, there will be thirty-five hundred members of the security service, in turquoise-blue uniforms, to protect no more than twelve thousand inhabitants. The Israeli building will have extraordinary protection, around the clock.'

"I then asked this gentleman to look at a map of the Village with me. Using a pencil as pointer, I showed him how our future building would be located in relation to the fences, other delegations, security-service posts, and so on. I said, 'Why did they put us there? It's a little house that's wide open, and isolated at the end of the Village! We have scarcely any friendly delegations near us! If you can't put us elsewhere, you must guarantee me that we will be guarded in an absolutely special way!'

"He got up, shook my hand, and said emphatically: 'Don't worry, Mr. Lalkin. Trust us to do it!'"

On his return to Israel, Lalkin filed a report. Some delegations, whose proximity to the Israelis did not seem really desirable, were moved. But nothing more.

Each country participating in the Munich Games had an Olympic attaché. The big ones, such as France, sent a special representative to the Bavarian capital for this purpose. But most selected a diplomat already stationed in West Germany or a neighboring country. Thus, Israel turned these functions over to Mr. Werner Nachmann, stationed somewhat farther north.

One of these attachés' main jobs was to select their delegations' lodgings in the Village. The Organizing Committee held frequent meetings to this end. Some of the arguments were bitter, but the Germans always ended up by working out friendly compromises. The French, first set to share with other teams the huge building finally given to the Soviets at 26–32 Nadistrasse, were switched to other quarters close by, at 131–135 and 137 Nadistrasse. Many factors were considered: neighboring teams, noise, assembly and surveillance facilities, and so on.

"The fact is the Israeli Olympic attaché never protested over the delegation occupying part of 31 Connollystrasse," one of Mr. Nachmann's colleagues asured me. "I must say that, having conscientiously attended all the meetings, I never saw Mr. Nachmann there once."

Bundles of Neglect

The Israeli Olympic authorities all had the same reaction as Lalkin when they saw their men were to be in a little, far-out, isolated building. What they wanted was to be high in a tower.

Would that have been any better?

It might have been harder for the fedayeen to get in. The terrorists might not have escaped detection, even if they all came underground. The towers seemed to me to be particularly well superintended: they had a charge of quarters in the lobby. If the fedayeen had gotten to the Israeli floors, they would immediately have awakened occupants of neighboring floors. The alarm would have been much faster: the great majority of the Jews would have had time to lock themselves in.

At 31 Connollystrasse, the Black September guerrillas commanded approaches in all directions. In a tower, there would have been many blind spots, traps, and hidden approaches: they could have been tightly surrounded. Their liquidation would have been much more feasible in an upper story of a tower, at any move they tried to make, if only because they would have had to use the elevator, or be trapped in the narrow dark of an underground lobby.

That very special guard that was to be set up over the Israelis just plain never existed. The delegation was aware of this the moment it emplaned on Lufthansa. The flight stopped at Zurich. There, as well as when they landed at Riem, the Israelis were continually alone, without a shadow of any escort.

They also noted, once moved into Block 31, that no security-service person was ever on sentry duty at the building, nor anywhere near it. Lalkin, Hershkowitz, and several others made a test of it personally, several times, before the attack; never a soul, day or night.

"All we saw between seven AM and seven PM," Lalkin told me, "was twice or three times a fellow in turquoise blue with a walkie-talkie. The night guards had 7.65 pistols. Big deal!"

The wrestler Gad Tsobari told me that one night he got back to 31 Connollystrasse after 2:00 AM. That was September 1. His events had just finished. With a head full of Bavarian songs, and feeling fine and at peace because he had competed well, he walked several friends back to their respective quarters, and then for a long time took a walk in the area of Block 31 far into the night, before going up to bed.

"Well, I did not see a single policeman. Zilch!"

I asked Tsobari whether he had his key; yes, he did. He was to be the last one in, so the apartment leader, Yossef Romano, had given him one.

"What happened if one of you came back in the middle of the night," I asked, "without expecting to? That must have happened."

"Sure! He'd ring, and we opened, and he got hell!"

Remember that these apartments can be opened from the outside only with a key; during the day, the Israelis generally left their keys with the concierge.

The *Dokumentation* of September 20 naturally discusses the relations of the organizers and police with the Israeli representatives before the start of the Games. It unfortunately fails to mention Lalkin's visit to Munich in June 1972, or his worries at that time. Beyond that, it asserts that on August 9, 1972, a "member of Israeli security" came to inspect the Munich arrangements for his countrymen. Everything was explained to him and he left without voicing the slightest complaint.

The same report also refers to interviews on August 24 and 25 with "a representative of the Israeli delegation," who does not appear then to have been so reassured, since he asked to have the police and special services go to Connollystrasse with him. But that was too late: the Games were about to begin, and all arrangements had been made.

In fact, Olympic Village was virtually wide open. To stress the peaceful image of the Federal Republic, they dispensed with barbed wire, using simple wiremesh fences, used no night sentries near the barriers, and made no identity checks within the *Dorf*. The delegations were expected to watch out for themselves! Except that—firearms were strictly forbidden within the Village! Only the night security service was allowed to have them, and they were hidden. Even the weapons of the shooting teams were not allowed off the range at Hochbrück—which did not keep some of the contestants from bringing their pistols back with them and firing blanks for fun in the Village.

Bundles of Neglect

The Israeli and West German special services until the Games exchanged information concerning possible acts against the Israeli delegation or any of the groups of citizens of the Jewish State who were going to Munich. But none of it suggested any actual threat to the Israelis—even though Palestinian circles had been carefully watched.

On October 17, 1972, Prime Minister Golda Meir was to make a statement to the Knesset about the Munich events. It was her second. In between, she had received the results of an investigating committee she had set up, including Messrs. Pinhas Koppel, Avigdor Bartle, and Moshe Kashti.

What the so-called "Koppel Commission" reported was very severe on West German reaction against the terrorists. It also criticized the flightiness of the Germans concerning their Jewish guests' security. "It was a grave error to provide mere routine security precautions for the Israeli delegation," she said. "Security . . . is the obligation and responsibility of the host country." The Israeli Prime Minister especially condemned the Germans for having refused to allow armed guards either in front of or inside 31 Connollystrasse.

If only, even without specific guards assigned to the Israelis, even without unusual precautions, the German security officials of the Village had set up careful patrolling, day and night . . . especially at night! But, worse luck, everything that seemed good about the Village worked to the disadvantage of Jewish security. Mere patrols on bicycle, going by several times an hour at irregular intervals on Connollystrasse, would have been a tough nut for the terrorists to crack.

The Koppel Commission, with Prime Minister Meir echoing it, was honest enough to point out the failings of Israel's special services: they did not foresee events; they were asleep.

"I am convinced," she said, "that the adoption of more comprehensive and intensive security measures, in accord with the German authorities, might have hamstrung the terrorists and lessened their chances." And she dismissed three key members of the Israeli secret service.

But there are degrees of error. Dr. Schreiber continually touted the impressive figure of the number of officers guarding the Games, and insisted Germany could not have done more to protect her guests. But he did not mention how they were deployed.

There is the case of Juan Carlos of Spain, the pretender to the throne named by Generalissimo Franco as his successor, who was entered in the Olympic regatta at Kiel as Juan Carlos de Borbón. The official record of participants lists him as born January 5, 1938, standing 1.82 meters (6 ft. 1) and weighing 79 kg. (174 lbs.). His team finished 15th out of 24 in the Dragon class. Not bad for a first Olympic competition, especially since his boat ran into technical problems. From the moment of his arrival at Kiel, he was tailed and guarded day and night, step by step, by two German police officers, to say nothing of the agents Madrid must have sent. And that was right. If the Israeli delegation had had three guards around the clock at Connollystrasse, one outside and two indoors, things might have been different.

8:45 AM *(Diary):* The blonde interpreter is back in front of Building 31, and I've found a great observation post at the top of an iron spiral staircase. The staircase just happens to be there, for no special reason, inside a domed cage set up on a concrete rise between Connollystrasse and Nadistrasse.

The nine-o'clock deadline is near. What will happen?

She knocks lightly at the door, with her fingertips. Some twenty seconds later, it opens and the leader in the little white linen hat sticks his head out. Behind him, you can see one of his cronies with a white scarf with red polka dots around his face, a huge scarf that might be twisted into a kaffiyeh.

The policewoman and the fedayee exchange a few words. He acquiesces, condescendingly. She gives two approving headshakes toward someone invisible. And with the studied care of an advancing column, Herren Tröger and Schreiber appear; accompanied by a large, heavy man, A.D. Touny, an Egyptian member of the International Committee for the past dozen years, an agronomist and political VIP.

This is my first view of Herr Tröger: baby face, air of assurance, he is rather small, well built, plumpish. He is supposed to be very nice, an excellent organizer, and he has done a fine job of setting up the Village.

Behind him, Schreiber, tough and determined, is looking toward Issa with an imperial face.

While the three argue with the fedayee, each side is deploying its bodyguards. Issa, for good measure, has in hand a Tokagypt, the Egyptian-adapted version of the Tokarev 9-mm Soviet automatic, a good pistol with a protected grip.

Herr Tröger announces to Issa that he, Ministers Merk and Genscher, Police Chief Schreiber, and Herr Vogel want to take the Israeli athletes' place as hostages.

"No. You are not our enemies. The Israelis are!" is the terrorist's reply. (This offer was to be repeated four times by the Germans.)

"In fifteen minutes," Issa goes on, "with my own hand I will kill a hostage right here, unless we have an affirmative answer to our ultimatum."

Touny intercedes: Israel has just barely received the list; no one has been able to reach Prime Minister Meir yet. If the guerrillas are fair, they should agree to a postponement of at least six hours. They compromise on three. New deadline: Noon . . . /

Chancellor Willy Brandt reached Mrs. Meir by phone. The Bonn-Jerusalem call lasted some ten minutes. Brandt acknowledged it had taken place, whereas Mrs. Meir merely said, "No comment." Though she did add that "the German Federal Government at no time tried to pressure Israel during the Munich events."

Here is a faithful summary of their conversation.

Brandt told of the new noon deadline, and said: "I want to assure you that I will do everything possible to free the Israeli athletes. I am worried about those fedayeen in the Village. Without trying to influence your decisions, I must say that, in your place, I would make some gesture, if only the slightest, to calm them down."

"My position," said Mrs. Meir, "is that under no conditions will Israel make the slightest concession to terrorist blackmail. My Government is unanimously behind me in this."

Brandt tried to get Mrs. Meir to agree to some partial promise: if the hostages were freed, Israel would promise after a period, say, of several days, to turn loose a portion of the political prisoners.

She answered she would submit the idea to her Cabinet, but she herself was against it.

"Munich is a German city," she said. "Weinberg's murder and the attack on the Olympic Village, the taking hostage of ten athletes and officials, are domestic German crimes."

Brandt: "I, at my end, have decided to advise the fedayeen before noon that we agree to free the two German prisoners they are asking for. That is all I have the power to do."

Mrs. Meir: "In the name of my country, I ask you not to abandon those ten Israeli athletes in the terrorists' hands."

The talk ended on a cordial note; the two prime ministers respect each other, and have long been friends. They are of the same political stripe, for Mrs. Meir's Mapai is the Israeli Socialist Party, and Brandt's SPD is the German Socialist (Social Democratic) Party. They were truly in harmony. But, today . . .

9:00 AM: Mark Spitz went through with the press conference that had been announced in advance and so anxiously anticipated until the dawn of September 5. Not that there was anything to reveal: everything had been said and done already. It was to be an apotheosis: the last Olympic meeting between the written and spoken media and the greatest, most impressive swimmer ever; a tribute from the world press and public to the recordholder for the largest number of gold medals won in one Olympics.

Out of twelve individual events, Spitz was first in four: 100-meter freestyle, 200-meter freestyle, 100-meter butterfly, and 200-meter butterfly. In each event he set a new record (breaking the old record he held in every case). In the three relay events on the schedule, first place in all: 4x100 meters freestyle, 4x200 meters freestyle, and 4x100 meters four styles. In these, too, the world records fell. Seven gold medals!

While the Indiana University student answered the questions, some of which were so obvious ("How did you feel when you won your first event at Munich?"—"Happy."), an effort was made not to dwell too much on the horror of the hostages. Two policemen guarded the doorway on either side, submachine guns at the ready. The buzz of helicopters above could be heard through the thick windowpanes. Awkwardly commingled in the journalistic crowd were dozens of turquoise-blue uniforms, and almost as many hefty fellows, chewing gum, in civvies with two lumps under their jackets like bulging brassieres. People were packed like sardines in the room, so artfully lighted you were unaware of it.

Mark Spitz was a Jew.

"What do you think about the death of Moshe Weinberg and the five Israeli hostages being held by the fedayeen in the Olympic Village?"

"No comment. It is a very tragic thing." The reply in his almost dry voice might have seemed banal and disappointing, were it not for the drawn lines of the face, the twitching eyelids, the proud and modest effort Spitz was making to keep from tears.

He had previously announced he would stay for all the Olympic ceremonies, the receptions and benefit shows.

"Are you still staying till September 11?"

"No."

"When are you leaving?"

"Right away."

"Where to? New York or Los Angeles?"

One of the coaches standing near him, flanked by the gum-chewing operatives, snarled, "No answer! Security reasons!" But, as if he had not heard, Mark answered, "Los Angeles."

He remained a distance from the mike. When it was pointed out to him, he just shook his head. Obviously terribly watchful, his eyes kept darting about the crowd; maybe he had been told to hold back in case the mike had been rigged to blow up if he talked right into it. In such an atmosphere, it had taken a huge effort of self-composure to face hundreds of journalists and technicians, of whom at least 15-odd could be recognized as Arabs. It was easy to get fake plasticized presscards. An American official later said that that very morning Mark had gotten more than ten warnings and death threats, in less than an hour. . . .

"Mark Spitz, born February 10, 1950, at Carmichael, California. 1.85 m. (6 ft. 2); 77 kg. (160 lbs.). Dental student . . ." said the official biographical note. It might have added: Jewish, from a religious family.

He had been a heavy favorite already in the 1968 Mexico City Games. But the strain had been too much: two gold medals in the relays, and one silver and one bronze in the 100-meter free-style and butterfly respectively, were all he got instead of the six first places he had hoped for. He had been called "too proud." Some said he was "finished." But he buckled down to the toughest, driest, longest training in the world: eight to ten miles in the pool every day, spending over four hours in the water, not to mention the rest-time between. All year 'round.

The main reason for his leaving Santa Clara in 1969 and breaking with his famous coach George Haines was Mark's Jewish-ness. He had been invited to Israel to take part in the Maccabean Games. He had accepted. But then the University of Santa Clara, at Haines' urging, had tried to stop him, on the pretext that the school needed him to swim for it in quite unimportant meets. He had just won a flock of national and college titles for Santa Clara. So he defied the dictate, and went on to win seven firsts at the Maccabean Games.

The journalists were disappointed by his reserve (though they were just as prone to criticize medalists whose prizes went to their heads). He never left a question unanswered, and was as polite as could be. He stayed with them for forty minutes. But his first action, when it was over, was to go looking for news of the Connollystrasse hostages.

For he knew them all.

I had met him at the reception for the Israeli delegation at the Holiday Inn, on August 24 or 25. When Spitz got there, Moshe Weinberg ran over and hugged him. Mark fired questions at him, about one Israeli and another, and then congratulated him on the birth of his son.

"You mean you know about it?"

"Sure. You wouldn't think of letting me know! But Shlomit told me!"

Shlomit Nir was a woman breaststroke swimmer on the Israeli team; a gorgeous hunk of girl. Weinberg had put Spitz up at the Orde Wingate Institute on Mark's last visit to Israel.

A lot has been written about Mark's $5,000,000 commercial contracts—but they detract in no way from the fantastic beauty of his Olympic feats. In Mark Spitz' triumphs, history got the last laugh. I watched him every time he went to the podium and the U.S. flag was raised. He looked like a new Saul. Who says competitive sports bring out only freaks and supermen? . . .

How Mark's eyes shone when "The Star-Spangled Banner" rang out. He has narrow, dark eyes, a blackish brown, the proud and clear eyes of a son of Judea. His face was tanned, chiseled, mobile as the sea, longish, with dark beard, thick brows, and a lusty smile beneath the peaked mustache. He stood out in all of his events, as superb and powerful as a shark. In the water, his mane seemed like a jet black plume.

He briefly smiled good-bye to the press and the broken spell of Olympic charm, and went off, with his nonchalant step and his long legs that bend in at the knees. The toughs in the swollen jackets formed a wedge around him, sweeping the terrain with their eyes like searchlights. . . .

Outside, you could feel the tragedy: police dogs, without barking, tugged at their chains, when you came too near.

There was no wind to cut the heat; it was heavy, muggy. Blue sky, dotted with stationary white balloons. I went to the top of the panoramic hill in *Olympiapark:* the Alps could barely be divined on the horizon. It was as if, way down at their first foothills, a huge screen miles high had been erected, made of some flexible material, transparent but dirty, distorting, and waving. And that screen seemed to be moving, closing in on our Bavarian plateau.

9:10 AM: Two fedayeen (the one, painted red, big Tony, the other in a hood no doubt Abu Halla, from his graceful kittenlike motions) appeared at the second-floor window and signaled. The interpreter, Fräulein Graes, came over. One of the men had a gun and in his telescopic sight was aiming at something. They demanded that the crowd—and the police barriers holding them— be moved back. This was to happen several times: the security services moved the people back. Then Tony gave the interpreter a sheet of paper.

It was another ultimatum, somewhat repetitious of the earlier one, but worth reproducing here in full:

> The arrogant attitude of Israel's militaristic authorities and
> their refusal to comply with our demands have not caused us to

forget our humane feelings, and we will continue to try to find a way to spare the Israeli prisoners, on the following terms:

1. The German Federal Republic must announce that it agrees to have the Israeli prisoners transferred to any other location designated by our revolutionary forces in Olympic Village.

2. The G.F.R. must put at the disposal of our forces three airplanes on which the Israeli prisoners and our armed forces will fly, in three successive departures, toward a destination chosen by us. Each plane will leave Munich about one hour after the previous one arrives at its destination.

3. Any attempt to sabotage our operation will result in immediate liquidation of all the Israeli prisoners, for which the G.F.R. will bear total responsibility.

4. This ultimatum expires three hours from now; that is, at noon. The G.F.R. will be responsible for the results of this decision.

5. At the expiration of this ultimatum, if our demand to leave German territory has not been complied with, our revolutionary forces are instructed to use just and revolutionary force to give a severe lesson to the warmongering heads of the Israeli military machine and the G.F.R. for its arrogance.

REVOLUTIONARIES OF THE WORLD, UNITE!
(*signed*) I. B. S. O.

This was all written out in a ballpoint pen, in German. The initials were mysterious, as the fedayeen wanted them, but probably stood for the English *International Black September Organization* (or the *I* could have been for *Islamic*).

It is notable that there is no direct mention here of the 236 political prisoners whose freedom they had demanded as the price of the lives of the hostages. Now they were merely attacking Israel's "arrogant attitude." Of course, the fact that all of the earlier demands still obtained was self-evident: they wanted to take their prisoners to a friendly country. There, they themselves would be safe, and nothing could stop them from carrying to the extreme the blackmail of threatening to execute the hostages if all of their demands were not met.

9:15 AM: Fräulein Graes, or Echler (no first name), the lieutenant of Munich's criminal police, always seemed to have plenty of time, never in a hurry. She had now come to the street door of Block 31's lobby to tell the terror-squatters that their memorandum was being telexed to Israel, but atmospheric conditions were poor.

"Let's hope for the hostages' sakes that they quickly improve," Issa said. He switched easily from Arabic to German with her. She spoke Arabic exclusively. Later she was to say that it seemed to her that while Issa spoke Arabic fluently and without mistakes, he spoke in a careful, watchful way, as if there were something acquired about it.

Fräulein Graes waved good-bye with her head. Unhurriedly, she went down toward the end of Connollystrasse, i.e., westward, toward the wiremesh enclosure—opposite to where she had come from.

She knew she was being intensely watched by the attackers as well as the two Israeli physicians locked up in No. 4. She walked even straighter than usual; chest out, gut in, head high, looking slightly to her left, toward Block 31.

A pretty girl with a round face, she walked like someone out for a stroll, lazily. Her back was to the terrorists. She was getting close to the windows of No. 4, from which Drs. Kranz and Weigel could see her.

Looking up at their rectangular windows, she made motions that were as sharp as they were clear. She brought in the hand holding the strap to her bag and four or five times waved it impetuously out from her chest and at the same time upward—in a gesture that under any clime means "Fly away! Beat it!"—while her lips very clearly mouthed in English: "Go! Go out! Now! Go!" There was a spark in her eye; her face seemed to change, to become excited, imperious.

The doctors understood. The Olympic staff member could only be trying to help them, and everything about her said: NOW! They perked up their courage, opened the French door on the garden side, and out they shot.

The terrorists had a man standing guard on the balcony of Apt. 1. Seeing the two physicians, he yelled "Halt!" and shouldered his gun. He would have had plenty of time to aim carefully and to bring down one of the two fleeing figures, especially since they were deplorably awkward, and did not dodge at all. Witnesses who saw it firsthand said that one of the two doctors stumbled, and they thought the fedayee had fired. But he had not. There was no shot. He was not sure that they were Israelis at all, since he could see only their backs.

VI
THE FEDAYEEN

Then said all the trees unto the
bramble: Come thou, and reign over us.
 And the bramble said unto the trees:
If in truth ye anoint me king over you,
then come and take refuge in my shadow;
and if not, let fire come out of the
bramble, and devour the cedars of Lebanon.
Judges 9:14, 15

ALL THE ORGANIZATIONS OF PALESTINIAN GUERRILLA WARFARE HAVE
the same aim: to fight Israel, without letup or respite, "so long as
Zionists occupy Palestinian land," to quote Yasir Arafat; in other
words, so long as there is a Jewish state.

It was King Farouk's Egypt, in 1949, that first had the idea of
sending Palestinian guerrillas against Israel. They immediately
took the name of *fedayeen* (fighters for the faith), but their activity
remained relatively minor until the end of 1954. Then Col. Gamal
Abdel Nasser ordered the Egyptian counterespionage service
(Mukhabarat el Kharbeyyah) to beef up the fedayeen. The Syrians
also set out to ape their "brothers" and rivals on the Nile. Terrorist
raids into Israel were at their height when the Sinai campaign of
October 1956 took place. Then they let up, only to resume the
next year.

Little by little, several parallel organizations, more and more
in competition with one another, sprang up. Each Middle Eastern
Arab state had its own. The Egyptian-controlled fedayeen, whether
in terrorist networks or regular military units, began to operate
not only against Israel, but also against so-called "reactionary"
Arab governments. . . .

The groups proliferated: OLP (Organization for the Liberation
of Palestine); PLA (Palestinian Liberation Army); NLF (National
Liberation Front) with its NLA (National Liberation Army);
PFLP (Popular Front for the Liberation of Palestine); and mainly

El Fatah, meaning Conquest, or Military Victory. The name was also an anagram, reversed in the typically Arabic love for playing with words, of more or less the initials of *Harakat At Tahrir Elwatani El Falas-tini* (National Movement for the Liberation of Palestine). . . .

Headed by Yasir Arafat, this last became the dominant group of them all, with a program that was, and remains, crystal clear (summarizing from various Arafat pronouncements):

1. Total war, with no thought of parleying with the Zionists . . .
2. War alone . . . Palestinian land must be liberated before the people can be free . . . Political doctrines applied to the Palestinian people today are as paralyzing as bureaucracy. Until we gain victory, we must have unity, apart from any ideology.
3. [Palestinianism is the prerequisite]: The Palestinians must free themselves.
4. [Arab states must give total support to the liberation movements] not with men, but with the means to conduct our struggle, from arms to bases, and including total freedom for our action. . . .

El Fatah has stated that Black September was created at the end of 1970, out of humiliation, frustration, and the desire for revenge. Its founders, members of Al Assifa, El Fatah's military arm, had lived through the "ten terrible September days" of 1970, on the battlefields of Jordan. A handful of survivors among the soldiers crushed by King Hussein's forces and exiled to Lebanon took the name of *Ailul al Asswad* (Black September), resolving to carry punishment and total war to the Jews of the world and the Husseinites. They are no longer connected with El Fatah, although they sprang from it. Nor do they hesitate to criticize the heads of El Fatah, albeit in what might be called a reasonable and fraternal way.

Or that, at least, is what they would have us believe.

To get at one of the basic facts, let us again consider El Fatah's stand. One of Yasir Arafat's leitmotifs before the bloody showdown with King Hussein was (again piecing together a number of his statements):

The Fedayeen

We have only one enemy, Israel. Our only battlefield should be Palestine. To attack Westerners and undertake guerrilla warfare outside our own country, to indulge in blind terrorism, to take innocent people as hostages, would mobilize world opinion against us and tie us indissolubly to the Communists. We are fighters for the faith. We would never be such cowards as to shed civilian blood. We will not sully our just cause . . .

This indeed is why El Fatah had never wanted its name associated with the savage acts of the "Palestinian resistance." However, in light, for instance, of the innumerable mortar or Katyusha shellings of Israeli villages from Lebanon, Syria, or Jordan, or the many acts of sabotage and other violence committed within Israel . . . there was a great load of hypocrisy in the Fatah leader's statements, for his group was always ready to accept credit for these atrocities.

Yet, Yasir Arafat and his movement would still like to be thought of as "pure and tough fighters," which they can the more easily achieve because they control the OLP, with its connections in virtually every country in which Black September has struck.

In fact, from the very first reverses of the Assifa in Jordan (October 1970), some of Arafat's lieutenants conceived the idea of a terrorist branch whose No. 1 aim would be the liquidation of Hussein and his whole family. Abu Hassan strongly supported such a proposal before the Central Committee, but he was voted down.

In the summer of 1971, the so-called revolutionary movements, PFLP at the head, were multiplying their terrorist actions, and Fatah by contrast seemed less dynamic than once it had. Arafat and the heads of his Assifa then made their decisive mistake. On June 5, El Fatah and six other movements joined in a manifesto calling for the ouster of King Hussein, at a time when Arafat's organization alone had a strong base in Jordan. Shortly afterward, the Assifa challenged Jordan's Arab Legion by spreading over the northern part of the country. The fighting broke out on July 13; by July 19, Fatah's army was no more.

On July 27, 1971, at Beirut, the movement's Central Committee met. Abu Hassan, Abu Jihad, and Abu Yussef urged their companions to resort to "total guerrilla warfare." The Hashemite dynasty and its backers had to be punished. El Fatah needed an underground branch that nothing could stop.

The new setup, intended as the spearhead of organized terrorism, could subsist and succeed only with the powerful support of Fatah, though it retained broad freedom of operation. Absolute secrecy; impenetrable compartmentalization; careful and detailed planning; maximum elimination of time-lapse between conception, implementation, and execution; power of immediate decision, even including summary death sentences for culpable agents and last-minute changes of plans (e.g., the murder of a VIP suddenly found accessible): this set of provisions showed that Black September was to have full autonomy as well as unlimited capabilities.

When Arafat and Abu Sabri demurred, the majority of the nine Committee members retorted that under any circumstances they ought to create a special section for organized terrorism, haphazard strikes really accomplishing nothing. Since the Arab collapse in the Six Days' War, the Popular Front for the Liberation of Palestine had emerged as the leader of all-out guerrilla warfare, terrorism, and extension throughout the world of anti-Israeli actions. Among the desperate and highly conditioned masses of refugees, PFLP was becoming more and more popular. And when the heads of El Fatah recently got wind of a strange attempt at mass assassination of all their Central Committee, they suspected not Israel, but certain PFLP elements.

Under such conditions, why not give a chance to the team of intelligent fanatics at hand? Yasir Arafat at the end of the meeting suddenly decided in favor of it. But he said he first wanted to make sure that the future terrorist network would from the start have significant financial wherewithal—"not out of Fatah's treasury," he specified.

At the beginning of August he went to Tripoli to negotiate with Libyan Colonel Khaddafi for a large subsidy earmarked for the future terrorist setup. Libya, seventh largest oil producer in the world (132,000,000 tonnes in 1971), had a colossal source of income therefrom, but its new leaders had gone into ruinous prestige expenditures. Arafat, assisted by his aide Abu Ayad, to whom Khaddafi owed a debt of gratitude, was successful. Coming back from Libya, he gave the green light, and Black September took off. The name of the organization reflects internecine Arab hatred; Arafat is said to have chosen it.

He and the El Fatah leaders felt that the links between their organization and Black September had to remain absolutely secret, at least until the first overt terrorist actions. After that, the game would be more complex, but it would still consist of officially denying any Fatah-Black September collusion.

He had come a far way since that January 1965 when a still-unknown Arafat, graying and worried as now, but solid, lively, muscular, strong as a mule, and a crack shot, had anonymously led El Fatah commandos in their first sabotage operations in Israel.

Now, despite the Jordanian misadventure, El Fatah was the sole colossus among the Palestinian movements. Its dream was still to bring down the Hashemite dynasty and proclaim a Palestinian Republic in Amman. It was intended to keep its respectable front so that, when that time came, such a takeover would be acceptable to the Western powers. It was still Israel's implacable enemy; it built up solid classical military units; it carried out guerrilla activities—all of which helped its image with the Arabs. But blind terrorism, killing of hostages, skyjacking, these might prove embarrassing to a powerful movement fully intending soon to govern a portion of Palestine.

Yasir Arafat, at that highly delicate point of setting up the terrorist network, had another reason for wanting maximum secrecy about anything to do with Black September, including its connections with the mother body: that was the infiltration of El Fatah by Israeli secret agents. Arafat was the first to realize that what with the swelling of his ranks and the living conditions of Palestinian Moslems the Jews were able to penetrate his movement more and more. Only the nine Central Committee members dealt with Black September affairs.

Some specialists have said that the first Black September head was Mohammed Mustafa Shyein, an old comrade of Arafat's and a Fatah Central Committee member from 1962 to 1971. Coming from a well-known Jerusalem family of Palestinian traders, Shyein —called Ali Abu Iyad, which is how we shall henceforth refer to him—was for total violence. He had been urging the creation of a terrorist group in the shadow of El Fatah for ten years. . . . But he was killed before Black September started, so he could not have headed it.

Abu Iyad at Baalbek ran the principal training and refresher camp for commando leaders. He also commanded the first shock *katiba* (company) of Assifa, stationed at Madaba, southeast of Amman, near the Dead Sea. . . . He was captured on July 17, 1971, outside Djerash, in a cave in which he and a few of his men were hiding after the company was wiped out. He had shown no quarter to Jordanian officers who fell into his hands. And none was shown him. El Fatah accused the Arab Legion of torturing him before his death. Mr. Wasfi Tal, Jordan's Prime Minister and Minister of Defense, replied that Abu Iyad had been killed in the heat of battle, but further stressed the cruelties attributed to that warrior chief. El Fatah then announced its death sentence on the Amman Prime Minister: the first Black September exploit was the murder of Wasfi Tal in Cairo, November 28, 1971. . . .

At any rate, there can no longer be any doubt that Black September is the terror arm of El Fatah. *Al Gomhuriya (The Republic)*, the influential Cairene morning newspaper and official organ of Egypt's single political party, on September 21, 1972, printed under the byline of its specialist in Palestinian affairs, Mohamed El Azbi, "Black September is a secret branch directly controlled by El Fatah."

Let us now move a step closer to Connollystrasse, with mention of two names that were to crop up many times during that tragedy.

Fuad Chemali, under the direction of Abu Hassan, was the organizer and most trusted adviser of Black September in Europe, until his death from cancer in mid-August 1972.

A Lebanese Christian, he had belonged to El Fatah from its start. In Geneva, he housed and saw to the treatment of two of Arafat's close kin. Never hiding his membership in El Fatah, until his final days he kept feeding the mass media news of it and of OLP. Naturally, he never referred to his role in Black September. He often went to Lebanon and Egypt, and had close connections with Daoud Barakat, of whom more anon.

Fuad Chemali died at about forty-five years of age. He was a

Marat, with a haunting bony face, eroded by a gleaming, fanatical look. Skinny, pallid, knowing he was dying and watching himself go, he was hatred and method incarnate. He thought up and helped organize at least five big Black September operations, including the major one, ours at Munich. His thesis, bought and put into action, was that terrorist acts had to be increased on the one hand against well-known or important Israelis (scientists, artists, writers) and on the other hand against Israeli delegations to meetings of world scope (U.N., festivals, sports events, international congresses).

Ramdane Abane, one of the toughest leaders of the Algerian NLF in the first years of its insurrection, once said:

> It is more profitable to shoot down a single VIP or plastic-bomb a large café in the heart of Algiers, even if only women and children are to die in it, than to wipe out a whole French squad in the brush. In the first case, we get star billing all around the world. In the second, we are dismissed in a few lines, if not completely blacked out.

Fuad Chemali lived five or six years in Geneva. His cover: Arab League delegate to the U.N. institutions headquartered there. In Beirut, this strange diplomat was especially famous, on account of his marriage. He had married Mlle. Elissa Saadé, someone to reckon with at the time of Connollystrasse.

Saadé is a famous name: her father, Antoine Saadé, had founded the prewar Syrian People's Party, which plumped for a merger of Syria and Lebanon, a dream the British shared. Like them, M. Saadé hoped to see this "Greater Syria" ruled by a sovereign of the Hashemite dynasty, already enthroned at both Baghdad and Amman. So, his party was serving Britain against France, then the mandatory power in both Syria and Lebanon.

When the two countries gained independence, Antoine Saadé swung to the Left, against the West and in opposition to the Lebanese regime, which executed him in 1950. His party, in his image, boldly came out in favor of the fedayeen. As the husband of Elissa Saadé, herself a passionate party militant, Fuad Chemali became the guiding light of the party, which remained significant,

101

if only as an excellent propaganda outlet. About a quarter of its membership was made up of Palestinian refugees. The Saadés remained important people in Beirut. . . .

Fuad Chemali's widow, still young, and a very striking black-eyed brunette, dressing in the height of fashion and with the best of social connections, tried to be as discreet as her late husband; but well-informed circles in Geneva were all more or less aware that the couple worked not for El Fatah alone, but also represented Black September.

From the morning of September 5 on, floods of cables and broadcasts linked the names of the Fuad Chemalis with the Block 31 attack. Before noon, the rumors had become more specific, although circumscribed by the wire services with the usual "alleged" and "reputed." About the dead man, the sheaves of evidence were so overwhelming there could be no doubt of his links to Black September (in the days that followed, more proof appeared—including documents discovered at Frankfort—concerning his part in planning the attack).

As for the young widow, many informants stated quite simply that, replacing her husband, she had masterminded the Olympic Village affair. Others, less positive, said she had contributed greatly to the operation. Thanks to her diplomatic passport (both she and her husband had been given Arab League credentials by the Lebanese Ministry of Foreign Affairs), she was alleged personally to have driven three of the terrorists to Munich in her Chevrolet.

These statements spread like wildfire in Beirut. By 1:00 PM, September 5, the SPP had put out a denial of any direct or indirect participation by Mme. Elissa Chemali in the attack, specifying that it had been in contact with her at Geneva. Then her mother, the widow of Antoine Saadé, also put out a statement, saying she had just spoken by phone with her daughter, who had not stirred out of Geneva in a week, and was in the process of selling her furniture before moving out of the apartment she and her husband had occupied. The mother specified: "Madame Elissa Chemali asked me to stress that she has had absolutely nothing to do with the Munich fedayeen operation."

The Chemalis are not in the phonebook, and it is no easy job to get their address. Yet a few newspeople succeeded in doing that. In

102

one of the towers on Rue Marzin, facing the park, they were greeted by courteous gentlemen in bulging jackets who intimated to them not to loiter near the door, since the Widow Chemali was in no condition to see them.

Around 3:00 PM, Swiss plainclothes police appeared in their turn. They were immediately shown in. Only later in the evening did the *Krisenstab* allow another item to leak out that brought in her name. This will appear in our chronological narration at the entry for *3:55* PM.

The other pivotal Black September name in Europe is that of Daoud Barakat, previously mentioned. He is a diplomat of the Democratic Republic of Yemen, living in Geneva, on Rue Gautier. . . . Arnaud de Borchgrave in an article in *Newsweek* at the end of September 1972 was the first to put the spotlight on Barakat, naming him as West European head of Black September. He went on to specify that Barakat was fully accredited to the U.N. and other international organizations in Geneva, and that, with a diplomatic passport issued by the Aden Government, he came and went with the greatest of ease between Geneva and the Middle East. (Barakat issued denial after denial, but in the spring of 1973 he was to be officially so identified by Swiss authorities.)

"Black September is merely the action section of Rasd [El Fatah's secret service]," some authoritative writers have stated. This is not quite so, even though Rasd has at times lent men to the terrorist group, and vice versa. . . .

The U.S. Central Intelligence Agency admits having monitored "almost" all the communications between Beirut and Khartoum, at the time of the March 1973 attack on the Saudi Arabian embassy in the latter capital. A month later, the CIA revealed that on the evening of March 2 it had recorded the following exchange between Arafat's Beirut office and the Khartoum terrorists: "The organization orders—repeat: orders—you to carry out Operation Cold River on Numbers One, Two, and Three."

The terrorists acknowledged the message and five minutes later reported back, "Cold River successfully completed on Numbers One, Two, and Three." These obviously were the three victims, the Belgian diplomat Eidet and the Americans Moore and Noel.

The sentence ordering the assassinations was spoken by Arafat's El Fatah second-in-command, Salah Khalaf (also known as Abu Ayad, who heads Rasd). But when Khartoum reported its successful operation, it was the voice of Yasir Arafat himself that was heard saying, "Brothers, I congratulate you and thank you! Long live Arab Palestine!"

That "Long live Arab Palestine" is the sign-off of all El Fatah broadcasts.

A "highly authorized CIA source," in revealing this, noted that "this is the first time that Mr. Arafat is incontrovertibly implicated personally in a Black September terrorist attack."

Despite all of which, El Fatah denied any part in the Khartoum butchery. Yet, instead of condemning it, Arafat thought it proper, after the denial, to state without any proof whatsoever that one of the three murdered diplomats, Mr. Curtis Moore, "had been involved in the September 1970 massacres in Jordan." . . .

Black September, though still young, has not remained silent. Mohamed Daoud el Odeh (known as Abu Daoud) spoke so freely to the Hashemite authorities at Amman that the 1973 Khartoum fedayeen put him at the head of the list of those they wanted released—presumably so he could fight again, but in fact so they might see to it he never opened his mouth again. . . . Let us see what he had to say about the preparation for Munich:

> The Olympic Village operation was planned by Abu Ayad at Sofia. I had been in Bulgaria since mid-August to make arms purchases for our mother organization [El Fatah]. On September 1, 1972, Abu Ayad arrived at Sofia, from Switzerland, and stopped at the hotel I was at. He was accompanied by Fakhry al Omari [a well-known Fatah leader]. That evening, these two comrades told me of an unusually large action that was to take place at Munich.
>
> Abu Ayad said, "Do you have a passport with an entry visa for West Germany?" When I said I did, he bade me give it to Al Omari, since my picture could be taken for him if not inspected too closely.
>
> The financing of the Munich job and the arming of the personnel involved were handled by Mohamed Masalha. The latter, based in Tripoli, was called in to confer with us in preparing the

104

attack; he had had a part in building the Olympic Village and spoke several languages, including German.

It is not true that Germans or Arab nationals living in West Germany were involved in the Munich operation. It was carried out by six fedayeen who came from Tripoli in Libya, three via Rome and three via Belgrade . . .

This seems an authentic confession, for the CIA has checked out the presence of Khalaf, Omari, and Masalha at Sofia.

However, Abu Daoud's revelations still contain some errors. Deliberate, perhaps? The most obvious: that only six fedayeen pulled off the Connollystrasse attack, when we well know there were eight. Secondly, denying any Arabs living in Germany had taken part. Daoud, fourth in command of Black September, must surely have known that when the attack took place three of the fedayeen had been living in the Village for months already. . . .

Quick, Munich's great mass-circulation weekly, never afraid to follow a story, wherever it may lead, tried in every way to shed light on the September 5–6 butchery. After the events related in our Afterword, its investigative reporters, in early December 1972, succeeded in getting to the brother of one of the skyjackers. This gentleman was leading a life totally above suspicion on the French Riviera, at Nice. He told *Quick*:

A French couple, a Latin Quarter bookseller named Raymond and his wife, a pharmacist named Viviane, drove the Palestinians involved to Munich, in their Mercedes, between July 20 and July 29. The fedayeen then went into training at a farm near Munich, belonging to a twenty-eight-year-old German engineer named Hans. This Hans drove the fedayeen near the Olympic Village on the night of September 4–5. Another German had supplied them with a detailed layout of the site.

Quick asked for proof, and the Nice man supplied convincing ones, according to the magazine, never one to go off half-cocked. The skyjacker's brother was not talking out of altruism. *Quick* paid him—and handsomely, it is said. He too was working for Black September which, like all underground organizations, always needs money. Some even say it deals in hashish to replenish its coffers.

Having spoken and collected, this fellow from Nice disappeared.

As for the Parisian couple, many people, including us, know their last name, but we cannot use it, for the word of a fugitive, even if undenied, cannot be considered evidence.

However, if, like this author, you were to go through Munich and talk to some of the *Quick* staff or connections at the Hall of Justice of that city, you would find that one of the surviving terrorists of September 5, during his brief detention, did mention a Parisian couple, the wife named Viviane, a white Mercedes, and so on. . . .

Yet, the man from Nice does appear to have thrown in a few red herrings, too, for the Bavarian police never did catch the Hans in question, whom they certainly would have apprehended, had that part of the information been correct.

The name of Palestinians which Black September and its Nice informant use for the eight Connollystrasse fedayeen does not hold up either, when closely examined, in at least two of their cases. Nor did they need a layout supplied by "a German," since we know that Issa—whose real name the Bavarian authorities have withheld, although they know it perfectly well—had himself worked on the construction of buildings such as Block 31.

Once again, a tissue of truths, half-truths, and lies. For reasons of its own, Black September decided to "blow the cover" of Raymond-Viviane, who indeed were involved in preparing the attack. The man from Nice, by alleging that all the terrorists came in from Paris, was supposedly covering other leads.

But, then, let us stay in Paris to deal with one more character. Between December 10 and 15, 1972, several large Israeli dailies printed stories to the effect that Mahamud Hamchari, the OLP representative recently executed in Paris, had been in the Munich area at the time of the Olympic Games; adding that Israeli secret services did not rule out his having been one of the brains of the September 5 attack.

Many Western newsmen specializing in the Middle East were familiar with the affable, often smiling, cultivated gentleman known as Mahamud Hamchari. Looking solidly built in his well-tailored dark suits, stocky, reserved, but easy to get on with, very much the respectable bourgeois, Hamchari was indeed the OLP representative, but beyond that, and more ostentatiously, an El

Fatah official. In Paris, he published a newsletter called *Faht-Information,* and he had diplomatic franking privileges.

A North African by birth, having studied at the University of Algiers after independence, and presumably taken a degree in economics, Hamchari lived at 175 Rue d'Alésia—where he was killed on December 8, 1972, by an explosive charge placed under his telephone table, that went off when the phone was raised.

Propaganda was only one of his occupations. In three years, with the cooperation of an Arab UNESCO delegate, he had set up a network covering all of France and made up essentially of French people. This clandestine group, commonly called "Fatah-France," had (and still has) its hideouts, depots, fake-document manufactories, letter-drops, and terrorists. With Hamchari's very efficient help, apart from the Munich job, three other successful Black September operations were prepared: the explosions at the Trieste-West Germany oil pipeline terminal, August 5, 1973; the execution of Adel Wael Zwaiter in Rome, October 16, 1972; and the execution in Paris of Khodr Kannu, November 13, 1972.

It is now possible to reconstruct dependably the principal steps by which the eight Connollystrasse participants got to Munich. . . .

Three of them, as we know, had long been on the spot: Issa, their leader; Tony, also called Guevara, a cook in a Village restaurant; and Abu Halla, or Abu Laban, a gardener there.

Three, Salah also known as Atif, Abdullah Mohamed Samir, and Abdelkader el Denawi, came from Tripoli (Libya).

The last two, Paulo also known as Saïd, and Ibrahim Messaud Badran, came from Beirut.

The three from Tripoli met with Fakhry al Omari in Belgrade. The two from Beirut were welcomed in Rome by Abu Hassan. These first legs took place between July 15 and 20. None of the men at the time was aware of the final destination.

Two of the three fedayeen already in the Olympic Village, Issa and Tony, the two leaders, had been "in" on the deal for a long time. Issa arrived in Munich in January 1971, shortly after being graduated, and learned of the plan in October 1971. Tony arrived in February 1972, knowing all about it. Their job was to blaze the trail and make preparations. The third, Abu Halla, in Munich

107

since March 1972, while theoretically not in on the planning, had been given too many assignments by Issa and Tony to have remained long unaware of what was afoot.

Two of the five fedayeen who came from Tripoli or Beirut, Badran and Paulo, did certainly come through Paris. They went to Munich, along with Hamchari, in the Parisian couple's Mercedes, around July 29. They did end up at a farm, where Hamchari left the two men, still unaware of what lay ahead.

The other three, Denawi, Salah, and Samir, waited out part of their time in Austria, coming to the Munich region much later, around August 25 or 26. They were convoyed there by Al Omari and Mohamed Masalha, who did not fill them in on the plan of operation, either.

On the evening of September 4, then, Badran and Paulo were on the farm of "Hans," while Denawi, Salah, and Samir had found lodgings within Munich itself, through the efforts of the president of the Munich branch of the General Union of Palestinian Workers, a skilled worker of Jordanian nationality, Abdhel Jabber Hamad, thirty-two, residing in the G.F.R. since 1960. Hamad was deported on Tuesday, September 26, 1972, without the Bavarian authorities giving any grounds for his expulsion.

Two cars, one driven by "Hans," the other by Hamad or another member of his Union, around 3:00 AM on September 5, dropped the five fedayeen from abroad on Petuelring, the avenue that separated the Village from the stadia complex.

At this point, Paulo, No. 3 in the group, explained their mission to them. He himself had been briefed by Issa in a *Konditorei* of Marienplatz, across from the new Munich City Hall.

"For over a month, we all knew we were to take part in an operation of the greatest significance," the surviving fedayeen would later tell the investigating officers.

Badran and Paulo, being set up in the environs of Munich, had guessed that what they were involved in had to do with the Olympic Games, and therefore with Israeli athletes.

Mohamed Masalha and Fakhry al Omari, after going away, returned to the Munich region around August 31. From September 2 to September 4, they stayed at "Hans'" farm, with Badran and Paulo. On the afternoon of September 4, Masalha joined

Denawi, Salah, and Samir at Hamad's. Fakhry al Omari took a room at the Eden Hotel Wolff, near the railway station, under an alias.

"We were all alerted on the morning of September 4," the surviving fedayeen were to relate. "There were final briefings, switches in orders, instructions about the amount of rest to be taken during the day, what to have ready . . . We could not fail to know that H-hour was at hand. Having been split into several groups, we were truly surprised when we met in the lobby of Block 31, to see how many of us there suddenly were. . . ."

VII
NIGHTMARE
UNDERGROUND

Yea, though I walk through the valley
of the shadow of death,
I will fear no evil,
For Thou art with me . . .
Psalms 23:4

9:20 AM: THERE WAS A SCURRY OF ALARM AROUND THE METAL DOOR
leading to the stairs and elevator of Block 31. The police watchers
darted for hiding. They just saw the door start to open. One
terrorist came out, then another. The two masked Arabs were
loaded down with artillery. They took a few steps to either side
of the slanting pavement. The door of the elevator whined. A
third fedayee emerged, in black shirt and trousers, very short,
and bowlegged. His oval face was not masked. The hump of his
wide-nostriled nose went off like a comma to the right. This was
Salah, whom Mr. Young of Hong Kong had run into at dawn.

The policemen were all attention. Suddenly they heard a voice
speaking German, in a sharp, strong tone: "Policemen! If you do
not immediately cease spying on us from behind pillars and doors,
we will shoot down one of the prisoners who are on the stairs.
You have one minute."

Could the cops know whether the Arabs had seen them? Or
how many of their number had been seen? But their orders were
clear: "In case of doubt, do what involves least danger for the
hostages." Six of the police came into the clear, and walked off in
the middle of the street. They seemed to be giving up the section
of underground that, on the Israeli sidewalk side, went from
Building 11 to Building 33. On the other side, the East German
side, no policeman left.

A second warning by the German-speaking Arab brought no

result. If there were any watchers left (and there were), their leader felt that the terrorists would not dare cross the wide pathway to ferret through the many possible hiding places.

What was happening here was typical of what went on during all of that day.

Did the fedayeen want to leave Olympic Village with half of their hostages? If so, to go where? Did they think they were upsetting a trap or a planned attack? Were they trying merely to disorient and worry the Germans? However that may be, four hostages, walking like paraplegics, now came out, their hands tied behind their backs, their ankles hobbled by a rope with a slipknot in a figure eight. Three fedayeen were with them. The captives started a sort of slow-motion trot in a herky-jerky fashion toward the underground entrance to Block 33, beyond which there was a large opening through which daylight streamed in. The first two Israelis were one behind the other, and each had a fedayee behind him with a muzzle of his gun at the back of his neck. The third and fourth were side by side: one terrorist was behind them, but he held a pistol against the ribs of each of them.

They got to the door to No. 33.

Who were these four Israelis? The German police were supposed to be carrying special cameras that they used a lot, but if they identified those bound prisoners through pictures or in any way, they never said. The witnesses I was able to question all mentioned the presence of a huge man, with broad face and broken nose: Yossef Gutfreund.

Block 33 was occupied by Zambia and Dahomey, but Schreiber had had it evacuated as early as 6:00 AM.

The seven figures out of Dante stopped. They remained where they were for perhaps four minutes. The Arabs pushed their hostages to the side, shoulder to shoulder, noses to the wall. This was easiest for all concerned. The AK-47 submachine guns and the Tokagypt automatics in the hands of the fedayeen could be seen moving up and down, right and left; obviously, they were stretching and working their muscles. They allowed the prisoners to jump up and down a bit, too. The latter were normally dressed, in street trousers, with sports or polo shirts. None had a jacket on. They were unshaven. The heat was penetrating.

111

The policemen's light walkie-talkies kept headquarters abreast of the strange doings minute by minute. Those undergrounds are always noisy, and this one echoed with the innumerable activities brought on by the attack—from the awful whirr of the helicopters to the sputtering explosions of the motorcycles going about at almost a walking pace.

There was much commotion at the emergency staff HQ and around Dr. Schreiber. Shooting down the three fedayeen in the underground would have been child's play. But how many were left up above? "Two at most!" the police insisted. Those two had certainly arranged something with their accomplices about a deadline for their return, or a renewal of contact. Barring which, they still had five hostages up in No. 1 . . .

In truth, the *Krisenstab* believed there were not five but six Israelis in Block 31, for there was no way for them to know that Romano was dead (Inbar, after careful checking, had thus concluded the fedayeen held ten of the Israelis captive).

There has been much surprise expressed because as early as 8:00 AM a rumor was about that there was a second Israeli casualty on Connollystrasse. Some said a seriously wounded man, others a fatality. The main source of that information was the terrorists themselves. Fräulein Graes had asked their spokesman whether there were any other dead or wounded, outside of Weinberg, and Issa had said, "Yes, a weight lifter. A big brute."

She asked for more details, but the terrorist cut her off.

Beyond that, two hours earlier, when Hershkowitz, the flag-bearer, and his four companions finally escaped from Apt. 2, they reported, "We all heard groans coming from Apartment One. They lasted a long time."

They could not have come from Romano, who had died in less than thirty seconds. He had made an awful sound when he was hit by the first burst, probably fatal in itself, and then he had shouted defiantly as he fell, knife in hand, sliced through the back by a salvo that never gave him time to know he was dying.

Then whose groans were they? Weinberg's at first. In the hallway and the kitchen, when with superhuman efforts he dragged himself there to grab, as Romano had, a long-bladed knife, one of those slicers the delegation had brought along but used only at breakfast, since the authorities had seen to providing kosher fare at the two main meals. Then Weinberg had panted noisily, uttered deep involuntary groans that had sounded like calls for help among mountaineers. But Hershkowit and the others had been able to hear none of that. It was something else, moans that lasted far beyond Weinberg's execution.

The fact is, it was David Marc Berger. He had been knocked cold when he first tried to escape. Once Romano was brought down, the terrorists had turned back to Berger lying below, and gone to work on him with their feet and riflebutts, even though he was unconscious. He had awakened with several broken ribs, his face puffed, one thumb smashed by heel stamps. In his half-torpor, he began to moan. The fedayeen were afraid the interpreter and negotiators might hear him. The group's first-aid man, called Abdelkader el Denawi—addressed at times as Kader, and at others as Denawi—took care of him. He was a little fellow with a 1935 mustache and thick crow-black hair. He had a very efficient kit; everything they had was well prepared. Berger was brought around; his wounds were not in themselves serious. The medic applied some salve, gave him a sedative shot, and he was able to go up to the bedroom where his comrades sat, trussed up, around Romano's broken cadaver.

When Hershkowitz and the others had made their report, Messrs. Inbar and Glovinsky were certain one of the Israelis was dying. They begged the *Krisenstab* to ask the terrorists to permit a physician into Block 31. The interpreter tried. The man in the white hat merely shrugged.

At 9:15, before she had been able to get the two doctors to escape, the young woman, indefatigable, friendly, and firm, had come back to the subject. Issa replied: "No one here needs a doctor any longer."

"Did the wounded man die?"

"Yes. Quickly. And it was better for all of us that way. The Israelis took it to heart. We are not going to be tricked by humanitarian pretexts, the way our comrades at Lod were last May. If the Israelis got that Sabena plane, it was only because the Red Cross hoodwinked the fedayeen. There's not going to be any Red Cross here, Fräulein. Not even if we are forced to shoot an unruly prisoner."

The interpreter said she could not see how it would hurt the fedayeen to give the West German authorities the name of the second fatality. "That's done in the fiercest wars, and we are not at war against the fedayeen."

"His name is Romano, or something like that," Issa hissed.

Yes, only because the Arabs had been so careful never to expose more than one of their two groups, and shown their stubbornness already several times since dawn, had the three who went down into the Connollystrasse underground with their four hostages not been shot when it would have been so easy.

Now the seven were leaving again! In the same way; the muzzles of the guns stuck to each hostage like suction-cups. They went beyond No. 33—a silent, phantasmagoric parade of seven oh-so-fragile humans. For no reason, they walked through this realm of bare cement, the huge network of driveways, parking spaces, cellars, and control booths. They rubbed against the gray pillars. At a command, the prisoners did an about-face, with their hoppy little steps trying to keep the rope from biting into their flesh, and the fedayeen breathing down their necks.

They were back before the iron door to 31. It had remained ajar. A rifle barrel, with glaring reflections, peeked through the opening. One of the hostages first, they all went into the vestibule, and were swallowed by silence.

After this strange episode was detailed, some contended this was when Gad Tsobari escaped. But the wrestler corrected the misstatement: he was long gone, when his friends were taken on this hoppity outing.

None of the four hostages in the underground had any chance to get away. If they ran, they would have lost their balance and fallen, even supposing they had not been shot.

All seven were back in Apt. 1 at 9:30. Herr Schreiber was concerned about this underground walk, and he was not the only one. The police thought the terrorists were planning to try to make it out with their hostages. Perhaps they had accomplices outside. The law-and-order forces started literally piling in to the underground passageways. They were instructed to shoot at the fedayeen under three conditions: 1. They were so close as to be virtually sure to kill them at the first shot; 2. There was only minimal risk of wounding any hostage or third person; 3. All—or nearly all—the hostages were in the group or groups that killing the fedayeen would free.

9:30 AM (Diary): The huge *U-Bahn* station called *Olympiazentrum* is turning out tens of thousands of passengers. These masses of would-be-gawkers find Lerchenauerstrasse strangely calm but the armed police out in force. The authorities have decided (for the moment only, because things change so fast!) to let the pedestrians use the wide roadway from which vehicular traffic is banned, but only to cross over.

The *BMW-Turm,* on the east side of Lerchenauerstrasse, is what the crowds want to see, even today when the bloody news has spread like wildfire, albeit late. The new general offices of BMW *(Bayerischen Motoren Werke AG)* cars house a fantastic museum of virtually everything the Munich firm has ever produced—not only cars, but planes, cycles, and so on . . . The museum is inside a huge reddened concrete bowl. The tower with the blue-and-white insignia of BMW, some 100 meters (110 yds.) high, looks like four turbines, or better, like four round transistor batteries standing on end. This is 1972's hymn to aluminum and glass.

Many of those arriving, as usual, take one of the concrete footbridges over Petuelring, the border artery between the Village and the park of sports arenas—most often the one that takes them near the TV tower and the all-sports hall. But instead of dashing across it as they usually do, this morning under the intensifying sun they are lingering, pressing against the guardrails to see the commotion in the Village, the armored vehicles parked at the ends of the pedestrian walks. The result is a fantastic jam of people up there, a few angry set-tos, and several old people fainting. Meantime, sail- and rowboats are crisscrossing the blue-green surface of *Künstlicher See,* the artificial lake in the valley of *Olympiapark* that looks like a reptile swollen with food, beneath the tower and the sports arenas shimmering under their acrylic-glass roofs. /

All during this day, people in alternate periods were admitted and ruthlessly barred from Lerchenauerstrasse.

The German Democratic Republic's delegation had been carrying on since dawn in its pyramidal tower, facing Block 31 like a large cat opposite a mouse. An hour before, they had been ordered to get out. But Herr Manfred Ewald, their leader and high muckamuck of all sports in East Germany, was not obeying: "We need no one to protect us! We have our own security service!"

The head of the Munich police patiently explained to him that the assault forces had to be able to use the facade of the building unimpededly. Herr Ewald was indignant, as were his assistants, at the idea that the lodgings of East Germany's Olympic competitors might serve as a theater of war. The *Polizeichef* tried to keep calm, facing his half-countryman. Relations between East and West Germans were so fragile and complicated! For a high official, no banana peel was slipperier. He tried to make the point that the GDR team was for the nonce the responsibility of Munich and the Federal Republic, and if an East German were shot there might be the gravest of consequences.

After an hour and a half, the East Germans agreed to clear, not the whole building, but only the south facade. Obviously, Israel did not cut much ice with them. In view of Communist Germany's violently pro-Arab and pro-Fatah stand, it was madness to have put the Israeli delegation under its shadow.

9:40 AM: The fedayeen made themselves heard as soon as their underground outing was over. They were phoning from the Israelis' Apt. 1 to the number given them at 5:30 by the first of the policewomen. In impeccable German, the voice that one of Herr Dr. Schreiber's seconds heard was instructing the *Krisenstab* to see to it that no more "people in military uniforms" were around Block 31. The Arab—or supposed one—hung up without awaiting an answer. It was decided to accept: the front lines of police barrages, around 31, were visible to the fedayeen, and until now had been manned by uniformed agents of the *Land*'s security police. After 9:45, they were replaced by the regular Village security people, at least if one judges by the turquoise outfits and white caps worn by the newcomers. Actually, of course, Dr.

116

Schreiber had merely had a group of Munich and Bavarian cops dress up in the Olympic uniform.

This may be a good time to take a look at the terrain on which the site of the Games (and the attack) was built . . .

Oberwiesenfeld (the traditional name of the area, meaning roughly "upper meadowfield") had the basic advantage of not having been developed. The south part of its verdant but stony plateau was made up of the humps of several small hills, about 60 meters (200 ft.) in altitude; they faced southwest, with sharp gradations.

In 1945, another hill had arisen, made of the rubble left by the World War II bombings. It had also reached the 200-foot height, and gave a depressing tone to the landscape: it was too full of memories. As a result, Oberwiesenfeld was deserted. It became a huge empty field, just 4 km. (2½ mi.) from the heart of Munich symbolized by the two green copper domes of the *Frauenkirche* (Church of the Virgin), the cathedral of this traditionally Catholic city.

Mayor Hans-Jochen Vogel of Munich had decided to turn the Oberwiesenfeld into a park, just at the time that Herr Daume and he got the sudden idea to apply for hosting the 1972 Games. That made Oberwiesenfeld the obvious choice as the site for them.

Olympiapark is split into a north and south part: the north has the two Olympic Villages, the men's much larger than the women's. As it turned out, the women's area was just a thin slice at the southwest of the men's. This made sense, since there were six times as many men competing as women. So their Village housed the soul of things, the Plaza, the solemn esplanade with the 123 flags (122 competing nations plus the Olympic banner), stores, recreation and meeting spots, banks, information booths, and so on. To all intents and purposes, then, "The Village" means the men's area exclusively. . . .

The three most important sports sites, Olympic Stadium, Sports Palace, and Water Stadium, were in the south half, on the southern shore of the artificial lake built for the Games, jointly covered by the legendary crescent-shaped tent-roof, the biggest and most amazing in the world. Everyone in 1972 knew of this covering of acrylic-glass slabs set in metallic frames, that left the eastern half of the Olympic Stadium in the open and completely protected the other two areas.

These three monuments of the Games, however, were dwarfed by our friend the tower, that huge *Olympiaturm* that suggested a lighthouse for spaceships, or a huge rocket with ringed cockpits. It was Munich's new trademark, unlike anything else ever, and visible from everywhere. It was better than a compass. The rounded walls housed tiered lights that, even in a fog, somehow seemed to shine through, in strange halos.

The ex-Oberwiesenfeld had other buildings, such as the red cycling arena with its track of African wood.

Or, the sort of hut and chapel that were the domain of a hermit named Timofeo Prokorov, appealing despite his weirdness. He was a strange character who claimed to be the two-thousand-year-old man. Around 1950, he set up on one of the humps of Oberwiesenfeld, with his mate, Natasha, whom he called his sister in religion. Timeless, with his shapeless clothing and worn-out high shoes, he was something out of a Gogol story. Beside him, Natasha glided about in the shadows. Age had ennobled the appearance of little Father Timofeo: I liked the long, serious, wrinkled face, the snowy whiteness of his hair parted in the middle, and the heavy drooping mustache that came down to a well-combed, if less purely white beard. After all, what he wanted was solitude for the two of them, with prayer and nature.

So he started a church. And why not? No one knew what he lived on, raising vegetables and flowers, planting some fruit trees. He had long since been accepted as a political refugee. People came on Sundays to look at his movingly ugly setup, made of sheet metal, zinc, tin, wood, and salvage, and topped by three or four uneven belltowers. It was decided to evict Father Timofeo from the future Olympic site, along with his quiet Natasha of the long blue eyes, and knock his building down. He objected, and called in the press. The newspapermen, seeing a good story in the picturesque patriarch and his Russian simplicity, took his side.

After all, leaving him where he was would only be a bit of an eyesore; and besides, the whole area was going to be planted with grass. So they decided not to move Father Timofeo, and tried to cash in on their magnanimity. The Russian émigré became more and more of a celebrity; more and more people came to see him. And, naturally, he made a large almsbox in which, when people came and disturbed Natasha or him, it was now customary to make an offering.

9:55 AM: One of the heads of the International Amateur Swimming Federation, in the wine-colored jacket with the two-globed emblem, Mr. A. de Oliveira Sales, came to palaver with the terrorists. His main title was President of the Amateur Sports Federation and Olympic Committee of Hong Kong, and as such he was British. He was recognizable at a distance, by his sharp profile beneath a balding skull, his heavy gold glasses, thin frame, and whitening thin hair. What he was after was to obtain release of the three Hong Kong athletes trapped by the attack in their own quarters in Block 31, with their mission head, Mr. R. Young. The man in the white hat agreed to release the Asians and told Mr. de Sales to go and get them from the third floor. Now the director appeared at the rail of the open gallery, up there, above Apt. 1. . . .

Mr. de Sales could soon be seen getting impatient: it took a good fifteen minutes for the accidental prisoners to emerge, hands over their heads. They had had to wait while one of the Chinese, asleep naked as a jaybird, got up and dressed.

Hong Kong had been occupying half of the third floor, and both penthouses. Except for the unfortunate Israelis, the other tenants of the building, Uruguayans, concierge, and steward, had all been able to get away in time.

Half-a-dozen Chinese had also believed in "God helps those who help themselves," and by way of the balconies they had gotten to one of the apartments at the corner of the building farthest from the terrorists. From there, they acrobated it down, landing first on the balcony below. They had no idea that huge cameras were following them with zoom lenses, and that in the speck of land they called home, their countrymen and their families were witnessing their escape, virtually "live." They bounced like springs when they hit the pavement and headed out toward the fence and Kusoczinskidamm.

119

The fedayeen were not the least interested of the televiewers. But instead of going after the Asians, they just smiled, for they had immediately placed them. The terrorists never did take charge of the top floor. All they wanted was for it not to be used against them. And so, till the end, they made rounds up there. But they were just as happy to see the two non-Jewish delegations off the premises as soon as possible.

10:00 AM *(Diary):* West Germany has three TV networks (soon to be four). The first, ARD, has a station in each *Land*. The second, ZDF, has only one, extremely powerful, station, that reaches all of the Federal Republic. The third is educational *(Studienprogramm)*. ARD and ZDF both use color, and both have pooled their resources in ZOD, to make exclusive films of the Olympic events. Each then makes its own selection within the body of takes.

Today's programs are naturally upset. ZDF, which is Channel 2, covers virtually nothing but what is happening with the Israeli hostages. ARD—Channel 4—does its best to cover the dressage competition and the kayak-one men's and women's events. It, too, keeps viewers abreast of the awful affair, by bulletins and newscasts. It shows a few striking shots, such as the one of Issa, thin and blackfaced, under the little beach hat, casting his square smile at the blonde policewoman. But then, back to sports!

I have a coffee at the pressroom snackbar in *Volleyballhalle*. In the pretty little arena, 3510 paying customers are wildly cheering on the West German men's team, which has just lost the first two sets of its match against Japan. The Federal Republic's sextet doesn't have a chance against one of the three best teams in the world; the Nipponese took the bronze medal at Toyko and the silver at Mexico City. But, like Paul Reynaud who, over thirty-two years ago, just before being replaced as French Premier by Marshal Pétain, had exclaimed, "I believe in miracles because I believe in France!" the fanatical German fans watching the volleyball here expect a miracle on the morning of September 5, 1972. And they are not thinking of 31 Connollystrasse.

Making these notes in my little black leather notebook, I am not unaware of the facile unfairness of what I just put down. Certainly, most of them are good folks. Many of them are not even aware yet of what happened to the Israelis before dawn. But if they did know and still piled in to see the Olympic events, what difference would that make? What would they be guilty of? They arranged their vacations so they could come to the Games, or got special permission to have this day off, and paid for their tickets, and the event is taking place . . . It is also true that the horrible attack would doubtless have been organized anywhere else, had the XXth Olympiad been held elsewhere than in Germany. I've seen all kinds of catastrophes, as a soldier, as an underground fighter, as a victim, as a witness. One of the most constant things that struck me is: When their country was collapsing, or was in its worst trials, the vast majority of city-dwellers went about their business, as normally as possible; theaters stayed open, and lines were long; daily life seemed more precious than ever.

Yes. I know. Not to be unfair. And yet, looking at these by-standing men and women, I am struck more than usually by the fact that they are talking German. I try to figure how old they are. That plump blonde woman so well-preserved and light afoot, with her hair up like the Gretchens of our darkest years, how old can she be? Forty-five? If so, she was eighteen in 1945; thirteen in June 1940. Many the *Sieg Heil!*s she must have shouted. Many the times she must have cheered the Führer. Many the yellow stars she must have seen! And didn't she on occasion go out to that pretty little country town of Dachau, along the Amper River with its rapids, just 17 km. (10½ mi.) northwest of Munich?

Its restful church with the bulb-shaped dome, its Rathaus with the gaily flowered balconies, its calm country homes. The two Dachaus, the old and the new, lie on the flank of a hill, and at its top there is the castle that belonged to the Wittelsbachs. From its towers, you see Munich, and the huge green-and-white waves of the Alps to the South.

All about, beneath the eye of the romantic castle, the even plateau, the marshy, hostile stretch, planted in sad woods, and called the *Dachauer Moos* (Dachau Marsh: *Moos* being Bavarian dialect). This is where the Dachau *Konzentrationslager* (KZ), the infamous concentration camp, was built. Some 230,000 prisoners went through it. Some 65,000 of them died, most in the camp itself, the rest during the forced marches of April 1945. More than

121

half the survivors came out with health badly impaired, often to die in short order.

Among the prisoners, in the last months, there were many Jews, for, because of the Russian advances, it became hard to transfer them to the extermination camps in the east, which now proved unprofitable (as to work accomplished, salvaging of corpses, experiments to be made, and so on). The life of the average Jew in the Dachau camp was two months.

To our children, these things mean little: they can't even imagine what that hellish Germany was like. But there are a lot of us older ones out here, looking at what is going on in Connolly-strasse, and finding ourselves thinking: "This is Germany's curse: the swastika descending on Munich again. Jeremiah said, 'They have sown wheat, but shall reap thorns: they have put themselves to pain, *but* shall have no profit: and they shall be ashamed of your revenues because of the fierce anger of the LORD.' Six million ghosts come back to haunt them."

Our sons just say, "The Germans sure aren't lucky. Tough break for them. They did a great job on the Games! The atmosphere was terrif."

September 5 is not a day of very sensational sports events. On the contrary. It was one of the truly off-days of the schedule. The terrorists had guessed right in selecting it. Even if the sports go on, all eyes will be on them.

Not that it would have been a boring Olympic day, if there had not been Connollystrasse. At exactly eight this morning in the Romantic Nervalesque park of Nymphenburg castle, the Grand Prix of individual dressage began. And just a little while ago, right here, in this reception room that looks out on the Village Plaza, I stopped for a moment before the set on which I could see Frau Liselott Linsenhoff performing on her horse Piaff. That was the triumphal number, the obvious gold medal. Change feet, prance, extended trot, passage. What style! The dazzling horsewoman, a discreet smile on her lips, the dignity of a Garbo, a long, svelte line, gave the jury an elegant salute, after the last volt, from the center of the track, with the sun playing on the auburn chignon sticking out under her high hat.

On the little screen, the GFR-Japan match is over. The fans

left somewhat downhearted: their German volleyers were badly beaten.

Now the kayak-one women's 500-meter eliminations are taking place. They are being held at Oberschleissheim, in that fabulous hole they dug 7 km. (4 mi.) northwest of Munich: it is a body of water unique in the world, in which they stocked 10,000 trout for the eventual delight of fishermen. The rowing took place here, too. The young ladies' double paddles fly back and forth on the light waters of the artificial lake: girls with royal shoulders, sitting nobly up, their dorsals rippling, nipples standing out hard as wood, arms like pistons smelling of salt and liniment, they are all bust and tautened neck, and on the skintight waterproof skirtlet, the drops accumulate. This is total concentration.

10:15 AM: The *Krisenstab* (crisis staff) met, and approved all the measures taken. Herr Manfred Schreiber got all of the Olympic Village forces placed directly under his command, regardless of whom they were answerable to.

Then, the main question on the agenda: Should the Games be suspended, or not; and, if so, how?

Mr. Brundage, President of the IOC, and Willi Daume, President of the Organizing Committee for the Munich Games and a member of the IOC, did not object to an interruption of the events. The IOC, together with the Organizing Committee, had to decide. But Messrs. Brundage and Daume left it up to the *Krisenstab*, since any decision had to be considered in terms of what it might mean to the Israeli hostages. Daume indicated that a great many members of the IOC were for a temporary suspension of the Games.

Herr Schreiber was against any cancellation. If the events were put off, tens of thousands of suddenly idle people would come crushing around the site of the attack: such mobs would badly hinder the law-and-order forces as well as vehicles. Hundreds of officers would have to be assigned just to keep the crowds in check. There would be incidents. Some overenthusiastic individuals might try stunts that could prove catastrophic. Why run such risks? The best thing would be not to suspend the Games till the end of the afternoon, when there is a normal break anyway, unless the matter had resolved itself by then.

Herr Schreiber carried the day.

An outsider might have felt that the administrative tower of the Village was devoted to nothing but saving the hostages. But that would have been impossible . . . Only the *Krisenstab,* in its ten or so offices, was looking for a lifesaving way out.

All day long, September 5, from top to bottom of G-1, the normal administration of Olympic Village ran its course, seeing to its daily tasks. The Games were on, full swing, and the Village had to go on living, eating, being entertained; transport and repairs had to be furnished as usual. The whole huge machine had to keep running smoothly . . .

10:30 AM: Two armored cars, apparently from the Hof base, brought a detachment of federal frontier guards *(Bundesgrenzschutzpolizei)* to the Village. Hof is a flourishing industrial town in the northwest end of Bavaria, just a few kilometers from the East German and Czechoslovak frontiers. Some thirty men were in the group, already dressed in camouflage outfits. One of Dr. Schreiber's assistants told us two-thirds of them were certified marksmen. They deployed around Block 31. . . .

"Hello, sir! What a pity!"

The tall blonde smiling sadly at me and addressing me in English was Leni Riefenstahl, who made the most wonderful sports film ever, *Olympia.* She shot it in August 1936, a documentary—but what a documentary!—on the Berlin Olympics. She was thirty-four at the time; Adolf Hitler had a liking for her. Even more than just a platonic liking, it is said. While never having actually been a Nazi Party member, let us say that Leni Riefenstahl served it well. Shortly before coming here, I had seen *The Triumph of the Will,* the amazing film she had done on the Nuremberg Party Rally of September 1934.

Now she was appalled, horrified. Behind the smoked glasses, her gray-blue eyes had lost their eager love of life. The two cameras hung around her neck seemed forgotten, with all their special lenses. The *Sunday Times Magazine* had hired her to do photographic coverage of the Munich Games. The picture pros were impressed with her, a celebrity of a world buried twenty-seven years before under the ruins, who now came back, full of vivacity, and perfectly at ease in the crush.

124

She accepted her age, and overcame it! There were still flashes of youth in her smooth oval face. Her cheekbones were prominent, her nose slightly hooked, her chin sharp; her body was well proportioned, in good shape, and responsive, with a dancer's legs. She was a woman who could cope. She was very friendly with the former Armaments Minister of the Third Reich, Albert Speer. Like him, she would have made it to the top under any regime, but she was cut down in full flight, because she had had the misfortune of appealing to Hitler—and being devoted to him.

"Do you believe this is God's judgment on Germany?" I asked.

"No. That would be too easy, blaming God for the sins of men."

"Have you gotten any shots of Block 31?"

She shook her head. Then, in a muffled tone: "I ought to. That's what I'm getting paid for." And she headed toward Panoramic Hill, with its good view of the building with the hostages.

There was Yossef Romano.

Born December 30, 1940, in Tripoli's ghetto, now destroyed. He was a small rock of a man standing 5 feet 6, and solid muscle for all of his 165 pounds. Wild jet-black woolly hair topped his head exuberantly, and he wore it in an "Afro."

No need to stress the difficult training conditions for Israeli weight lifters. A national champion for six years, Romano had spent long years in the armed services. He fought the Six Days' War on the West Bank and then the Golan Heights. In 1968, he was in on several clashes with organized El Fatah units, along the Jordan. In Israel, every top athlete is also a good soldier. Married, and the father of three girls, the youngest of whom had just been born at the end of April, his devotion to sport caused his family some concern. They lived at the resort town of Herzliya, where his parents had a grocery.

Shmuel Lalkin told me, during that September 5: "Romano was a brave one; courage was his religion. Where others might have been able to keep still and bide their time, he would have attacked the Arabs without concern for the outcome. He was a packet of muscles, an explosive bundle, but also a softie, an artist. You know what he did for a living? He was a window dresser, and very gifted. He had already been around inspecting all the shops

125

in Munich, their windows, their furnishings . . . He was also interested in interior decorating. But his wife and his three kids were his whole life. Just yesterday he said to me, 'This is going to be my last international event, because sport doesn't leave me enough time to spend with my kids. And I have to work, instead of training so much . . .' You know, our athletes get no special privileges, no subsidies or exemptions from military service, nothing."

On the souvenir-picture of the Israeli delegation the eve of their fateful departure for Munich, twenty-two of the twenty-eight had been together to pose happily. And Yossef Romano with his thick black mane and heavy sideburns, his broad tanned face smiling confidently, his bull neck and hefty drooping shoulders, was just to the right of his coach, Tuvia Sokolsky.

Among all of his charges whom he cared for so, little friendly mustached Sokolsky liked Romano best, not only because the little Libyan Jew whose mother tongue was Arabic was the best of all Israel's weight-lifting stars, but because of the mixture in him of extreme gentleness and extreme pride.

We had met two days before the tragic events: his light eyes reflected a straightforward soul.

Romano's well-tempered body had been like a living sculpture to him. And he had finally put it forward to defy the barbarians. When he was in military action, Romano had always been first to volunteer for dangerous missions. "This old carcass has to be put to some good use!" he would declare with a laugh as bright as his hair was dark. He would have wished to die no other way.

VIII

WHILE THE WHOLE WORLD WATCHED

And the LORD said unto Cain:
'Where is Abel thy brother?'
And he said: 'I know not; am I
my brother's keeper?'
Genesis 4:9

10:45 AM (DIARY): ONE HUNDRED-ODD NEWSMEN HAVE INVADED THE lobby of the G-1 tower. Herr Willi Daume emerges, rapid-paced, a brown face, sharply chiseled, with prominent cheekbones.

"*Herr Präsident,* won't you give us a statement, please? *Bitte? S'il vous plaît? Pazhalista? ¿Por favor? Per favore?*"

Completely surrounded, he has to stop. It's surprising to see the weight he has lost. He had put on a great deal, but in 1971 he decided to get back to his old shape. He must have dropped a good 35 lbs. He's still solid: his body is that of an ex-champion who has kept up his training.

"Later, Mr. Hans Klein [head of the Organizing Committee's p.r.] will let you know what has happened. Our first task is to save the hostages. I am not the one to say whether the Games will be interrupted. But if we canceled them, that would be giving in to crime, wouldn't it?"

He makes his way out through the willing crowd. But there is no cajoling smile on his determined countenance this morning: I'll bet he's ready to fight for "his" Games tooth and nail. He has never willingly admitted defeat.

Daume was born May 23, 1913, at Hückeswagen (Rhineland), right near the Ruhr, where he made his career. He was always opposed to the Nazi regime, which conferred neither favors nor honors on him, but sent him to the front like tens of millions of others. He is a great industrialist, heading many companies (steel,

127

commerce, banking, and so on). Living in Dortmund, he has been athletic all his life, and in 1936 was a member of the German Olympic handball team.

Becoming a leading sports organizer right after the war, Willi Daume quickly rose to be president of the German Sports Federation. In the Federal Republic, devoted to democracy and decentralization, there is no place for an official sports commissar, especially since so many of the sports are more professional than amateur. But within that framework, Willie Daume can be said to be the national head of all amateur athletics.

In 1956, at age forty-three, he was elected to the IOC. Five years later, he became President of the German Olympic Committee (*Nationales Olympisches Komitee für Deutschland,* often referred to as NOK). He is a lover of modern art, with a special interest in abstracts: his tastes in this direction, his daring concepts, played a large part in determining the construction of all of Olympia Park.

To this habitual meeter of challenges, who, at the head of the Organizing Committee for the Munich Olympiad, brilliantly set up this titanic enterprise, the bloody attack on Connollystrasse is a personal tragedy. He had been eminently successful. The Munich Games were the object of everyone's admiration. There were only six days left till the final apotheosis . . . /

11:00 AM: Israel's ambassador to Bonn, H. E. Eliashiv Ben Horin, arrived at Riem in a Luftwaffe plane, and went directly to Olympic Village. He was immediately received by Ministers Merk and Genscher, at the *Krisenstab* HQ, on the third floor of the Administrative Building, also known as G-1.

Mr. Ben Horin was bringing the West German ministers the following message from the Israeli Government, assembled in Council from 9:00 to 10:00 AM, dictated to him at 9:30 from Jerusalem, and personally confirmed to him by the Israeli Premier, Mrs. Golda Meir:

> 1. The Israeli Government does not negotiate with terrorists. The entire responsibility for these events belongs to the West German authorities. The Government of Israel expects the German authorities to do everything in their power to free the hostages and save their lives.

2. Israel will understand if the German authorities promise to free the terrorists, in case such a promise might improve the chances of assuring the safety of all the hostages.

"In a word," the Bavarian Minister of the Interior countered, "the Israeli Government is refusing to free a single one of the two hundred and thirty-four political prisoners whose names were given us by the terrorists, right?"

"Correct."

"Is this an irrevocable decision?"

"I believe so."

"Mr. Ambassador, do you realize what this means? The only way to try to save the hostages now is by force, unless the terrorists should collapse. Are you willing to risk that?"

"Mrs. Golda Meir answered that in advance. She told me before I left Bonn that our Government was depending entirely on the German authorities to free the hostages."

Mr. Ben Horin's face is round, with a soft but immovable frankness; he had been a fine figure of an underground fighter before the rebirth of the State of Israel.

"What if the terrorists suggest leaving Germany with the hostages, and continuing the negotiations later from their destination?" Herr Genscher asked.

"My whole country is convinced that Germany would never agree to abandon to terrorists Israelis who were its guests and were taken hostage in its territory."

Bayerns Innenminister Bruno Merk placed at Mr. Ben Horin's disposal an office on the same floor, in fact with communicating door to the one being used by Messrs. Merk, Genscher, and Schreiber. The latter, though, was often away, at his forward command post, an ultramodern communications van: armored, luxuriously outfitted, and with fantastic technical equipment.

Mr. Ben Horin had a direct phone line from this private office. In order to avoid delay, once he had gotten Jerusalem on the line at 11:30, the phone would remain off the hook. At the other end, it would be continually monitored. The phone was to remain that way till 3:45 the next morning . . .

No one knew what was going on in Apt. 1, where the hostages had apparently now been permanently settled. They supposed the nine Israelis were tied up. The apartment itself was typical of the Village: its tan, orange, or light-blue walls were covered with Olympic posters, and other funny ones. Two beds in each room. Metal furniture, painted green or blue, but always some other yellow or bright-red thing around to make a contrast. Green plants. Potted flowers on the balconies. Small TV set. A functional setup, with everything supplied, from refrigerator to electric-shaver outlet.

Dr. Hans-Jochen Vogel now met in front of Apt. 1 with the inevitable white hat over the almost transparent body, Issa in his Prussian arrogance. The former Mayor of Munich kept feverishly busy as long as the hostages remained in the Village. His viewpoint was said to be: under no conditions can we allow them to be removed from Connollystrasse, else they are lost.

He was an amiable man, with a thoughtful rounded-oval face, framed by heavy brown hair, and very popular, having left his position as mayor of his own free will, to seek national office.

Now he was the advance man of the negotiations that were to take place to extend the ultimatum, set for noon, an hour away.

It would take some tight playing. At ten o'clock, the terrorists had given the interpreter a note repeating that if at noon the 236 requested political prisoners had not been freed, the hostages would be massacred. The mind boggled at such a prospect, but what had the three Japanese kamikazes of the Popular Front for the Liberation of Palestine done three months earlier at Lod Airport, when, as calmly as the Nazis at Oradour during the war, in a few moments they killed twenty-eight persons, and wounded ninety, ten or so of them so critically that they were still between life and death?

After having reiterated the offer to replace the Israeli hostages with four Munich VIPs (at which the terrorist leader just shrugged), Herr Vogel offered the attackers as much money as they might want: they had only to set the figure. They could have that and a plane to take them wherever they wished. It was turned down with a sneer . . .

"Money means nothing to us. We are ready to die for our country."

Vogel retorted, in vain, that the organizations the gentlemen belonged to certainly could use additional funds for their treasuries. White Hat did no more than repeat that noon was the deadline.

One of Dr. Hans-Jochen Vogel's pet ideas was: our period is out of joint, because our techniques and production belong to the twentieth century, while our customs and institutions are still in the nineteenth.

The vital statistics on this human beacon of the Munich Games make interesting reading, for they demonstrate how high-competition sport becomes a matter of national politics.

Born in 1926, Herr Vogel came from a well-known old Munich family. At seventeen, the Third Reich put him in uniform and sent him to the Eastern Front in 1943. Twice wounded, he was made a prisoner. After the war, he became a judge.

In 1958, he was given charge of the whole justice system of the Bavarian capital. On May 1, 1960, aged only thirty-four, the young war veteran was elected Mayor of Munich; he had joined the *Sozialdemokratische Partei Deutschland* (SPD), the German Social-Democratic (Socialist) Party, in 1950, and quickly gained importance within its Bavarian ranks. This *Land* being predominantly Social-Christian, Munich was a Socialist enclave within it. The SPD on many occasions tried to extend its control to all of the old province of the Wittelsbachs, but up to now had not succeeded.

Reelected in 1966, Herr Vogel did not stand again when his term ran out; his Party comrade Georg Kronawitter was elected Mayor on June 30, 1972, after 4,444 days of the Vogel mayoralty. The main reason for Vogel's abandonment of this position was that being *Oberbürgermeister* stood in the way of his becoming a Cabinet member, and Chancellor Brandt had promised him an appointment if the governing coalition was reelected in the elections to be held November 19, 1972. Secondarily, he had run into opposition from the *Jusos* (Young Socialists), who accused the Party leaders of having foresworn Marxism and for several years had formed an agitating and threatening minority within the Party's ranks.

Herr Vogel remained highly popular in Munich. Because of the Olympic Games, which would never have been awarded the city without the joint efforts of Herren Daume and Vogel, Munich had made an unhoped-for leap forward, "gaining fifteen years of infrastructure," to quote the former Mayor. At any rate, Munich's growth and modernization under the Vogel regime were unquestionably a record in the city's history. . . .

Tall and well-built, Herr Vogel looked young for his age, but also responsible and attentive behind his dark-rimmed glasses. He knew how to take his time. His pen was persuasive, as was his personality. No one denied him intelligence, distinction, or tenacity: these attributes could take him far.

11:40 AM: Following a Cabinet meeting, Mrs. Golda Meir in the name of the Jerusalem Government instructed Eliashiv Ben Horin to ask the competent authorities immediately to suspend the Games, "out of respect for the two murdered athletes and the hostages being held on Connollystrasse."

The ambassador of Israel personally transmitted this to Herren Genscher, Merk, and Daume. His mobile face, topped by silvery waves, hardened as he was met with a regretful rejection, but he remained in control of himself.

11:50 AM: *Münchens Polizeipräsident* Manfred Schreiber, and Mr. A. D. Touny, the Egyptian member of the IOC who had been so helpful three hours before, appeared before the door of Apt. 1. They had first conferred in the communications van parked underground in front of the metal door leading to the lobby of 20–24 Connollystrasse, the building with the East Germans in it, just across the street from 31. Then they emerged in the street right under a fountain.

Following them was a very well-dressed Arab-looking gentleman, who I was told was Mr. Mohammed Khadif, head of the unofficial legation of the Arab League to West Germany in Bonn. The three were engaged in discussion, and they were shortly joined by a rather young man, somewhat bulging in his blue blazer, wearing metal insignia which my field glasses could read as the initials of the Munich police. He had a clear lump in the front of his blazer that seemed very real.

Only ten more minutes!

The salutary policewoman-interpreter was talking with an unidentified someone through the opened door. She now wore oval glasses instead of the earlier round ones, and the lenses were tinted pink. She was quite formal, with her slight smile, not indicating gaiety, but just relaxation. She was soberly carrying out a job that must have been nerve-racking.

And here now was *Bürgermeister* Walter Tröger, looking very justifiably worried. All five of them waited out on the rectangular tiles, saying nothing. But Issa came out, blacker than ever under his plaster-white beach hat. He surely must have charcoaled his face again. His great hooked nose shone beneath the huge dark glasses. Behind him was a long skinny fellow, stoop-shouldered, with a tropical hat, dark glasses, and a cashmere print shirt: Tony. He had taken off the buttercup sweater: it was too warm.

But he had made up like a Red Indian. He had a revolver on his right hip, two grenades stuck through his wide belt set with colored stones and held by a gold buckle, and in his hand a Kalachnikov AK-47, the abovementioned submachine gun of which the last defenders of the French Empire had tasted the fruits at the hands of the Algerian fellaghas. His index finger never left its trigger. He wore his hair long, and had remarkably high lifts on his heels.

Issa went calmly toward the group that had taken a position before the east corner of Block 31. He was smiling; he had plenty of confidence—in this case buoyed by the cocked hand grenade he had in his right hand and laughingly showed the visitors. He was holding the pin carefully down with the palm of his hand. Once he got back to the apartment, one of his men would carefully put the safety back on it. In his other hand, he also had a grenade, but this one was not cocked.

The negotiation was lively. Issa's bodyguard, at his instructions, moved around, so as to be out of reach of any bodily attack. From a second-story window, a rifle with a telescopic sight stuck out. Issa was gesticulating a great deal. He shook his left hand suddenly and made a V-sign with his first and middle fingers.

Later it would be apparent he had not been signifying V for victory, but 2, for he was saying: "If at one PM, we are not informed by the agreed-upon code that Israel has freed the two hundred thirty-four patriots it holds prisoner, whose names we listed, and if we are not in a position at that time to start our move back to an Arab country, we will execute two hostages right here in this street, for the world press and television."

Mr. Touny repeated the bases for his new request for a postponement of the ultimatum: diplomatic negotiations with Jerusalem were difficult because of poor phone connections, and because of the fact that Israel's whole Cabinet, not just a single person, had to take the responsibility of the decision. And the cabinet, meeting from 9:00 to 10:00 AM, had asked the proper services to supply it with the details on the prisoners, as the fedayeen must have heard on the radio.[1]

Only once the Cabinet had this information would it be able to meet again and come to a decision.

Issa and Tony held a brief conference; the assistant went back into the building. A minute later, a face hidden in a dark-blue hood appeared in the opening of the Munich-blue door, and shook its head negatively, while Tony was slipping back out. Issa and the hooded one had a whispered exchange. Mr. A. D. Touny made a sign to Dr. Mohammed Khadif to talk to the commandos, something that diplomat had hardly done until then.

According to his later statements, the Arab League's Bonn representative offered the terrorists, in the name of the German authorities, safe-conduct out of the country and "a very large sum of money," the figure to be determined by later negotiations, if the fedayeen would release their hostages. Mr. Khadif added: "I am merely transmitting a message. If you want my personal opinion, I think you might get the Israelis to let out ten prisoners or so, but no more. And the money would really come in handy for your organizations."

Issa and Tony listened respectfully to the Arab League representative. Where the dark-blue hood had been, there was now only the muzzle of a rifle.

The head of the attackers answered in Arabic: "Brother, you mean well, but why do they bother sending us such useless proposals? Our only aim is to get our comrades out of Israeli prisons. We don't want to hurt anyone."

[1] It must be said that the various radio stations, according to their reporters' imaginations, deductions, or political bias, were broadcasting just about anything—as well as the opposite.

After which, Issa turned toward the group of Germans, headed by Dr. Schreiber, which had moved nearer, and told them the same thing in their tongue. Khadif reiterated that a further delay was imperative: "The German authorities assured me that, during this interval, nothing will be tried against you. Otherwise, I would not have come."

It was obvious Issa liked Khadif; he finally granted an additional hour. So the deadline was now 1:00 PM, instead of noon. The fedayeen went back into Block 31, while the gentlemen and the policewoman moved away.

Though his associates looked relieved, Dr. Schreiber left Connollystrasse looking very concerned. Once back at HQ, in the Administration Bldg., he was quick to say he did not believe they would be able to get it moved back beyond 1:00. . . .

He went in to see the Israeli ambassador, asking Dr. Merk to come along.[1] The Munich commissioner of police assured Mr. Ben Horin that he was not trying to influence the decisions of another government, but added: "I would ask your Excellency to inform your Government of my opinion. These terrorists have shown us they are not afraid to kill; and I say they are ready to die themselves. They are fanatics. If Israel continues to refuse to negotiate, we will attack. But it will take a miracle to keep the hostages from suffering terrible losses."

Dr. Merk agreed with Dr. Schreiber, who was adding that if there were an armed confrontation the West German police would probably have to use "overwhelming power" to avoid spilling too much German blood. Such power, involving heavy weapons and the use of armor, would unfortunately make it even riskier for the hostages.

The ambassador replied that he would immediately transmit the message. Israel, he reminded them, had already stated that all the steps to be taken to free the hostages were entirely up to the federal and Bavarian governments.

12:30 PM: Dan Schillon, the head of Israeli TV's sports department, was giving a long interview. His strong and even-featured face was visibly shaken. Young, darkish, with black hair, he did not

[1] Germans regularly address as "Dr." not only physicians, but anyone holding a doctorate in anything.

135

mince words about the security that had been afforded the Olympic athletes.

"To get into the Village," he was saying, "it was easier to go in a sweat suit, on a bike, or carrying equipment, than to present legal documents. Anyone could get in. Fences? Anybody who wanted jumped them!"

"Do you think the security given the Israeli delegation was defective?"

"Obviously! Nothing was done. I was at the airport when our team came in. I asked an important Munich police official, who was there to welcome a Minister from Bonn, whether anything had been done to protect Israelis, and especially our delegation, which would be an ideal target for attacks in Munich. He assured me that there was no need for that, for the Village was powerfully guarded, as were all the athletic stadia. I pointed out that, however that might be, there were plenty of strangers and gawkers mixing in with the travelers at the airport: any of them might take a shot at the athletes. He said, 'We only take precautions for El Al planes, and your team is coming in on Lufthansa.'

"I was in daily contact with our delegation. I can say with certainty that they were never given any special protection, either in their quarters at Block Thirty-one, or outside . . ."

Today, ABC-TV had the best spot of all: it was at the front of a hillock from which the whole extended cube of Block 31 could be seen, with all of its southern-exposure balconies. ABC was just where Kusoczinskidamm widens and starts octopusing between the Media Center (*Presse-Rundfunk-und-Fernsehzentrum*) and the Village fence. This was where Connollystrasse and its offshoots came to their end; and it was halfway up ABC's hillock that the terrorists from the outside had scaled the fence, at dawn.

ABC had paid a high price for exclusive TV (but not film) rights to the Games for the U.S. That was why it had been allowed to set up two communications vans on the roadway. The tops of the two came together, making a platform for the ABC cameramen and their magnificent equipment: for any company could film anything it wanted—excepting only the Olympic events.

Now the technicians were putting away their equipment, coming down and getting into the vans, on which the huge A-B-C logo was colored to match Waldi, the mascot dachshund of the Munich Games—a tactful tribute, since usually it is always done in red, white, and blue.

ABC was being made to leave—for the time being—like everyone else, for all the networks and cameramen had been instructed to stop shooting in the area of the action, i.e., a broad area around Block 31. The reason: The fedayeen had a TV set in Apt. 1, where they were holding the hostages. They must be monitoring it in relays; so they were able to see every detail of how the area was being sealed off, the mass arrival of the first batch of city police, and even the arrival of the black-tarped trucks of the frontier guards, who, as the TV commentators obligingly specified, included many marksmen. Henceforth, the small screen would be kept from showing anything that might help the fedayeen plan their movements. Might the authorities not have asked the Jewish escapees earlier whether there was a TV set in Apt. 1 of Block 31? . . .

12:45 PM: From *Olympiapark,* I returned to the Olympic Village, on a coach's I.D. that had been lent me: there were five successive checks to pass through. My regular badge and personal presscard never would have done it.

I went into 8 Connollystrasse, at the head of the broad avenue that crosses the Village from East to West. This building was a mastodon, covering three street numbers. Its endless, crushing facade was eleven stories high—a breathtaking concrete ocean liner. Inside it, among others, was the Italian delegation, in which I had friends. In one of their sheltering offices a fine color set was on continuously. . . . The modishly outfitted commentator was explaining what we already knew, that the fedayeen had a TV set and consequently all telecasts had been suspended that might give them, etc., etc.

A strange effect: Once such a wise if belated decision was made, should those it was aimed at have been so informed?

". . . Therefore, we will no longer be telecasting the Israeli quarters, so that the guerrillas [which was what they were now being called] may not be aware of what preparations are made . . ."

My Italian friend and I held our heads. "Oh, well!" he said, after a bit, "whatever they think, will it change anything?"

"The terrorists have two crates of explosives," the commentator on Channel 2 (ZDF) was going on. How did he know? "Olympic Village has been totally sealed off, and the security forces have left the immediate neighborhood of the Israeli building, at the request of the fedayeen." They would be glad to have the world know they were now dictating terms.

This 8–12 Connollystrasse housed the Puerto Ricans in addition to the Italians. The former were closest to the bend the street makes toward the southwest, as it heads on to 31 and the fence. It straightens out again when it gets to the corner of the huge pyramidal building occupied by the East Germans. Then it runs due west again, between the East German giant and the little Israeli block.

My Italian friend advised me, "Try to get to the roof of our building, over the Puerto Ricans'. From there, you'll have an unbeatable view on Thirty-one, and you'll get some surprises."

I went up the emergency stairs, skillfully using them to avoid the cops policing the corridors. I got up to the roof area, and was not really so surprised to see a score of newsmen there ahead of me. Down below, cordons of police had the street sealed off—the street which was supposed never to have any motor vehicles on it, but now had a caterpillared troop carrier, probably come in through the underground and up the pedestrian ramp.

Two East German-sweat-shirted athletes were showing their credentials, being searched, and made to wait until two officers could escort them to the entrance-hall to their building.

Helicopters. Tropical sun. Pavement burning through one's soles. Over there, the other side of the fence, from north to south, there was a crestline with greenery and transplanted little pines that stood out as on a sketch. Outsize cameras with meter-long lenses were set up in batteries along it, and looked ready to open fire on the besieged building.

Across from the corner of our building, a yellow TV van was parking next to the sidewalk; this was the one that had been underground a little while before. How did it get up to Connollystrasse? It must have plowed over a grassy slope. But, of course, it was the HQ of the crisis staff, with a license-plate by now known to probably half the world: D-309. The two Interior Ministers, Merk of Bavaria and Genscher of Bonn, as well as Herr Vogel, had joined Herr Schreiber inside it. Around it, uniforms buzzed in a busy ballet.

The policewoman-interpreter reappeared, no telling from where, and went back to Door 1 of No. 31. Issa shortly was visible through its opening. He seemed terribly near, through my field glasses. The big round lenses of his glasses were full of reflections. He was laughing in a friendly, relaxed way, his white teeth showing between his drawn lips. Before him, the young woman moved from one foot to the other; he was smoking and offered her a cigarette. She took it, and he lighted it for her.

You have to act that way. She was right.

12:55 PM: Herren Genscher and Merk now went over to the north face of Block 31, shortly followed by Dr. Schreiber.

I had heard good things about Genscher. A large, solid man, with light eyes, he was a refugee from Behind the Curtain. He came from Reideburg, not far from Leipzig. In 1952, he had left East Germany to become a lawyer at Bremen, and joined the Free Democratic Party. He was one of the opinion-makers of the young liberal wave. Aged forty-three, he had self-control, authority, and was reputed to know more than he let on. A hard worker.

It was to be hoped the TV was not picking up the flea-hops of the sharpshooters who were surrounding the small bloody space. No communiqué was needed to tell the world what this reappearance of the *Krisenstab* before the terrorists was about: they wanted a further delay on the current 1:00 PM deadline, now just five minutes away. The Palestinians had made a psychological mistake, and shown weakness and lack of judgment in giving only a one-hour reprieve if they were not ready for the killings in the next few minutes. Only a little while ago, Colonel Crespin had said: "They know a thing like this can't be settled in one hour, unless the Israelis were to give in to them all along the line, and that's unthinkable!"

Beneath his reassuringly bald pate, Bruno Merk was smiling—circumspectly, but relievedly, when the meeting was over. The deadline had been set back to 3:00 PM, "in view of the negotiations with the Israeli authorities." The Arabs had radios. They had surely brought some, and found others in the rooms. One of these, at least, "little" Mark Slavin's, was very powerful. So they were able to get the broadcasts that would inform them that "according to the best-informed sources," the Israeli Cabinet had irrevocably turned down any freeing of prisoners whatsoever.

Mr. Woolen, head of security for the British delegation, who had served in many hot spots in the Middle East, told me: "If I were the Germans, I would not under any circumstances let the Israelis be taken out of Olympic Village. You can only overcome people like these by attrition. Wait them out, and attack by dark. Or else, with gas . . ."

Everyone was thinking of gas. Around 11:30, near the fountains at the head of Connollystrasse, I had bumped into Mr. and Mrs. Alexandru Siperco. The Rumanian IOC member had headed the Communist student groups in the anti-Nazi underground. I asked his expert opinion.

"Of course," he said, "chemicals could be wafted in through the ventilation ducts. There are a lot of nonfatal gases that work very fast and are easy to use. Yet, there is always a risk. Even odorless gases can sometimes be detected . . ."

The *Dokumentation* would explain the nonuse of gas with, "All experts agree, no gas works instantly. . . . If a nonfatal gas were used, the terrorists would have had plenty of time to do away with their hostages."

Still, the new forms of chloropicrin, bromoacetone, and many others, to say nothing of the various combinations of the classical carbon oxide, could at almost no risk of permanent damage quickly knock their victims out, without the latter being aware of their presence. Of course, as Mr. Siperco had said, there is always some danger; but when an operation seems to have a good chance of saving a patient, you chance it. Perhaps the Munich experts had reasons other than those given by the *Dokumentation;* it would be interesting to know what they were.

Zigzagging through *Olympiapark,* I had the strange feeling that people and things seemed as if Block 31 and the hostages just didn't exist. It might be any normal place. . . .

In its northern part, i.e., the Village, ex-Oberwiesenfeld, for all the painting and exposed pipes made to look like art, was nothing but a collection of rabbit hutches. The south side, with its difficult terrain, had become a symphony of vales and slopes, meadowlets and buttes, harboring an armada of stadia, paths intoxicated with colors, and the charm of the artificial lake snaking unevenly along. Everywhere, the overbearing TV tower dominated.

I ran into my brother Robert, an Olympic tourist. . . . We tried to reconstruct the path of the killers as they came in from the outside. We followed the fence, through which we could see the Village with all of its busyness and its submachine-gun-armed cops.

To the west, the Village was flanked along its entire length by the future Institute of Physical Education and Sports, of the University of Munich. The builders had not gone at it by half-measures: seventy-three different training or competing areas, field hockey, track and field, basketball, volleyball, you name it. Plus twelve enclosed halls, also suitable for competition, training, or just calisthenics. All of it of course intended for the sole use of the Olympic athletes, but today a number of these places held armored vehicles or armed men.

The fine Institute complex, completed just in time for the Games, also included some large buildings of tinted glass and steel, the dormitories for its students, as well as school offices and classrooms. Since dawn, the mass media of every continent had been passionately concerned with these buildings, where the *Deutsches Olympia Rundfunk und Fernsehzentrum* (German Olympic Radio/TV Center) (DOZ) was, including the studios, offices, and equipment of that fabulous audiovisual unit. . . .

Back in the Village, there were the unfailingly pretty young hostesses in their soft-blue miniskirts and boleros, with white balloon-sleeved blouses and aprons. White, too, their shoes and socks. In the Bavarian mode, this made for very attractive damsels, albeit they came from all over the globe. Usually all smiles, they were now doing their best to seem cheerful. But their mouths were tense, hiding behind icy masks.

The three floors of monster restaurant facing the Plaza were overflowing with athletes. They had to eat, after all. And here, there was food for every taste, every religion—despite a sudden drop in the demand for kosher cooking.

Below the Plaza, in an endless courtyard sunk among the masses of concrete, the 18-hole golf setup had as many takers as it could handle. All twelve Ping-Pong tables were in use. And there too were the huge chessboards with crowds around them. I went over to one: a Russian weight lifter and an English-speaking fair-haired fellow, who I am told plays hockey, were playing. Each in turn carefully picked up the two-foot-high wooden chessmen. The black and white squares were traced on the ground. What might they be doing if they were not playing? A priest in a street suit of dark synthetic, with a discreet golden cross on the lapel, hurried by toward the ecumenical center, his hands squeezing his missal as he mumbled his prayers.

Going back up the business street, I noticed Shmuel Lalkin. The head of the Israeli mission had come out of G-1 to relax for a moment. He was drinking tea at one of the two rival free carts in the Plaza. The pretty Sinhalese fairy dispensing the cardboard cups had recognized him, even though he was in shirtsleeves, without insignia. She smiled at him, with a great deal of warmth.

1:00 PM: In Cairo, diplomatic offices, notables, and several press agencies received a release signed by Black September, and dealing with the reasons for the Munich attack. Here are extensive passages from it:

> Our revolutionary forces made an entry in strength into the Israeli quarters at the Olympic Village, at Munich, in order to get the Israeli military authorities to adopt a more humane attitude toward the Palestinian people, whether now under Israeli oppression or forced unwillingly into diaspora.
>
> The massacre Israel has carried out against the population of Palestine has created a condition of racial persecution against 3,000,000 Palestinians, as well as against Oriental Jews, by uprooting an entire nation and depriving it of any existence.
>
> The temporary victory of the Israelis in their conquest of Palestine will never be able to keep the Palestinian people from enjoying their rights in their own country nor give the occupier [Israel] the right to represent Occupied Palestine in a world meet such as the Olympic Games.
>
> At the same time, all peaceloving peoples of Europe and the world will forever reject the transplanting into the Middle East

142

of a foreign body such as Israel, an emanation of American imperialism. The only aim of such a transplant is to create in the region a client state of the U.S., putting the peoples of the Middle East under a permanent threat, militarizing the Mediterranean, and thus making impossible the neutralization of this cradle of civilization.

An appended sheet stated that the Connollystrasse operation had been given the operational name of *Berem and Ikrit*. These were two Arab villages in Israel whose inhabitants were expelled in 1948 for security reasons. In the spring of 1972, the inhabitants and their descendants asked to be allowed to return to their homes, but the Israeli Government refused to let them, because they were too near the borders. There were violent polemics on the subject in Israel at the time.

There was David Marc Berger, weight lifter, born June 24, 1944.

His was a stocky silhouette, swollen with rounded muscles; a thick mane of raven-black hair, curly and readily tousled, covered his whole head from skull to jawbones, swelling out on the nape of the neck.

Shmuel Lalkin, on September 5, said of him to me: "If Berger is still alive, he's just waiting for his chance. Then he'll jump them, even if he knows he won't get out of it alive. The only thing that might hold him back would be reprisals that might affect his comrades. Berger is an idealist and a real champion, a man of amazing culture."

The woodsman's body, the heavily sculptured leonine face, round cheeks and thick lips, shadowed by a heavy beard he was not unaccustomed to shaving twice a day, his swinging walk, and the impressive size of pectorals and thighs, these were what struck you about him: his solidity, his health, his virility. He was on the short side, 5 feet 6½, but that frame carried some 182 pounds of power. And then, in total contrast to the tough physique, you saw his eyes, deep and narrowed beneath the heavy brows: dark eyes, with long Oriental lashes, that grabbed at you like hands. Warm eyes—courageous, contagious with intelligence.

David Berger had been born at Shaker Heights, outside of

Cleveland, Ohio. His father is a physician, and the Bergers are people of substance. After high school in Cleveland, David went to Columbia University in New York, for a master's in law.

He was practicing already when he visited Israel in 1970. But it was love at first sight. Dr. and Mrs. Benjamin Berger, good Jews, were not surprised when, on his return, their son told them he had decided to emigrate to Israel.

David was engaged to an Israeli student, and was to marry her as soon as he got back from the Olympics. He was set to start his military service on October 1, 1972. That would last thirty months, as it does for men (twenty months for women), but of course Israelis knew they might often be called back for active service, in addition to yearly refreshers. David planned to open a law office in Haifa as soon as he became a civilian again. He was a devoted member of the Tel-Aviv Maccabee athletic club.

Dr. and Mrs. Berger watched the rebroadcast of the Munich Games every evening: Cleveland is six hours earlier than Munich, so the Bergers, since they were busy during the day, usually watched the rebroadcasts. But on September 2, at 4:30 PM, their time (10:30 in Munich), they watched the live telecast of their David's appearance in the middle-heavyweight category of weight lifting. He was disqualified at the third movement, the clean-and-jerk, after starting out rather well. He might have done better: he had taken a silver medal at the Asian Games in Manila in 1971.

September 4, they turned the TV off at about 11:00 PM. That, then, was 5:00 AM, September 5, in Munich. They went to sleep unaware of a thing. A phone call awoke them before dawn in Ohio to tell them of what had happened, and that their son was one of the hostages. From then on, the Bergers never left their set . . .

The next morning, September 6, Governor John J. Gilligan, of Ohio, ordered that all flags in the State be kept at half-mast for a week, in honor of David Berger. He personally phoned David's parents to express the condolences of all.

The father of the martyred young lawyer met with the news-papermen who had gathered outside his door that morning, and told them that the way David ended was terrible, but he had

144

decided to devote his life entirely to Israel. He accepted in advance whatever might happen. His father was sure that if David was aware of what was happening to him, he regretted nothing, because he knew that sacrifices such as his are necessary.

IX

THE INTERNATIONAL OLYMPIC COMMITTEE

> . . . not with thy sword, nor with thy bow.
> *Joshua* 24:12

THE CONNOLLYSTRASSE ATTACK WOULD NOT HAVE TAKEN PLACE WERE it not for the XXth Olympiad, and the Games would not have been held without the International Olympic Committee. So, it may be useful to us here to consider the role of the IOC.

Each country has its own national Olympic Committee, "recognized and approved by the IOC" for the purpose of "development and protection of the Olympic Movement and of amateur sport" within its country and to enforce the regulations of the IOC. The Olympic Movement was made up in 1972 of twenty-six international amateur federations covering virtually every sport.

The IOC has tended to increase its functions: it now arranges for both the Winter Games and the regular quadrennial Olympics. It watches over the maintenance of the Olympic ideal. It encourages, promotes, and organizes any sports events that tend to help the Olympic Movement and keep athletics in the Olympic spirit. It advises organizations that request its help and devotes all of its surplus income "to the promotion of the Olympic Movement or to the development of amateur sport."

The IOC is filled by co-optation. Pierre de Coubertin, the father of the modern Olympics, who formed the IOC in 1894, felt that there was no other way to assure its independence. This is done by the Executive Board nominating a candidate, whom up to the present the IOC as a whole has invariably confirmed. No woman has as yet ever been co-opted.

146

Upon election, the new member swears to the following very noble declaration:

> Recognizing the responsibilities that go with the great honor of serving as (one of) the representative(s) of the International Olympic Committee in my country (name of his country), I bind myself to promote the Olympic Movement to the best of my ability and to guard and preserve its fundamental principles as conceived by the Baron Pierre de Coubertin, keeping myself as a member free from all political, sectarian or commercial influence.

In September 1972, it had seventy-five active members. It also has nine honorary members, all former active members now retired because of age or other reasons, sometimes political. Members elected since 1966 are required to retire at age seventy-two, at which time they may request being made honorary members. Prior to 1966, members were co-opted for life.

There is no mechanical rule as to national representation, but no country is allowed more than two active members. The IOC tries ever more carefully to maintain geographical equality.

The governing Executive Board has nine members: the President, elected for eight years and eligible for further terms of four years each; First, Second, and Third Vice-Presidents, elected for a single four-year term, but moving up by seniority; and five members elected for four years, ineligible for reelection.

Each of these positions is voted for separately by the full IOC, so a member can move readily from one "grade" to another in the Executive Board; defeated for President, or a Vice-Presidency, a member may still be elected to the Executive. Mr. Constantin Andrianov (USSR) has been on the Board since 1962, as either a Vice-President or member.

The IOC is not loath to change its rules. The Board meets three times per year apart from the annual full IOC meetings (two in leap, or Games, years).

IOC decisions are carried out by its secretariat-general, located at the Château de Vidy, Lausanne, Switzerland. This secretariat has a director who since January 1972 has been Mme. Monique Berlioux (France); she had actually been fulfilling the same functions, under another title, since January 10, 1969. This director is assisted by a technical director, who at the time of the Munich Games was Mr. Artur Takac (Yugoslavia), in office since the spring of 1969. (He was replaced in March 1973 by Mr. Henry R. Banks [Great Britain].) . . .

Though the IOC is a famous international organization, neither the U.N. nor any government recognizes it officially. It has no Vatican, and no treasury; only since April 10, 1915, does it occupy the château HQ that the City of Lausanne supplies without fee; so, it does not even have a roof of its own.

Thanks to its share of the Olympic TV rights, it has at last begun to be able to operate on a somewhat decent basis. But this has been true only since Sapporo; before that, the IOC lived entirely on loans. Now, apparently, the great TV networks plan to present a united front so as to pay much less for rights to the next Winter Games and the Montreal 1976 Olympics.

Apart from TV rights, all other fees of all kinds relating to commercial or other tie-ins are paid to the Organizing Committee of each Olympiad—which is only right, else the taxpayers of the cities where they are held would be sorely imposed upon. Out of the TV rights, the IOC retains but a portion, with the balance going to the Organizing Committee and the various International Federations of different sports. With excess funds available, they will now be used to promote "Olympism" and for "Olympic Solidarity," through an Olympic Foundation voted into existence in 1972. . . .

The IOC has changed a great deal since its founding by an old-line baron who, in his lifetime, surrounded himself with other men of illustrious lineage, generals, and millionaires. Despite Constantine II, King of the Hellenes, Ruling Prince François-Joseph of Liechtenstein, and Grand-Duke Jean of Luxembourg, commoners were the rule on the IOC of 1972, accounting for fifty-nine of the seventy-five members. Social, political, and racial diversities were on the increase. Most of the members had no great personal means. Their average age was fifty-seven, so that the standard old complaint about "old fogies on the IOC" was at best somewhat exaggerated.

Of the seventy-five members, eleven were former Olympic competitors, who among them had won four gold medals (400-meter hurdles, 100-meter backstroke, pentathlon, and yachting) and four bronze. Moreover, they included two former tennis champions and the conqueror of Annapurna. All were once practicing athletes, a good half of them ranking competitors. The hackneyed, "What do they know about sports?" was also meaningless, if we are to be fair.

The IOC above all is a sort of club; its members all feel special, and stand by each other. The citizens of Communist countries, once co-opted, abide by the setup and the rules, and are careful not to upset their fellows by their actions, even when as a solid bloc they support some party-lining stand that is at odds with traditional attitudes.

Mr. Avery Brundage was at this point winding up his tenure as President of the IOC, but that seemed impossible! As a living legend, the apostle of amateurism had for so many years dominated the Olympic spirit! We will see how he acted this day, but for now let us look into his unusual story.

Avery Brundage was born in Detroit on September 28, 1887. So his youth was spent in a period of stability, without great leaps forward or mass genocides, without a mad race toward progress in every area. A period when people took their time; and the world was still on a human scale.

Brundage is usually referred to as a millionaire; true, he came from a good family, but his father early deserted it, and young Avery started life with no fortune behind him. An honor student at the University of Illinois, he was graduated in 1909 as a civil engineer, having edited the college magazine and managed the track team, as well as being intercollegiate discus champion, a member of the basketball squad, and winner of a special medal for athletic achievement.

A solid fellow (over 6 ft. and 175 lbs.), he was a strict disciplinarian, for himself as for others, and a sports maniac. For the next ten years, as a member of the Chicago Athletic Association team, he was three times All-Around Amateur Champion of the U.S. This was comparable to the decathlon, but much more strenuous, since the ten all-around events were held within the same day. As a member of the 1912 U.S. Olympic team, he competed in the Vth Olympiad at Stockholm, in the discus throw, the decathlon (then spread over three days), and the pentathlon.

By 1915, with six years' experience behind him, he created the Avery Brundage Co., which was to put up many a great building in Chicago, and make him a millionaire indeed. His creed: devotion to work; absolute respect for his word; no time off, except for athletic events; and the most modern and efficient methods available.

Ruined a first time by the Crash of 1929, he was back in the saddle two years later, but his great fortune was smashed again in the postwar depression of 1946 as he met with a series of reverses: fire, losses at sea, and government reconversion. By dint of hard work, and pitching in to take the place of missing architects and subcontractors, within a year he was a big boss again, quoted as feeling "young as a draftee" as he entered his sixtieth year.

He had long since become a leading international athletic organizer. He was President of the A.A.U. (Amateur Athletic Union of the U.S.) from 1928 to 1934, withdrawing only because of the (still unsettled) rivalry between it and the N.C.A.A. (National Collegiate Athletic Association). As President of the U.S. Olympic Committee since 1928, he felt he had to remain outside such internecine struggles.

He was, however, often a controversial figure. The 1936 Olympics had been set for Berlin in 1931, during the IOC's 29th meeting, at Barcelona. When the Nazis came to power on January 30, 1933, and imposed their anti-Semitic decrees throughout the Third Reich, there was a strong movement in the U.S. for a boycott of Hitler's Games.

Especially after promulgation of the Nuremberg Laws on September 15, 1935, stripping Jews of German nationality, forbidding marriages between Jews and "Germans," making it a crime for Jews to employ German charwomen under forty-five years of age, or even to fly the German flag, this feeling grew. Anyone with two Jewish grandparents fell into this category, and mass arrests and persecutions ensued, until the start of the "final solution" of the Jewish problem through total liquidation, in 1938 and after. Jewish communities in Germany were sorely oppressed, and emigration was increasingly difficult, what with the general lack of good will on the part of foreign countries in accepting Jewish refugees.

In the face of this, Brundage went to Berlin and, when asked about Nazi anti-Semitism on his return, was quoted as feeling, frankly, that it would not be to our interest to mix into this. We are, he said, an athletic organization, created to watch over purity of competition, and the honesty and honor of competitors. If politics, racial questions, or religious or social quarrels were allowed to interfere with our action, we would get into the deepest kind of trouble. He had been assured we could send to the Olympic Games any athletes we wished. What else, he asked, can we ask?

To say that not everyone agreed with him, that millions outside the athletic world were shocked, is understatement.

But Avery Brundage stuck to his guns in the deep, sonorous voice that rang from the depths of his lungs up through his nostrils, to make him sound like some fanatical evangelist preaching scouting. His stand was backed by the USOC. The new President of the A.A.U., the Hon. Jeremiah Mahoney, a highly respected former New York judge, tried to get his federation to withdraw its members from participation in the Berlin Games, but lost by a narrow margin, and promptly resigned. Brundage jumped to the platform to announce his own candidacy as his successor, so the stand of the A.A.U. might be made even clearer: he was elected by an eyelash.

Thereupon, three months before the *Führer und Reichskanzler* Adolf Hitler formally opened the Games of the XIth Olympiad at 3:00 PM on August 1, 1936, Brundage stated that "the anti-Nazi outcry in this country is the work of alien agitators, Communists and certain Jews." And a pamphlet issued by his USOC decreed, "The persecution of minorities is as old as history and no Olympic committee should pay any attention to it."

During its 35th meeting, held at Berlin just before the Games, the IOC co-opted Avery Brundage, July 30, 1936, under most illuminating circumstances. Among the fiercest opponents of U.S. participation in the Berlin Games was one of the two American members of the IOC, Ernest Lee Jahncke, a former Assistant Secretary of the Navy under President Herbert Hoover. With courage, in the face of the otherwise-unanimous view of the IOC, Lee Jahncke carried on his campaign against the sending of a U.S. team and stood up to Brundage in violent public exchanges. The

IOC called on Jahncke to change his stand, accusing him of betraying the interests of the Committee, violating its rules, and being ungentlemanly toward his colleagues.

Lee Jahncke refused to apologize, and, in a letter that was couched very politely, also refused to attend the Berlin meeting, to be held in racist Nazi territory. He added that he would forever feel it a blemish on the honor of the U.S. that it had sent a delegation to Games sponsored by Adolf Hitler and used for the propaganda of the Third Reich.[1]

In a move which had had but one precedent, the then-President, the Belgian Henri de Baillet-Latour, asked for a vote of expulsion against Lee Jahncke. It was unanimous, with the sole abstention of the other U.S. member of the IOC, William May Garland, who did however record his "deep disapproval" of his fellow American's position. The Executive Board then immediately co-opted Mr. Brundage, a move ratified by the IOC.[2]

It is strange that Avery Brundage's membership in the IOC, brought about by the awful tragedy that befell the Jewish people, should have ended with the terrible bloodshed of the Israeli Olympic athletes.

For, is he an anti-Semite? No, not specifically.

Why is there no Jew on the IOC? That is a question that remains unanswered.

At the end of the Berlin Games, Brundage was all compliments for them and the German people. On his return to New York, he appeared in Madison Square Garden at a large political rally for the close of German Day: he lauded the Nazis for their accomplishments in stopping the decline of patriotism!

With the start of World War II in Europe, the Chicago master builder was one of the founders and president of the Citizens' Keep

---

[1] It is interesting to note that the official press-release biography of Mr. Brundage, given out by the USOC and presumably prepared in his personal office, reads: "In 1936, when there was an organized international movement to boycott the Olympic Games and all other countries were watching developments in the United States, he at considerable personal sacrifice led the furious battle to keep Olympic sport from being used as a political weapon. Overcoming all obstacles, he organized and financed a large and victorious U.S. team and *this insured the success of the XI Olympiad.*" (Italics ours; Tr. Note)

[2] Today, there is no U.S. representation on the IOC. (Tr. Note)

America Out of War Committee, as well as a director of the notoriously isolationist America First Committee.

On July 20, 1944 [the very day of the generals' abortive attempt on the life of a Hitler they could no longer abide], he amazed the world by coming out in favor of inclusion of America's wartime enemies, Germany and Japan, in the postwar Olympics: GIs at the time were fighting both these countries, and daily dying by the hundreds in Normandy and the Pacific, but Mr. Brundage has never been under fire.

That was the way he was. He was always ready to assume responsibility for making decisions, even if he had to backtrack later in the face of adverse reactions, only to come back to his original stand once the storm had passed. His whole life long he remained willful, opinionated, and solitary. In 1927, aged forty, he married a well-known singer-pianist, Miss Elizabeth Dunlop, a beautiful vigorous woman, with a great deal of dash and deep culture. They were a very happy couple, though they had no children. Mrs. Brundage, who often accompanied her husband abroad, but preferred living on their sumptuous estate at Santa Barbara, California, died in 1971.

Unlike others, Brundage was elected to the Executive Board of the IOC as early as 1937. He had once again (this time for good) given up the presidency of the A.A.U. Now, in his own silent way (incessantly at it, though never formally a candidate), he was out to become President of the IOC. A key man thought most highly of him: Pierre de Coubertin. The brilliant little baron, now white-haired and withered, with the huge Gaulish mustache across his pinched countenance, saw Brundage as a disciple: they were united in their Germanophilia. But, to be fair, we must admit there was another bond: their uncompromising passion for a traditional Olympic spirit, devoid of scandal or professionalism, an Olympic spirit that might be seen as a school for present-day knighthood, universal brotherhood, noble virility. But Coubertin, after being instrumental in Brundage's election, was to die in poverty at Lausanne, the very year his American protégé stepped into the saddle.

In 1945, Brundage became Vice-President of the IOC. Mr. J.

Sigfrid Edström, a patrician Swede, was then the temporary President, since January 1942, when Count de Baillet-Latour had died. Mr. Edström, who would officially become President in 1946, sponsored Brundage's promotion, with the feeling that the very rich and dynamic American would be his best successor. Indeed, in 1952, at the IOC's 47th meeting, at Helsinki, on the occasion of the XVth Olympiad, Brundage was elected President, to follow Edström, retiring at eighty-two.

His most serious rival had been Lord Burghley, later Marquess of Exeter, whom Brundage defeated, 32 to 17.

David George Brownlow Cecil, Lord Burghley, sixth Marquess of Exeter, belongs to Britain's oldest, highest nobility; he is related to the royal family. A longtime M.P., stalwart Tory, and later important businessman, for ten years he headed British Overseas Airways (BOAC). Since 1946, he was at the head of the International Amateur Athletic Federation, the most powerful of all the sports internationals (embracing track and field events). Fine-looking, sturdy, with aquiline nose and authoritative voice, speaking clearly and succinctly, he had an impressive presence.

Lord Burghley won the gold medal for the 400-meter hurdles at the Amsterdam Olympics (1928), and the silver medal in the 4x400 meters relays at Los Angeles (1932). He had earlier come in fifth in the 400-meter hurdles at Paris (1924), and was again fifth in them at Los Angeles. He won hundreds of international meets, and as a great champion would have had the finest chances of becoming President of the IOC, had he not been afflicted with arthritis of the hip, which forced him to walk with a cane. A member of the IOC since 1933, when he was twenty-eight (setting a record for youthful co-optation), he was therefore the senior member of the organization.

In his very first speech after his election on September 1, 1952, at the Villa Mon Repos at Lausanne, the new IOC President, Avery Brundage, showed his colors: "I will assume the full responsibility of my office. I will never hesitate to make the decisions I feel best serve the Olympic spirit."

Thus began a one-man reign that was to go on for twenty years, marked by what has been called the Olympics explosion. From the

Rome Games of 1960 on, they have been accused of gigantism, an aggressive, antagonistic, and untrue accusation, since human qualities can be preserved even with huge success. At the same time, the Winter Games were also undergoing fantastic development with their apotheosis to come at Sapporo in February 1972.

Avery Brundage, while voicing pious qualms about the dangers of overexpansion, was always delighted by the continual prodigious growth of the quadrennial summer event, for he quickly came to look upon the post-World War II Olympics as his baby. Which, to a degree, was correct. The main promoter of the Olympics' galloping rise in size was the promoter of construction whose impress was felt not only in Chicago, but throughout the Midwest, and even in California.

His role in it, all to his honor although at times he denies it, is obvious despite the fog he has so consciously spread around many of his actions. It would have been so easy for him to keep the leap-year Games within the parameters of Helsinki. But that was the last thing he wanted. One has to read his scoldings at Melbourne in 1955, when he felt the organizers had done things on much too mean a scale, and the work was far behind schedule. Every city to host the Summer as well as the Winter Games got ten visits from him rather than one, mixing into every detail and delighting in each fact that would further glamorize the great meet. The organizers, each in turn, were warmly congratulated. The greater their plans and accomplishments, the more ardent Brundage's tone, reaching its climax with the fantastic Olympic extravaganzas of Mexico City, Sapporo, and Munich.

The very lances with which this would-be Don Quixote tilted so noisily against the windmills of creeping professionalism or the alleged invasion of commercialism were often the shrewdest of publicity stunts. I have seen him roar with delight at the huge coverage the mass media and press gave to his thundering ukases, his threats, and his crashing undertakings.

He had a sense of the dramatic. Each quadrennial Games was a theater to him, in which he was the one to cast the leads and the heavies, the good parts and the bad. In an ever-more-clamorous setting, he stage-managed his play, always with a very careful plot. The central idea was clear, inevitably spectacular, alternately wor-

155

rying and delighting the organizers, enthralling the contestants, raising the hackles of the host city's taxpayers, and never failing to create the vast, if secret, delight of the thousand heads of that hydra that Brundage, without admitting it, felt to be ungrateful: the press. Would the Games take place? Who would be disqualified? How many teams would withdraw, or would any? Would he succeed in killing off the Winter Games? Would he change his mind? Would the IOC go along with him? Would he be reelected? Oh, yes, he knew that drama could not be good without a plot—and he was one devil of a plot-hatcher.

I have been speaking of him in the past tense. Yet, in his eighty-sixth year, he remains intensely alive, full of plans, highly active, still as straight as a ramrod, chest out, gut in, an indefatigable walker, with his powerful ex-discus-thrower's handshake and his deep voice that grinds and keeps going like the indestructible old automobiles they used to make in Detroit.

In truth, there is but one chink in that amazingly resistant carcass: the eyes. He never had good sight. With age, it has gotten worse. He is said still to be driving his car on the broad avenues of Santa Barbara, but I would not like to ride with him. In 1972, he sold the Spanish colonial-style mansion he had built, with its cream-colored walls and manorial garden. Putting behind him the site of his long, happy marriage, he had an apartment built on the terrace of the Montecito Country Club, overlooking Santa Barbara. It in no way disfigures the property, of which Brundage, naturally, is the principal stockholder. From his balcony, the former IOC President can look out over the green-and-white landscape beyond the Montecito golf course, at the mushrooming city tapering down toward the bay. And beyond, the broad expanse of the imperial Pacific, all green-gray.

So he was all alone again, the old wolf who had known how to roar in the morning and negotiate at night, the autocrat who, while remaining true to his somewhat outdated athletic ideals, in two decades multiplied by ten the market value of the Olympics business in his charge.

But the loneliness was too much, too hard. In August 1973, nearing his eighty-sixth birthday, he married at Garmisch Princess Marianne Reuss, thirty-six. Described in his press release as "an

156

accomplished international sportswoman," she had been working in the protocol division of the Munich Organizir g Committee when he met her. Precise, a hard worker, with a feel for command and a good rearing, the new Mrs. Brundage is a tall, very slim person, with long regular features and a contralto voice: her Prussian princely family, related to the Mecklenburgs, was ruined by World War II, in which her father, a general, served well on the Russian front. She is a cousin of Joachim von Ribbentrop, Hitler's well-known Foreign Minister.

Brundage is not athletics alone. For all his deep American roots, he is passionately interested in Chinese art. He is a born collector, and ever since his first visits to Europe had become an habitué of antique-shops and galleries. But he remained very eclectic until in 1935 in Shanghai he happened on a batch of Chang Dynasty bronze ritual vases. After amassing the finest collection of its kind in the world, he gave it in 1959 to the city of San Francisco, which built a special museum for it in Golden Gate Park, overlooking the bay. Then, starting from scratch, Brundage set out after another master collection.

Still with him, assisting him in all of his many business enterprises, is an aide well-known to the IOC members, Mr. Frederick Ruegsegger, a Swiss by birth, courteous and secretive, very large and businesslike behind his glasses on a dark, square face. The heart of the Brundage empire remains in Chicago, and the former czar of the Olympics visits there regularly.

This was the man who on the morning of September 5 was at the helm of the IOC. A sacred cow. An historical figure. As we shall see, he had little effect on the tragedy that took place but, deaf to all else, he kept the huge, magnificent Olympic ship headed toward port. Perhaps it was in that that, as he was about to bow out, he rendered his last significant service to the Olympic spirit. [Retiring as both President and member of the IOC the week after the 1972 Games, he was awarded the lifetime title of "Honorary President" of the organization.]

X

TWO HELPFUL ARAB DIPLOMATS

> . . . Oh, that Thou wouldest rend the
> heavens, that Thou wouldest come down,
> That the mountains might quake at
> Thy presence,
> As when fire kindleth the brush-wood,
> And the fire causeth the waters to boil;
> To make Thy name known to Thine
> adversaries,
> That the nations might tremble at
> Thy presence . . .
> *Isaiah* 63:19, 64:1

1:15 PM: DR. MANFRED SCHREIBER APPEARED AT THE *Pressezentrum;*
the newsmen, stormy captive forces, were bumping into people and
things, trying to do their job, feeling sorrow, hope, and perhaps
some of them secret joy, for like any collective group they were but
reflections of the passersby that all of us are.

They came from everywhere, prompted by instinct, or by that
grapevine which it would today be unseemly to refer to, as we used
to in North Africa, as the "Arab telephone." More than a third of
the 4200 correspondents assigned to the Games were here, in the
luxurious auditorium with all its up-to-date comfort and its impeccable air conditioning, suddenly smelling of the blood and
bestiality of a gladiatorial arena.

"No, I cannot say exactly how many hostages there are. No, I do
not know exactly how many terrorists are at Number Thirty-one.
Until now, we know of only one fatality, Moshe Weinberg, whose
body has been recovered. Anything else is speculation.

"Es ist fertig!" (That is all!), said Dr. Schreiber. "Even if I had
any other information, I would have to hold it back, for the
fedayeen are watching TV and listening to the radio."

And he left. There was a huge buzz throughout the ground floor.
Lines formed at the various windows: post office, banks, travel
agencies, car rentals. . . .

What could be seen on the faces of these pros, as if superimposed
on everything else, was surprise, and sadness. They reacted immedi-

ately, writing, phoning, wiring, turning it all into news—but still they were stunned.

Also at 1:15, the spokesman for the Free State of Bavaria, on TV, was saying: "The Government of the German Federal Republic is not authorized to stop the Games. Only the IOC can make that decision."

That may be called partially true partiality. I have known Chancellor Willy Brandt long enough: he is a brave, loyal man, with intelligence as well as instinct, and full of the virtue so many statesmen scorn: heart. He would not approve this manner of defining responsibilities. Yes, in the abstract, the IOC alone could decide whether the Olympics stopped or went on. But concretely, as we have seen, this problem had been discussed by the authorities in the administrative building of *Olympisches Dorf*.

Remember: the crisis staff, which made all the decisions that day, had two IOC representatives on it, Avery Brundage and Willi Daume, the latter being there, however, as head of the Organizing Committee. We might add our regret that the outgoing IOC President did not see fit to have his successor, Lord Killanin, immediately included in the group. Messrs. Brundage and Daume, while not wanting to see the Games interrupted, stated they would abide by the will of the *Krisenstab*'s majority.

On the other hand, the leading politicos, Messrs. Genscher, Merk, and the like, were for immediate suspension of all Olympic events. Manfred Schreiber, the head of the Munich police, was the one who, very convincingly, got his compatriots to change their minds. So, both Bavarian and federal authorities were as much involved in the decision as the IOC. To put it mildly.

I have a good friend that sometimes I forget to turn off, and his eight transistors can be heard through my attaché case. Today, he was not the only noisy one in Olympic Park. Why would one expect all the hippies sitting on the grass between two multicolored steel poles of the Olympic Stadium's acrylic-glass tent not to be letting theirs blare out the old Nat King Cole tune that was being broadcast? I had just turned mine off, after hearing that at 12:58 at Kiel Schilksee, the Israeli team of Yaïr Michaeli and Yitzhak Nir was competing. Today was the sixth regatta, in each of the six Olympic yachting events.

159

THE BLOOD OF ISRAEL

The Jewish crew was in the Flying Dutchman category. I wondered how come they were doing their acrobatic sailing around the buoys on their spinnakered centerboarder when they could not be unaware of what had happened to their fellows, 930 km. (app. 580 mi.) to the south. They were in the charge of Mr. Elie Friedlander; he was responsible for their sailing in this next-to-the-last round of the tourney. They had done very well, but they had no chance at all for a medal . . . Maybe they had not heard all the news up there. Surely, no one had sent them any directives . . .

1:20 PM: Of course, *they* were not telecasting it any more, but *they* kept talking, and talking . . .

> Armored vehicles have just taken aboard a group of persons near 31 Connollystrasse. Perhaps they are some of the hostages. Near Connollyplatz, a landing area has been cleared for a helicopter. Is this a trick or has some kind of deal actually been arranged? No one knows . . .

These were the things that German TV commentators were putting out. Remember: the terrorists were following it all.

It was hot and windless, humid, heavy; the very blue sky was dotted with motionless white balloons.

Between attempts to get a view of the fedayeen, people were massing on Spielstrasse, which ran along 250 meters of the south shore of the lake. They had to do something with their time. There were crowds around the sales-stands, and many others were watching the pretty outdoor scenes beyond the blue lake. At the multivision center, people were vying for pictures of the dramatic events. Some of them—horrible to say—were very good. I bought a batch.

1:30 PM: "The Olympic Movement is living through its most tragic moments, and the IOC is being left out of the decisions made in its name by a lame-duck President all by himself!" said Count Jean de Beaumont, in the huge upholstered parlor of the Vierjahreszeiten Hotel, in which the perfumed ghost of Lola Montez still seemed to be hovering.

The French banker, who looked like a dashing horseman, had a right to feel bitter. Not because Lord Killanin had beaten him for the presidency of the IOC on August 23 by 39 votes to 29, and

160

one abstention (only those present being allowed to vote). Once the election was over, the two candidates resumed being what they had always been: best friends. Jean Bonnin de la Bonninière, Count de Beaumont, was not a man to bear grudges, and Lord Killanin was loyalty incarnate, so they would go forward as a team. What bothered the former President of the French Olympic Committee (1967–1972), and onetime world shooting champion, was the immediate situation. He had been a member of the IOC since 1951 and was very devoted to the Olympic Movement.

Michel Clare, of the French sports paper *L'Equipe,* asked him whether Mr. Brundage, w·ose name appeared so frequently in the *Krisenstab*'s reports, had been in touch with his constituency.

"Absolutely not!" exploded the French official with the adventurous life-story. "That's the last thing he did. To Brundage, *he* is the IOC—no one else, just him! One week before he goes out of office, and he's playing pope without cardinals, when the very existence of the organization and the movement he is the head of is at stake! Lord Killanin, First Vice-President, soon to be President, went to Kiel last night to represent the IOC there. He's stuck there against his will, when the outgoing President might at least have wanted to reach him. And I'm second VP and have not been told a thing—nor have any of the other members." . . .

Meantime, Señor Juan Antonio Samaranch was efficiently and discreetly getting together all the available members of the Executive Board, despite Mr. Brundage. The elegant Spaniard was deploying all of his skill to try to arrange for Lord Killanin, as well as Jonkheer van Karnebeek and Prince Takeda, both also on the Board, to get back from Kiel.

2:00 PM: Herr Conrad Ahlers, spokesman for the Federal Government, was on West German radio/TV, as he had been several times since morning. "The federal authorities," he said, "for good reasons, wish for the Games to continue." And he went into an explanation about how, if the IOC had called for suspension of the Olympics, Bonn would have overridden it.

There were once three cooks . . .
Trying to make his aging-gladiator's face expressionless, tighten-

ing his jaws, Dr. Schreiber, the head of the Munich police himself, was now coming forward with three hefty characters, dressed in cooks' whites, each carrying a heavy box.

If it had not been tragic, it would have been farcical. For, with all due respect to Herr Schreiber, could anyone for a second have thought a child would not immediately know these were three disguised flatfeet? Later it would come out that, without any faith in the plan, he merely attempted to do what several of the VIPs had urged on him. The idea was to carry the three boxes inside of Building 31, so as to get a chance to see the ground floor and the location of Apt. 1. The fake chefs were armed to the teeth with trusty pistols, and it was hoped that, once in the lobby of the building, they might get a chance to pull a lightning-annihilation of all or almost all the fedayeen.

The first step of this magniloquent plot was the fact that, at 1:15, the man in the white hat, the obvious leader whom the interpreter-policewoman had heard called Issa, let it be known he would allow food to be brought in for the hostages, but that his comrades and he would not touch it, since they had supplies of their own.

When the "chefs" now appeared, with their boxes and a Dr. Schreiber very obviously controlling his exasperation, the watchman on guard—cowboy hat, orange-on-blue print scarf, black shirt and pants, bowlegs, very small and frail: this had to be Salah, who had scared the Hong Kong Chinese—ordered them to freeze. Issa came out alone, to meet the head of the Munich police and his men who were stopped stock still some ten meters or so from the corner of 31, in the middle of the street, next to a big square bed flowered with pansies and four-o'clocks. He carried the boxes in himself. And the three impromptu chefs went back the way they came.

2:20 PM *(Diary):* Before getting to 31 Connollystrasse, coming from the east, there is a last turn that widens into a square, sickle-like. This space goes as far as the terraced stairs that lead up to the East German pyramidal building. On those steps, a German team-member was arguing with a member of the *Ordnungsdienst*. The East German, I was told, is famous for one of the field events, but I won't try his name, not being sure of it. Anyway, a huge hulk!

The Olympic service-man was skinny, with pale blond locks down his neck and the body of a dragonfly; he had to lean back to look up at Mr. 275-Pounds.

I saw the sweat-suited athlete shove the employee's shoulder full-strength with the palm of his hand, bringing his right leg back and twisting his torso the way one does in the shotput.

The order-service man in his white shirt with the Waldi tie and turquoise trousers rolled down to the bottom of the steps, picked himself up, jumped toward the colossus, feinted as if trying to get around him, and then let him have a kick square on the shin, with the point of his shoe. The trackman faltered, got a second kick, near the knee, then fell, and got back up, very fast, purple with rage, getting ready to counter with clenched fists against his little opponent, who seemed to be dancing, when a group of members of the order service and East German athletes separated them. /

2:40 PM: Ministers Genscher and Merk, as well as *Polizeichef* Schreiber (wearing a pretty springtime blue-green jacket over his 9-mm Mauser parabellum in its brown leather holster), confronted Issa again; alongside him, his assistant Tony, the tropical dandy. Tony had put on more base makeup, and with his big, long wide head, and his vulture's nose with the nostrils that could smell the presence of palefaces on the prairie winds, he looked like a Technicolor Red Indian.

Each time, the same question: Would the Germans get another reprieve? Nine Israeli families, too, were living through a hell of waiting. It is easier to kill than to go knowingly to one's death: that was the note the negotiators had to hit. You kill them, and we'll kill you.

These repeated encounters—deadlines successively at 9:00 AM, noon, 1:00, 3:00 PM—may seem monotonous, in reading about them or having them all played back in full, with the tenseness of the participants, the repetition of the arguments, Issa's screaming meemies, the same actions and reactions over again, like a whole ceremonial routine. In fact, they were awful—awful and horrible as the whole of the tragedy.

Never in history had such blackmail over the lives of innocent people been carried on in the name of a national struggle. Or, at least, not before the Nazis systematized collective responsibility and the executions of hostages. Then it had been thought such depths of horror were forever behind us. The abjectness of Connollystrasse was of a piece with Hitler Germany's annihilation of 6,000,000 Jews. And this abjectness was happening at Munich, Hitler's most "sacred" place, the starting-point of his march toward total war.

Polizeipräsident Schreiber had been very skeptical of the whole thing; he remained practically silent.

"We still have nothing definite," Merk started abruptly. "If you want to murder the Israelis you are holding, we can do nothing to stop you. Whether you shoot one or several five minutes from now, nothing will be changed."

"What did Israel say?"

"Jerusalem has still not been able to get together the files on the two hundred thirty-four prisoners you're interested in. That's a Herculean job. They'll have them in about half an hour. Then they'll make a decision. I don't think they'll free them all. Not by a long shot."

Issa began to fume. He was not playacting. His wolf's teeth gleamed: he was howling in German, waving his AK-47 submachine gun under the nose of the Bavarian Interior Minister, almost touching it. Schreiber took a step forward, livid with contained rage. Tony turned sharply toward the middle of the street, while a rifle muzzle began to poke out of a second-story window. The Germans were making no moves, but the tension was almost tangible. The fingers of the sharpshooters placed around the area must have been itching on the gunmetal.

The fedayee was saying that if in five minutes he was not given more acceptable proposals, he would have one of the hostages brought down in the street and shoot him himself.

"Do you think that between the life of a Jew and the freedom of our brothers who are Israeli prisoners, we would hesitate?"

This was when, at a sign from Herr Bruno Merk, who simply asked Issa to be patient a moment, one the aides of the Munich police head went for H. E. Mahmoud Mestiri, ambassador of Tunisia at Bonn, and Dr. Mohammed Khadif, head of the Arab League office for West Germany.

Two Helpful Arab Diplomats

Seeing them, the faces of the two terrorists lit up. Issa with a broad gesture invited the two Arabs to come over to the threshold. He shook hands effusively with both of them, even though he had seen Dr. Khadif just a little while ago. Behind the two diplomats, Herr Walter Tröger, who had come with them this far, stepped a few steps forward, between the group with the two ministers and the group of Moslems. Suddenly full of hospitality, Issa invited the Mayor of Olympic Village—and by indirection also one of Schreiber's aides who had come over to say something to Tröger— also to come up to the threshold of the tragic building. Now he was shaking their hands, too, even though he had spoken several times— rudely—to Tröger, since the start of the morning.

Thereafter, Issa and Messrs. Mestiri and Khadif talked in Arabic. The Tunisian ambassador started by assuring that if a new reprieve were granted, the Germans undertook to make no moves against the fedayeen. He added, "I would advise you to give the Germans two more hours, so they can get a final answer from the Israelis."

From upstairs, a fedayee with a Tokarev assault rifle was following the conversation. The bottom of his face was covered by a sky-blue-and-white scarf, one of the Israelis' scarves. He yelled, "We refuse." Issa looked up and bade him come down. This was big Badran, of the charcoaled face and almond eyes. He was one of those Moshe Weinberg had knocked out, and his swollen jaw, cut lip, and broken teeth were one of the reasons for the half-mask. There was a discussion, while Tröger waited, as did the Germans farther away. Badran, stumbling over his words, was vehement at first, but after a look from his chief he fell silent.

Dr. Mohammed Khadif later told *Le Monde:* "The Palestinian [who says he was a Palestinian?] in charge gave us the impression a compromise was possible, provided there was a discussion of the commando's basic demands. It is very probable that if Israel had agreed to release a part of the prisoners asked for by the fedayeen, the latter would have accepted such a solution . . ."

Of course! But that was just what the Israeli Government was not going to agree to at any cost.

The Federal Minister of the Interior, Herr Genscher, cut in, coldly and officially: "*Bundeskanzler* Willy Brandt has come from

165

Bonn to Olympic Village with the sole purpose of settling this thing. I have been authorized by him to inform you officially that, at the proper exchange time, the Federal Republic will turn over to you the two German prisoners you asked for."

Issa replied that it was the Arab prisoners in Israel that mattered—"and not just a few, but all of them!" However, he did not seem unimpressed, and stared at the federal minister through his round glasses. A few more words between the fedayeen and the Arab diplomats, then suddenly, Issa, "without hesitating, without even looking over at his comrade," as Mr. Mestiri would later say to *Le Monde* and the Tunisian press, agreed to postponing the deadline until 5:00 PM, but asked the two Arabs not to come back to him "except with new, concrete proposals." It was a deal.

Mestiri also said of Issa, "He sent his armed comrade away with a wave of the head and gave us all the feeling that he was the sole boss there."

Dr. Mohammed Khadif said later: "The Tunisian ambassador and I told the German representatives that only some consideration for the demands of the Palestinians would bring a humane solution, for they were determined not to give in unconditionally . . ."

Exeunt. . . .

Counterpoint: Waldi. During the collapse of one of the last sanctuaries of brotherhood, protected by the essential fragility of the Olympic flame, Waldi remained everpresent, in whole or in part, made of every imaginable material. He wagged his tail, barked, wiggled his ears, or else he was a poster, in which he was admirably portrayed, or a keyring, a can opener, or . . .

Waldi was a dachshund, that typically German hound. He was chosen by Willi Daume as official mascot of the Munich Games. God knows how many manufacturers, paying impressive royalties, were given the right to reproduce the six-colored Olympic model: turquoise-blue head and tail, with a body, if you followed the official order, of successive stripes of dark green, purple, light green, yellow, and orange.

Second counterpoint, hardly less popular: the emblem of the Munich Games, the (stylized) Spiral, which, with all due respect, reminded me of the emblem of Louis XIV, that sun with the rays that illuminated the globe. It was truly original, elegant, and simple, traced in bars, with each of the teardrops, each of the sticks, having a different design as they skated around the heart.

Unbelievable: middle-distance and long-distance runners, as well as marathoners, kept tirelessly training, blind to the tragedy. To harden themselves, they prefer the cross-country. Dressed in track suits, under the hot sun, they went out of the Village, up and down greenswards, cutting through cordons of green police, and blue, and white, sprinting, panting, with the shining sweat and absorbed stare of the snipers on the lookout, passed some 30 meters outside the building the hostages were in, came back into the Village, then out again, then in. . . .

From the windows of towers and bungalows, bits of music could be heard, and laughter. The recreation places of the Village remained constantly full. On the Plaza, a group of Kenyans, Sudanese, Ugandans, and Nigériens had two transistors going full-blast, on the same station. They danced with huge good humor, shimmying, swinging their hips, and giving each other great pats with the palms of their hands. A beautiful and well-known girl swimmer, against a pillar of *Olympia Stadion*, was all but having intercourse (and perhaps even that) with a husky lad from one of the islands. That was what it was like as 3:00 PM hove in view. There was quite a wave of cynical egocentrism. But, as the hours went by, we were to see the whole gamut of collective attitudes.

I suppose all of them—or, anyway, most—had some guilt feeling. One of the Kenyans came trotting into Kennedy Platz, and went through the rotunda. He was a perfect being in ripe-date tone, a wholly balanced sculpture, with nothing departing from the norm. From the white sleeveless shirt and yellow-green shorts, youthfully ebullient arms and legs with long muscles burst and swung like a silent mechanism, to the rhythm of an even breath. This was Julius Sang (bronze medal in the 400 meters and gold medal in the 4x400 meters). We had had an interview on August 25, on one of the training fields. Now he was hailed by the dancers with the raucous radios. He stopped, swinging back and forth on one foot, and looked at them. His fine African head with the sharp chin and deep wide black eyes, looked sad.

He said in a singing, soft, lisping English, that slurred its *r*'s: "Oh, no! No songs for me today, friends! Today is so sad, today is awful . . ." He shook his head, stopped running as if his inspiration had been broken. His hands came together, fingers intertwined, his head was bent.

He went off toward his own building, at 42 Strasseberger Strasse, in the northeast corner of the Village, very far from the tragedy. Two of the gesticulating Africans watched him go, shrugged their shoulders, and shook their heads to the tall Nigérien in a necklace who was asking them to go on with the dance. Looking sad now in turn they went off toward the crowd of athletes and officials forming down there, as close as possible to the bloody building.

Chancellor Brandt, arriving in Munich, or more exactly at the Fürstenfeldbruck air base, in a Luftwaffe twinjet, took off in a helicopter for the Village. Silent, tall, and solid in his gray suit, he could be seen looking at his watch as he walked away from the craft—as if time were on his mind. Shortly after 3:15, he would be off again, destination unknown. The even but heavy lines of his face, virile and full of energy, with the direct blue eyes full of human communion, looked terribly upset. But he was the kind of man who would fight to the end.

Juan Antonio Samaranch happened to be near me when the news of the Chancellor's arrival spread like wildfire through the Village. Señor Samaranch reminded me, "Think about Chancellor Brandt's life. He never gave in. He never surrendered. He won't give those hostages up to the fedayeen."

One of the strongest personalities of the IOC, the Spaniard had the face and figure of a romantic leading man. A textile king, and big industrialist with huge and varied interests, Señor Samaranch was presently a member of the Executive Board and Chief of Protocol for the IOC. Until September 1970, as National Delegate for Physical Education and Sports, virtually a Cabinet post, Samaranch brought Spain into the class of the great athletic nations. When Francisco Ochoa won the gold medal in the slalom at the Sapporo Games and we were all clustering around him on the way to the podium, it was Samaranch that the onetime sheepherder mainly wanted to see, to embrace him and dedicate his victory to him.

"He won't give those hostages up to the fedayeen." No truer words could have been spoken. And speaking them, Juan Antonio Samaranch sounded very grave, almost anguished.

2:45 PM: Back on the air:

> It has been decided once again to allow viewers to see events in a usual and normal way, but this will be done so as to pose no threat to the hostages. The negotiations so far have had no result. The police are prepared for all eventualities.

There followed a vitriolic attack on the IOC on Channel 2. Since morning, how many accusations, how much badmouthing, on both Channels 4 and 2, against the Olympic officials! This was one way of trying to relieve Bonn, Bavaria, and the City of Munich of some of their responsibility in the awful affair. There had to be a patsy. Here are a few samples:

> It was the IOC that refused to interrupt the Games . . . The IOC refuses to ask Israel to satisfy the demands of the fedayeen . . . Everything that has to do with the Games is essentially the responsibility of the IOC, so if not for the IOC there would have been no terrorist tragedy in Munich . . . The IOC did not call on its Arab members to condemn the Connollystrasse fedayeen . . . The IOC has not called its Executive Board into session . . .

Enough of these pearls. Most of us spend most of our lives talking about things we know nothing about—but at least it is not in front of millions of viewers.

The funniest part was the so-called Leftists accusing the IOC of—take your pick—decrepitude, blind capitalism, ignorance of sports, or what have you. They carefully failed to mention that one of the members of the Executive Board, long a Vice-President, was named Constantin Andrianov, one of the key organizers of Soviet sports. They made no mention of the fact that the Soviet Union had never ceased within the IOC being one of the foremost defenders of amateurism as defined in Article 26 of the Olympic Rules and Regulations. They deliberately overlooked the strong constant influence of the Communist bloc on Olympic activities, the concerted effort of that bloc to garner the largest possible number of medals in each of the Games, Moscow's strong push for getting the 1976 Games and then—with 99 chances for success out of 100—the 1980 Games, and the enthusiasm all over Eastern Europe for every Olympics, and the Red countries' sincere devotion to the Olympic Movement.

Nor did they mention that within the IOC the Communist countries had comparatively as many members as the others. There are still Communist countries not included in the ruling Assembly: China, for instance. But China will surely have two members as soon as it takes steps to qualify in the Olympic Movement. Israel, the two Vietnams, Burma, Albania, and others, have not had any members on the highest body of the Olympic Movement, either.

Whereupon, the commentator knowledgeably announced: "There are five terrorists all told."

2:50 PM (Diary): A UPI flash says the terrorists included on the list of prisoners to be freed several of their close relatives. The best sources, at the administrative building, confirmed the following to me. It is believed that two of the Connollystrasse fedayeen have been identified. One is said to be a civil engineer who was graduated in Germany; he supposedly worked on building the Olympic Village and is still employed there (Issa). The other, a law student at Munich, is said to have worked as a librarian at the University. Since August 20, he is supposed to have been a cook in the Village (Tony). Both are said to have had regular lodgings within the Olympic Village. /

This information proved to be correct. In their joint desire to build a wall of silence, the various political and police authorities concerned were not always in harmony. Several times, Bruno Merk's offices confirmed that at least two of the fedayeen were working and living in the Village on September 5. The Federal Interior Ministry also admitted it. Then, suddenly, their lips were sealed.

Here, for instance, is a dialogue that was to take place in the studios of DOZ and be broadcast several times on the evenings of September 11 and 12. There was a round table of journalists interviewing various important officials, with the Bavarian Min-

170

ister Bruno Merk giving many of the answers himself and not contradicting any of those that came from his associates.

"Is it true that the head of the Palestinian commando had worked as a civil engineer on the building of the Village?"

"It seems to be."

"Is it true that this Arab worked on Building Thirty-one Connollystrasse?"

"Why not? At the time no one could suppose the building would be housing Israelis!"

"Is it true that the head of the terrorists was already known to the police as a militant in the 'Palestinian resistance'?"

"If we had to worry about that, we would have to get rid of all political refugees. There are many in our country. They are not supposed to have to beg. As far as we know, he had done nothing illegal."

"Is it true this engineer lived in the Village after the start of the Games?"

"He succeeded in getting through the checks that our security services made, as far as our present information goes."

"Is it true that a second of the eight terrorists was employed as a cook in the Village?"

"That seems to have been so."

"Was he living in the Village since the start of the Games?"

"That may well be. It was necessary to house two thousand employees in the Village. All cities have needs of that scale."

"Since the real names of some of the members of the Connollystrasse commando are known to the German authorities, why not give them to us?"

"You will understand that I cannot answer that question."

3:00 PM: Chancellor Willy Brandt personally issued an appeal to heads of state and heads of government in all the Arab nations: "I call on you to do all in your power so that the hostages held by the terrorists may regain their freedom. The whole world is waiting for you immediately to bring all of your influence into play."

3:10 PM *(Diary)*: I enter the Vierjahreszeiten Hotel and find myself praying the events of Connollystrasse are not true. Here, in the elegant Maximilianstrasse neighborhood, crime and misery are what seem unreal. Even at the height of the Games, there is a select crowd in Maximilianstrasse. The majestic, wealthy avenue, somewhat like a Parisian Grand Boulevard, is a showcase for quality West German products. Chic, expensive shops! And a succession of well-heeled edifices, luxurious private homes that were spared by the deluge of Allied bombs. The memory of the Wittelsbachs lingers beneath the chestnut trees.

At the foot of the slanting street, a lively merry-go-round of cars in the traffic circle at the brink of the Isar River makes this day seem just like any other. Doormen and bellhops of the Vierjahreszeiten, all in their becoming wine-colored uniforms, by voice and whistle regulate the ballet of high-powered cars, the Mercedeses and BMWs of the VIPs.

This No. 1 hotel of Munich (indeed of all Bavaria) has plenty of class. And now its capacity will soon have to be considerably increased. The rooms, large and chicly furnished, with thick carpeting and heavy curtains, have sleep-inducing armchairs and absolute silence at night. An all-year swimming pool will soon add to its high tone.

What can I, what can the organizers of the Games and the leaders of the sincerely peaceloving and prosperous Federal Republic do about it, if the blood spilled at dawn on September 5 over the Israeli slumbers of Connollystrasse brutally reminds us of so many things—e.g., that the Vierjahreszeiten in its long history has played host to the greatest and most awful names of twentieth-century Germany? For it was here, where now I am writing these lines on a low, round, brilliantly waxed mahogany table, in this huge gallery-flanked hall, that Reinhardt Heydrich, head of Hitler's terrible *Sicherheitsdienst,* the domestic-espionage service of the Third Reich, sat with his henchmen, at the start of Kristallnacht.

On the night of November 9–10, 1938, and then on into the evening of November 11, Himmler and Heydrich organized pogroms throughout Germany, on the Führer's express orders (allegedly in reprisal for the murder by Herschel Grynszpan, a Polish Jew, of the diplomat von Rath at the Reich's Paris embassy). At least 35,000 Jews were arrested; some 6,000 were massacred. Shops were looted, synagogues burned, homes pillaged, and cemeteries profaned. Probably 1500 committed suicide. The Nazis named the occasion after the fact, because of the tinkle of glass from the broken Jewish windows heard throughout their homeland, the Crystal Night.

The outsize TV set at the back of the hall alternately shows Olympic events that keep taking place in spite of everything, and chilling pictures of Connollystrasse earlier this morning. . . .

"Anything of importance, in the last few minutes?" asks Ivar Emil Vind, a Danish IOC member.

"No, alas! Just waiting."

"I don't like these long waits."

A very handsome man out of the Viking picturebook, he had been a great track champion. Very well-born, he had become an agribusinessman and his products had reaped many international awards and marketing successes. At fifty-one, he had real clout within the IOC. /

Hostages! Oh, yes, the Germans knew them well, for having made use of them throughout occupied Europe under the Third Reich. I would not mean to insinuate that the important figures of the Federal Republic or the *Land* of Bavaria who had to deal with the Palestinian terrorists in Munich's Olympic Village had had any responsibility whatsoever, under Hitler, for arrests or executions of hostages. I believe indeed that today's West German dignitaries are good people who at worst, among those who were of age, passively accepted their fate during the Nazi years. Just the same, they must have found that word "hostages," applied to Jews on German soil in 1972, to have a sinister, snarling connotation. Lady Macbeth had not awaited the hell of Fürstenfeldbruck for her ironic, "Here's the smell of blood still: All the perfumes of Arabia will not sweeten this little hand."

We would always remember those clear and fascinating first ten days, August 26 to September 4. It took real effort to find any shadows of swastikas on the graying people of Munich. It was strange, to walk along the iron fences and, through the mesh, watch the masses of police and especially the Games employees in their turquoise blue, on the move without a machine pistol or assault rifle in their hands. The young members of the security guard had been so friendly that until then, consciously or not, everyone forgot they were actually police officers.

The police are a noble and necessary body. Yet they tend sometimes to take themselves too seriously, even to be overbearing. Not so, these modish cops of the New Germany, with their hair grown long, and all kinds of gadgets stuffed in their coat pockets. On the hot continental-summer afternoons, they went about in shirtsleeves. They laughed, kidded around, and tried to be as helpful as possible. But now here they were, under the mounting sun, hair still long and dress still fashionable, but with submachine guns at the ready and that tough look in their eyes; once again they reflected the blue steel I had seen in their fathers'. Yet it is wrong to put it that way; it's too facile, and unfair, if only because they felt their fathers had been silly old men who fought that idiotic war, instead of making money. And also because all you had to do was look at them to see how unhappy they were, how heartbroken at seeing the end of the fine memories they had expected to have, the victory of German peace, the wiping out of the old saws about militarism, Nazism, and the whole shebang.

Not their guests alone—Jewish guests, to boot!—were being massacred, but also the most grandiose, splendid, and fascinating of all modern Olympics.

Refined and mournful, suddenly seeming disguised, severe, like people under siege, they were now pacing inside the Village, along the fences.

At 31 Connollystrasse, on the blue doorframes of their apartments—the blue of the Games, both lively and soft—the Israelis (did I remember to mention this?) had put the first and last names of each of them, in both Hebrew and Roman lettering. Those lists were still there when the Games were over, carefully pasted at the very place where Jews, when they are living in a place for any length of time, place the mezuzah, the little tube with two quotations from Deuteronomy on a parchment roll. It was unutterably moving, later, to stand on the threshold of Block 31 and spell out the names—somewhat washed away by the rains but made eternal through death: Moshe Weinberg, Yossef Romano, Mark Slavin . . .

Until the evening of September 9, there was a circular taped to the glass door of the lobby: Signed by Herr Werner Nachmann, *Vorsitzender des Zentralrats der Juden* (President of the Central Council of the Jewish Community of Germany), it was an invitation to all Jews in the Olympic Village to join with the Jewish colony of Munich, beginning at 8:30 PM on September 7, at the Holiday Inn, to celebrate Rosh Hashanah, the Jewish New Year. The piece of paper flapped more and more in the winds and showers of September, on the smoked glass of the door which narrow strips of steel cut into green-gray slices, and at its feet, before the door, the floral tributes, crowns, triangles, six-pointed stars, were slowly fading, while the inscriptions chipped away from their streamers.

There was Mark Slavin, born January 31, 1954, at Minsk, the capital of White Russia.

He was entered in the Olympics in Greco-Roman wrestling, 74 kg. (163 lbs.) category. He stood 5 feet 9 and was the youngest of those murdered on September 5–6. He was also the most recent immigrant to the Promised Land. Finally, he was one of the most symbolic—but, then, all of them were symbols.

When Mark landed at Lod Airport, three and a half months before that dawn on Connollystrasse, and kissed the ground of Israel, two newspapermen were waiting for him, for they had been told that a potential champion was coming in. A Russian interpreter was found, and Mark Slavin told his story.

"In Minsk, as in all cities of Soviet Russia, or the world, there are the good neighborhoods and the others. We lived in one of the others. My parents raised me to respect the Hebrew traditions, which was not an easy thing. I felt different from my schoolmates, right from the start, and they felt it, too. So, when school let out, they would gang up on me, yelling, 'Hey, dirty kike!' Whenever I could catch one of them alone, I trounced him. But then, after that, they'd gang up again, and I would get it. We Jews of Minsk were used to that. My family had always lived under that kind of conditions. And we were the first to admit that we weren't like the others. But we did not accept that it should be thrown up to us." Mark's father carried on from there: "It could not go on that way. Mark came home all black and blue. We taught him how to defend himself, no holds barred. So the neighborhood kids finally stopped riding him. He made sure he was always one to one against them. And anyway, he did have some good friends. The gym teacher heard about what a tough fighter he was. And he was entered in the youngest classes' wrestling matches. He won every time. But Minsk mainly needed some good men in Greco-Roman, so that was what they taught him. And from then on . . ."

Mark quickly came to the attention of the USSR's top sports officials, for he had won almost everything. They had him come to Moscow, and, in an unusual honor, admitted him to the Physical Education Teachers' Training Institute of the USSR. He had not been there long when, in February 1971, aged seventeen, he won the junior Greco-Roman championship of the USSR, middleweight category, outclassing all the others, and creating a sensation, because he had been matched against boys trained under much better conditions and for a much longer period.

Mark had hardly won this title, which guaranteed him an assured future, first as a national athlete and then as a sports instructor, when his whole family, himself included, officially requested visas for emigration to Israel. The Soviet sports organizers were even more amazed by this than they had been by the young Minsk Jew's victories.

The national sports authorities and his patrons at the Physical Education Institute all tried to get him to stay in Russia, by stressing the fine future he was assured of in the Socialist fatherland. But he stubbornly said no. After several weeks of this impasse, he was expelled from the Institute. He had no affiliation now, no place to train, and he was turned down when he tried to enter events. His former comrades turned their backs on him.

Mark went home to Minsk, and renewed contacts with his Zionist friends. Russian Jews' resistance to arbitrary decisions, persecution, and the refusal of exit permits, was growing daily. Massive arrests, general firings, leading to starvation, could not stop it. In the front rank of Minsk Zionists, Mark demonstrated before the offices of the KGB (secret police) and Hall of Justice, with banners flying and picket signs aloft. He was among those arrested, released, called in again, tailed, and hounded . . .

Mark's maternal grandfather, Mr. Grisha Cerniak, distraught

and weeping, but in a voice proud with the memory of the young champion, told us: "He was a real Jew. He always felt he was an Israeli. He told those people at the Institute, 'You with your security and your fatherland. What do I care about security if I have to let my parents leave without me; and they simply will not stay in Minsk? My fatherland is Israel. I want to represent Israel, as a wrestler and as a soldier, when the time comes.' "

The last months the Slavins spent in Russia were terribly trying. But their kind of "stiff necks," the uncompromising ones who will go to any lengths, sometimes make the Russians realize it is better not to court too much scandal and let them quietly go. At any rate, there was no more question of Mark becoming a great Soviet wrestler. His father was a professional photographer, and a very good one. But that trade is not in short supply. So, after fifteen months, the Slavins were allowed visas.

On May 20, 1972, the whole family arrived in Israel. There was the mother's father, Mr. and Mrs. Slavin, Mark himself, and a brother and little sister.

Mark joined a local branch of Hapoël, the national sports organization, which is an offshoot of the trade-union federation, Histadruth. Moshe Weinberg often came by to give the young champion a workout.

The Slavins found lodgings at B'nei B'rak, one of the outlying suburbs of Tel Aviv, which had been founded in 1924 by orthodox Polish Jews and remained a gathering-point for Jews from Eastern Europe. It had a number of Yeshivoth (Talmudic schools), and everything concerned with religion, as well as its cigarette and textile factories. Nine km. (5½ mi.) to the southwest was the very heart of Tel Aviv, drunk with its own activity, the fantastic metropolis where the Mosaic Law has to fend for itself, which the Jewish pioneers had caused to bubble up from the dunes of the Palestinian coast, near the mouth of the Yarkon, starting from scratch in 1909.

The Slavins were immediately at home. The father found a good job in photography. They piled into a tiny apartment of Kiryat Herzog, a whole colony of Russian Jews. They were happy.

Shortly after the Slavins set up at B'nei B'rak, at the urging of Moshe Weinberg, Mark was admitted to the Orde Wingate

Institute. There, the national wrestling coach was able to give his white hope daily attention. Mark studied Hebrew at a nearby kibbutz, and was again living under conditions that must have reminded him, on an Israeli scale, of what it was like at the Russian Phys. Ed. Institute, where he had spent those months in 1970–71. He found it all wonderful. He was eighteen.

The French champion Daniel Robin spent August 2–5, 1972, at the Wingate Institute, mainly to size up Mark Slavin's chances. After watching him train and fight, he said, "Mark is short on experience and practice. He has practically not wrestled for a year and a half now. But potentially, he is a great international champion. You have to send him to Munich, because what he will learn there will be inestimable."

Mark Slavin, who until then had never met any wrestlers other than Soviet or Israeli in official competition, was to make his international debut on the night of September 5, at 9:30, in the Olympic Greco-Roman tournament, at the Ringerhalle of Exposition Park, in Munich. He must have thought of it very often during those twenty hours of waiting, as he watched the muzzles of those guns pointing at him.

XI
THE FRIEDMANS
AMONG OTHERS

Like a lion, they are at my hands and my feet.
I may count all my bones;
They look and gloat over me.
They part my garments among them.
And for my vestments do they cast lots.
Psalms 22:17–19

3:30 PM: THE TV WAS BROADCASTING THE SWEDEN-CZECHOSLOVAKIA handball match beginning in the well-filled Sporthalle; fine shots of the ball and rough clashes of the men.

The radio was announcing that Egypt had just forfeited its semifinal basketball match against the Philippines, by not appearing at the Siegenburgerstrasse gym. This confirmed the withdrawal of the Egyptians from the Games, rumored since midmorning. The order had come from Cairo. So, where was the vaunted independence of the National Olympic Committees? At any rate, the withdrawal was unexplained: President Anwar el-Sadat was afraid of reprisals against the Egyptian team, according to one of its officials. Reprisals by whom? Israel? Unthinkable. So? An irrational decision? A silent rebuff to the Germans, guilty of not having been able to insure security? At any rate, the first newscasts from Cairo Radio were lavishing approving comments on the "exploit of the Black September fedayeen."

3:31 PM: The Organizing Committee officially announced that Egypt had withdrawn from the Games, the announcement coming from the indefatigable spokesman Hans Klein, "press chief" of the *Organisationskomitee*. Roundfaced, brimming with happy laughter, bow tie gleaming like a plume, he was a gnome right out of a Grimm Brothers' fairy tale with his black goatee and his eyes laughing to themselves behind the thick glasses. Always on the go, he was never short on news tips or helpful favors. He knew how to get a bit of humor into the most routine events. He knew his job and the people he had to deal with.

The Connollystrasse attack filled him with horror, but did not throw him. It would be up to him to keep the press of five continents patiently waiting until the over-delayed revelation of the ending. He had had six years of experience in the Moslem world of the Middle East and Indonesia as press attaché of West German embassies there.

As for the wasted blood, he had seen enough of that during the war. In April 1945, he had been sixteen. Unconnected with Nazism, repelled by the Hitlerian hysterics, he had been patriotic as only a pure young heart can be. He was drafted, along with his high-school buddies, in the *Volkssturm;* in the Sudetenland, I think. The old noncoms had hardly had time to start the child-conscripts' basic training, when the Allies arrived. "A high SS officer," as he recalled it, "sent us toward the front. The other way, the catastrophic retreat was coming, exhausted soldiers, truckloads of wounded, refugees. To tell the truth, we were all ready to get ourselves killed. A graying old captain saw us there, buried with our *Panzerfauste* and rifles, waiting for the Americans, in silence. 'Are you kids crazy?' he said. 'You want to get yourselves wiped out for nothing? Go on, get rid of those uniforms and guns. Go on back home quietly, and get your noses back in your books! *Schnell!* On the double!' "

Yes, and today was as horrible as the worst of those moments.

3:40 PM: Back to Olympic Village. To tell the truth, the bottlenecks were no laughing matter. Colonel Marceau Crespin, head of sports and physical education in the French Fifth Republic, let me ride in his official car, and dropped me at the entrance to the underground passages. At his instructions, the driver tore along in true French style.

From the administrative building, I had planned to go deeper into the Village, until I saw Moshe Weinberg's mother get out of a car.

Herr Willi Daume, accompanied by the Israeli ambassador, moved out to head her off before she came into the building. The head of the police patrol had quickly identified her to one of his men, while the Mercedes was just pulling up to the sidewalk. Silence fell like a stone. We all stood stock-still where we were.

The Friedmans Among Others

She is an elegant lady with fine Oriental features. I was told her maiden name was Henriette Mars. She was in full control of herself, but extraordinarily pale, her face bespeaking tragedy. She had insisted on viewing her son's remains. Shaul Ladani, the heel-and-toe man, bent, haggard, had been telling the story of his escape, repeating over and over again that there was no hope for the hostages without a resort to force. No one was paying attention to him any more.

I started walking through the crowds of fine-looking young people again. Nothing was transpiring from Block 31. Was despair finally catching up with them in there?

Dr. Manfred Schreiber appeared and started barking, at the corner of Connollyplatz, where Connollystrasse begins. He set two lines of green-uniformed cops out to close off the little narrow stairways off the Platz into the various roadways and service roads all called Connollystrasse. They were to keep the press and athletes out. There was yelling, and insults. Schreiber, in a while silk shirt, two-toned blue tie, and light gray slacks, straight as an I, thrust out his hammerlike chin. Gorgeous weather.

3:45 PM: Severely dressed in dark blue, and taking quick little steps, the Tunisian ambassador, Mahmoud Mestiri, appeared before fateful Block 31. Eight minutes later (at 3:53), he was back at the telecommunications van, conversing with Dr. Schreiber. The police head had changed his shirt: this one was pale blue. His granite face with its thin lips betrayed nothing. But Antonio Vellani, of the Italian *L'Europeo*, who apparently knew him well, was saying: "It's not going well, according to Schreiber." Actually, the Tunisian diplomat had only been able to confirm that the deadline remained 5:00 PM.

3:51 PM: A release was issued by the Organizing Committee. It was signed by its President, Willi Daume, and the President of the IOC, Avery Brundage:

> Olympic Peace was broken by a murder committed by criminal terrorists. The whole of the civilized world condemns with horror their barbaric crime. As a sign of deep respect for the victims and sympathy for the hostages still being held, this afternoon's athletic events have been canceled. The IOC and the Organizing Committee of the Games, Wednesday morning at 10:00 AM, with all

181

participants in the Games, will hold a ceremony in memory of the victims in the Olympic Stadium. This ceremony will demonstrate that the Olympic idea is more powerful than terror and violence.

The reaction of the IOC members, whether at the Vierjahreszeiten or here in the Village where so many of them were today, was generally surprise and irritation. Not against Daume, who was courageously trying to face up to his crushing responsibilities, but against Avery Brundage. The President of the Organizing Committee was supposed to be sure that Brundage had checked the text out by phone with the Executive Board members present in Munich, before submitting it to the *Krisenstab*. . . .

3:55 PM: For the third time, the Connollystrasse fedayeen phoned Mrs. Fuad Chemali, at Geneva. The young widow did not seem surprised that they should have her number, even though it was unlisted.

I have already said that only the head of each delegation in the Village had a phone (generally green) on which long-distance calls could be made. The Organizing Committee had received deposits from the delegations against such charges. So, to get Geneva, the terrorists each time had to go through the Village switchboard. And their conversations were recorded. The fedayeen (specifically, Issa and Tony, in turn) spoke in Arabic. They repeatedly apologized to the widow for disturbing her, "for, while we have heard many wonderful things about brother Fuad Chemali and his devotion to the just cause of the Palestinians, we have not had the honor of meeting you personally." Mrs. Chemali was always available to them, and replied politely and succinctly.

They kept her abreast of the negotiations with the *Krisenstab*, and asked her to transmit the information to two numbers in Cairo, for two people referred to by aliases. One of the numbers belonged to the Palestine Liberation Organization.

There was nothing specially interesting in what they said, unless they were speaking in code. The specialists did feel that, in the 3:55 call, Issa was asking Mrs. Chemali to pass the word that the group in Block 31 felt the nervous tension growing and was asking for Arab intervention.

The Friedmans Among Others

The widow had conscientiously transmitted their messages to Cairo earlier. Now she called there again as soon as she hung up, and the Geneva phone service got her the number rather quickly, something not always so easy because of atmospheric conditions. Mrs. Chemali repeated word for word what Issa had said to her. Cairo told her to transmit its permission and affection to the brothers in the Olympic Village, and to assure them that no one doubted their unshakable determination. After that, Mrs. Chemali was not able to reach anyone: her phone was out of order. And fortunately she did not try to go out before the next morning; she probably would have been unable to. Visitors had found that the way to her door was barred.

4:00 PM: Among the 122 nations entered in the Olympics, there was Israel. Before the eyes of the whole world, a commando had grabbed eleven of its members and held them hostage right in the Olympic Village. Most of the Arab countries (Libya, Egypt, Syria, Iraq, Algeria, and Saudi Arabia) applauded. The others so far kept still, except for Jordan, whose king had the courage and dash to condemn the attack. But the Arab League, which all of them belonged to, had broadcast a communiqué on Radio Cairo saluting "our heroic brothers who are covering themselves with holy glory at Munich."[1]

The countries subservient to the USSR or the Chinese People's Republic were also silent—or else, like the German Democratic Republic, they were already blaming Israel for the whole affair, truly the height of something. Virtually every one of these nations had representatives at the Games. But they were not much concerned right now with Olympic solidarity, athletic camaraderie, or decency.

The deadline was less than an hour away, and the *Krisenstab* could only hope for further postponement. The main thing seemed to be: stall as much as possible. A sign of the times.

---

[1] There were 18 members in the Arab League: Algeria, Bahrein, Egypt, Iraq, Jordan, Kuwait, Lebanon, Libya, Morocco, Oman, Qatar, Saudi Arabia, Sudan, Syria, Trucial States, Tunisia, Yemen, and Democratic Republic of Yemen, with a total population of 130,000,000 inhabitants on some 12,000,000 sq. km. (4,600,000 sq. mi.). And this did not include all actual or so-called Arabs (as, say, in Mauritania). The League thus had 43 times the population of Israel, and 570 times its territory.

183

THE BLOOD OF ISRAEL

Here were the 10,000 finest athletes in the world brought together, in a festival of brotherly youth. The grandiose organization of these Games cost six years of hard work and well over half a billion dollars. Four and a half million sports fans had come, or would come, here from all over the world during these Olympics. The TV networks had set up on a global scale, to show the events to a billion viewers at once. But all that was being defied, endangered, perhaps smashed, by a tiny grouplet of a few unknowns with guns in their hands.

And the German Federal Republic, third most powerful industrial nation in the world (surpassed only by the U.S.A. and USSR, but ahead of China and Japan—a fantastic feat for a people of only 63,000,000 on 248,649 sq. km., or some 99,460 sq. mi.), with all of its superdevelopment and its most advanced of techniques, was being checkmated, rendered powerless, by a handful of terrorists who had already with impunity murdered two of the hostages and were threatening to do the same to the rest.

Bundesgrenzschutzmajor Konrad Müller, heading the detachments of border guards put at the disposal of the *Krisenstab,* at 4:00 PM presented himself at Block 31, accompanied by Fräulein Graes. He was still a young man, all muscle, and a fine figure of a career soldier.

In a mechanical tone, his eyes boring in to Issa's smoked lenses, he repeated in the name of Chancellor Brandt the offers of Ministers Genscher and Merk: as much money as they wished, safe-conduct or right of asylum, and liberation of the German prisoners asked for, in exchange for the hostages. He added: "I give you my word as an officer that everything will be faithfully carried out if you accept. The Federal Chancellor has authorized me, in that case, to stay with you until the whole affair is ended, if you wish."

Issa glared silently and sneeringly at him, then replied violently in perfect German: "You're wasting my time and yours. Every minute counts."

The head of the terrorists turned his back on Major Konrad Müller and headed back into the building. . . .

There were new developments over at the U.S. delegation. It

184

was located in one of the huge buildings done in the typical Village architecture: whitewashed concrete, balconies to the south, huge glass expanses, at Nos. 12–16 Nadistrasse.

The ground floor was surrounded on all sides by solid fellows all uniformly dressed in green waterproof fatigues with huge pockets in front and on the buttocks, of the kind worn by Air Force mechanics, but on the back, what should have been the identifying label was covered with a taped circle. Inside the lobby, gentlemen "in civvies" stopped everyone and carefully examined their identification.

Those responsible for the 447 U.S. athletes and their 168 officials were right to be on their guard. Blackmail and murder are contagious. No sooner was the attack on Connollystrasse bruited about, than not only did Mark Spitz get innumerable death threats, but several correspondents announced that the Nadistrasse building would be blown up.

I looked at the picture of James B. Connolly, the Olympic champion whose name had been given to the fateful street, at the back of the varicolored lobby. It was discreetly placed among scores of others: a manly head, with a blond crew cut, and a heavy chin above a solid neck. A close friend of Brundage's, he had died under fire, on French soil, in 1918.

There was Zeev Friedman, born June 10, 1944, at Prokopevsk, Siberia.

This family of Ashkenazim (or Northern Jews) had no real connection with Asia. Zeev's father, Shlomo Friedman, came of a poor family, and lived for a long time at Czerniakow, a suburb to the south of Warsaw. He was twenty-three when the Nazis attacked Poland, on September 1, 1939. He was drafted into the auxiliary forces, for few Polish Jews were taken into the regular army. In January 1941, all of the Friedmans were taken to a Nazi camp, some 10 km. (a little over 6 mi.) outside Warsaw, near Zbytki, on the right bank of the Vistula.

I saw Shlomo Friedman at home, at Kiryat Hayim, a workers' suburb 8 km. from Haifa, on that admirable bay. He was small, with tortured features, his head sparsely covered by thin graying

185

strands. He spoke a mixture of Yiddish and Russian, perhaps because he was dealing with a foreigner. But he had no trouble in making himself understood.

"That camp at Zbytki: they locked us all up there. The four grandparents, my father Moshe, my mother Chaya, my five brothers and sisters. With my family's blessing, I escaped, one rainy evening, in the fall of 1941. Twice I missed by a pond's distance being caught by police dogs. I didn't trust anyone. By day, I hid in the woods."

After several nights' walking, Shlomo crossed the line between the German and Russian occupation zones, at which the two powers had divided the country. He thought he was saved. And he was. But he was arrested, interrogated at length, and then sent to Prokopevsk, in the southwestern part of Siberia, 150 km. (90-odd mi.) from Novosibirsk.

The Russians had set up a ghetto there, with some 10,000-odd Jews from Poland and Slovakia. And there Shlomo met Hannah, his future bride. Coming from Lodz, in Poland, she too had missed by a hair being grabbed by the SS. Her whole family had also been sent to concentration camps. She and Shlomo quickly united their respective lonelinesses, in this godforsaken place: he was a laborer in an armaments factory; she ran a machine.

Their first child was Zeev. Nina, the girl, was born in 1950. By that time, for five years already, the Friedmans had been dreaming of nothing but getting away from their Siberian plateau with its cruel winters, and its exclusive atmosphere. They wanted to flee this Soviet Union which, for all that it had saved them, kept them separate, even more than prewar Poland, silent, with their identity cards stamped *Ievrei* (Jew). There were pitilessly strict quotas in every profession; they were absolutely forbidden from moving away; discrimination was present from the cradle to the grave. The household kept pestering the Prokopevsk authorities with requests to return to Poland—but in vain.

No Jew was allowed to leave for elsewhere, even deeper in Siberia. So, Poland was out of the question!

The arms factory had reconverted to metals. Shlomo—by his own admission—was no Stakhanovite laminator. A foreman ("An anti-Semite!") turned him in as a saboteur. He was given a year in prison; and spent it under very hard conditions.

In 1957, the Friedmans learned that Poles were being allowed to go back home. This time, they got permission. But when they detrained in Czerniakow, there was nothing left of the Friedman family. The building they had lived in was destroyed, all their kith and kin gone. Shlomo desperately tried to find out what had happened to his family, and in this he succeeded: all of them, without exception, from the grandparents down to the youngest nieces, had been fed into the ovens. The annihilation was complete.

Hannah also tried to trace her family. Through persons who somehow had miraculously survived Treblinka and Auschwitz, she learned also of their death throes and their final extinction, one and all. They had gone up into thin air, leaving no pinch of ashes nor the slightest other memento.

By the end of 1957, they had made their request for emigration to Israel. Ever since they got married, they had planned to go to the Promised Land, but first they had had to make this pilgrimage to Poland. Besides, if they had told the Prokopevsk police that they were headed for Israel, they never would have been let out of Siberia. After many a turndown, and worsening conditions that reduced them almost to starvation, they were finally allowed to leave Poland in 1961. Since getting to Israel, he as a worker, then a small clerk, she as a housewife, they had been able to lead a decent, if modest, life.

Among the few things they were able to take out of the Soviet Union, the Friedmans particularly loved a picture taken on Red Square in 1956. The metalworkers' union of Prokopevsk had made it possible for Shlomo and his family to take a vacation tour to Moscow with some 100-odd other comrades. It was their one great adventure! All four had been snapped together, in front of St. Basil's. What a picture those four Friedmans made, in front of the marvelous domes with their brilliant scales, topped by the golden crosses. A picture of resigned sadness, of a familiarity as old as they themselves with misfortune, and of dignity. Shlomo, already balding, with heavy wrinkles between the hooked nose and lips, and his son Zeev, already a sturdy twelve-year-old, were doing their best to smile. Nina, the girl, all stretchiness and braided hair, looked mistrustfully at the Kremlin wall. And Hannah, not so small as her husband, stared fixedly at the camera as if she expected nothing good from anyone or anything not her own.

They live in a somewhat small but sunny apartment, in the populous neighborhood, full of activity and childware, known as Kiryat Hayim. From their windows, you could not see the Mediterranean, but you could guess where it was by the color of the sky. When the wind was from the sea, you could hear the boat whistles in the port.

Zeev Friedman was very attached to home, and always lived with his parents. He was a pocket Apollo, of ideal measurements: 5 ft. 2½, 135 lbs. A miniaturized explosive; a spring coiled taut. Clear and mobile features, with the dimpled smile that had earned him the nickname of "Bambino" at the Orde Wingate Institute. Intellectually very gifted, at sixteen and a half, when he arrived in Israel, Zeev had already finished his secondary schooling in Poland, and it seemed that at the Czerniakow high school some of the teachers had deliberately lowered his grades to keep him from being at the top of the class.

In view of his credentials, he was immediately accepted at an advanced school in 1961—as soon as he and his parents and sister were able to leave the temporary camp where they had stayed, waiting for a permanent home and suitable employment, as was normal.

Zeev was explosively enthusiastic, at home in Eretz Israel, among free Jews. All the novelty, the passionate acquisition of the Hebrew tongue, the inevitable family problems in the arrival camps and then during the first days at Kiryat Hayim, and finally the demon of sport: all combined to interrupt Zeev's devotion to his studies. His forte had been math, but he stopped before finishing college. Still living at home, he wanted to help in supporting them, and started to earn his own living at eighteen. He tutored mathematics and Slavic languages, then took a certificate in physical education, and thus became completely thrust into the fascinating sports world.

At nineteen, he left for his military service, with enthusiasm and gratitude. During one of the first operations against the fedayeen, in the rocky hills near the frontier village of Metullah, a few hundred meters from Lebanon, Zeev Friedman distinguished himself. On a scouting patrol, he surprised two terrorists hiding in a clump of brush. One of them fired. Zeev, very slightly hit— a scratch on the neck—shot back, wounding him seriously, and stopping the other Arab too, though wounding him less seriously. With the rest of his squad, who had come to his rescue, Zeev carried the two Arabs back to an aid station. The closest was in one of the pretty red houses at Metullah, the old frontier village from which one could see the majestic mass of Mount Hermon, in Lebanon, the three-toothed cone of its summit spotted with snow.

To their amazement, the more seriously hurt of the two fedayeen turned out to be a woman. She had been hit several times, one of the bullets disfiguring her. She was bleeding profusely. Only a transfusion could save her, and fortunately the station was set up for it. But the only available donor with the right blood type was Zeev. Her life was saved, and she later confessed having taken part in several attacks on Israeli soil. Remember, this was in 1964, well before the Six Days' War.

Zeev went to visit the girl he had wounded, at the Haifa military hospital, then in prison, after having testified at her trial. Her name was Farida. Born at Nablus, she had spent her childhood in refugee camps. With plastic surgery, Israeli doctors had restored her severed nose, her smashed jaw. Only twenty, she was like a dark little vine full of life and, a thoughtful person, she became attached to the sweet intelligent boy. He felt the same way. In hospitals, courtrooms, and visitors' parlors where they had met up to now, the affair could go no further.

Farida told Zeev, "All I hope is that they keep me in jail as long as possible, because I don't want to go back to fighting like before."

She was not speaking out of fear, but because now she knew these Israelis, whom she had never approached before, except as enemies.

Farida eventually was let out. Zeev by then was far away, on military maneuvers. She wrote him at length. And then, it was Jerusalem, the Mandelbaum Gate, and back toward Lebanon.

After that, only silence. But the affair had left a deep mark on the young Jew from Siberia.

"You can see," he would tell his folks, "this proves how stupid war and violence are. All it took was a few talks, a few nice gestures, and her heart and mine both changed completely. I'll still fight the terrorists, because they are trying to kill Israel in its own home. But now I will know that if they and we can only get to meet, to know each other, we'll all be able to win out over hate."

Kiryat Hayim is a cooperative commune, meaning that everything there belongs to all and nothing is private property, whether real estate or shops. It has a big stadium, and several sports clubs. The first among the latter is the local chapter of Hapoël. There, Zeev quickly specialized in weight lifting. He became bantamweight champion of Israel. In weight lifting, around thirty is when champions often "blossom." Zeev Friedman was well on his way. At Munich, he had just finished in 12th place. Israeli TV had featured him as in the three movements he lifted a total of 330 kg. (app. 725 lbs.).

Tuesday, September 5, 1972, his father Shlomo appeared on TV for the first time in his life. It was on a worldwide telecast around 4:00 PM. In pathetic, halting phrases, he begged the Connollystrasse fedayeen to spare the hostages. He recalled the horrible end of his family. The terrorists certainly must have seen him on the screen, with his irresistible appeal.

September 6, at 1:30 AM, Israeli radio, quoting Munich sources, broadcast that all the hostages had been saved. The Friedmans, in their time of trouble, like the other families involved, were surrounded by friends and newspapermen. The exulting of Zeev's parents, who invited all present to share their Carmel champagne with them, gave shivers of fear to some who, having seen and listened to the broadcasts from one end to the other, found too many unexplained things about them: the sporadic shooting at Fürstenfeldbruck, for instance, around the two helicopters and the Boeing, or the fact that none of the hostages who were said to be freed had been shown to the flocks of newspapermen waiting outside the military airport.

Today, with his wife, his daughter, and his son-in-law, Shlomo Friedman thinks back on the mountains of suffering and bloodshed that have dotted his life and his family's. His monotone of a voice is something you never forget. It rang out through Zeev's bedroom, where all the dead boy's things remain, pictures of his dear ones, his guitar, his books, the Israeli landscapes, and the couch, for which his mother had embroidered the antimacassar.

"To think that I was always known as what they called a dove," he says. "Against all war, any policy of force and annexation, you understand? Now it's over. Over and done with. Blood must answer for blood. If not, they will get what they want: there will be nothing left of the Jewish people. Hitler will triumph from beyond the grave."

Silence. He is in a white shirt, and his short arms with the knotted biceps remind you of his son's muscles. He tightens his fists, and lowers his head. Nina, his tall, beautiful daughter, with her long straight reddish hair, listens to her father without apparent reaction. Her face reflects despair and ferocious determination. If there be degrees of despair, then the face of Hannah Friedman, Zeev's mother, is more terrible still. A while back, as she brought in a photograph of her son taken just before his takeoff for Munich, she let out a sigh that sounded almost like a roar.

Nina said to her, "There are still my two children."

Hannah calmly replied, "Your father's family and mine, counting him and me, came to forty heads. We are the only ones left. Two out of forty. Well, Nina, adding you and your husband to those forty, makes forty-two. And for those forty-two head of people, there are only two descendants, that's all, just your two children. All it would take is one little pogrom . . ."

XII
NINE PROUD SOULS

And if our time is come, let us die
manfully for our brethren's sake and not
leave a cause (of reproach) against
our glory.

I Maccabees 9:10

4:10 PM: THE AFTERNOON WAS A SCORCHER. I WANDERED ABOUT trying to understand, racking my brains as so many others were doing, going up and down stairway and ramp, seeing again Moshe Weinberg's smiling face that flashed his friendliness and strength at you.

I took an elevator up one of the fifteen-story towers on Helene-Mayer-Ring. It was at the spot where this avenue becomes the Village's business street, Ladenstrasse, after having gone along the administration building. This tower, No. 14, held twenty-three teams as well as representatives of private companies, an amusing, very very dimly lit bar, and who knows what else.

No one asked me anything. The guards and stewards today seemed concerned only with what was happening on Connolly-strasse. At the top, I went through a huge, empty, greenish corridor, and out a swinging door that led to a narrow cement spiral stairway. This took you to the terrace. A soft wind was blowing, barely more than a breath, but I was surprised not to have been conscious of it down on the street. A huge aerial made a grating noise. Before me stretched the whole Village with its bumps, its solid gray concrete masses, its green tongues and young trees that would some day be beautiful. From here, nothing appeared to have changed, as you got this overview of the landscape of the suburb and its sports complex.

Pigeons were pecking (at what? their own reflections perhaps?) on the translucent roofs of the Olympic Stadium, the all-sports hall, and the swimming pool, which were really only one continuous roof that steeplechased among the taller buildings, looking like a set of Chinese hats. Their unending panes of acrylic glass must have accumulated all kinds of windfalls from vegetation or the city, tons of refuse blown here. And the oily, coaly, dusty air had also deposited its scoria there, on the 8300 rectangular panes, set on an angle into the steel rods that held everything together. The deposits ended up as a viscous crust that the rains might wash away, but meantime were a kind of scattered paste the gray pigeons were pecking.

Yes, everything seemed as it had been, until you looked more closely.

Olympic Village actually was like a port. The administration buildings were at the east, and the towers ran like three jetties, irregular but parallel, from east to west. The smaller houses attached to them suggested wharves. And the hollows, the green spots, the lakes, the sinuous walks were all the water, the harbor. Over there, beyond the Village, to the west, there seemed to be a sort of cape that closed the harbor off; a cape or perhaps an archipelago, with islands separated from each other only by very narrow waterways.

It all formed a crestline. And that whole line, including everything anyone might climb up on, hillocks, bridges, terraces on the Radio/TV Center, all had been stormed by multicolored crowds, pressed dense, who in their immobility seemed to pitch and toss in brilliant, noisy waves never to calm down. They were trying to seize on some vision of what was going on over at 31 Connollystrasse. Out of sympathy? Out of sadistic delight? No, just out of curiosity. One did not often get a chance to see terrorists at work who had just committed murder and were getting ready for a repeat performance.

In the insolently happy sky, an armada of helicopters buzzed, going in circles. Some skimmed the tops of the towers, others climbed into space like the rungs of a ladder with invisible supports. Actually, there were no more than four or so at any one time, but what a noise they made! Through the Plexiglas of the Alouettes and Bells I could see tense faces made even more livid by their flying helmets. . . .

193

At the highest spots, where the crestline is closest to Gate 25A and the end of Connollystrasse, there was a fantastic concentration of tripods and zoom-lensed cameras. Photographers had climbed up on whatever they could, swiped chairs or boxes, to aim their telescopic lenses at the facade or rear of No. 31, where from time to time there were threatening signs of life. I did a full swing around, like the panoramic restaurant on the *Fernsehturm,* on which, despite the height of 200 meters (some 220 yds.), the shining muzzle of a super-zoomer was continually pointed at Block 31. At every spot from which any view at all of the tragic southwest corner of Olympic Village could be gained, there were bunches of humans.

Panoramic Hill no longer had any grass or bushes: they were crushed under the mob. So, on this elevation that human hands had created from the rubble and ruins of Munich knocked out by the Allies and laid low by bombing, here now were the survivors of the Nazi disaster, along with their descendants and fellow countrymen, and samples of all the peoples who were their enemies or friends twenty-seven years ago, looking on at the long silent martyrdom of nine Jews on their soil, 12 km. (7 mi.) from the Dachau concentration camp. Nine survivors. Two already dead. All of them brothers or sons of the 6,000,000 Jews murdered by the subjects of a madman who lived here for so long, before this fine Panoramic Hill had arisen to offer a view for the fine summers of the West German miracle.

4:15 PM: Hey! There are three of the sharpshooting frontier cops mountainclimbing, roped together like real ones. They started from the twelfth floor of the pyramidal building where there were still some of the East Germans, despite Dr. Schreiber's exasperated strictures. The building (it will be recalled) faces 31, so the terrorists could watch it at their ease. The marksmen took off on the other, north side, like elves flying out a window, up toward the roof, which is covered with small structures, basins, ropes, and the communal aerial. Once there, they stayed prone. Hidden by a revetment or the foot of a pillar, they were able to zero in on the bay windows in which, from time to time, with or without masks one or another of the fedayeen could be seen. The windows made easy targets for an expert shot; barely 50 meters

(55 yds.) down, in perfect view, due south. But the subjects inside were in shadow. The still-bright sun was beating right down on the roof; the marksmen wore large flat caps with broad visors.

Adjusting my field glasses from Mitsukoshi of Tokyo, the policemen seemed very broad-chested to me. But of course they were all wearing bulletproof vests under the sweat jackets of attractive colors. The arsenal that had now been deployed in the symbolic space of peace and brotherhood was striking. What the snipers had was best of all: Heckler-Koch rifles with Zeiss sights, the *ne plus ultra* of precision guns, and of course, since every kind of fight had to be anticipated, machine pistols, good old 9-caliber Lügers, stub-barreled automatic pistols, and automatic carbines with their 30-degree slanted barrels for shooting with less personal exposure. "Thirty recently certified marksmen of the *Bundesgrenzschutzpolizei* came in by truck at two PM," said a Belgian coach.

Olympic Village, dressed for war! Near Gate 25A, two green light-armored cars, with rubberized caterpillar treads, were lined up out of sight in the exit tunnel from the underground. The black lettering on their hoods: POLIZEI. It would be a cinch for them, despite the obstructions, to go right over in front of Apt. 1. The fedayeen could not see them, any more than they could the heavily armed group hiding behind the west wall of 33 Connollystrasse. Two ambulances, their red crosses halfway up the exit ramp in front of G-1, blocked the whole ramp. Verdigris-colored motorcops were patrolling the underground streets, their cycles backfiring, machine guns slung.

4:20 PM (Diary): Elegant as a fashion plate, lithe as a jockey, but with worried brow, M. Maurice Herzog, on the Village Plaza, is walking down the tiered steps. I've known him since his return from the fantastic expedition up Annapurna that he headed in 1950, to become one of the world's purest celebrities. The man who won the "First 8000 meters" (roughly Annapurna's elevation; actually 26,492 ft.) then was being carried into the American Hospital at Neuilly, where he was to stay for more than a year and have scores of operations. He was shockingly pale, but had smiled serenely.

I watch him walk: you can't tell he has no toes; yet, he has just

195

had still another foot operation. His green-brown eyes meet mine, and we head toward each other. With his fine aquiline nose above the stiff mustache, the tanned skin under the long curling pepper-and-salt hair, he suddenly brings to my mind a British major.

"Looking for signatures?" I ask.

Since the end of morning, he has been circulating a petition within the IOC asking for the calling of a plenary meeting. He is No. 2 French representative on the IOC, with Count de Beaumont (now First Vice-President-elect).

The former French Secretary for Youth and Sports shakes his head. "No, not looking for anything. I came over to see whether I could help with this misfortune. Every major event from now on will have to beware of the escalation of violence."

Silence. We take a few steps among the athletes who all seem preoccupied with their own problems.

"If the Games were to be called, what a victory for terrorism!" Herzog goes on, continuing his thought: "I wonder whether the Games can still make sense here in Munich, against a tragedy that is shocking the whole world. I think the whole IOC has to meet on it. All together, we can see where we stand, and make a decision. The time of single rule in the organization must come to an end, or else we mean nothing at all."

I watch Maurice Herzog go off toward the French quarters. Like his feet, his hands were frozen and the better part of his fingers had to be amputated. His sharer of glory atop Annapurna, Louis Lachenal, died in the mountains; and Lionel Terray, too. /

The full meeting of the IOC finally did take place this day, at 10:00 PM, in one of the dining halls of the Vierjahreszeiten. But not through the efforts of M. Herzog, Deputy-Mayor of Chamonix. . . .

Avery Brundage, only six (actually, because of the one-day postponement of the Games, seven) days away from the end of his term, had, as we shall see, intended to act as IOC all by himself that morning and afternoon.

Only at 7:00 PM did the Executive Board, at the height of the drama that was shaking the columns of Olympia, finally officially meet at the demand of its members in the Vierjahreszeiten Hotel, under the chairmanship of (President-elect) Lord Killanin.

The IOC avoids scandal. It does not wash its dirty linen in public, or at least so far never has. That is why most of the members resisted M. Herzog's petition; but their "paper silence" did not mean they kept still. All the newsmen of five continents had to do was lend an ear to hear tens of members raising their voices not against the interruption of the Munich Games as such, but against the fact that so serious a decision, absolutely unprecedented, had been made by Avery Brundage alone—in defiance of Article 16 of the Olympic Rules and Regulations:

> The President may take action or make a decision where circumstances do not permit it to be taken by the International Olympic Committee or its Executive Board. Such action or decision is subject to ratification by the IOC at its next meeting.

Similarly, a storm that did not escape the notice of the international press broke out within the IOC when it learned that, before coming to the Hotel Vierjahreszeiten at the urgent and firm demand of the Executive Board, Brundage had again made a serious decision, which would undoubtedly have been approved by the Board, had he deigned to consult it. In spite of which, Avery Brundage was a great IOC President, universally respected by his peers. He just did not understand what democracy was; that's all. And methods that may well have been all right in the IOC of the 1950s or 1960s simply were no longer acceptable today. . . .

4:30 PM *(Diary):* The frontier-guard "good shots" are now in place on every roof from which they can get No. 31 in their sights, without being seen. On Connollystrasse, at the beginning of the straight part that runs along the side of No. 31, two small buildings face each other: No. 18 (on the right when coming from the east) and No. 11.

At 18, are Luxembourg and Burma; at 11, Bolivia. All of them should have been moved out until the affray was over, but as a result of the compromise with the East Germans who snarlingly refused to be evacuated and largely remain in their quarters, for the time being occupants of 11 and 18 have been allowed to stay where they are, at their own risk. Then, bingo! No more sharpshooters on the two roofs! A member of Schreiber's staff confirms what we had guessed: the fedayeen finally—they seem to have excellent binoculars, no doubt of German make!—noticed some prone or kneeling characters up there, who from their equipment did not exactly seem to be on a peaceful mission. So the terrorists phoned the *Krisenstab,* whose most secret unlisted numbers are at their disposal.

And now what? Two disguised cops reappear. One with a telescopic-sighted rifle, the other with a slant-barreled assault gun, moving along the roof of 18 again. But this time they're careful not to come forward of the community aerial. How many similar rubber-band trips since this morning! It's like our childhood yo-yo—or the trooper chasing Punchinello, who gets locked in the box, and then, zip! springs back up.

No. 11 is immediately to the east of 31. The way these buildings were numbered boggles logic, at least so far as I can see. So that, to the south of Nos. 11, 31, and 33, from east to west on the first of the Connollystrasse service roads, there are 25–27 (a single, and rather small, building), 15 (much larger), and 17–23 (a really tiny one). Behind, therefore farther south, and below, is 29, on the second service road. Riddle me that. It's worse than the mazes of Tokyo.

While I'm criticizing, let me mention the kind of colored charm the Village has, or had before the horror. Its calm, its pure, fresh air, its greenery, the transplanted lindens, the silvery poplars and baby-oaks pushing up, for those who live here after the Games, will make an admirably up-to-date suburb. The apartments will be modern and varied, the garages roomy, the underground passages huge and convenient, to say nothing of the availability of sports fields and playgrounds, subway stations, commuter trains, streetcars, and buses.

Some of the bigger buildings will have to come down, to reduce the crushing presence of concrete in the Men's Village. Part of the Women's Village may have to be leveled, too, so as to be replaced by one or two more towers. For the 12,000 future inhabitants of the onetime Oberwiesenfeld, it will be a convenient, busy, youthful, middle-class suburb near the heart of Munich.

I wonder who'll live in Apts. 1 and 3 of Block 31.

At the bend in the square that is Connollystrasse before it turns

into its final straightaway—the one with No. 31 and the tragedy—
there is a fountain with daubed piping. Against it, there is now a
command-car with its treads full of weeds, just where a couple of
minutes ago telecommunications van D-309 was standing. But instead of the 9-mm machine rifle the wheeled police command-cars
have, this apple-green vehicle with black markings is equipped
with a batch of loudspeakers. The driver is sighing, and sweating
under his helmet.

There is an enormous patient line waiting before the Gulliver-
ian tower, with its arrow glinting 292 meters (320 yds.) up in the
blue sky. What a beautiful, proud gray creature she is, suggesting
as she does, magnified tenfold, the minarets of St. Sophia's of
Istanbul. Everyone would like to find a seat in the Atrium, that
revolving café-restaurant, from which the whole of the Munich
plateau is visible. Today, they are all fascinated by the southwest
corner of the Village, where fate's "On your marks! Ready!
Set! . . ." have already been heard. They will try to pick out Block
31, with its long white shape, down there on the earth of mortal
men. /

4:35 PM: Fräulein Graes, the light-blue-clad criminal-division
officer, who for hours already had acted as interpreter and liaison
person, came forward in deserted Connollystrasse. She had changed
her shoes, and was wearing square-heeled white sandals instead of
her heavy white uniform leather pumps. She stopped calmly, seem-
ingly as relaxed as ever, before the door of No. 1. If they only
knew she had guided the two physicians in No. 4 out of their
clutches . . .

Behind her, alone, Dr. Bruno Merk, head of the *Krisenstab*,
was ambling along the flowerbeds and decorative things in the
middle of the roadway. He finally caught up with her, but instead
of staying with her walked on beyond No. 31, and started pacing
at the level of the three-sprayed varicolored fountain, that nice
gurgling fountain, happy as the Games themselves.

There was a conventional conversation between the policewoman and the terrorist in the white hat, Issa playing the beau in
his light-gray suit, with his ultra-slim figure. Behind him, someone

invisible was shaking an AK-47, its muzzle wagging like a dog's tail. The girl motioned to the Bavarian minister, who came over, standoffish but dignified.

Issa was waiting for him on the threshold, with an athletic-looking character in a hood, or rather a light-blue cotton kind of knit bonnet, down under his chin, with holes cut in it for the eyes. He must have been warm, for the sun was still shining hard. Dark hairs were visible on the backs of his dark hands. In his synthetic shirt and slacks of the same shiny black, this bodyguard (Paulo) was a living advertisement for handguns. The most precious seemed to be his submachine gun: he was petting its barrel as I had seen the Bavarian police, a few steps away from No. 31, pet their guard dogs, those German shepherds who looked strangely at you while tugging at their chains. The harmonious little interpreter stayed alongside the minister.

After a few moments, the latter gave a signal, holding up three fingers. In reply, *Bundesinnenminister* Hans-Dietrich Genscher, Dr. Schreiber, and *Bürgermeister* Tröger came over. Behind them stood a new gorilla, or perhaps an assistant to the police head. The conversation was lively, with the young policewoman continuously translating. The pugilistically built fedayee who was covering Issa disappeared. Two rifle muzzles now were sticking out of windows, one on the ground floor, the other one flight up. Issa had empty hands, instead of holding the grenades he liked to display. What was more, he was now completely surrounded by the Germans he was talking with, all of them out in the sun, in front of the house, with pigeons pecking around them.

During this time, within a narrow perimeter about the building, observers could see the mad tearing of police groups, variously in sweat shirts, black leather jackets, or shirts with green ties. They were dangerously likely to be seen, as they tried to get in closer and closer. Four of them had crawled, on their stomachs and sides, as close as leeches against the corner wall at the end of Block 31, the wall just beyond Apt. 11, on the fence side of the building; two now were kneeling and two prone. The newsmen, watching all this from every available vantage point, thought they were getting ready to rush the place.

Herr Merk spoke first. In a tone that was not abject, but rather terribly upset, as against his previously authoritarian manner, he said, "The Free Bavarian and Federal authorities are obliged to ask you for an additional reprieve. The Israeli Government has still not given a final answer. Munich and Jerusalem are in constant consultation, but I did not want to wait until the last minute to let you know."

"You're not going to trick us the way they did at Lod!" Issa shouted. "You're trying to play around with us."

He was fuming. Dr. Merk raised his hand to interrupt him, and calmly countered, "I can only tell you once more, in the name of all the gentlemen here and Mr. Vogel and myself, that we are ready now to take the place of the hostages you are holding . . ."

The fedayeen leader majestically gestured his irritation, then erupted again with, "Germany will be responsible for the blood of the Jews we are going to kill! What happens to us doesn't matter one bit!"

Herr Genscher, a solid and forceful heavyweight, cut in with his impersonal politeness: "Germany cannot force its view either on Israel or on you. She is doing all she can. So no one is going to hold Germany responsible for your doings. All of your demands that we could reasonably meet have been met. We are ready to listen to any further demands you have."

Issa seemed to think it over. He lit a cigarette. He asked his visitors to stay where they were a moment, and disappeared inside the building.

A few minutes later he came out. He turned toward the interpreter-policewoman, to speak in Arabic instead of in the German he so often used, and stated a new demand that seemed to surprise the negotiators: "Our commando has decided to leave Olympic Village with the hostages, and not wait any longer for the Israeli Zionist imperialists to make up their minds. So we will need two planes. We will head for Egypt. These planes are to be ready to leave within the hour. When we land in Cairo, we expect to find waiting for us each and every one of the prisoners whose release we demanded. If not, before getting out of the plane, we will execute all of the hostages, without exception."

The later reports published by the Bonn and Bavarian governments presented this demand for emplaning as something totally unexpected. However, all one has to do is look back at the fedayeen's first ultimatums to see that right off they had demanded three long-distance planes, on which they said they would take their prisoners to a friendly country. After half a day, they were simply lowering their demands by one craft.

What *was* new was important, though: until now they had insisted on Israel's agreement to release the Arab prisoners *before* their takeoff. They had insisted so heavily on this agreement beforehand that it seemed they had overlooked the fact that, in any case, according to their own basic statements, the exchange could take place only outside of West Germany, at an airport of their designation. For twelve hours, the terrorists on every occasion had threatened to execute all their hostages right outside Block 31 unless Jerusalem agreed to release the prisoners they had listed. But since they had not repeated their intentions to take the hostages with them, they had seemed ready to stay in West Germany until the matter was settled.

Now, suddenly, they were getting ready to leave, with their hostages, posthaste. They were dismissing the Germans as negotiators, and sending them off to become taxi-plane dispatchers. They were trying to force Israel into direct dialogue, overtly or tacitly: either you send all of our imprisoned comrades to Cairo forthwith, or else . . .

The problem was still the same. But suddenly the tactical situation had been completely altered.

Herr Genscher temporized, "I might as well warn you immediately that trying to get two planes at this hour in the time you allowed would be impossible. It would be hard enough to get even one."

"All right! One will do!" Issa agreed.

He gave them another surprise in accepting this way—so fast, and without consultation with his group.

Merk explained they had to find a long-range plane, get it serviced, and work out the transfer of the fedayeen and their hostages to one of the Munich airports. "You can see we are only too willing. But there are a lot of imponderables. How can you expect us to work all that out in one hour? Give us three hours, at the least."

The head terrorist promptly agreed, with his unnerving calmness, to set the deadline back to 7:00 PM.

The German negotiators had a short-term relaxation in the new deadline, but the sudden demand of the terrorists to fly out of Germany was none the less a terrible problem.

For if Germany accepted this demand, it would be abandoning guests captured on its land, within the Munich Olympic area—and delivering the Israeli hostages to their bitter enemies, under the worst possible conditions.

Dr. Merk asked Issa, "Are you sure the Egyptian government will welcome you and let you have your way?"

"In flight," Issa quietly answered, "we will use the plane's radio to contact the Arab nations. Cairo will be our anticipated destination, but the plane will have to be equipped to change its direction until the last possible moment."

Merk asked insistently how many hostages there were, and approximately how many fedayeen.

"Just prepare us a large-size plane, without any booby traps," was all Issa would tell him, as he grinned like a tiger-cat.

Salah, charcoaled up again, hopping around and making faces, was keeping Issa covered, until the latter motioned to leave more space between them. The dialogue had at no time been tenser, despite the phony relaxation Issa was putting on. They all felt they were at a decisive turn. Herr Merk took his federal opposite-number aside: they whispered to each other for a moment. The Bavarian minister came back toward Issa who was making small talk with Fräulein Graes (asking her whether she had found time to have lunch), and firmly replied, "We cannot carry these negotiations any further without being assured that there are still living hostages. We must insist you show us the hostages before we set about fulfilling your latest demand."

Issa thought it over, or pretended to. He raised his arm suddenly toward Apt. 1. A panel of the bay window opened and Tony's jungle-hat appeared: the two exchanged a few words ("Issa asked him to pick out one of the Jews and bring him to the window right away; Tony agreed," Fräulein Graes translated).

In a moment, Tony was back down in the street, his gun pointed at the Germans. Salah had taken up a position on the threshold of the building. A rifle muzzle stuck out through the open window, and a fedayee in a jungle-hat like Tony's, his features hidden behind a scarf, appeared there with one of the hostages, Andrei Spitzer.

Spitzer was in a white body shirt, his arms tightly back behind his very narrow body, meaning his wrists were bound together, very low. He, so careful of his grooming, had not been able to shave. He was very pale, yet remained totally dignified. His long Osiris-face stood out clearly, and an interview took place in English.

Spitzer: Good day, gentlemen.

Merk: Good day, dear sir. I am Bruno Merk, Minister of the Interior for the Free State of Bavaria.

Spitzer: I am Andrei Spitzer, fencing master, and coach of the Israeli team for the Olympic Games.

Merk: How many of you are still alive?

Spitzer was about to answer, when Issa shouted: "No, do not answer!" There was a short exchange between Merk and Issa, then Merk asked Spitzer again, "Are your comrades with you in good health?"

Spitzer: All the hostages who survived the dawn attack are alive and in fair condition.

Genscher: We are doing everything humanly possible to get you released under the best conditions. I am Interior Minister of the German Federal Republic; my name is Hans-Dietrich Genscher. Chancellor Willy Brandt came to Munich specially. He is fighting for your safety. We will be concerned only with you until you are freed.

Merk: We are all concerned about you.

Spitzer: Thanks, in the name of all my comrades.

He spoke with assurance, in a well-modulated voice. He was calm itself. Suddenly, he tottered and seemed to pitch backward. He must have been grabbed by the belt and jerked back in.

The fedayee masked by the blue-and-white scarf and wearing the tropical hat even indoors appeared in Spitzer's place. Later, pictures would identify him as Badran. He shouted something angry at Issa. Before the interpreter could translate, the Black September leader was shouting something at his men. A second Israeli appeared in the window, in a jacket, with his wrists tightly tied in front of him: a sturdy fellow, the wrestler Eliezer Halfin. Two brown hands could be seen grappling his shoulders.

Issa turned on the Germans, who were somewhat surprised. He shouted, pointing at Halfin: "You are trying to trick us. Your soldiers have just surrounded the building. They are getting ready to attack us. Take a good look at that Jew. If you do not immediately order your men away, we will shoot him down, where he is, before your eyes, and throw his corpse out to you. It is now exactly five o'clock. In another five minutes, two more hostages will be shot right on the spot where you are now standing."

He did an about-face and went back into Apt. 1. Eliezer Halfin remained as dignified, as self-composed as Spitzer had before. He bowed his head in greeting to the Germans, and at the same time was violently jerked back in.

Dr. Schreiber and his aide left to instruct their troops to abandon all forward positions—at least any that the Arabs might have been able to see. Once more, the plan of attack was shattered.

Merk, Genscher, and Tröger told the interpreter to call to the head terrorist and ask him to come back to the door, so she could stress to him that if his comrades and he really wanted to get somewhere, they had to resume the interrupted discussion. If not, everything would stand still. A moment later, cigarette in hand, Issa was back, swinging from hip to hip in his well-cut safari suit, and still unarmed.

"I repeat," Merk stated stiffly, "that we must know how many of the hostages you took this morning are still alive. Moreover, we cannot allow you to take them away unless they themselves agree to it."

Issa smiled his biting smile. Since dawn, his square face with the pointed chin had become more drawn, beneath the thick coating of charcoal. He motioned to the ministers to remain where they were, and went back inside. Dr. Schreiber returned from his nearby forward command post, legs tensed, jaws set, like a wild animal on a leash.

Silently, Halfin and Spitzer appeared in the window together. As if alerted, the Germans looked up at them. The two hostages still had their hands tied, and retained in their bearing the great dignity which Herr Genscher would later term unforgettable, moving beyond the power of words.

Issa was back in the doorway. Now he was carrying a sub-machine gun with a safety belt around the stock. He said: "Just ask the agreed-upon questions. No conversation." Around him, there was the same security setup as before.

Merk: Do you know the commando's decision to take all of you to Cairo?

Spitzer: Yes, Mr. Minister.

Merk: We cannot allow this unless you and your comrades clearly inform us you are willing to leave the Olympic Village.

Spitzer: We are willing to be flown to an Arab country, provided the Israeli Government has agreed to carry out an exchange of prisoners at the airport we land at, at the time of our landing.

Some of the watchers on the roof of the East German building could get a good view down on the two Jewish prisoners. They were bound together like Siamese twins, by a thick cord cutting in to their wrists. As soon as Spitzer stopped talking, a hand pulled the cord that bound them, and the watchers saw the two hostages collapse backwards, their legs stiff: they were also tied to each other at the ankles.

The four West German negotiators put their hands together a moment, and Merk then addressed Issa, emphasizing each word: "We cannot be satisfied with the word of just one Israeli hostage. No blackmail can make us accept that. We will get nothing started unless you let us see how many of them are still alive, and how they feel at the idea of being taken out of Germany."

At this point (5:12 PM), Issa displayed more authority than at any other time. He replied without hesitation, "I agree, if only to show you the good will and humaneness of Arab revolutionary fighters. This favor will be granted only one personality, the *Herr Bundesinnenminister.* I will go and tell my comrades. One of the fedayeen will be down in a moment to escort the *Herr Minister* up."

Three minutes later, Herr Genscher was entering Apt. 1. He went up the stairs behind two fedayeen. Issa met him at the landing and took him into a room darkened by closed curtains. This was the bedroom with balcony on the garden side. The French door was closed and the air in the room stale.

There were nine living Israelis. Six were seated, in groups of three, on the two single beds pushed back against the perpendicular walls. The other three were on chairs set side by side, in the space between the beds.

All the Israelis were tied hand and foot. Each group of three was bound together by a thick rope wound around their arms and attached to the tubular legs of the chairs. In the semidarkness, it was hard to tell them apart. They were a glob of silent prisoners. It was hell.

Two terrorists, Salah and Tony, submachine guns on their hips, stood in the middle of the room, guarding them. Issa, back a bit, leaned against the door, holding a cocked hand grenade. Before the hostages were open baskets of food.

One could feel there were other fedayeen on that floor, but they were not visible. Despite the poor light, Herr Genscher could see that the faces of at least two of the nine living hostages showed marks of recent blows. Yossef Gutfreund had a very swollen, puffy ear. David Berger had all kinds of bruises and, in spite of a big band of adhesive tape, it could be seen that over one cheekbone his face was badly split open. (Around 10:15 PM, several observers would be able to see that the veteran Yacov Springer, easily identifiable by his rough old pirate's face, his balding forehead, and his lumpy nose, had a very swollen and discolored lower lip on the left side; as it would turn out, two of his teeth had been knocked out.)

Yossef Romano's body lay on the floor in the middle of the room. A soaking bloody towel covered his head. He was horribly wounded, almost cut in two at the waist. Around him, there were black puddles, and on the walls, the floor, the furniture, the ceiling, everywhere, splatterings of blood and gelatinous matter. Bulletholes could be seen all around.

Issa warned Genscher to ask only two questions, adding, "If you do not abide by our agreement, we will kill a hostage before your eyes."

The West German Interior Minister introduced himself. Then

he repeated his question about how the hostages felt at the idea of being flown to an Arab country.

One after another, the shooting coach Kehat Shorr, weight-lifting judge Yacov Springer, and wrestling referee Yossef Gutfreund, speaking for all of them, agreed to leave for an Arab country. "However," they insisted, "we would assume that, if we leave under such conditions, our government would meet the demands of the terrorists [that was the way they referred to their captors in their presence], for otherwise we would all be shot."

Genscher stated, word by word: "In other words, if your government did not agree to the exchange, you would not be willing to leave German territory."

"Naturally," Kehat Shorr, the senior man, answered with everyone else agreeing. "In that case, there'd be no point to it."

The Federal Minister had by now recognized all of them, from having studied an emergency file with their pictures and vital statistics in the morning at the Village administration building.

"Chancellor Brandt, and I, and all the German authorities," he said, "will fight with all our strength for you. You will not be abandoned. You have our word for it."

The attitude of the nine hostages overwhelmed the German statesman through its nobility. He would forever be seeing the pride of those faces, the intensity and mastery of the eyes turned toward him.

Kehatt Shorr said, "I am speaking for all of my comrades in thanking you, Mr. Minister, for having come to see us and for doing your best to help us."

The eight others warmly joined in these sentiments, including Mark Slavin, so young, yet not looking in the least depressed, and interested in everything. He spoke only Russian and embryos of Hebrew, but Zeev Friedman was alongside him and in a low voice translated each word for him. Slavin listened with rapt attention.

Herr Genscher, although he was not supposed to ask any further questions, inquired how their spirits were.

Yacov Springer smilingly replied, "Just fine, sir. Our morale is high. We are Israelis."

All of them seconded that.

Issa announced the meeting was at an end. The West German

Minister of the Interior bade good-bye to the hostages without being able to get near them. Back on Connollystrasse, one could read the intense emotion in his face.

He had just witnessed courage. The nine hostages had not uttered a single complaint. Not one had even sighed. None looked defeated.

Herr Genscher was sorry he had not been able to ask the hostages whether they needed anything; the terrorists had been on the watch; they had forbidden any personal exchanges.

Herr Tröger was waiting for him before the blue door. The two men looked into each other's eyes. Genscher tapped the Mayor of Olympic Village lightly on the shoulder. They went over to Merk and Schreiber.

Subways, railways, streetcars were unloading stunned, curious, irritated crowds, inclined no doubt to the worst mob reactions, had any skillful leader called on them. At the slightest signal, by the thousands they would have surrounded Block 31, demonstrating mindlessly, confronting the forces of law and order.

The business street was still crowded with shoppers and strollers. They were jostling in the big drugstore, pushing toward the free milkbar; the rival Adidas and Puma sporting-goods shops, souvenir stands, fine stores with catchy window displays, and the while-U-wait shoe-repair were all doing a brisk business. The athletes looked more than they bought, but the officials, today worried and at a loss, seemed to find consolation in spending.

As always, the Men's Village teemed with women. "The Girls' Village has been absolutely empty since noon," Leni Riefsenstahl had told me just a little while back. "There is a terrible feeling of desertion there."

The *Olympisches Dorf Frauen* (Women's Village) was, in fact, rather forbidding. Not only because it was absolutely off limits to men, nor because its 2.5-meter (8-ft.)-high fences were harder to scale than those of the Men's Village. Mostly, it was because it looked like a mining-company town. It was a gray assemblage of identical little buildings, pressed close to one another, poor-looking and sad despite its colored daubings and the flowerbeds that were not to bloom this year.

THE BLOOD OF ISRAEL

Bicycle roadracers and marathon-runners this afternoon kept going by on the pathways of the Olympic Village. One's first reaction was irritation. But, after all, neither they nor the other athletes could stop training as their events drew closer, after having driven themselves through long hard years to get ready for them. They were tortured by the tragedy that was unfolding. But the Games were not canceled, and had they been it would have seemed terribly unfair to these young people who had sacrificed so much to be able to participate in them.

All along Spielstrasse, that followed the contour of the artificial lake like a ring of the seven deadly sins, the daily round went on in all its animation. That it may have been an act, that the pros were merely doing their job, in no way lessened the spirit of it.

Olympiapark, Village included, was a business too. Today, the sausage-sellers were as busy as the soft-drink stands, the outdoor cafés, and the little notions shops. There were mobs at the puppet show, the pantomimes, and the improvised play by a Hamburg troupe about the loves and ideological differences of six athletes, only survivors of a mysterious catastrophe that had befallen the Universal Games. Naturally, the last six people on earth soon discover an A-bomb wiped out everything around them.

They were not being allowed into the Village, of course, but they were not really objecting. It was past 5:00 PM, and the young Jews kept relaying each other: there were continuously hundreds of them out there. There was also a crowd of them outside the Radio/TV Center, watching DOZ.

I have already described the long sinewy street called Kusoczin-skidamm, that ran from south to north like a high dike, along the west flank of the Village. As Kusoczinskidamm passes between the DOZ parking lots and the service roads of Connollystrasse, the elevated roadway widens into a ridge dotted with transplanted trees. Apts. 1 and 3 of Block 31 are only some 60 meters (66 yds.) below the point of the tongue-shaped ridge.

An ideal observation point, mobbed by picture pros shoving each other around as they trampled the grass and maltreated the young lindens. The police were there, too, and not playacting. But both groups left a share of this narrow space for Jews.

210

Nine Proud Souls

They were adolescents, mostly Israelis, coming from the International Youth Camp, with the fine well-planned and gaily colored tents, over near Riem airport. Before today, they had been so happy, in the constantly fraternal atmosphere.

Every quarter of an hour, they started to sing pioneer folksongs, the ones of the earliest kibbutzim, that were still as sorrowful as psalms. Then there were marching-songs, especially the ones used in the Negev. And, at least twice every hour, a full-bodied *Hatikvah*, the national anthem of Israel, the sharp, grave music that had marked nothing but Jewish victories, and would probably never accompany their defeat—for to lose, for them, would mean to die.

Near them, in the late afternoon, were other young people, wanting to show their solidarity with the hostages. Most of these were black or yellow, and their numbers were a ringing denial of the propaganda lies. They generally sang in English, usually "We Shall Overcome." . . .

When Israel's Olympic athletes took off from Lod Airport, according to the Lufthansa crew and hostess that took them to Munich, they were tense and pensive. One immediate reason was their concern over skyjacking or sabotage; they felt the security measures taken by the West German company were inadequate. Why, then, had they not gone via El Al?

The survivors of the Israeli team who spoke to me told me there was something else. It was the mere fact that they were going to Germany. Not that Israelis hate or even mistrust West Germany. They know it is a new nation, with peaceful intentions, and that most of its inhabitants are ashamed of the Nazi horrors. They also know that by now the great majority of West Germans are too young to have had any part of the swastika madness. But most of these athletes, though born after Hitlerism, had an instinctual reaction—like a weight on their chests. Their throats caught, just the least bit, as they said before leaving, "I'm going to spend two or three weeks in Germany, at Munich."

They went with banners flying high in their national outfit, under the sign of the seven-armed candelabrum and the Shield of David. They went in the name of their country. To Munich. To the city where National Socialism was born, where Hitler had attempted his 1923 November "Beer Hall Putsch," where he completed *Mein Kampf* on his release from Landsberg Prison, and lived from May 1913 until he came to power on January 30, 1933. The holy city of Nazism—just 12 km. from Dachau. The city that had been the monster marshaling-yard for all the trains of deportees going to nearby Dachau, as well as the camps in Eastern Bavaria, Austria, and the Sudetenland. The city in which Czechoslovakia had been condemned to die. Munich—*München*—Germany.

Even the very young ones, even the youngest, Mark Slavin, had that tightness in the throat because, with Jews, from birth on there is awareness of anti-Semitism, persecution, pogroms, genocide.

There was Kehat Shorr, fifty-three, civil servant at the Defense Ministry and coach of the national shooting team.

He left a wife and married daughter. He came from Rumania, which he had left for Israel in 1963. A former champion of Israel, he remained one of the country's best pistol shots, but had stopped competing a few years before, since it was not compatible with the position he held as coach.

He was rather tall, well built, with sharp laughing eyes. His face had the color of ripe wheat, lightened by the pepper-and-salt hair.

He was both open and reserved. Before *Aliyah* (the "return" to Israel), he had been champion of Rumania. The Shorrs and Halfins were now neighbors in Neve Sharrett, a Tel Aviv suburb, not far from B'nei B'rak, where Mark Slavin's family lived.

I was unfortunately not able to get any other information on Kehat Shorr's life than this: Rumania entered the war against the USSR in June 1941, hoping to get back Bessarabia and Northern Bukovina, which Moscow had taken from her. In December 1942, as the claws of the Iron Guard were closing in on Jews, young Shorr, marked for internment, took to the *maquis* with some of his friends. They hid in a redoubt in the southern Carpathians, from which over a period of twenty months they made many sorties into the largest Rumanian cities, to save hidden young Jews from the clutches of dictator Antonescu's forces.

Nine Proud Souls

When, in August 1944, national insurrection broke out against General Antonescu and the Germans, the Jewish mountain underground came down from their hideouts to harass the Axis troops on their communications lines. Shorr proved his outstanding marksmanship in many of these encounters. He was awarded the highest decorations. But then he preferred to lapse into anonymity. Although many fine offers were made him, he turned a deaf ear on them all: perhaps because in his own eyes he knew that he had gone into the maquis, not for Rumania, but for the Jewish people.

XIII

ISRAEL DEFENDS ITSELF

And David said: 'The LORD that
delivered me out of the paw of the
lion, and out of the paw of the bear, He
will deliver me out of the hand of this
Philistine.' And Saul said unto David:
'Go, and the LORD shall be with thee.'
First Samuel 17:37

"NO MEMBER OF OUR SPECIAL SERVICES, NOR OF ANY OTHER ISRAELI
civil or military body, took any part whatsover in what happened
during the events of September 5–6, either at the Olympic Village
or at Fürstenfeldbruck. There was not a single instance of Israeli
participation. The German authorities made the decisions and
acted entirely on their own from one end of the tragedy to the
other. I already specified this to the Knesset on September 12 and
again on October 16. I repeat it again. How can I be any clearer?
The official reports of the Free State of Bavaria and the German
Federal Republic, dated September 7 and 20, 1972, fully and un-
equivocally confirm what I am ready to repeat to you once more,
if necessary. Is it necessary, gentlemen?"

"No, ma'am. It is not."

Thus, Mrs. Golda Meir, in a TV interview.

When people say "Israel's secret services," they seem to think
this means one simple structure. But no country in the world,
not even the Soviet Union, has achieved unity in that area, if only
because it is more wholesome for no one branch to hold all the
keys. Political stability and solidness of power, efficiency of intelligence and security of action are results of hermetic partitioning,
rivalries, division of jobs, just as much as of technical proficiency.

Israel's secret services are broken down into three kingdoms
and three baronies.

The first kingdom is *Mossad* (Hebrew for: Organization).

Oversimplified, this is a counterpart of the CIA. It is directly under the power of the Prime Minister, and operates only abroad. . . . It grew out of the 1937 setup created to help further Jewish immigration into Palestine in defiance of the wishes of the mandatory power, Great Britain. . . .

The second kingdom, the Armed Forces Intelligence Service, is known to Israelis generally as *Aman* (contracted from *Agaf Modiin*, or Information Service) or *Modiin*. It operates purely in military matters, and like Mossad has two main branches, Information and Action. Its personnel, made up entirely of career military, brings together the specialized intelligence services of land, sea, and air arms. . . .

The third kingdom is the General Security Service of the State of Israel. The first three Hebrew words of its name, *Sherut Bitachon Klali,* telescoped into *Shabak,* are what all the specialists call this virtual equivalent of the FBI. The man in the street sometimes calls it *Shin-Beth,* the initials of Sherut Bitachon. It handles internal security and counterintelligence. While theoretically confined to working within Israel's borders (including the occupied territories), its agents sometimes have to go abroad, or at least did so prior to the fall of 1972, when this practice was significantly curtailed. It is broken down into six divisions, the first three of which (Arab countries, Eastern Europe, and International, meaning the rest of the world) are devoted to counterintelligence; the fourth, highly autonomous, is very specialized (anti-terrorist activities), while the last two (Israeli Arabs, and Administered Territories) assure the systematic safety of the country.

The first of the three baronies is the Ministry of Foreign Affairs' Investigative Service. It has no Action section, but its intelligence services are first-rate. Their adaptability and familiarity with the problems involved are greatly helped by the ease and speed with which Israelis may switch or be transferred from one area to another, from regular army to civilian life, from public service to the private sector. Politically and economically, this service has listening posts everywhere.

Second barony: Persecuted Jews, a self-defining title. This service deals with all Jews who are persecuted or immobilized where they are: USSR, Poland, Arab countries. No Action branch here, either, but fantastic documentation and huge research resources. It is headed by Shaul Avigur, a real old-timer, a famous veteran of the pre-independence struggles and then of Mossad. Born in Russia, he is one of the last of Ben-Gurion's companions still active.

Third barony: the policy's Special Flying Squad. This group, on request, comes to the assistance of the three kingdoms of the secret services, particularly when they need specialists to track people down, set up dossiers on individuals, check out archives, make routine double checks or certain arrests.

Israel has a Ministry of Police, whose members have a very high *esprit de corps*. They consider that the operatives of the three kingdoms are barred from carrying out certain operations on home territory, and feel very strongly the need for the existence and employment of their special section. . . .

As a Christian, I must state here that, beyond the current problem of the Palestinian refugees, Israel has to put up with the consequences of the unspeakable attitude toward Jews of a certain school of Christianity. Jesus berated Israel as had been done before him by the Prophets, whom he so favored quoting, whom he venerated and set on high. But that was a father scolding his children. The Gospels bespeak his deep support within the Jewish people, and the fact that he fell victim to temporal powers, as was to happen to so many of the Church Fathers: the Roman master force and occupying power decreed the Crucifixion. But all of this was not to keep some, centuries after Christ had returned to his Father, from teaching pious masses that Jews held some kind of collective guilt for the death of Our Saviour. By the same token, Islam had found it convenient to allege that Israel suffered a divine curse. . . .

XIV
THE LAST DEADLINE

Naked came I out of my mother's womb,
And naked shall I return thither;
The LORD gave, and the LORD hath taken away;
Blessed be the name of the LORD.
                                                Job 1:21

5:15 PM (DIARY): SIGN OF THE TIMES: WHEREAS THREE DECADES AGO, as time went on, the control would have become tighter, now, despite the continuing tragedy, in the declining afternoon, it is less hard to slip into the Village. Two American newsmen, totaling well over a century in age between them, show up with the I.D.s of two swimmers who together are barely thirty-six. They get in./

Avery Brundage was still in G-1, telling the *Krisenstab* that the IOC would not tolerate participants in the Games, guests of Olympic Village, being carried off by terrorists and taken out of West Germany.

Calculated leaks got this information to IOC members trying to be helpful in the Village. From there, it spread like wildfire to the Vierjahreszeiten, where the remaining heads of Olympia were stewing. Once again, he had acted entirely on his own. Not only had there been no general meeting, but even the Executive Board had not yet been called together. This was all unprecedented in IOC history.

Michael Morris, Lord Killanin, should obviously have been called in by Brundage right at the start, both as First Vice-President and as President-elect due to take office as soon as the Games ended. But, by prearrangement, Lord Killanin the night before had flown to Kiel with two other members of the Executive, Jonkheer Herman von Karnebeek, of Holland, and Prince Tsuneyoshi Takeda, of Japan. The general staff of IOC had to be represented in the Olympic second city during the Games. These 1800-km. (1125-mi.)-flights were not easy; a small group of other members also went to Kiel with the three executives.

Brundage had heard of the attack on Connollystrasse at about 6:00 AM on September 5. He sent no word of it to Lord Killanin, who first heard of it on the radio in his hotel room at Kiel, while shaving, at 8:00 AM. The news was still fragmentary, and confused. According to the commentators, it would be a short affray, that might end tragically or happily, but could not last long. Weinberg's murder was reported, as well as several seriously wounded terrorists and Israelis.

Lord Killanin inquired as to whether a plane might be immediately available or whether there was any room on a scheduled flight to Munich, for the IOC group had not been intending to go back till ten that night. Unfortunately, he was told, there was absolutely no way to fly to Munich before evening, and the organizers of the Olympic regattas would be considerably put out if the members of the ruling body of IOC were to leave and deprive all the scheduled events of their participation, for it would appear that they were censuring the Kiel Olympic organizers, whereas the latter in carrying on as planned were acting no differently from Munich. Lord Killanin and Messrs. van Karnebeek and Takeda decided to go to sea to follow a boat race as they had promised, but insisted that transportation be found to take them back to Munich by early afternoon.

Immediately, by his actions, and answering his friends' questions, Lord Killanin privately established his position: the IOC did not have to get involved in handling this terrible occurrence. That could be left to the Organizing Committee, the board of Olympic Village, the authorities of the City of Munich, the Free State of Bavaria, and the German Federal Republic. All of them were directly affected by the attack, and had the data, the means, and the experience and power needed to effect saving the Israeli athletes. The IOC should urgently respond to any request from the *Krisenstab*. It might, in conjunction with the abovementioned authorities, decide to suspend or continue the Games. It might issue an appeal to the conscience of the world (which it failed to do). But it had no reason to get involved in the operations proper. It was not called upon to participate in, underwrite, agree to, or reject them. It had to restate its support of the Organizing Committee, and then let the latter handle matters.

When Lord Killanin, still at Kiel, heard that Brundage was sitting with the crisis staff and publicly making decisions in the name of the IOC, and Brundage's name appeared more and more frequently in the official pronouncements of the *Krisenstab,* in which he was mentioned as taking part in their deliberations and approving their actions, the First Vice-President of the IOC held his tongue, but intended to express himself once back at Munich.

While watching the boat race, Lord Killanin and the others kept abreast of events in Connollystrasse as best they could. The Irish lord and his fellow Executive Board members were more and more surprised as time went by that the lame-duck president of the IOC made no effort to hurry them back to Munich nor to reach his next-in-command and soon-to-be-successor by phone.

The IOC directorship, unable to meet personally with Brundage, who was sequestered on the third floor of G-1, sent him note after note to ask whether it was not highly desirable, on the one hand, for Lord Killanin and the other two Executive Board members to come back from Kiel at the soonest, and on the other, for the Executive Board to have a meeting at the earliest convenience. The IOC President replied that he saw no reason to call an Executive Board meeting. He merely instructed all of his members not to leave the Vierjahreszeiten Hotel.

Obviously, he did not want any IOC members to be in the Village. His order was disregarded, even though Mr. Brundage had used every available channel to transmit it: most of the IOC members, properly haunted by what was happening on Connollystrasse, crisscrossed the Village very often until the epilogue.

The IOC directorship had, very early, telegraphed Lord Killanin to ask whether he did not think he should make an emergency return to Munich. But President Brundage, at the same time, had gotten directly in touch with Herr Berthold Beitz. The latter, elected to the IOC at Sapporo in February last, had been named by the Organizing Committee to head the Kiel sector of the Games. Brundage asked him to keep Lord Killanin and the others in Kiel as long as possible, specifying, "Take them out to sea! Don't get them a special plane!"

Herr Beitz did not agree. But he had to move heaven and earth to find a plane that could take the IOC members back to Munich. Berthold Beitz, a fine-looking and impressive man, eager to please though reserved, with bushy salt-and-pepper eyebrows, was none other than the president and chief operating officer of the Friedrich Krupp enterprises, the famous, legendary Krupp armaments works, and as such had access to private planes. He finally got a jet that delivered Killanin and his group to the Vierjahreszeiten by 5:30 PM. From then on, it was blood and thunder in the red-and-gold parlors and the large overstuffed bedrooms of the noble traditional hotel.

Not that the internal upheavals within the IOC had any bearing on the outcome of the tragedy. For, even if Mr. Brundage had gone personally to ask the terrorists to free their hostages, or if the IOC had sent an appeal to all the countries of the world, things would not have changed one iota.

Yet—what if Mr. Brundage had tried something else?

What if he had appealed to all 10,500 athletes and officials of Olympic Village to surround Block 31, along with the members of the IOC? Just imagine: all those competitors who felt the abomination of this attack and believed in Olympic solidarity laying siege to the building! Unarmed. In sweat shirts with the names of their countries. Empty-handed. After having gotten all the police personnel to leave the Village and all the helicopters taken out of its skies.

They would advise the terrorists of their determination. They would promise to undertake no violent action. But would also assure them they would keep their vigil until all the hostages were freed, saying, "If you try to get out with your prisoners, you won't be able to. We will not let you through. You kill them? You shoot us? We'll see. But you shall not pass."

Obviously, it would have been good if in the front ranks of this enclosure of athletes there had been a sufficient number of Arabs to represent the majority of the Moslem countries. The terrorists would then have seen that they had to break out not only over the bodies of "infidels," but also over those of their brothers in Islam.

220

The Last Deadline

The Connollystrasse fedayeen might have bitten their knuckles in rage, but they would have been stopped by the idea of the catastrophic setback to their undertaking if they killed non-Jewish athletes in trying to break out of the barrage.

Was it illogical to think they might have finally decided not to try to break out of Block 31, and that their decision really to gamble with the lives of the hostages might have weakened before worldwide disapproval so symbolized?

They would have negotiated their own safety, and left alone, by plane, for some Libya or other where they still would have been welcomed as heroes, in recognition of the two Jews they had fortunately murdered for openers.

5:20 PM: Entertainment was going full swing on the boards and stages that Spielstrasse ran through like a moving sidewalk: fascination of multimedia! Light shows, rock, jazz and blues, clowns and puppets, mimes and jugglers, competing with sound montages and filmed newsreels showing the armored cars in the Village Plaza. Sidewalk painter Klaus Mittenhauer was offering a choice of charcoal or pencil drawings: your instant portrait, an Olympic champion, or a hooded terrorist, any of them only 25 marks each. A nearby competitor accused him of cutthroating.

Kids were buying all-day suckers in the shape of Waldi.

I was pacing up and down before the towers at the start of Connollystrasse. Bending way back to be able to see the top of one of those skyscrapers, you had the feeling of a fantastic stairway ending up in space, a Gulliver stairway, decorated with plants and flowers that, when seen from below, seemed to be growing right out of the concrete.

On every balcony of the concrete explosion, petunias and geraniums spread their bright-red and delicate-mauve music.

At the beginning, before the start of the Games, the Village was a colorful splash of native outfits: burnooses and dashikis, turbans and sombreros, saris and leather pants; but now they had all been replaced by sweat suits and body shirts.

And the mammoth pillars of the roof-tent over there were reminiscent of launchpads at Cape Kennedy.

Just before you reached 31, on Connollystrasse, a gilded reinforced pipe split into a four-headed siphon to become the fountain in a minibasin.

221

5:30 PM (Diary): At G-1 they're saying that Chancellor Willy Brandt is not in Munich at all, but 26 km. (16 mi.) away, to the south, on one of the many lakes that dot these foothills of the Alps. At any rate, since his arrival at Riem airport, the West German leader has not been seen in the Village. I inquire. Yes, at Willi Daume's invitation, the Chancellor, with his retinue and secretariat, has set up in a fine villa that the president of the Organizing Committee put at his disposal, at Feldafing, on the west bank of Starnberger See.

This Starnberg Lake is famous not only for being bucolic and beautiful of aspect, but because Ludwig II of Wittelsbach, the Mad King of Bavaria, finally deposed, came here to end his days, by suicide or murder, on June 13, 1886. . . . /

5:45 PM: This was how the *Dokumentation* would relate it:

> Mr. Manfred Schreiber, in the presence of the Minister of the Interior of the German Federal Republic and the Minister of the Interior of the Free State of Bavaria, ordered the chief of the assault forces to prepare an action for the liberation of the hostages at the arifield of Fürstenfeldbruck. This action was to take place some time after 6:40 PM. One of the chiefs of the Bavarian criminal police was given the order to have a long-distance plane brought into position at Fürstenfeldbruck. As soon as the meeting ended, a shock group of the police's special forces, accompanied by five marksmen, went by helicopter to Fürstenfeldbruck.

This was a logical decision; here is why.

At this moment, the only thing the fedayeen wanted was to leave Connollystrasse with their hostages and take them to Egypt or some other Arab country. The *Krisenstab* had to pretend to go along. But they decided to save the athletes from the terrorists.

Supposing the nine hostages could not be freed during the trip from Block 31 to the departure airfield. In that case, the last chance to try to save the hostages would be on the airfield itself. Such an action would have to be undertaken at whatever cost, for, barring a change of orders from Chancellor Brandt, the *Krisenstab* had no intention of letting the hostages be taken off of German territory, since Israel had rejected the fedayeen's demands. The problem then was: What airfield lent itself best to a move against the terrorists?

The Last Deadline

The international airport of Munich-Riem had just been renovated, and was now one of the biggest and most modern in Europe. Yet it would have serious drawbacks if a fight were to take place there. It was constantly jammed with traffic. At the height of the Olympics, it would be a catastrophe to upset foreign airlines' schedules by forbidding them the use of the field for an indefinite period. It would also be a catastrophe suddenly to get rid of all the transit or waiting passengers, and the visitors, at Riem. The public facilities at Riem were very compact, to be as convenient as possible for people in a hurry; so really isolating the terrorists and their hostages there to make an attack on them would be impossible without great dangers to innocent bystanders; in particular, the fedayeen might even get a chance to seize additional hostages.

Finally, Riem was 8 km. (5 mi.) from Munich. Compared to other big European cities, that was practically downtown. But, in the drama of September 5, the nearness became a calamity. How could the terrorists be convinced to take a helicopter for so short a distance? And Dr. Merk forbade any trip by bus, no matter how short, as too dangerous to the regular population. The police, too, were opposed to automobile transport, for the terrorists might then demand that the car be driven right up to the plane gangway. The use of a helicopter offered a reasonable variety of possibilities. The terrorists, after all, would have to alight from it and walk in the open over to their plane.

So? There was another plausible field: Fürstenfeldbruck. It was a military base, long used by the U.S.A.F., but now belonging to the Luftwaffe. The West German air army is less exclusive than some of its neighbors across the Rhine: it sometimes allows civilian traffic on its fields. So Fürstenfeldbruck each year is used to relieve Riem of some of its congestion, during the *Oktoberfest,* October's festival of beer and folksay, sixteen days of unleashed imbibing, stuffing, and general merrymaking. Unbelievable crowds converge on Munich for it: five million people in 1972.

During the Games, Fürstenfeldbruck was being used so extensively that the military virtually "surrendered" it to civil aviation. All charters landed there, as did all VIP planes.

Actually, the base was 5 km. (3 mi.) north of Fürstenfeldbruck, and extended from there to the limits of a sleepy, quiet little town called Maisach. It was isolated, and easy to close off; no plane unrelated to the eventual operation needed to land there this evening; and it was 25 km. (a little over 15 mi.) from Munich. In fact, the terrorists might be told it was 35 km. away, not too great a distance for an airport located near a great city. And in view of traffic on the roads, which, the fedayeen would be told, were bottlenecked, the use of a helicopter would be fully justified.

Fürstenfeldbruck, apart from the airport, was a little town in the Amper valley, on the same river that flows by Dachau, a bit downstream, before going into the Isar. And it is a spa. The pure-water baths, set up by the doctor-priest Sebastian Kneipp, are famous: they are prescribed for delicate stomachs and fragile intestines.

On September 6, when it was already all over, I went for a walk in the little town: spared by the war, it had not changed since the 1920s when, it is said, Adolf Hitler used it for discreet assignations. It is a nice little artistic, middle-class town, lazing a bit on its hilly plateau; average elevation, 528 meters (some 1743 ft.). Clean as a new-minted penny, full of flowered balconies, and half-timbered fine houses, it boasts an old Cistercian monastery with a brilliant, sumptuous, shimmering baroque church.

The monastery has a history. First known as Fürstenfeld, it was founded in 1263 by an earlier Ludwig II von Wittelsbach, appropriately named "The Strict." This Duke of Bavaria did it as an act of contrition because he (the Prince or Fürst) had felt obliged to have his wife, Marie of Brabant, decapitated. Of that original munificent edifice not a stone is left standing.

Fürstenfeldbruck's quiet streets, that lead down, as if secretly, to the green-flowing Amper below, abound in frescoed house-fronts, pink-cheeked young girls, and retired gents in brush-decorated hats. The beer halls of Hauptstrasse exhale powerful scents of hot sausage. But as soon as one gets a bit away, the sweet odor of honeysuckle overpowers them.

No one was talking about the massacre of the night before. But it was on everybody's mind.

6:10 PM: A communiqué from the West German Government issued on radio and TV denied the rumor that the Bundeswehr (regular army) had sent shock troops into Olympic Village. The golden rule of keeping the army out of confrontations between police and civilians still applied.

Sixty thousand spectators were beginning to file out of the *Olympiastadion*. They had come to see the West Germany-Hungary soccer match, an Olympics semifinal, and just heard the very belated announcement that it was postponed until tomorrow. They were leaving in deep silence. It was an impressive crowd to watch: expressionless; passive.

More than a third of them were walking over the fine bridge across Petuelring to go toward the two green roads that belt the Village: Kusoczinskidamm and Kolehmainen Weg. Pushed back in one place, getting through in another, elsewhere moving across the greenswards like slugs, they headed for the buttes, the rising paths, the unobstructed spots from which there was a view on some part of Connollystrasse and Block 31, now famous on all continents. They coalesced at these vantage points in the remaining light of the declining afternoon.

An armored reconnaissance vehicle (ARV), probably no boon to the pavement, barred Kusoczinskidamm to the southwest of 31, right in front of a little stall of assorted gadgets and snacks run by a one-legged man. He was so old one might have assumed he was a veteran of World War I, but at my questioning he said he lost his leg at Kharkov in 1942, and then spent nine years as a prisoner of the Soviets. The Olympic Park concession people had rented the spot to his son, but the latter had had to give up the idea of taking his vacation during the Games. He did his street-vending only in his spare time, his main work being in a Munich beer hall, which, precisely because of the Games, needed all the manpower it could get. So he had asked his father to take his place. The father, normally a cashier in a clinic—but sick of that job and ready to retire, since he already had his disability pension —accepted. Then, the gentlemen in charge of the Village told him he would not do at all, because it was not nice for the visitors and all those young people to have to look at an old amputee who would remind them of the g—d— war. So the amputee said: Let them just try to shut down his stand, he would mobilize all his comrades, the veterans' associations, the TV guys and the

THE BLOOD OF ISRAEL

press, and everybody, with his artificial leg and the other good one, and they'd see what they would see . . .

At the same level as the amputee and the police ARV, on the west side, at the foot of the crestline, began the red steel buildings of the *Deutsches Olympia Zentrum* (DOZ), covered on facades and roofs with "Cor-Ten" steel, of a granular red they said would fade into rosewood color. On the east, below, practically at the foot of the grassy knoll, ran the metal fence.

Another ARV was stationed just outside the Village, due north, on Kusoczinskidamm, beyond the bridge that takes that street across the crest. The armored vehicle, its heavy machine gun appearing to pivot of its own accord, stood crosswise on the pavement. Some sparrows were perched on its rubberized treads.

And, more tenacious than an army of locusts, the human mobs, deprived of soccer, were making their way, little by little invading even those 300 meters of Kusoczinskidamm that were blocked off by the ARVs. The police lines, the bullhorned appeals, the jostling, or the fact that often one could see nothing through the wall of heads and backs—none of that slowed the monster push toward the rises in terrain from which one could look down, very close (less than 100 meters most of the time, sometimes as little as 50) to Block 31.

It was a fantastic human tide. An anthill of loud colors, although dominated by tanned skins. Once at the top, it turned entirely eastward, toward the long white building with the light-blue doors. It condensed, as if trying to crush itself, and beat like an indefatigable angry swell against a double line of cops in blue-gray summer uniforms, holding hands, facing the pressing hordes, yet indiscernibly, despite their yelling and their steadiest efforts, giving ground.

What was most extraordinary was the silence of this crowd moving forward like a huge bulldozer. Twenty thousand human beings reacting like a bunch of sheep. They merged into one, hallucinated, sweating in the heat that lingered despite the setting sun. Centimeter by centimeter, the teeming mobs of would-be eyewitnesses to terrorism in action succeeded in setting foot on Kusoczinskidamm, like a cowcatcher driving back the double chain of police, drenched in sweat and anger. And as the day waned, the mob waxed.

There came a series of whistles. The two lines of cops suddenly broke. The blue-gray uniforms jumped back. There was a brief hesitation in the shapeless human mass of apparent sleepwalkers. The voiceless mass could be seen swaying where it stood, rolling, despite its compactness: it wanted to move forward, but its carcasses guessed what was going to happen. Half a thousand other policemen now ran up, elbow to elbow, swinging long black nightsticks. They reached the first row of the mob and, without reaching back and swinging, gave light taps on the solidly packed shoulders. Nothing gave. The nightsticks went down and started to hit at legs, still restrainedly. Tens of officers had their whistles in their mouths. They all started to whistle as loud as they could. The nightsticks started to beat on chests. The bullhorns announced the police were getting ready to make an all-out charge. The enunciated words came out like a bark. At that moment, like a rotten fabric that suddenly gives way all along its length, the entire human mob about-faced, and dispersal slowly, regretfully began.

Until the dark of night, a great many people remained outside the besieged Village.

6:15 PM: The Israeli Government's reaction to the terrorists' sudden decision to take their hostages to an Arab country without further delay was brought to the *Krisenstab* by Ambassador Ben Horin. Prime Minister Golda Meir was still personally handling the Connollystrasse incident. In this, she was being assisted by a restricted council that included at all times some or all of the following: Deputy Prime Minister Yigal Allon, Minister of Defense Moshe Dayan, Minister of Transportation Shimon Peres, and General Aaron Yariv (until he emplaned). What Jerusalem said was:

> The Government of Israel in no way modifies its decision not to release any of the political prisoners it is holding. This position is irreversible. Concerning the eventual transfer of the Israeli hostages to Cairo, the Government of Israel would like a reply to the following questions:
> 1. Has the German Federal Republic or has it not received clear assurances from the Government of Egypt on two points: *a*) Will Egypt undertake to insure the safety of the hostages from the moment the plane lands? *b*) Is Egypt ready to send the hos-

tages out of its territory immediately, so they may return to Israel under proper conditions of safety?

2. Will transportation from Munich to Cairo be in a German plane?

3. Will the hostages be accompanied until their return to Israel by a high official German personality who will assume in the name of Germany the responsibility for their fate?

If the answers to all of these questions are positive, and if the German Federal Republic asserts that it is in position to neutralize the terrorists in case the latter should try during the flight to make the transport plane veer off toward another Arab country, the Government of Israel would not go on record as being opposed to the eventuality of such a transfer.

Mr. Ben Horin added that he was ready to transmit forthwith to Jerusalem the G.F.R.'s answer to the message. Chancellor Willy Brandt was very disappointed by the inflexibility of the Israeli position. However, contrary to what has been published about it, the German *Bundeskanzler* never brought any pressure to bear on his Israeli opposite-number to try to get Jerusalem to soften its stand. In her September 12 declaration to the Knesset, Mrs. Golda Meir said, "Neither the German Government, nor any political authority, asked the Government of Israel at any time during the events of Munich to submit to the demands of the Munich terrorists and free the Arab terrorists imprisoned in Israel."

This is only technically exact. There were many indirect pressures to try to get Israel to release at least part of the prisoners demanded by the fedayeen in Munich. The heads of the crisis staff, namely Herren Genscher and Merk, said to Ben Horin: "If your Government maintains its intransigence, if it refuses to make a gesture, however slight, that might help the terrorists not to lose face, we run the risk of seeing the whole tragedy played out."

Dr. Manfred Schreiber went much more brutally to the point: "Since Israel totally rejected the terrorists' demands, the hostages are as good as dead."

Willy Brandt himself, at least twice, once at about 4:00 PM, and again at about 9:00 PM, asked Mr. Ben Horin to plead with Jerusalem to make a gesture. The Chancellor reminded the ambassador of the attitude of the late Prime Minister Levi Eshkol, when, on

The Last Deadline

July 23, 1968, a commando of terrorists skyjacked an El Al plane en route from Rome to Tel Aviv: he negotiated, secretly. Some fedayeen were released. The hostages and the plane, long held at Algiers, were returned to Israel.

But both of these initiatives of Brandt's were made privately, through third parties. It is to be noted that in her October 16, 1972, speech to the Knesset, covering the general outline of the Pinhas Koppel Report, Mrs. Meir lauded the firmness of Chancellor Brandt, for, after all, it was he who finally made the decision not to give in to the fedayeen. "We must consider it," she said, "to be a positive act of great value when any government decides not to give in to anti-Israeli and anti-Jewish terrorist violence perpetrated on its territory. Even the failure of the operation at Fürstenfeldbruck does not alter the scope of our positive appreciation."

6:15 PM (Diary): What is this handsome twelve-year-old, so lively and delicate, his big eyes like two pearls in an angelic face, doing in the Plaza of the poor old Village? He is the son of the Samaranches, the Little Lord Fauntleroy of the IOC. With his Instamatic slung over his shoulder, he is lithely wandering among the painted pipes and the tea and Ovaltine stands.

¡Buenas tardes, caballero! ¿Qué tal? A shadow passes over his even skin, and under the dark bangs coming down to his eyebrows, I have the feeling he is creasing his forehead.

The child of Spain answers courteously and then, no longer able to refrain from passing judgment on criminal adult madness: "People feel just fine, out for a stroll. And over there, right next door, misfortune is rising, and it seems nobody can do anything about it. Can you imagine that, sir? Right in the Olympic Village!"

He says "Olympic" in a tone that implies sacrilege, and I realize once again that children grasp events as much by reflection as by instinct.

Usually, the son of the famous Barcelona industrialist wears an unbelievable collection of insignia and Olympic shields. His armada runs all along the seams of his trousers and like a striking bouquet invades the breast of his jacket. But this afternoon there is nothing but the obligatory identification badge on his elegant brown suit, that looks formal as a result.

"I'm here because I went out with Mother. She's supposed to

meet me in the Plaza. I don't know why I brought my camera. I don't want to take any pictures."

6:25 PM (Diary): The TV has just shown the finish of the sixth Flying Dutchman race live. Among the last to start, the Israeli crew came in at about 6:10. One of the crew members, Yitzhak Nir, is huge, athletic, with a long neck. Beside him, his teammate looks rather small. They came on camera, but did not say a word; tragedy was written all over their faces. They must have understood at once on seeing the expression of their delegation official awaiting them on the dock. Had they hoped that by the time they got back the hostages would be free? Asked by a TV newsman, neither they nor Mr. Friedlander replied. Big Nir just shook his head despondently. Friedlander seemed to be crying.

The reporter points out that all the events scheduled for this day at Kiel are to take place, for the arrangements involved are too complicated to allow their postponement.

Anyway there has been plenty to keep the crowds excited at Munich this afternoon, even after the solemn 3:51 PM announcement that the Games would be suspended. The suspension was planned for the end of the afternoon, that is, about 6:00 PM, for reasons that, as we have seen, made sense to Dr. Schreiber.

For instance, the hall was chock-full and frenzied, on Siegenburgerstrasse, for the basketball game between West Germany and Australia. It was nip-and-tuck until 6:08:20 PM, when the end of the game was called, not by a whistle, which is no longer done, but by two strange trumpet blasts, long, sad, and loud. West Germany lost by one point, 70 to 69. The faces of the Germans seen exiting on TV were something to watch: poignant consternation. On the other hand, the Aussies' fans were delirious! They rushed down and embraced the winners, especially the other Australian athletes, who had come in their green-and-lemon sweat suits to cheer their buddies on, between training sessions of their own. Then, all at once, they seemed to get over their happiness: they turned serious again.

I bump into Daniel Mortureux, who had been a shock officer in Indochina. "What do you think?" I ask.

"When faced with killers, you either attack or give in." /

6:30 PM: Out at Fürstenfeldbruck, twenty members of the police

230

assault group had been disguised as employees of the military air-field of Lufthansa. Some were wearing blue overalls, others gray-blue fireproof coveralls, and still others the uniforms of flying personnel or airport hands.

What an expression of pain and contempt, what dignity holding back tears, what fits of powerless rage, could be read on the faces of the Israelis all during this day of September 5!

In the administration building, Shmuel Lalkin, the head of the Israeli delegation, had been given a third-floor office, along with Herr Werner Nachmann, President of the Central Council of German Jews, previously mentioned. It was next to the big conference room in which Messrs. Brundage, Daume, Tröger, and Vogel were to meet.

Starting at midmorning, Lalkin was in frequent phone contact with Jerusalem. Of course he remained in touch with the Israeli ambassador to Bonn, Mr. Ben Horin, whose office was on the opposite side of the corridor. Frequently, until the three helicopters left for Fürstenfeldbruck, Lalkin went back as close as he could get to Block 31. He looked with hatred at long skinny Tony with his stooped shoulders, tiny febrile Salah, and especially Issa, the civil engineer, so full of nervous solemnity beneath his beach hat, prissy as a fashion plate, and short, but so thin and straight that he seemed taller.

Lalkin did not stop urging the Germans to invade Apt. 1 without delay, or to send in nonfatal neutralizing gas through the air-conditioning ducts. "The longer you negotiate," he kept saying, "the more important they feel, and the tougher they get. When they feel they're weakening, it'll be a massacre. I don't see how this can last over twenty-four hours: it will have to be settled either by force or by the deaths of our people."

"What do you expect us to do?" Dr. Merk finally asked. "Send our men in with orders to shoot only at sight and only on the terrorists? It would be suicide. Those people have a whole arsenal. The only way to get in would be in a torrent of overwhelming firepower. We would have to break in through both ground-floor entrances, the one on the garden and the one on Connollystrasse. Other elements would swoop in to the second floor through the balconies, coming down from the roof. The attack would have to be covered by an intense, sustained, and systematic curtain of machine-gun fire. Can you imagine what state your hostages would be in after a couple of minutes of that?"

Lalkin kept at it: "Some of our people may die, but others will be saved. Whereas your parleying will end up by having them all killed."

One statement particularly made Lalkin furious, as he said: "German TV and press lied in saying that anti-terrorist specialists arrived from Israel during the day of September 5 to help set up the measures to be taken in the Village and at Fürstenfeldbruck. The Germans handled the whole matter entirely by themselves. They asked everybody's opinion, but in the final analysis, from beginning to end, they did just as they pleased."

After it was all over, Mrs. Golda Meir also several times reiterated officially, as clearly and as heavily as possible, that no Israeli had had the least share in any of the decisions made during the twenty hours of the Munich tragedy. Several papers, on the basis of "information" received from the offices of Herren Schreiber and Genscher, had, for instance, asserted that Shimon Peres (at the time, the Israeli Cabinet minister in charge of liaison with the secret services) had arrived at Olympic Village during the afternoon. This was absolutely untrue.

I have already quoted Mrs. Meir's very clear statements about Israel's noninterference with the decisions made by the Germans to try to save the hostages. Here is another quotation from the Prime Minister's speech to the Knesset on Monday, October 16, 1972:

> The Israeli Government never had any opportunity to use its forces or its experience in liberating our dear brothers, and this was true from one end to the other of the awful events that took place at the Olympic Village and the airfield. The Germans alone were responsible for the preparation as well as the execution of the operations they carried out, they alone made all the decisions, and never asked the approval of any Israeli representative.

As early as September 7 (and I was not the only one), I had in my hands a non-exhaustive list of key members of Rasd (El Fatah's secret service). It was shortly published in *Quick*.

This was a calculated leak, engineered by Bonn's intelligence.

It was a list dating back to the end of July, and gave "the list of cadres of the secret organization Rasd, of which Black September is a terrorist section. Rasd is part of El Fatah."

Quick, let us say, "interpreted" the cryptic notes of the federal intelligence service, by inserting for instance above "Group B": *Fuehrer der Ermordungstruppen* (Leader of the Murder Units). But it was an excellent job of journalism, with a profusion of details about the true or assumed identities of the gentlemen in question. The list gave, as commander-in-chief of Rasd, Mahmud Abbas. It so happens that Salah Khalaf, known as Abu Ayad, current No. 1 man in Rasd, did use the pseudonym of Mahmud Abbas when he first set up in Libya in the days of Idris I.

The other names were known: Sayyid Hamadallah, "the Child of Gaza," Khaled Ali Hassan Salamah, and so on. All of them, being important in El Fatah, were or are high up in Rasd.

What the German intelligence service was trying to show, by leaking this document, was that it had long known the measures that El Fatah, through Rasd and its terrorist branch Black September, had aimed at the Games. At the end of July, it had given the Bavarians an approximate list of the key men in Rasd. They had annotated the names of these *caïds* with "Killer," "Highly dangerous," and stressed the multiplicity of fake passports, assumed names, and covers. In this way, it thought, it had alerted its Bavarian counterparts, so that they might keep tabs on the Arabs present around Munich.

This time it was the fedayeen who summoned (the term is not too strong) the crisis staff to meet with them.

"Is the plane ready?" Issa barked, chewing on an American cigarette.

His hands trembled from time to time. The principal member on the other side, Dr. Merk, answered coldly: "We are doing everything we can to see to it. But it is technically impossible before eight PM to get our hands on a long-range plane in flying condition with an adequate crew."

Thereupon, Merk "revealed" to the Black September man that one of the unsolved problems so far was getting a crew of volunteers.

"Come on! Your army has enough qualified pilots!"

"The heads of the Luftwaffe," the Bavarian minister replied in a tone of regret, "would never permit one of their planes to be taken over by hostile elements, and foreign to boot. No army, no military leader in the world would agree to being so humiliated. Besides, our hands are tied by the federal constitution and the military code: no soldier can place himself under the orders of a person of foreign nationality without committing high treason."

What Dr. Merk was saying about the strictures of German laws concerning the use of the army was to be frightfully confirmed that very night. Herr Brandt offered the Government of Bavaria the loan of some federal sharpshooters, but Munich refused, on the grounds that in time of peace federal soldiers are forbidden from firing at civilians unless the latter are attacking military installations or the army itself. This Bavarian interpretation was moot, since in fact Fürstenfeldbruck was a military airfield and the fedayeen were acting as enemies there. The real fact is that the Bavarian police believed, until it was too late, that its own marksmen would be sufficient in number and quality. States' rights here came into play as well as interservice jealousy.

Issa's threats and imprecations were now heard for the last time. Tony started to yell even louder than he until Issa ordered him to stop.

"Have the Israelis given your Government any answer on our demands for the Arab patriots they are holding?" Tony then asked, soothingly.

"We must admit they have not. The Federal Chancellor himself has just asked them for one again. We are as surprised as you . . ."

"Every radio station in Europe is saying you got that answer a long time ago, and it was negative."

"There is absolutely no basis for such allegations, for the Israeli Government is still discussing the matter, and has made no statement. I can give you my word on that."

True, the radio stations had merely been broadcasting probabilities, stressing that no one could know for sure.

"Listen!" Genscher cut in. "You can kill all of us right here, but that won't alter matters any: we need two hours to make ready for your flight."

There was a long aside between Issa, Tony, and another fedayee

234

who remained out of sight inside the door. The safari outfit came back to say that his friends and he were agreeing to a final postponement of two hours more.

"It will be better for you," he said, "if you understand we will not go any further. We have been at this since last night. We are afraid that we will get tired and lose some of our effectiveness. So, watch out: if we find we are exhausted, even if it means our lives, all the hostages will be killed. Don't try to stall any longer."

So, the deadline now was 9:00 PM. This time, Ministers Merk and Genscher were convinced the Black September contingent would agree to no new "delay."

The fedayeen of course knew before they started that the contretemps would be many: that is the rule in this kind of thing. And they were ready for them. But the tension of the motionless waiting, the arguments, the incessant watchfulness, were beginning to tell, more than they had anticipated. They kept trying to foresee all the possible traps ahead.

After having agreed to 9:00 PM, Issa now lost his temper again when he saw *Krisenstab* people getting ready to leave.

"I have something to tell you!" he yelled. And went on to explain that his comrades and he intended to go to the airfield not by helicopter but by bus. "We need two large buses. They can pick us up near the metal door to Thirty-one" (that being, we may remember, the door leading from the underground to the lobby of Apt. 1).

Merk and Genscher, after staying away for a few minutes (to give the impression they were considering the fedayeen's new wish), returned to say that was utterly impossible.

"The whole population is furious at you," Merk said. "We could in no way insure the safety of the hostages. For, what would you do, if you were attacked and the vehicle stopped in its tracks? Besides, you can't imagine the traffic jams in Munich and throughout the area, tonight. Your actions have helped upset everything. There are over a million people in the streets. We'd be going along at five kilometers [three miles] an hour, and before we got there it would be a bloodbath."

"But from here to Riem is only eight kilometers. With motorcops to clear the way, we ought to be able to get through."

"The people would knock the motorcycles over and try to lynch you. The atmosphere is revolutionary. Besides, we don't feel we can let you take off from Riem."

Merk then explained the "extraordinary traffic jam-up" at Riem, and the presence there of mobs equally determined to do whatever they could to foil the fedayeen. And he and Genscher for the first time mentioned Fürstenfeldbruck, describing it as the only airfield from which they could take off without interference.

The real reason that made the fedayeen want to get away from their stronghold at 31 Connollystrasse as soon as possible became apparent when Issa and Tony so quickly agreed to Fürstenfeldbruck. They did not even look into its ramifications, did not ask for a map of the area, or any details about the air base.

They wanted to get this thing over: they were afraid their nerves were wearing thin. They felt their control of the situation dwindling hour by hour. The negotiators could see they were getting more and more nervous, irritable, and edgy. It seemed that they must be bucking themselves up with pills.

The question will always remain whether, all things considered, it would not have been preferable not to let them get away from Block 31, even if the ambush at the airfield had been set up the way it should have been.

There was Yacov Springer, fifty-two years old, phys. ed. teacher at Bat Yam high school, south of Jaffa.

The only Israeli weight-lifting judge in the international A category, he was at Munich in that capacity. He was refereeing his fourth Olympic Games.

He was born in the Warsaw ghetto, and from childhood had had to be able to fight like a wolf.

He was the son of petty craftsmen. He had guts. His energetic bursts of laughter underlined the zigzagging wrinkles across his tanned face with the protruding ears and underslung chin. His nose, broken several times and reset, was impetuous. He had a real fighter's look, beneath the highly receding hairline.

He had gotten into the Jewish Resistance early. He had been in the Warsaw Ghetto uprising, and was one of its miraculous survivors. He had blown up an armored vehicle in Muranowski

236

Square, by bolting up the side of the armor and tossing a grenade into the turret. He was one of the last holdouts of Mila Street, spending a week down in the sewers getting away.

Strangely, for a militant Zionist of the dark years, once the war was over he willingly stayed on in Poland: perhaps he saw it only as a waystation.

Among this author's closest companions during wartime deportation, there were some Poles. A people full of dash and heart, with a dramatic and courage-marked history, they were never very fond of Jews, let's admit it. That is why Yacov Springer pulled off something quite unusual in the popularity he gained after 1945. He had wasted too many years, undergone too many ordeals and deprivations to become the kind of champion he might have been. But he nevertheless won the Polish weight-lifting championship, and represented that country in London at the 1948 Olympics. Indefatigable, with his brimming energy, he took up amateur boxing, and quickly cut a swath through welterweight ranks, twice qualifying as finalist for the championship of Poland. But his vocation was coaching and organizing, and there he ran into insurmountable prejudice.

He arrived in Israel in 1957, with his wife and two children. At the beginning, he did a bit of everything, including long military stints, even though he was past thirty-four when he got there. Weight lifting was in an embryonic stage in Israel at the time. Springer brought it to life. He wheedled a little space in gymnasiums, imported old secondhand equipment from West European clubs, hounded the newspapers to get them to cover the events.

On June 5, 1967, past military age, he hitched a ride on a jeep of reserve members heading for a motorized-infantry unit in Judea, on the east flank of Jerusalem. He was finally given a uniform and carbine, for it was all too obvious how expert he was. And in this guise he fought as a private in the reconquest of the Old City.

The murder of Yacov Springer revealed the extent of his influence. Everything in Bat Yam shut down completely, at 2:00 PM on September 6. The mayor and city council, followed by seven hundred high-school students, paraded across the town, behind the furled flags. They stopped before the Springers' home. The whole town was assembled there on the sidewalk. The day of the funeral, there was an innumerable, silent, meditative crowd. Shoshana, Yacov's daughter, had come in from the Sinai, where she was doing her military service. She was truly a vision of haughty beauty. The son, Alex, just gritted his teeth.

XV
"FIVE TERRORISTS, AT MOST!"

> Remember then thy Creator in the days
>   of thy youth,
> Before the evil days come . . .
> *Ecclesiastes* 12:1

FÜRSTENFELDBRUCK! I'VE WRITTEN THE NAME OFTEN NOW, BUT I must tell about it. Those four syllables will not be soon forgotten.

It is so easy to get to, by road: 26 km. (15-plus mi.) west of Marienplatz, the center of Munich. You leave the Bavarian capital by Landsberger Strasse, which changes its name to Bodensee Strasse as it goes through the residential Pasing quarter.

You follow Federal Highway 12, as it winds toward the Boden-see, Lake Constance to you, but not far, for after 5 or 6 km. there is a fork in the road. Go off to the right, toward Augsburg, on Highway 2. It curves gracefully, to accommodate slight bends in direction, and after the small town of Puchheim, it is countryside. Milch cows own the prairies. Truck gardens rub elbows with hop-fields. Silver poplars and oaks in the hollows, beeches and firs on the crests, make up deep woods full of game. Coming out of a turn, you see the first houses of Fürstenfeldbruck. You cross the fast-running Amper. The city of 16,000 then begins to grow, com-bining the Tudor-style paneled houses with middle-income hous-ing projects, and well-to-do villas brightened by flowerpots, Virginia creeper, the green or red of the shutters, and the white curtains of the tall windows.

After Fürstenfeldbruck, you turn away from Augsburg, on to a secondary road to the right, a gray strip in the green-and-black setting of wooded hills, pastures, and ponds. That leads toward Maisach, Einsbach, and points north, through huge twists.

Some 5 km. farther, the air base looms on the right, with its fences, its control tower, and a few buildings. It is unobtrusive, but enormous. Since, outside the airfield proper, it is dotted with copses and green fields, that follow the accidents of terrain, it takes patient girdling to appreciate its size: perhaps 6 sq. km. (some 2⅓ sq. mi.). Its barracks buildings, mostly long and low, sometimes look like farmhouses. The underground facilities are also supposed to be extensive. The base was reconditioned by the Americans at the start of the cold war, and they gave it the works.

You have to be at some height to see the runway used by the super-Boeings. Farther along, there is the town of Maisach, that starts just the other side of the airfield enclosure, and then a river also called Maisach, that flows into the Amper—at Dachau.

Yes, Dachau, just 19 km. (12-minus mi.) northeast of Fürstenfeldbruck, with its idyllic charm and its *Konzentrationslager*. I know it is facile—and not too fair—to point to the hell of the Nazi death camps as significant in relation to the Israeli athletes massacred during the Munich Games. Well, memories cannot be erased. I know that Munich was also the founding-place of the White Rose, the heroic network of German students and teachers who tried to organize an effective Resistance against Hitlerism. The leaders of *die weisse Rose*, Professor Kurt Huber, Sophie Scholl and her brother Hans, along with a still-unknown number of their friends, were executed in the Munich prison in 1943. They were admirable—if all too few.

That is the décor of the peaceful region in which Fürstenfeldbruck had so long stood. It is classical Bavaria, with its moors and forests, its *Lederhosen,* and the silver-pated blue of the Alpine crests, on a clear day. Its people had been so quiet! No one even dredged up the nasty old tales of Hitler horrors any more. But they would not soon forget the Games!

6:35 PM: The live telecast of the Denmark-Morocco soccer game from Passau was ending. Denmark was ahead. It had been 6:09 at Augsburg when the Poland-USSR match ended in the surprising Polish victory. At Ingoldstadt, the G.D.R. (East Germany) in three minutes would conclude its 7–0 trimming of Mexico. So, three of the four scheduled games in the second round of Olympic soccer did take place this afternoon.

240

"Five Terrorists, at Most!"

The scheduled canoe and kayak events all took place this day; the last one at 12:37. Now there was another Poland-USSR encounter on the TV, this one in volleyball. It was in its fifth set. Brief interruption of the rebroadcast: the announcer informed viewers that the men's individual épée semifinals had concluded at 6:40. The finals in the event, originally scheduled for tonight, had been postponed until tomorrow.

All day long, the TV and radio were never turned off in Apt. 1. The shouts of the nearby crowds easily reached the bloody room on the second floor: so the hostages in Block 31 knew that the Olympic celebration was going full speed ahead.

But, let's not overdo it. Even before the official proclamation of postponement, some events were canceled: the Grand Prix Dressage did not resume at 2:00 PM. The third preliminary matches of boxing, scheduled for 1:00, were canceled, although the West German Magazine, *Sport Illustrierte,* contradicting the official records of Munich results, stated that after 3:45 at least two fights had been held, both won by West German champions: heavyweight Peter Hussing knocking out the Peruvian Oscar Ludena in the first round and in the light-middleweights Dieter Kottysch by decision over the Tunisian Mohammed Majeri. In weight lifting, the super-heavyweight contest, due to start at 1:00 PM, had also been postponed until tomorrow. But it could be noted that certain events were going on beyond the 6:00 PM cutoff.

This was not the case for the Greco-Roman wrestling eliminations, scheduled to start at 7:00 PM, in the heavier categories. The "small weights" had competed, as scheduled, in the morning. But this evening was just when Israel's one big hope, Mark Slavin, was to make his international Greco-Roman debut, in the 74 kg. (163 lbs.) category. He was the one, it will be recalled, who as recently as last May 2–3, was still demonstrating with his Jewish comrades outside the KGB HQ in Minsk. He was in the first row, and there is a picture showing him waving a sign that reads: "Freedom for Jews to leave!" He did leave, and now he was bound hand and foot, tied to his fellows, gazing at the corpse of Yossef Romano, riddled with holes, emptied of life.

6:48 PM: When Herr Genscher visited the Israeli hostages he had been able to hear the cheers from the stadia, distantly.

The *Volleyballhalle* was only 100-odd meters from Block 31.

241

It was full for the Poland-USSR match: 3,708 paid attendance, with some 309 complimentaries, to overtax the 4,000 capacity. The Soviet Union had won the gold medal in 1968. The two teams— all outsize, as in basketball—had had to go five sets, the last ending 15–13 for the Russians, after a fierce struggle, with opposing hands slugging it out over the net, miraculous recoveries, and wild jumps to get at the white ball.

Yells, applause, whistles, and group cheers of fans surrounding the white-eagled Polish banners or the little Red flags could easily be heard in the East Germans' pyramidal building. So the Israelis also to an extent, behind the drawn raw-silk curtains of their prison-apartment, could hear the partisan outbursts.

The hostages must have wondered why the celebration—their celebration—still went on.

It was 6:47 when the team in the red jerseys with the gold splashes of hammer-and-sickle emblems scored the winning point on a cannonball smash. The place went wild with yelling, clapping, and stamping of feet.

I was in the Plaza, where the fountains' running waters take on precious silver shimmers in the twilight. I was not the only one who saw the two athletes whom I might identify much more closely (others have), a New Zealand field athlete and, let us say, a Balkan, waving rolls of film. "There are terrific shots of the terrorists in here! On the balcony, and in the street! I got the guy in the white hat with the cocked grenade in his hand. Live color! Fifty bucks!"

6:55 PM: All together, the lights in Apt. 1 went on, on both floors. The fedayeen wanted to make it appear they were all over the place. Evening brought some slight shadows.

"This is an awful night that's beginning. It may clear up for us, but what a wait!" said Dan Schillon, head of the Israeli TV sports service, near me.

The Games of Joy, and now this nightmare. Would the night do away with the crowds? Were they surrounding the Village, or was the Village holding them, hypnotizing them, with its big concrete towers like snarling shark's teeth?

7:00 PM: The Executive Board of the IOC was in special session in the Vierjahreszeiten Hotel. Unusual circumstances, obviously; unusual place, Suite 410, occupied by M. and Mme. Jean de

Beaumont. More unusual still: it was not called by the IOC President, but by eight of the other members.

Avery Brundage had been confronted with the accomplished fact and invited to come to the meeting. It had taken perseverance and long efforts for these eight to get together, no small thanks to Señor Samaranch. They were: Lord Killanin (Ireland), First Vice-President, Count Jean de Beaumont (France), Second Vice-President, Jonkheer Herman A. van Karnebeek (Netherlands), Third Vice-President, and Sir Ade Amola (Nigeria), Constantin Andrianov (USSR), Major Sylvio de Magalhaes Padilha (Brazil), Juan Antonio Samaranch (Spain), and Prince Tsuneyoshi Takeda (Japan).

They were tense and grave. They had been meeting for half an hour when President Brundage joined them. Since it was an ultrasecret meeting, we will not try to say what went on.

But the specialized press would know a few hours later. For the Executive Board voted to call together the full IOC in a special meeting at 10:00 PM. Following this plenary session, despite Brundage's appeals for absolute secrecy, a certain number of members were surrounded, tugged at, pressed, harassed, and finally overcome, by world press representatives who had been watching for them in the lobby of the hotel or its large public sitting room for the past two hours. That was when word leaked about what had gone on between 7:00 and 8:10 PM in the Beaumonts' suite.

The Executive Board, it transpired, unanimously (except for Mr. President) felt the IOC should have kept hands off the Connollystrasse events. They were none of their affair. They were the province of the Organizing Committee and the German authorities. Therefore, the Board expressed regret that President Brundage had deemed it proper to spend the day in the Village administration building, and especially agreed to sit on the crisis staff as an IOC representative. This had already been Lord Killanin's opinion when he was caught short in Kiel. He made no bones about reaffirming it in Suite 410.

The Board endorsed the idea of a commemorative service to be held the next morning at 10:00 in the *Olympiastadion*, as proposed by Messrs. Brundage and Daume. Finally, it unanimously felt that, come what might, the Games must go on.

The minute the meeting ended, there was a mad dash to alert

the other IOC members before the time of the special plenum, also to be held at the Hotel.

All these high athletic officials had a great deal of dignity, sadness, and worry, but also a determination that might have surprised their critics. On the main point, i.e., the supremacy of the Olympic Movement, they were of one mind. To them no matter how awful the events of Connollystrasse, however bloody their outcome, the first duty was not to give in to crime and horror. The Olympic Games had to come through the tragedy showing that the ideal they embodied was insuperable. The greatest cowardice, the unpardonable sin, would have been to cancel them.

And in all of this, the role of Lord Killanin, while hidden, was capital. Without him, to what extent would the IOC have been compromised, and in what ways?

It was through the President-elect's control of himself in public that the 4,200 newsmen covering the Olympics-now-turned-tragic came to know him. Lord Killanin speaks very well; but he can also be eloquently silent: his broad, large frame powerfully set before you, he looks at you with his blue eyes (shading toward Irish green), and the look says all there is to say, between the puffs of the pipe.

Michael Morris, son of an old Irish Catholic family, was born in Galway, on green Erin's west coast, July 30, 1914. In 1927, he inherited his uncle's title, to become third Lord Killanin. Now he had been elected to an eight-year term at the head of the IOC; eight unusual years for him, and decisive ones for the Olympic Movement. To get there, Lord Killanin, in his powerful stride, had covered a long hurdle-strewn road, the only one that could lead to the summit of this new Olympus.

In 1950, he had been elected President of the Irish Olympic Committee, and remained that until his new elevation. In 1952, he was elected to the IOC, at age thirty-eight, relatively very young, thus indicating the range of influence, organizational ability, and friendships of Lord Killanin. In 1967, he became a member of the Executive Board and head of its Press and Public Relations Committee; the next year, he was a vice-president.

Very popular and supported by many of his colleagues, Lord Killanin had been a clear favorite in the race to be Brundage's successor. The well-unified body of Anglo-Saxons were for him. He was threatened in the last straightaway by the spirited burst of Count Jean de Beaumont, who had the South American votes, among others. But English-speaking Africa and the Eastern bloc tipped the scales in favor of His Lordship.

Schooled at Eton and then Cambridge's Magdelene College, which in themselves bespeak his patrician origins, Lord Killanin took an M.A. and then went to the Sorbonne for advanced French literary courses; so he was naturally completely fluent in French.

He soon became an adventurous newsman, for the *Daily Express* and the *Daily Mail.* As a war correspondent in China, he covered the Chiang Kai-shek campaigns of 1937–38, when Communists and Kuomintang were both fighting against Japanese aggression.

From the start of World War II, he enlisted in the British Army, even though Eire remained neutral: out of loyalty. His father had died at the front during World War I as a colonel in the Irish Guards and is buried in France at Villers-Cotterets. Lord Killanin fought throughout the war, landing in Normandy as a major; he earned numerous decorations, including the prestigious Order of the British Empire.

After the war, he returned to writing. Two of his books, *Four Days,* and *The Shell Guide to Ireland* in collaboration with Prof. M. V. Duignan, were big sellers. He is a member of the Royal Irish Academy and, a great film buff and friend of the late John Ford, he also produced several movies.

A member of Lloyd's of London, he was on various other boards of directors, including Shell and BP oils, and Bovril. Yet, as against the stereotype of the IOC member, he is without personal fortune. When Lord Killanin says "I have to earn my living," he means just that.

In the harmonious Irish capital of Dublin, Lord Killanin and his spouse, née Mary Sheila Dunlop, live in a roomy but unostentatious red-brick house at 30 Lansdowne Road. It seems to be anywhere but in the heart of a great city, surrounded with trees and greenery, with a round blue pocket-size swimming pool in the garden, that reflects whatever sun there may be.

The new headman of the IOC is humorous, hard-working,

willful, and straightforward. He looks you right in the eye, and speaks his mind. The Killanins are a very close-knit family; and, fortunately for him as a family man, Lausanne is not too far from Dublin.

Lord and Lady Killanin have four children: Redmond Morris, currently an assistant film director; Michael Morris, probably the best gentleman-rider in Ireland, following a family tradition once upheld by a much slimmer Lord Killanin himself; John Morris, a photographer; and daughter Deborah, who is married to Bill Bryden, a popular playwright, author of the successful *Willie Rough,* and director of Edinburgh's Lyceum Theatre.

Lord Killanin is an impressive man, large, massive and square-cut, some 220 pounds of flesh and muscle. His face is high in color, and broad as his body, and it is crowned by a heavy head of silvering hair; his forehead is striking in its expanse. He laughs clear and loud, between sideburns out of Dickens, and his straight nose is scarcely marked by the long years in which he excelled at amateur boxing.

Once more, Lord Killanin was being called on to fight for a noble cause that, though mortal perhaps, would rise Phoenix-like from its ashes. One thing was certain: the new President at the helm of the gigantic Olympic ship would be a forceful skipper, schooled to weathering storms.

7:05 PM *(Diary):* In the square of honor in the Village, the 123 flags of participating nations are at half-mast. Should I remark they might have been lowered sooner? It is so tempting to be critical, in these off-the-cuff notes! Having alternately been participant in events and professional witness, I know how easy it is, when drama is at hand, to wield a judge's pen. It reflects a good conscience and sounds fine. But the truth is that a few criminals swooped down on the Games like a cyclone. Are those responsible for the security of the great event supposed to anticipate even (and especially) things like cyclones? /

7:30 PM: One helicopter took off from the field behind G-1, on the Lerchenauerstrasse side. There are still three more on the greenswards, south of the big car park.

The helicopter that took off was a Bell UG-1D, better known as an Iroquois. I saw them by the thousands in Vietnam, being

246

used as light troop carriers and patrol planes. Two of them were set to take the Israeli hostages to their rendezvous with fate.

The Bell looks like a beetle with a dragonfly's tail. Its maximum weight is 3,900 kg. (8,600 lbs.), length 13 meters (about 43 ft.). They are very dependable, solid craft, used more and more frequently by commercial airlines for short passenger hops from cities to airports, or between airports.

The green-blue Iroquois had Minister Merk and Dr. Schreiber aboard, as well as two individuals whose names have been kept determinedly off the record, perhaps to make it seem they were members of Israeli special services, whereas none such was in Munich until an hour and three-quarters later.

It was headed for Fürstenfeldbruck. The crisis staff was still far from certain that the terrorists and their prisoners would ever reach that base, but they did not plan to be taken off guard: if fight there had to be, it would undoubtedly be at the air base.

On their arrival, they were greeted by Schreiber's faithful aide, Dr. Georg Wolf, *Chef der Münchner Schutzpolizei* (head of the Munich security police), and as such *Vice Polizeipräsident.*

Herr Wolf, at fifty-one, was in charge of the planned airfield operations to try to free the hostages. His two superiors had come to inspect. They were highly satisfied, and would remain so in spite of everything, as shown on pages 57–58 of the *Dokumentation,* which set forth the reasons this field was chosen as the circumscribed area of the projected action.

We saw earlier why the *Krisenstab* had felt that Fürstenfeldbruck was best, if one may use that term, for the showdown. In later weeks, Herren Merk and Schreiber would fill in reams of technical detail to support that view, namely:

1. The base was far enough away from the Olympic Village so that the flight of the two helicopters carrying the fedayeen and their hostages could be extended by almost ten minutes without the former smelling a rat. This would allow a chance, if necessary, as soon as the two whirlybirds had taken off, to send additional specialized forces in on the fourth Bell Iroquois. Moreover, the principal people in charge would have plenty of leeway to get to the base in time to take whatever new measures were required.

2. The Fürstenfeldbruck air base was isolated, surrounded by

countryside with truck farms, woods that were mainly fir, oak, and elm, many ponds, and dogs that in the dark would bark at any untoward steps nearby. Only at the north did the perimeter of the base come near a town, the outskirts of Maisach. But, even there, the closest things were farmlands, fields, and houses with gardens. So, an armed confrontation was most unlikely to hurt anyone unconnected with the action.

3. Like any self-respecting military air base, this one discourages outside curiosity by being enclosed in rugged terrain, with lines of trees and metal fences and gates. A proper cordon of relatively few troops would make it impossible for any enemies caught on the site to get out. On the field itself, the space between buildings allowed armored vehicles to come through without problem, and discreetly, to get as close to the action as possible. The control tower was ideally located. The sharpshooters set up to surround the fedayeen would have perfect conditions, both from the viewpoint of shooting angles and as far as convenience and safety of their positions were concerned. This set of circumstances gave the air base operational advantages that could not be equaled in the region.

Herr Wolf had the reputation of a daredevil. After what it is customary to call a distinguished war record, his fame as a crook-catcher had long been established.

Each sniping-point was checked. The general lines of any eventual confrontation were perfectly clear.

Herr Wolf had one more question (a telling one): "Are we sure there are no more than five terrorists?"

"Yes, ninety-nine and a half percent sure," his superior replied. "The testimony of the two employees who saw them jump the fence was very definite on that score. The telephotos, films, and what we and the Israelis have seen give us no reason to feel there are any more. Some even doubt whether there are more than four."

Later, in the *Dokumentation,* the Bavarian authorities would go on at length about how, even if the correct number of terrorists had been known, no changes would have been made in the arrangements.

7:40 PM: The Luxembourg track coach was talking to me about

248

the dead or captured Israelis; he knew them well. His people were quartered at 18 Connollystrasse, a little building nestled between the huge 20–24 (East Germany) and 14–16 (Hungary). No. 31 was right close by 18, slightly to the west, the other side of Connollystrasse.

"The actions of wild beasts," he kept saying.

He was a very tall, thin, dark fellow, with a strong loyal face. He was nervously biting at his mustache. He suggested I go to see Dr. René Burger, physician to the Luxembourg team, who had seen very interesting things during the day. The doctor was now up on Panoramic Hill among the army of photographers; he was talking to a group of athletes, telling them that a little while before he was a virtual prisoner in the East German building. The security service had decided to forbid anyone who was not part of the East German team to leave the building. Before this was rescinded, Dr. Burger had spent several hours on a balcony, looking down on what was going on over at the Israelis'.

"Around four-thirty," he said, "there was a time when the cops could have gotten rid of all the fedayeen in one stroke.

"Their leader, the guy in the safari outfit, was in front of the door talking to the blonde interpreter and some German VIPs, including Schreiber. A second fedayee was behind him, at the corner of the door. A third was outlined in the open door as in a shadow play, and since we could see him, the sharpshooters hidden across from 31 would have seen him even better. The fourth fedayee was framed in a second-story window. And there was a fifth, up on the third floor, in the Hong Kong quarters, leaning over the balcony and aiming his submachine gun at a German. Of course, a lot of cops disguised as athletes were in various excellent aiming-spots, with rifles that had telescopic sights. They had an easy bead on the terrorists. Five shots, and it all would have been over, without blinking an eyelid. Why didn't they shoot?"

Dr. Burger added that through an open window he had seen the hostages, "all blindfolded and with their hands tied . . ."

Back through the Village, where nothing had changed, yet everything was different, like the double of someone who has died.

Here came a fine giant of a fellow, Roberto Vezzani, the Italian weight-lifting champ whom I had met at such exhibitions in Paris. He had just competed in the heavyweight division in the Games. This category goes up to 110 kg. (242 lbs.). Beyond that, they're superheavyweights.

Vezzani's face radiated light and warmth.

"Some nightmare, eh, Roberto?"

"*Mamma mia!* What barbarians! The vipers that did that . . ."

His thick nostrils trembled, his hairy fists clenched.

"I was so happy coming home last night. I had finished fifth and broken seven Italian records. The other guys and I got in late; we're not so far from the Israelis. [The reader will remember that the Italians were near the head of Connollystrasse.] I didn't hear a thing. Then, this morning, when I went out to get the papers . . ."

He shook his head, bull-like, then went on somberly: "Did I ever know them, all of the weight lifters! We used to work out together often. Little Friedman: he wore a little chain around his neck, with a Star of David on it, and some Hebrew letters engraved. He said to me, 'That's my name.' And Romano, they called him the desert bombshell. And Berger, as wide as two wardrobes, and his eyes looked right inside you. And Springer was their coach. The Poles used to sneak looks at him, respectfully too, because he had been one of the real big ones once, competing for them. And out of the four, one is dead, and three are hostages. Who knows what'll happen to those three?"

Vezzani was staying there, waiting for news. He had his light-blue sweat suit on. He paced back and forth, beneath the lowered flags.

Then there came another weight lifter, a Frenchman, Pierre Gourrier. His event had been the day before yesterday. He came in tenth among the light-heavies, the same place he had made at Mexico City. His young wife had just come to join him in Munich. Both of them were overwhelmed tonight. He said, "I know, it's a funny thing, the athletes don't look like they're affected. But just the same, all day long, there have been continual crowds of us here waiting to get word. We talk about the Israelis, our friends, the two of them who were dead. I feel like I've been drained. If

"Five Terrorists, at Most!"

I had to compete now, I wouldn't be able to. The whole world seems to be collapsing, if there can't be Olympic peace. Maybe the Palestinian Arabs have good reasons to be unhappy. But to do something as monstrous as they did—even a wolf wouldn't stoop that low!"

Pierre Gourrier is a gracefully developed man, with even features beneath his dark brown hair, crew cut, out of fashion. Hand in hand, he and his wife went back, as close as possible to where the Israelis were.

I continued wandering, too. Back up the business street. The crowd was calm in the early evening, despite the startling armored vehicle at the horizon. Cops in uniform were walking around with assault rifles and submachine guns as if they were sporting equipment.

In a bright-blue sweat suit adorned with the navy-blue French rooster on a tricolor shield, here was the hockey player from Lyons, Christian Honneger, who had also been to Mexico City. Tanned, with light eyes, he looked like a Viking with his ash-blond hair and his reflective, close-mouthed appearance. I asked him about how the athletes were feeling, considering what was going on.

"Most of them," he said, "are not the kind who say much. Eighty percent feel it doesn't affect them and don't want to get involved. The rest, well, most of them are pro-Israeli now, the more so because they're so indignant and disgusted. But there's still a constant minority who are, if not for the terrorists, at least for what they stand for, as the saying goes. That includes all the Arabs, a lot of Blacks, and quite a few from the East.

"We're sure far away from the Mexico City spirit! There, there was still an Olympic idea. Here, in this concrete suburb, with so many of the guys pros masquerading as amateurs, there's an emptiness in the soul. I believe in the Olympic idea. But we'll have to do something about it. This attack could never have taken place in the Olympic Village, if the Games weren't on the verge of turning into a circus!"

A few steps farther, and there, sitting on the steps was Patrick Vial, the judoka, his chin on his fist, thinking. A fine square virile face, with a flattened bumpy nose; violently black brows and hair. Fortunately for him, Vial had finished his events, too: he got to

251

the quarterfinals in the welterweights, a fine performance. He was certainly not thinking about it now.

In a few simple, direct, heartfelt words, he told me his horror of what was happening. If one just looked at him, it seemed to me, he might have appeared closed in on himself, unconcerned with anything else. Just as one might take for insensitivity the attitudes of all these magnificently built young people, going back and forth in the temperate evening. Girls in sweat suits, tight-fitting ones, attracted many an eye, but almost impersonally.

"To come and ruin the Olympic Games! To come and kill athletes in Olympic Village," Patrick Vial was muttering.

7:50 PM: At a sign from the young policewoman, ever discreet and self-controlled, Herren Genscher, Tröger, and Vogel went toward the doorway to Apt. 1. Issa still had his dark glasses on, even though now the light was dying. He was fingering a cigarette, and was overprotected: two assault rifles a short distance away were watching over him.

"We came to discuss the travel conditions with you," Tröger began. "Here's our plan: leave Building 31 at nine PM. You go by helicopter to Fürstenfeldbruck. The Boeing 727 to take you to Cairo is scheduled to take off from there about nine forty-five."

This time, Issa wanted to know about the airport. He was told it specialized in charter flights and VIP specials, which was true so far as it went. Issa started to remonstrate and ask why they could not leave from Riem, and Herr Genscher cut him off by saying that under no circumstances would he allow German blood to be shed in this affair. And there would be the worst risks if the fedayeen went to Riem, what with the mobs of young Bavarians assembled there since late morning, ready to grab at the fedayeen with their bare hands to free the hostages. It was true: several thousands of boys and girls, some from Munich, some from the international youth camp or elsewhere, had indeed deployed around Riem, and seemed quite determined to free the hostages, even if it meant rushing out on the runways if the terrorists came to the airport by helicopter.

Issa accepted that. The lights inside Apt. 1 made the tan curtains radiant This twilight hour seemed to teem with traps. The mobilization of armed men was fantastic.

"Five Terrorists, at Most!"

"Has Israel replied?" Issa wanted to know.

"Not definitely yet. There are severe disagreements in Jerusalem. That is why we would think it wiser to delay your flight till tomorrow," Vogel replied. "There would be a lot more light on the matter, in every sense."

Everyone smiled. But Issa shook his head.

"Let me remind you: if we are not on our way at nine sharp, two of the Zionist hostages will be shot right here before this door, for starters." And he pointed to one of the gun muzzles sticking out of the entryway.

"Where will we get the two helicopters that will take us?"

"Behind the Village Administration Building. It's not far at all, maybe two hundred meters. You can walk there underground."

"I don't agree with that estimate of the distance. You could bring the helicopters much closer to here."

There was another argument, that Tröger won, because he had technical points on his side.

"Then, I'll go in and talk to my comrades about it, and then I can go right off for the reconnaissance."

"That's a new demand, this rehearsal walk," said Genscher. "The sharing of responsibilities in this matter is very strict among the German authorities. The safety of the captured athletes, and therefore yours too, comes under the crisis chief of staff, Herr Bruno Merk, and the Munich police chief, Dr. Schreiber. They hold all the keys to this problem. We can't walk through the Village without them. And they are at dinner right now. Since five this morning, they've had a long day of it, too."

The Arab engineer uttered some loud curses that echoed through the wide avenue full of held breaths and lurking shadows. The sharp tone of them rang with rage. His release was met with a great stone face by the federal minister. Issa was shouting that everybody was tired, that it only took two seconds to do away with nine captives, and he didn't believe a word "of this dinner-party fairy tale." Herr Tröger answered that, however that might be, there was no way to get in touch with them at dinner, and they surely would not be back until 8:45 or 8:50, since they thought everything was all set. They hadn't had a minute's rest, he added, and had to stay in shape "until you people get away."

"Don't try to give us any of that," Issa said. "We're as smart as you are. And we don't care any more about other people's deaths than we do about our own."

"You have nothing to fear if you stay in the Israelis' building," Mr. Genscher said. "No one will come after you there. But I have come to tell you in the name of the German Federal Republic that there is one condition before you can leave. You must promise that none of the German citizens who furnish your transportation from the Olympic Village until your final destination will be taken hostage, whatever happens. I have been instructed to get your word of honor, and that of all your associates, on this."

"No German will be held hostage. You have my word."

"The interpreter will translate my request to your bodyguard and the man in the doorway. Your three answers will serve as word of honor for the whole commando."

Issa started talking Arabic in a very loud voice. As soon as he finished, the young policewoman went over to get the replies of the two fedayeen, both agreeing without the slightest reservation.

The usual Salah was jiggling around behind Issa; Tony was the one in the doorway. The fedayeen had taken care that only those three show their bare faces. The others were always hidden under hoods or scarves. Of course, a close scrutiny of the film footage and the individual photographs would have revealed the peculiarities of each of them, and probably allowed an exact count to be made. But they would have had to be good pictures, and technicians would have needed time to collate them. That was never tried. We might add that the masked terrorists continually switched their disguises and their demeanors, even going so far as to pad their clothing at times. They wanted to make it seem as if they were much more numerous than they were: the result they achieved was just the opposite.

Just as the three Germans were about to leave, Herr Vogel asked about sending some food in to the hostages. Issa said OK.

8:00 PM: Epilogue to that business of the Tunis telephone number:

We have to go back to early afternoon. The fedayeen, as we saw, were quick to capitalize on the fact that there was a phone in their captives' quarters. Twice, they called a number in Tunis.

"Five Terrorists, at Most!"

The Tunisian ambassador to Bonn, H.E. Mahmoud Mestiri, was in Munich, and offered to be of any service he could. It was he who got the postponement of one of the deadlines, which the fedayeen had set at 3:00 PM.

The *Staatssekretär* (State Secretary—the top grade of West German career civil servants) for Foreign Affairs, Sigismund von Braun—brother of the legendary now-American Wernher von Braun, who pioneered the V2s and aimed at the stars—was instructed, at 2:00 PM, to ask Ambassador Mestiri to try to find out whose number that was in Tunis.

Von Braun, who had been West German ambassador to Paris in 1968–1970, had been detached to the crisis staff at G-1 early this morning by Herr Scheel, the Federal Minister of Foreign Affairs. The nobly built Baron Sigismund von Braun had a lot of dash and sported a courteous face with glasses over his blue eyes, a determined chin, silvery locks falling down on to the collar of his dark jacket, and he gave of himself without stint, if discreetly, during these twenty hours.

Ambassador Mestiri reacted strangely, although his personal good will was never questioned. "I see no way at all in which my Government could have the slightest influence over any Tunisian nationals who might be acting as fedayeen," he exclaimed, and politely refused thereafter to discuss the matter any further.

G-1 buzzed with wonder after that at what his Excellency had meant: Did he know that some of the Connollystrasse terrorists were Tunisians by birth or happenstance? Did he have any idea of who their contacts were in Tunis? Having spoken, he did agree to try to find who was at the number that so interested Issa and his crew. But, despite honest efforts, he never could.

Herr von Braun, on the other hand, from 2:15 on, tried to reach the West German ambassador at Tunis. He did not get through until 3:45, which gives an idea of the physical problems that stood in the way of each effort undertaken at this time when every moment counted. The German ambassador at Tunis, Dr. Heinz Naupert, decided to go straight to M. Hédi Nouira, Prime Minister in President Habib Bourguiba's Cabinet. It was only at 8:00 PM that Bonn's distinguished representative at Tunis was able to get back to Munich by phone and inform Von Braun: "The Prime

Minister of Tunisia informed me that the number called in Tunis by the Munich fedayeen belongs to a very honorable personality. I asked, 'Well, does this personality seem to you to be connected with the Palestinian Resistance? And if so would he be willing to intervene?' M. Nouira replied, 'It is impossible for us to put such a request to the personality in question.' "

Some might say, if the phone was lousy, use the telex. But the telex was terribly crowded. And besides, there are many remarks, nuances, personal impressions, opinions, that a diplomat abroad or a statesman in office might say on the phone, but would be reluctant to put in writing, even by teletype.

As it turned out, Tunis was bowing out, out of the picture.

8:00 PM *(Diary): Bundeskanzler* Willy Brandt is on TV, both networks. In color you can see he's pale. His manly features, which maturity has etched deep, now reveal the traces of the sadness and frustrations of this long day. The clear Nordic eye looks squarely at you, with the kind of sincere candor that has marked his life.

Perhaps what he has just said, in his velvet tone that can at times swell like the sea, may sound banal, with the passage of time. For the moment, his emotion is contagious and his expression of it gives stature to the drama:

". . . These were the Games of Peace and Joy. Then, this morning, Arab terrorists broke into Olympic Village, and they destroyed the whole thing.

"Our whole country now is in mourning. During all of this day, the directly concerned authorities and I have made every effort to free the hostages, in vain. We offered ransoms, safe-conducts for the attackers out of our territory. Important political leaders offered to become hostages themselves in the place of the Israeli athletes. None of our offers was accepted . . .

"We are in constant touch with the Israeli Government, as well as with the Organizing Committee, and the law-enforcement services. Obviously, one of the first questions is, Were adequate security measures taken at the Olympic Games? Inquiries are already under way to determine this. At any rate, against desperadoes, there is no real protection. Condolences are not enough. All civilized countries must combine to put an end to such acts. This is not only the affair of the Arab nations.

"The question was raised: Should the Olympic Games be canceled? I would not wish to infringe on the International Olympic Committee's domain. But my personal feeling is that we don't want attacks of this kind to snowball. And that is what would happen, from the moment an extremist organization was able to determine whether or not any given large-scale undertaking should be allowed to continue through to its end."

General feeling: The fate of the nine hostages still alive will determine the fate of the Munich Games.

For the families of Moshe Weinberg and Yossef Romano, the depths of horror have already been plumbed. Since the Games were not stopped because the two of them died and nine others were taken hostage, should they be canceled because four, or five, or six more are killed? What is the measure? How much does a human body weigh? So much per head?

It strikes me that Chancellor Brandt has just stated a reasonable judgment. To draw the curtain on the Games would mean giving terrorism an unhoped-for victory, and opening the floodgates to the worst kinds of blackmail. Surrender never pays. The Games versus the Connollystrasse fedayeen are equivalent to civilization against the barbarians.

Willy Brandt's storm-tossed face fades from the screen. It is a large head. His wrinkles are an adornment, as they are in the face of Joseph Kessel. The two men, indeed, have much in common./

The *Bundeskanzler* had a more-than-difficult part to play in this world-shaking affair. He was the head of a coalition regime of Socialists and liberals. The governing group in Bavaria belonged to Herr Franz-Josef Strauss' CSU; Christian Democrats united closely with the Christian Social Union members federally to form the opposition bloc. Between Christian Democrats and the Socialist-liberal coalition, there was a very bitter struggle, especially since Willy Brandt had dissolved the *Bundestag* and set a new election for November 19 next.

So Willy Brandt would have thought twice, for several obvious reasons, before trying—unsuccessfully, in all likelihood—to mix in

257

to the control of operations in the Olympic Village, a control automatically falling solely to the Government of the Free State of Bavaria, specifically its Interior Minister, Dr. Bruno Merk.

Willy Brandt, born December 18, 1913, at Lübeck; real name, Herbert-Karl Frahm. His mother was in turn a laundry worker, a seamstress, and a saleswoman in a department store. Father unknown. The child was raised by his grandfather, a onetime agricultural worker turned truck driver and a devoted Socialist militant. In 1930, Herbert Frahm joined the extreme left wing of the old Social Democratic Party.

I met Herr Brandt for the first time in Lübeck. It was raining in the old Hanseatic capital. Twenty kilometers away, the Baltic was experiencing a raging storm. Big ships, anchored in the port, were bowing and scraping. We were just where the Holstenbrücke starts, the biggest of the bridges that lead in to the center of Lübeck. Behind us, the north wind was driving against the powerful twin towers of Holstentor, that majestic fifteenth-century fortified gateway that is the emblem of the city. Brandt pointed to the swollen waters of the Trave River and said: "The Nazis threw more than one in there, after knocking them out, of course. I was one of the first names in Lübeck on their list, because I was the organizer of the Young Socialist Workers. I got away from them by a hair."

He had to flee from Germany at the end of 1933, with the Nazis on his tail, and went into exile at Oslo. There he married a Norwegian woman, became naturalized, but never stopped working with his German comrades, now refugees throughout Europe. He became a reporter for a Scandinavian chain of papers. The Second International sent him to the Spanish Civil War fronts in the name of Socialist solidarity.

When war broke out, and the Wehrmacht occupied Norway in April 1940, Willy Brandt became one of the young leaders of the Socialist Resistance, in defiance of the Gestapo. He had taken the name of Willy Brandt when he first went to Oslo, at age twenty, and he kept it after he returned to Germany in January 1946 in the uniform of a Norwegian Army major. He became press attaché of the Norwegian mission to the Four-Power Control Commission in Berlin.

No need here to detail the gehenna that was Berlin and all Germany of those days, chastised, crushed, and streaming with all kinds of blood, including its own. The Socialists had not forgotten Herbert Frahm, and knew how much Willy Brandt had done for his native land, against the Nazis. The great humbled nation had few men who in Allied eyes were beyond reproach and eligible for the highest political positions.

Brandt did not hesitate. He resumed his German nationality in 1947, and joined the *Sozialdemokratische Partei Deutschland* (SPD), the German Socialist Party. In 1949, West Berlin, where Brandt now lived, elected him to the *Bundestag* (though only with a voice, and no vote, for Occupied Berlin did not qualify for full representation).

The onetime Norwegian Resister quickly became the No. 1 disciple of an extraordinary man, Ernst Reuter, first Mayor of West Berlin. In 1957, four years after Reuter's death, Brandt in turn became Mayor of West Berlin. He held that position for nine years, until he was named Vice-Chancellor and Minister of Foreign Affairs of the German Federal Republic in the CDU-SPD "grand coalition" Government of the Christian Democrat Kurt-Georg Kiesinger.

After the October 1969 election, through alliance with the liberals (FDP), Willy Brandt became the first Socialist chancellor in the history of the G.F.R. . . .

With his straightforward smiles that crinkle his boldly chiseled features and pointed chin, you feel this big man, built like a powerful workman, is exceptionally honest. He has sharp sensitivity, and a feeling for gesture. Remember how he knelt before the monument in the Warsaw Ghetto? How his lips shook with emotion as he received the 1971 Nobel Peace Prize, after his regime adopted the *Ostpolitik,* the reconciliation with the East?

I have often seen him at work in public meetings, at big German banquets, on the hustings. His presence, his radiation, his persuasiveness strike me as almost without equivalent. He loves life, good books, sailing, cognac, and good red wine. He smokes heavily, switching from cigars to pipes to cigarettes, as he tries to keep his nerves in check. One of his strengths is his spontaneity. He invited me once to share smoked fish and marzipan in his childhood Holstein, and was delighted at the simple fact that a foreigner should find those things to his taste. His second wife, Ruth, and his three sons, one of whom caused him some little embarrassment through his militant leftism, are the treasures of his life.

I do not believe he could have done better than he did during the Munich Olympic tragedy. Division of authority is too rigid in the German setup. The police operations at the Olympic Village and Fürstenfeldbruck were out of his hands: the Bavarians meant to hold the reins from one end to the other.

How they handled it, and their self-confidence, could not but impress the Federal Chancellor.

8:10 PM *(Diary):* Two men, dressed like waiters in white coats and black trousers, go toward Block 31 carrying two huge trays covered with food. There is none of the febrile agitation behind them that there was during the first feeding incident; no more idea of getting into Apt. 1 and knocking the terrorists off with a series of lightning bull's-eyes.

An upstairs window opens. A fedayee leans out. A navy-blue stocking cap, like the kind mountain climbers wear, is down over his eyebrows. A shrimp-pink scarf is rolled around his face up to the eyes. He signals to the "waiters" to stay where they are, 10 meters outside the building. They do. Then the fedayee, like a traffic cop, instructs the first one to come forward. They hesitate. He snaps his fingers irritatedly, but does not say a word. The "waiter" understands and comes forward with his load. Another fedayee appears in the doorway of Apt. 1, takes the tray, passes it in to invisible hands. Exit First Waiter. Now the Second Waiter is brought forward, to deliver the cold cuts he is carrying.

The upstairs terrorist (Paulo), powerfully built, healthy-looking, with the shoulders of a stevedore, is compressed in a light-gray pullover sweater, the same one worn at the beginning of the afternoon by another fedayee patrolling the balcony on the garden side of the building and aiming at phony "onlookers" who seemed to be too close. That fedayee on the balcony (Badran, trying to hide his mouth that Weinberg had roughed up) was tall and rather thin, with very black, very thick, woolly hair, and a scarf that came up to cover his face as far as the almond-shaped eyes, the swift sharp eyes. /

There was Andrei Spitzer, thirty, national fencing coach, head fencing-master of the Wingate Institute and the Ramat Gan Maccabi. He lived at Ramat Gan, an exurb east of Tel Aviv.

Slim as a vine, with a long narrow intellectual's bespectacled face, he had displayed determination throughout his short life. He could have lived perfectly quietly all his life in Europe, free and faithful to his beliefs.

Born in Rumania of an Orthodox Jewish family, he emigrated to the Netherlands in 1964 with part of his family. He was at the time one of the finest of Rumanian foilsmen. Once without a country, and therefore ineligible for official contests under good conditions, he became a fencing-master. This led him to meet a Dutch Jewish girl, also excellent with the foils, and they married and lived happily in Amsterdam. But they had both decided they wanted to live in Israel, and they arrived there in 1967. Andrei became coach of the national team, after completing his military service. His wife, who had also been in the service, was planning to get back to competitive fencing shortly. They were the parents of a little girl, just six weeks old on September 5. With her husband on his way to Munich, Mrs. Spitzer had gone on to Amsterdam, to show the baby to her parents. Andrei was to join her there after the Games.

Dov Atzmon, the special correspondent at the Games for *Yedioth Aharonoth*, the big Tel Aviv evening daily, was a friend of the Spitzers'. Wednesday, September 6, at about 5:00 AM, he was the one Andrei's wife reached by phone. She had arrived in Munich very late the night before, and turned off the radio just after Conrad Ahlers, the official spokesman of the Federal Government, announced that all the hostages had been saved. But she had not been able to sleep; she was wracked with worry.

Atzmon got all his courage together and simply said, "I am with you." Mrs. Spitzer understood; she whispered, "Thanks, Dov," and hung up. All that day, she remained fully in control of herself.

Andrei Spitzer's body was still warm when the terrorists and their henchmen started to attack his family. After the funeral ceremony at Ramat Gan, the young widow had gone back to her parents' in Amsterdam. Daily threats, accompanied by small wrapped coffins, warned the household it was marked for liquidation by Black September. The Dutch police, under the circumstances, felt they could not assure Mrs. Spitzer's safety, or that of her child or parents. A team of Israeli special-service people came expressly to the Netherlands, and secretly escorted the entire family back to Israel.

As I write this, I recall the tall silhouette of a young woman, on the early afternoon of Wednesday, September 6, in a glossy corridor of the G-1 tower, that had glowed with the happiness of the Games, until suddenly . . . It was Mrs. Spitzer, her pallor framed by long dark hair, her features dramatically tense. But her eyes were bone-dry. She had just gotten a small valise of his "effects." Jewish friends surrounded her. She was holding enlargements of the picture of Andrei Spitzer standing in the second-story window, with his hands tied, but his head high, and his expression proud. She had asked for them.

XVI
CAIRO TURNS A DEAF EAR

. . . For thine enemy hath persecuted thee;
But shortly thou shalt see his destruction,
And shalt tread upon their necks.
                    Baruch 4:25

8:10 PM: THE TWO-BLADED ROTOR OF THE BELL ON THE GROUND AT
the military air base of Fürstenfeldbruck was turning at takeoff
speed. The four passengers it was to take back to the Olympic
Village were seated and safety-belted. The pilots waited patiently,
as Schreiber and Wolf went over a last rundown of the attack measures they had just set up. Merk, listening to them, looked worried.
He was gazing at the control tower, which would be of funda-
mental importance in the ambush.

Let us describe this building in a few lines. It is in no way
original, and has a counterpart of a sort on every airfield on this
earth. But there were to be so many unexpected developments
there, in the hours ahead . . .

The Fürstenfeldbruck control tower to begin with is a thick,
high rectangular building, with a terraced roof. A little while ago,
Dr. Schreiber had lain there on his stomach, with an imaginary
rifle in his hands.

The roof has two rotundas, one atop the other, both glass-walled.
The upper of these two superstructures has a platform at its top,
jammed with aerials, cables, instruments, surrounding a globular
beacon that sends, or on the night of September 5–6 sent, beams
into the fliers' skies, in a rhythm of flashes that spells Fürstenfeldbruck to navigators.

What targets for automatic arms!

The tower faces north. On its right, it is extended by a one-storied cubic building.

Schreiber suddenly decided to get back out of the copter. Merk and the others followed, telling the crew to advise Genscher and the Village general staff. The Munich commissioner of police wanted to tour the positions that hostages and terrorists on one side and marksmen and support forces on the other would be in at the start of the fight.

What was hardest to say was just where the Black September members and their prisoners would be. The terrorists might indeed at first be all together, or split into two or three groups. They might be walking across the landing area, or standing still, or at the foot of the helicopters or the Boeing 727, or even inside the latter plane.

The planners were pacing back and forth on the prestressed concrete, and night was settling in on the base. It was so calm! A flock of cuckoos chimed in to the serenity. From the doorway of the little annex to the control tower, the colonel commanding the base was watching the men, ready to answer if they called.

The building in which the Luftwaffe colonel stood was the "technical center" of Fürstenfeldbruck: it housed the essential telecommunications instrumentation, radar, various kinds of warning signals, and so on.

During the entire unfolding of events, it was staffed by the military. It was also where tapes recorded the messages of the base's receiving/sending units and the intercoms. Everything was recorded, with a talking clock superimposing audible time signals. It has been asserted that the entire sound track of the tragedy that went on by fits and starts during that night was fully canned here. One thing is certain: the official film of events at the Village and Fürstenfeldbruck, shot without interruption by successive teams of Munich police from around 6:00 AM until the incarceration of the three surviving terrorists, is a priceless document—but just as totally secret.

The passengers got back in the Bell, looking more concerned than ever. Georg Wolf shook his head, perhaps to drive out ideas as black as the majestic night enfolding them.

8:23 PM: Dr. Merk, seated next to the Plexiglas windows, was

looking at the stationary or moving lights of the field: lamps, projectors, groundlights, strips, beacons, markers. The base was
marked out almost as in a sketch. Despite the lateness of the hour,
Merk asked the crew to circle over the field.

The only military drawback to Fürstenfeldbruck was that it
could be clearly observed from several nearby hilltops. It was not
included in lists of Class A fields, probably because of military
security, but it qualified fully for Class A, in that it could under
all circumstances accommodate normal long-range flights, imply-
ing the existence of a powerful infrastructure.

Herr Schreiber was also looking at the picture reduced to its
essential lines, and cut into multicolored bits that shook and
trembled with the intermittences of the discharge lamps. The
main airstrip, recently improved, seemed munificent, with its 3 km.
(almost 1.9 mi.) of length, and its width of 50 meters (165 ft.). The
secondary runway, called concurrent because it converged with
the main one, led off toward the north and was also of impressive
dimensions. Any large base in this region needs two runways, because all year around there may be unpredictable winds, in any
direction.

The control tower, facing all of the areas of movement, sparkled
with its panoramic windows. It was clear that it was located halfway
up the main airstrip. The paths connecting the two runways and
the standing pads were definitely less brilliantly lighted. Dr. Merk
was concerned about that. But there was worse. At the foot of the
control tower was an unusually wide and extended paved area that
was quite dark. The Bavarian Interior Minister pointed this out
to Dr. Schreiber.

"The projectors haven't been set up yet. All of it will be
lighted," he replied, sure of himself.

Merk shrugged.

To the east of the tower, the area spread into a broad crossroads: two roadways led into it, the first coming from the secondary
runway northeast, and the other from the southwest, or opposite,
corner of the field. In this crossroads, a sort of four-pointed star,
the Lufthansa 727 was to land: it would be almost impossible to
see.

"Well, right now you certainly couldn't make out a cat's tail

265

there," Schreiber added thoughtfully. "I'll call Wolf as soon as we land."

8:25 PM (Diary): First stage: At 7:00 PM, the Village was sealed off more firmly than ever. Yet it was still impossible to keep its legal residents out, or by indirection those who appeared with valid passes. Second stage, just now: Suddenly, with perplexing speed, the main streets of the neighborhood just to the east of the Village are all sealed off. The off-limits zone is a narrow rectangle of which Lerchenauerstrasse, the dilated avenue that runs the whole length of the Village, makes the long side.

Presto, not a vehicle or person on the banned surface. The huge subway station of *Olympiapark* is suddenly deserted.

The extensive esplanade around the subway station now seems endless, oppressive, suddenly so silent and empty, marked only by the marching of patrols, as if we had all been taken three decades back into Occupied France with the beat of Nazi jackboots.

Quick hop over to the Four Seasons Hotel (for that, for those who may not know, is the meaning of Vierjahreszeiten), and I can't forget the twinkling eye and dimpled laugh of Moshe Weinberg. Some things are unpardonable!

"Munich is in a state of siege," my transistor is saying. Indeed? No matter where I look, there is nothing of the sort, except in the Village. My taxi wisely sidesteps Marienplatz, but as I walk into the hotel, after having discharged the cab up the block, I encounter two helmeted soldiers, carrying carbines. A gentleman identifying himself as police asks to see my identity papers. He does.

Here are three IOC members. Two cars are waiting for them, *Bundeswehr* chauffeurs at the rear doors. As they pass, you feel a slight tremor of curiosity among the bystanders who are outside the hotel as they are every night. These are very middle-class bystanders, respectable and reassuring. They remind one that all is not horror, even on an infamous day like this.

The entirely male IOC is made up of people of all kinds of backgrounds, as I said: rich and poor, young and old, businessmen and politicians, reactionaries and Communists. The three who come out all belong to ruling families, and each is with his spouse.

At the head, H.R.H. the Grand Duke Jean de Luxembourg in

a double-breasted indigo-blue alpaca suit that brings out his jockey-type wiriness, and a dark agreeable face with black mustache. Next, H.H. the Ruling Prince François Joseph II de Liechtenstein, tall and slim, slightly stooped, with a thin arc of a mustache turning elegantly gray. Behind them, H.M. The King of the Hellenes Constantine II, athletic, with a kind round face combining humor and energy, accompanying blonde Princess Georgine, the highly attractive and impressive wife of François Joseph II. The Greek monarch, in exile since December 1967, has not lost that springtime-of-life look, that charm his people loved. Closing the ranks come Queen Anne-Marie of Greece, tall and distinguished, with a chic I might almost call imperial because of the purity of her features beneath the short chestnut locks, and Grand Duchess Josephine-Charlotte, almond-eyed, high cheek-boned, and all class. . . .

His sharp, mobile features showing weariness, Cheik Gabriel Gemayel, a twenty-year member of IOC and an important Lebanese of patrician birth, is pacing the sitting room, looking worried. The huge TV screen breaks the interminable suspense with repeated interviews in color with the Israelis who escaped. "This is a long and awful business," Cheik Gemayel says to me. "But I promise you, the Olympic spirit will survive it."

Mr. Alexandru Siperco takes my arm: "They say there's a mass demonstration heading toward Marienplatz. Want to come and watch it?"

We head for the revolving door, but two armed policemen in black helmets have closed it off. Exit now is only by one of the side panels, which responsible gentlemen are monitoring. But now two more cops, members of the action police in field uniforms, rush into the Olympic GHQ and head for the elevator near the restaurant! Mr. Siperco, amused, and I watch them at a distance, only to note that the fine red-carpeted corridors already harbor at least a score of their impressive colleagues.

In answer to my question, the hotel manager says, "There is some fear that gangs of Maoists may try to break into the Vierjahreszeiten and attack the IOC members . . ."

The shadow of a smile flits over Siperco's lips, and his clear eyes twinkle through the convex lenses. We go out.

At the foot of the stairs, beneath the entry arch, a security man is loudly announcing that the Maoist demonstrators, coming from Marienplatz, are heading toward us. Yet, the sidewalks are perfectly free. Law and order is heavy on the street, but the cops are gossiping, looking serene. We go up Maximilianstrasse. Siperco, his graying hair blown by the first gusts of wind of the day, looking both intellectual and powerful with his good shape and his former weight lifter's shoulders, says he is relatively confident about the outcome of the drama. So am I. We both believe in the practical efficiency of German organization.

Before the monumental neo-Gothic *Neues Rathaus* (New City Hall), we find a parade crossing the whole length of the great square reserved for pedestrians. There is a huge crowd out tonight. The Rathaus clock chimes the half-hour; the fact that one so clearly hears the chimes here, where at this hour there usually is an infernal din, is significant in itself. Everyone is looking at the demonstrators. They are mostly all young, going along slowly, in orderly fashion. At their head, two boys and two girls holding a huge Israeli flag, unfurled horizontally; then come two young men in blue jeans and long hair, holding up a sign that has a very fine picture of Moshe Weinberg pasted on it, draped in black crepe. The murdered coach is smiling his broad smile that lights up his forceful features and narrows his eyes. Then a portrait of the second Israeli killed this morning by the terrorists: Yossef Romano. His sideburns down to his jaws, his face filled with happiness, he is holding two of his three daughters in his arms. There are several thousand of them, from all backgrounds it would seem, walking along behind the flag and the portraits of the victims, waving small cardboard rectangles handpainted sky-blue-and-white with the Shield of David.

"Where are the Maoists?" I wonder aloud.

"Maybe in somebody's imagination," says the Rumanian IOC member.

Before the *Mariensäule* (Pillar of Holy Mary), the hymns resume as soon as the demonstrators have cleared the square. This is a nightly thing, the psalms powerfully sung by very large groups of young people who have assembled here from everywhere, come because of the Games. I can't say "for" the Games, because among these visitors there are many who are more interested in what

268

surrounds the Games than in the event itself. This evening, they are chanting the psalms of distress and pain, Nos. 51, 52, and 102:

He weakened my strength in the way; he shortened my days.
I said, O my God, take me not away in the midst of
    my days: thy years *are* throughout all generations.

They relay each other by the hundreds. What fervent youth! A curious harmony of their voices chanting in German, English, French, but without clash . . .

We go back along the new City Hall with its lacy facade, chiseled like a huge jewel. People in Munich tend to argue over this new City Hall, saying it is too heavy, overdone. But I find it has beauty, grandeur, and charm. The medieval characters of its carillon delight me with the colors of their enamels, and by the ballet they perform at 11:00 AM, that brings together at the foot of the belfry huge crowds returning at last to innocence. An Israeli journalist this afternoon in the Village was showing a picture taken a few mornings ago of Romano and Weinberg, side by side in front of the belfry, enjoying it.

The frenzy and delights sculpted into the stone are in tune with the exuberance of life that is Munich and Bavaria in the flesh. The *Münchener* had two catastrophes in their history, with no common denominator: Adolf Hitler, and September 5, 1972. They had not bid to get these Games only so as to restore to Germany, in the eyes of the world, a brilliant, happy athletic image, powerful, relaxed, and fraternal. It was also to affirm to the rest of Germany that Munich and Bavarian civilization remained perennially the same.

As we get back to the fine hotel, with the three mourning-draped flags flying in front, Mr. Siperco stage-whispers to me: "Just the same, I'm worried about the epilogue. Nerves wear out. And they've been at it sixteen hours . . ." /

8:32 PM: Chancellor Brandt's idea of trying to get Cairo to help was now in its decisive moments.

The idea had originated with State Secretary Sigismund von Braun. He can be said to have sent feelers throughout the entire world looking for useful support: a good reacher for the impossible! The minute the fedayeen demanded to be flown to Egypt with their hostages without waiting for Israel's reply, he had suggested to Brandt to go straight to Egypt's President Anwar el-Sadat.

"At this point, what do we have to lose?" said the Chancellor.

Herr von Braun had already alerted the German ambassador at Cairo, H.E. Hans Georg Steltzer. Diplomatic relations between West Germany and Egypt had been resumed three months before, after a rather long interruption due to Germany's refusal to observe the economic blockade of Israel decreed by the Arab League after the Six Days' War. Egypt was currently negotiating a series of economic agreements with Bonn that would be very advantageous, in that the G.F.R. was to give Egypt considerable financial and technical assistance.

Ambassador Steltzer at 5:15 PM had confirmed that President Sadat was in town; the President's personal secretariat had been alerted that they would shortly be receiving a call from a "very high German personality."

Chancellor Brandt placed the first person-to-person call to President Sadat at 5:20 (Cairo time being an hour later, it was 6:20 PM there). The connection was good, and the delay minimal. Ten minutes later, he was informed: The President's private office regretted infinitely, but the President was not in Cairo. He was on inspection "somewhere in Egypt."

Willy Brandt thereupon decided immediately to come in from his lakeside villa to join his staff in Munich. Three Luftwaffe helicopters had been standing by. They landed at 6:10 PM in the gardens on the east bank of the Isar, just north of the *Friedensengel* (Angel of Peace). This bronze angel spreads its wings at the top of a Corinthian column, set atop a massive fountain of Roman antecedents.

Just before taking off, Chancellor Brandt had had Cairo on the line a second time, and had himself spoken to President Sadat's personal assistant. The President was still unavailable.

The exact time of the decisive conversation, as well as that of all the fruitless attempts that preceded it, has as many versions as there are sources: Brandt, the Bavarian *Land,* the Egyptian Government, the *Bundesregierung,* you name it. And that point, unfortunately, applies to every aspect of the cursed Connollystrasse affair: times, figures, facts, analyses are never the same, and, what is worse, sometimes have no relation to each other, according to each of the most qualified informants, services most directly involved, and most dependable participants. However, it is rather feasible to allow for the honest errors, deliberate omissions, masqueradings, and lies that have cropped up around the massacre of September 5–6, 1972.

Where did Chancellor Brandt and his entourage set up in Munich? Some official services say in the DOZ tower; others, at 7 Prinzregenstrasse, the office of *Ministerpräsident* Dr. Alfons Goppel, head of the Bavarian State government; still others, in Olympic Village. The truth is, Brandt went to each of those places, but remained longest at the Maximilianeum. This grandiose building, made even more official by its broad arcades, lies like a château on the hill of Gasteig, overlooking the right bank of the Isar. It is where the Bavarian *Landtag* (Parliament) meets. The federal Chancellor's impressive security apparatus had plenty of room to spread out in there, and communications were good.

Today, Brandt had been scheduled to meet at Kiel with British Prime Minister Edward Heath, who is a great yachtsman. They were to discuss the next summit meeting of the extended European Economic Community. The Chancellor had worked on his notes far into the night. And then, the hammerblow at dawn. . . .

At 6:30, 7:00, and 7:20 PM, there were three more fruitless official calls from Munich to Cairo: "The President of Egypt has not yet returned to the capital."

Supposing that the President of Egypt were truly impressed by his title, he might feel he ought not to come to the phone for anyone less than an equal, that is, in the G.F.R., President Gustav Heinemann. However, whereas Mr. Sadat was the effective head of his country, Herr Heinemann, while having great moral influence and being as highly respected as he was popular, had no real governmental authority. Chancellor Brandt was the sole head of the executive.

At 7:20 PM, seeing time fly by, Willy Brandt thundered: "What if the President is not in Cairo? The state machine still operates, in Egypt as elsewhere. There is a head of the Government. Will he refuse to talk to the Chancellor of the German Federal Republic?"

They tried. At 7:30 PM, Mr. Aziz Sedki, Prime Minister, was "also out of Cairo." But Von Braun was not out of touch with the West German ambassador in Egypt, and Steltzer replied without equivocation: "Messrs. Sadat and Sedki are both here. Their appointments are all being kept as scheduled."

At this hour, connections always got more difficult, under the best of circumstances, because of atmospheric conditions and the like. Chancellor Brandt had Secretary von Braun advise the offices of Messrs. Sadat and Sedki that he would continue to call the two Arab leaders without a stop until he had talked to one of them. Mr. Sedki's office suggested that an Egyptian minister, name unspecified, call Chancellor Brandt back. The latter refused. The nervousness of the Cairene leaders was very evident: their dryness almost verged on discourtesy.

At 7:50, a member of President Sadat's office answered and was about to hang up after the usual negative reply, when he was stopped by the statement (which he was asked to pass along to his superiors) that the German Chancellor had made the following decision: "If, at his next call, Mr. Brandt were not put on the line directly to either the Egyptian President or his Prime Minister, the Chancellor would immediately issue a communiqué describing all of his unsuccessful attempts since 5:20 PM."

Such shocking airing of the conduct of President Sadat and his second-in-command would be most distressing to the Egyptian image, at the very time when the U.N. and all other possible platforms were echoing with their bitter complaints. Heads of governments are not supposed to act insultingly toward each other, even when relations between their states are strained. And it just happened that at the moment Bonn and Cairo were getting tenderly intimate, as we have seen.

Von Braun added to Cairo that, of course, the Chancellor, even after his press statement, would continue to try to reach either of the responsible Egyptian leaders.

At 8:12 PM, for the eighth time, they got through to Cairo. The connection was rather poor. But a voice said: "Is the Chancellor of the Federal Republic himself on the line? We will put the Prime Minister on."

Brandt took the phone, and waited. The interferences and modulations in the sound were such that a skeptic might conclude there was complicity between some Cairene technicians and the elements. It was 8:14 by the time Mr. Aziz Sedki, at the other end, was finally on.

After the usual greetings, Mr. Sedki said, "I am listening to you." The conversation took place in English.

As Mr. Brandt began to explain the situation to him, Mr. Sedki's irritated voice could be very clearly heard: "I can't hear you clearly." The Chancellor talked louder. Despite all the strain Brandt put on the vocal cords he would be needing in the up-coming election campaign, the Cairene Premier could not understand him. Or did he prefer not to?

The Egyptian deeply regretted, but felt there was no point in trying to make himself understood. The Chancellor, very calmly, replied that he would go on calling until they got a good connection. The Egyptian Premier hung up.

The truth was that three out of four of the parallel calls that Brandt's office had been making to various other members in Cairo for the past hour and a half had been excellent.

Mr. Aziz Sedki is very Westernized (I was about to say "very British"), with his English-tailored suits and Harrod's ties. He has agreeable features, a strong chin, wavy hair sprinkled with snow, and looks as if self-control to him would be child's play. Politically agile, he has been alternately reputed to be pro-American and pro-Soviet.

At ..20, then 8:25, Brandt and Sedki were both on the line, but could not talk, the connections being so bad, that was the fact. Finally, at 8:32 they were both able to hear each other adequately.

In a long interview with the Munich *Süddeutscher Zeitung* of September 9, Chancellor Brandt among other things recounted his conversation with the head of the Egyptian regime. He later confirmed this version several times, with the minor alterations that occur when one has only his memory to rely on and a turn of phrase suddenly comes back to mind. I heard him myself during

273

his whirlwind electoral campaign on his special train, relate it again at a televised press conference in Frankfort, as follows:

Brandt: Good evening again, Mr. Prime Minister.

Sedki: Yes, good evening to you too, Mr. Chancellor.

Brandt: Mr. Prime Minister, we both have a problem. I don't think I need explain mine to you. You must be equally concerned by what is going on in the Olympic Village, in view of the way it will discredit the whole of the Arab world and the Palestinian cause.

Sedki: Mr. Chancellor, you have your opinion and I have mine on what may or may not harm the Arab people and Palestinian Resistance. Our respective concerns are too urgent for us to try to argue this out on the telephone. May I know to what I owe the honor of your call?

Sedki's tone was just as cold as Brandt's was cordial. I was surprised by the way the Chancellor had begun his exposition: one of his attributes is his psychological sense. Was he not making a mistake by stating considerations that could only displease the listener? At any rate, had he not stated them, the result would have been the same.

Brandt: The perpetrators of the Connollystrasse attack have announced they want to go to Cairo with their hostages. Their final ultimatum expires at eight PM GMT [9:00 PM in Munich, and 10:00 PM in Cairo]. The German authorities would be willing to let them go through with this, if it were possible for my government and yours to cooperate in the matter. Would you agree to intervene the moment the plane lands at Cairo International Airport, to insure that the fedayeen do not shoot their hostages, and that the plane will be able to leave as quickly as possible to take the nine athletes on to Israel? Naturally, your word on it is all I ask.

Sedki: I don't believe your plan is a valid solution. And at any rate it is unworkable. This is not an Egyptian matter. I cannot understand how or why Egypt should be involved in what is taking place at Munich.

Brandt: I can then only express my regret, Mr. Prime Minister, that I was unable to come to agreement with you on a plan that would have saved human lives.

Sedki: Well, good night, Mr. Chancellor.

Brandt: Good-bye, Mr. Prime Minister.

On September 7, Mr. Aziz Sedki had his office release his version of the phone conversation with Mr. Brandt on the evening of the 5th. There are notable differences between it and the Chancellor's.[1]

The main clashes between the versions come in the second half of the conversation, after the Chancellor had presented his proposal. According to Cairo, it was:

Sedki (answering the Chancellor's proposal): Has this arrangement of yours been agreed to by the fedayeen?

Brandt: I don't know exactly what the fedayeen want.

But, of course, the Chancellor did. In Cairo or the Olympic Village, the deal was the same: the lives of the hostages against the release of the whole flock of Arab terrorists held by Israel. So one may wonder whether he could have answered in this way, which would have done no good anyway, since immediately on arrival the Egyptians would have been able to consult the terrorists and clear it all up, including their demands.

Cairo's version ends:

Sedki (answering the strange words attributed to Brandt): In that case, your proposal is unacceptable to Egypt. We can make no decision without previous agreement with the fedayeen.

Those around the Chancellor on the morning of September 6 let it be known that Mr. Sedki had been even icier than the later accounts suggested. The Egyptian Premier could be felt to be fuming with irritation at the other end. Mr. Brandt had let one of his close associates listen in, and two other people were in the room. Sedki hid his impatience with the whole thing so little that he tried to interrupt the Chancellor before the latter had finished his brief proposal, according to one of the witnesses. He is supposed to have said, "This is absolutely impossible. We can do nothing. We do not want to get involved." And hung up with an abrupt, "Good-bye, sir." (Such behavior may in part account for the troubles he ran into the following December with the usually docile Egyptian Na-

---

[1] Among others, Mr. Sedki claims that Mr. Brandt wanted the 727 to take the hostages back to Munich from Cairo, rather than to continue on to Israel. This may have been merely the Egyptian statesman's way of sticking to the Arab position: Israel does not exist.

tional Assembly, and the fact that he was relieved of his duties the following March.)

As for the Egyptian President, Mr. Anwar el-Sadat did not even bother to answer the German Chancellor's calls that evening, nor the next day, nor ever.

8:35 PM: The Bell Iroquois that had taken Herren Merk, Schreiber, and two others unidentified, to Fürstenfeldbruck, set down with all aboard on the green between the rear of G-1 and Lerchenauerstrasse.

Two Piper Cubs were circling over the Village.

8:38 PM: At the conclusion of his unsuccessful dialogue with Premier Sedki, Chancellor Brandt let himself go for a moment: "Such conduct is inadmissible! That man must think he's the Pharaoh! And such heartlessness!"

But Sedki had certainly been doing no more than reflecting President Sadat's position, albeit spiced with his own grating manners. Egypt had thereby forced the Germans to go over to the attack, and thus sealed the fate of victims and terrorists. Brandt understood instantly. He told several people, "History will hold Mr. Sadat and Mr. Sedki morally responsible in large part for the blood we are probably going to have to shed."

Obviously, once away with their hostages on a plane in the air, the fedayeen would without problem have been able to blackmail the crew into taking them to some airport other than Cairo. All the important German VIPs in the world being along would make no difference. But why should the terrorists suddenly have decided against going to Egypt, after insisting on it? They could know nothing of any negotiations between Bonn and Cairo.

Let us suppose, however, that Issa and company had decided to land in Libya, Iraq, or elsewhere, instead of Cairo. Let us suppose that Sadat and his second-in-command had agreed to protecting the lives of the hostages, although allowing the fedayeen to keep them prisoners. Let us suppose that, as soon as the fedayeen had forced the plane to veer off toward Tripoli, Baghdad, or Damascus, Brandt, with Sadat's agreement, had made public the mutual understanding they had worked out. It would have been extremely difficult for the Libyan, Iraqi, or Syrian governments to allow the massacre of innocent athletes on their territory. The terrorists in the landed plane would still be able to wound, torture, or kill all the hostages in the world at their leisure (as their fellows would do at Khartoum the following March). . . . So what, if there were some disagreements among Arabs about it?

The *Krisenstab* immediately was told of Sedki's verdict: thumbs down. It was time to settle the matter once and for all.

8:45 PM: There was a final discussion among Messrs. Brandt, Merk, and Dr. Alfons Goppel, the head of the Bavarian Government, an affable, well-turned-out man, with heavy, intelligent features lightened by silky-glinting silver hair, and given to cigar-smoking.

Some say that the Chancellor came to the Village for the final call to Cairo and this meeting. I don't think so. The commotion of official cars and motorcycle escorts would have been noticed. I rather think it was a phone consultation, with Brandt and Goppel at one end, and Merk at the other.

Dr. Goppel, as Minister-President of the Free State of Bavaria, was increasingly disturbed by this whole affair. He was not sorry he had put his Interior Minister, Bruno Merk, at the head of the crisis staff, with full authority to counter the attack by any measures required. But he was beginning to fear the worst. And he was most anxious to have the Federal Chancellor's approval on the capital options.

Constitutionally, the split of authority between the Bavarian and Federal governments, in a matter such as Connollystrasse, was not so simple. Everything concerning maintenance of order in Bavaria came under the local government. Therefore, as long as the fedayeen held their hostages in the Olympic Village, any effort to stop them had to come exclusively from the Bavarians, that is, Dr. Merk. But even there, the Chancellor's authority to get involved had good legal support.

1. The XXth Olympic Games at Munich were not a local, but a national, affair. The Federal Government had had to make guarantees to the IOC in order to get them at all, and constant and costly cooperation from Bonn was needed to make them so glamorous. The games were under the high patronage of President Gustav Heinemann of the G.F.R., and Brandt was Chairman of the Advisory Committee to the *Organisationskomitee*.

2. Olympic Village, legally and officially, was an international enclave within West Germany, for the duration of the Games. Germans without passes were no more entitled to enter than anyone else.

3. Members of Olympic delegations had been permitted to enter West German territory on presentation of an Olympic I.D. card recognized by the *Bundesregierung* (Federal Government) They had been able to come in at any frontier point—and any thing concerning German frontiers, including all personnel employed there, customsmen, guards, police, and so on, was the sole province of the Federal Government. So the West German Republic was the actual host of the Olympic Games.

4. The hostages were citizens of a foreign country. As such, they were under federal protection as well as Bavarian. The attack was thus an international affair. And all foreign relations, of course, were Bonn's exclusive concern.

5. What was more, they were Israelis, which, in light of the 1936 Olympics held under the swastika, the official anti-Semitism of the Third Reich, and the genocide of 6,000,000 Jews by the Nazis, made this a catastrophe for all Germany.

These were five grounds on which the Federal Chancellor might have superseded Minister Merk, by reason of national interest. Had the Bavarians "rebelled," he could have called his ministers together in an emergency meeting and had them vote full powers to him or to any designated member of the Government, and later have had this ratified by the Bundestag. But that would have raised a storm and perhaps reacted unfavorably for the SPD-FDP coalition at the next elections, for Germans were very concerned for states' rights.

In fact, Brandt had no desire to try to impose his views on the *Krisenstab,* the matter having gone too far, and the risk of a real disagreement between him and Merk being too great.

As Franz-Josef Strauss' CSU, since the creation of the G.F.R., had always held the majority in Bavaria, Dr. Merk's crisis staff was under Christian Democratic aegis. The only two exceptions on the *Krisenstab* were Federal Interior Minister Genscher, a liberal or Free Democrat, and the ex-Mayor of Munich, Hans-Jochen Vogel, leader of the Bavarian section of Brandt's Social Democrats. The

No. 2 man in the "loyal opposition," Herr Strauss himself, known as the "uncrowned King of Bavaria," was in constant touch with the *Krisenstab* and had now finally even moved in to the G-1 tower.

No, Brandt was not about to pound the table. Yet he had enthusiastically endorsed Genscher's unsuccessful effort at the beginning of the afternoon to get Dr. Schreiber to put the operational reins in federal hands. This had been turned down flat. Around 7:00 PM, Genscher, trying again, had suggested that operational command at Fürstenfeldbruck be given to Major Konrad Müller of the frontier guards. Again, Merk and Schreiber had replied with a sharp refusal.

The Bavarians felt that, if things turned out badly, under any circumstances they would be the first ones blamed. They believed in single command and conception, and felt themselves as well equipped and probably better informed than their Bonn colleagues. They firmly hoped, if it came to a fight, to come out on top handily. The two murders of the morning had gone badly against their grain: they had personal reasons for getting even with the terrorists who had spoiled their Games, the finest in history.

That had been before the fedayeen had decreed they were taking their hostages abroad. From then on, the decision of whether or not to let them go through with their plan was strictly a federal matter, that could be decided only by Chancellor Brandt. Moreover, the air base the *Krisenstab* had chosen, whether for the takeoff or the showdown, was a Luftwaffe base, thus federal, too. The fact that the German air army had agreed for the duration of the Games not to use it, so as to allow the charter flights and many supplementary planes to land there, in no way changed that. The military were still operating the base, taking care of maintenance, surveillance, and traffic control. Ancillary services were seen to by the Lufthansa, a federal corporation.

So, it would be a cop-out to say that Bonn had no say in the matter. In fact, the shadow cast before by the Bundestag elections to be held in two and a half months figured greatly in the reserve on the one hand and the touchy concern on the other.

Now, back to the two-way conversation among the Herren Brandt, Merk, and Goppel. "Gentlemen," Brandt began, "what we have to decide is where we draw the line."

THE BLOOD OF ISRAEL

What follows is a reconstruction from later reports of what they all said. I have lumped the statements of Goppel and Merk under the heading of *Krisenstab*, for, so far as I know there is no tape to show us who said just what, but the position of each individual is scrupulously reflected here.

Brandt: The Federal Republic's attitude toward acts of terrorism accompanied by taking of hostages has up to now been to put the safety of the prisoners above all else. That is why we have previously freed political prisoners and paid impressive sums of ransom to the fedayeen. The problem we face now is a diabolical one. The terrorists want nothing from us, except for us to let them have their head. Nothing we have offered interests them. What they want is the release of all of their friends who are prisoners in Israel, and we know Israel will refuse to make any compromise whatsoever. That's the background. Now what is the current situation?

Krisenstab: We have just gotten a final postponement. We won't be able to get them to extend it any further. And we also won't get them to give up going to an Arab country with their hostages.

Brandt: The question then is, since Cairo has said no, can we let the fedayeen leave German territory with their hostages, when we know that once they get where they are going both terrorists and hostages will be met by Israel's flat refusal?

Krisenstab: The leader of the fedayeen made it clear to us, if Israel has not released the Palestinian Resistance prisoners they listed by eight AM tomorrow, the nine hostages will be killed aboard the plane, whatever the destination. The fedayeen already shot in cold blood two of the unarmed athletes this morning. They're fanatics, and they won't be fazed by nine more murders, nor by their own deaths.

Brandt: Yes, they're ready for anything. The reputation of the German Federal Republic would be sullied if even one of the nine remaining hostages were killed outside our territory, because we gave in. We can't get rid of Germany's Olympic guests by shipping them outside the borders, tied up like packages of unregistered air freight. Moreover, the Israeli Government has sent word to me that it would agree to the departure of the hostages for Cairo only if it had our full assurance that the Israeli athletes would be immediately reshipped, safe and sound, to their own country. So, we are all agreed: we are not going to let the terrorists take the Israeli athletes out of Germany.

Krisenstab: Fine! But then there is a second question: Do we stand passively by, leaving the fedayeen and their prisoners at Block Thirty-one, and trust to fate? Or do we undertake an armed action, either at the Village, or elsewhere, while the nine hostages are still alive?

Brandt: An honorable nation can't stand by with arms crossed while its guests get murdered. We have to carry out a rescue operation, on German soil, as quickly as possible.

Krisenstab: We are all in agreement. Now, to put it into work.

Brandt: It will be horribly difficult. I'm terrified of a bloodbath.

Krisenstab: Aren't we all?

Mr. Abdelaziz Elshafei, head of the Egyptian delegation to the Munich Games and Secretary-General of the Egyptian Olympic Committee, went to the corner of Building 31, with the police-woman-interpreter, (said to be named) Fräulein Graes. The usual ritual took place: the young woman went to the door that was ajar and a few moments later signaled to the visitor to come over.

It was dark now, a fine warm night. Connollystrasse was normally lighted: in the middle of the roadway, among the greenswards and flowerbeds, among the basins, the flower tubs, and the mocking rumble of the varicolored pipes, stood black posts, no bigger than the ashtray-stands you find in the waiting rooms of every airport in the world. They were projectors, with powerful bulbs that spread amply into a yellow beam. Also, farther apart, there were the tall lampposts with their almost-white neon lights. And yet the street seemed darker than usual. That was because the surrounding facades, especially the one of the East German building, were only sparscly illuminated. In Block 31, the whole third-floor gallery was lighted, as were Apts. 1 and 3. But the rest of the building was dark.

The entertaining songs of color created by the phosphorescent materials in the waters spouting from the fountains tonight were less joyful than strange. The whole village, it seemed, was out of doors. The security people could not forbid the athletes, or those supposed to be, from walking around. Yes, everything was difficult.

First, let us see what was incontrovertible about this meeting between the young Arab athletic official and the terrorists. With the final—*but* final—deadline coming close, several members of the *Krisenstab* asked the Arab League representative, Mr. Khadif, and the Egyptian IOC member, Mr. Touny, whether they would make one more overture to the terrorists. Both said that, having nothing new to tell the fedayeen, they did not feel they could.

Someone mentioned Mr. Elshafei. Mr. Touny said he would not object to the head of the Egyptian delegation going, provided he was not asked to lie or mislead the fedayeen in any way.

"I was the very last Arab to be in touch with the Munich fedayeen," would be Mr. Elshafei's later emphatic statement.

But then there is another circus of conflicting versions.

The members of the *Krisenstab* I spoke to later said, "We had asked Mr. Elshafei to suggest that the terrorists stay in Building Thirty-one till the next morning, which would have given time to open things up again with Jerusalem, and perhaps find a solution. If they had said yes, we would have promised to try nothing against them during that time."

But Mr. Elshafei himself says the Germans gave him no specific message to relay to the fedayeen. He thought he was supposed to tell them merely that they would be leaving the Village shortly, and that they should not do anything rash if things dragged slightly on past the nine o'clock deadline.

He has the sharp features and wiry silhouette of the warriors shown on the frescoes of the Pharaohs' tombs. He is in the vanguard of the young Cairene intelligentsia. The son of a very distinguished family, a former swimming champion, and a chessplayer of Omar Sharif's caliber, he is solidly grounded in both Islamic and Western culture. I have on occasion had the pleasure of conversing with him. He has class.

According to a statement he gave to the great Egyptian daily, *Al-Goumhourya* (September 13, 1972), Issa greeted him at the door of Apt. 1 and told him some impressive things, namely, that Herr Genscher, the federal Minister of the Interior, had asserted (quoting Mr. Elshafei): "Israel has agreed to exchange two hundred Arab prisoners against the nine hostages. The exchange is to take place tomorrow morning at eight, at Cairo International Airport."

When Issa added that the West German authorities, through Herr Genscher, had undertaken to transport the commando and its hostages and guarantee their safety, he noted Mr. Elshafei's worried look, and asked whether it was true that Israel had agreed to the terms.

"I told him," the Egyptian official said, "to be very careful." Issa was very perplexed by this, but then the blonde policewoman, who had stepped aside for a moment at Issa's "request," came back. "Taking it on herself to join in the conversation," said Elshafei, "she announced that everything was going according to schedule and three helicopters had landed at the Village to take the fedayeen and their hostages to the airfield."

Returning to the *Krisenstab*, Mr. Elshafei found Herr Genscher with them, and, at Willi Daume's request, recounted his talk with Issa. The President of the Organizing Committee, according to the Egyptian official, seemed surprised that the Bonn Interior Minister should have said that Israel had agreed to the terrorists' terms.

Mr. Elshafei concluded, "The Federal Minister of the Interior seemed embarrassed. I suddenly realized what game the West German authorities were playing, but had no way of warning the commando of the trap that was being set."

As soon as this was published, Herr Conrad Ahlers, official spokesman for the Bonn Government, dcelared: "Mr. Abdelaziz Elshafei's statements have been fabricated out of whole cloth."

On November 24, 1972, the Beirut daily *An Nahar* published an interview with one of the Connollystrasse terrorists freed by the Germans in response to the ultimatum of the skyjackers of October 29. This man (tall Badran, the one who stood up to Issa) asserted: "West German Interior Minister Hans-Dietrich Genscher gave us his word of honor that a safe-conduct had been given us by his Government, and that we would take off with the hostages for Cairo in total safety."

As for the *Dokumentation*, it states, on p. 33, in contradiction of the Egyptian official: "The West German negotiators, during their final conversations on Connollystrasse, at 9:00 PM, drew the attention of the terrorists to the fact that the Israeli Government was still working on the list of Arabs whose release had been demanded. The Israeli Government had as yet made *no decision.*"

There was Eliezer Halfin, wrestler, born June 18, 1948, at Vilna; 5 ft. 7½, 150 lbs.

He was the son of a Lithuanian Jew whose first wife and children had all died during the extermination of the Vilna Ghetto. Eliezer "returned" from the USSR to Israel with his parents and sister in January 1970.

He was built like an Apollo of Delphi. His cheekbones were hollow, as if hammered in, and when he was making an effort, his face became emaciated, with a Caucasian kind of beauty. He had flat stiff hair with short wisps that came down on the stubborn forehead, huge black slashes of prominent brows, a craggy nose, and round chin, that all added up to a determined, virile face. But there was also the tender appeal that radiated from the clear burning look, a look that grabs you, even in pictures.

The Nazis had murdered his father's first wife, and some twenty others constituting all of Eliezer's ancestry and immediate family.

Born at the same time as independent Israel, Eliezer, like all Jews in the Soviet bloc, had been weaned on recollections of endless persecution, pogroms, and genocides, and had grown to maturity along with the miraculous faraway homeland, expecting the worst. He had gone in for freestyle wrestling in school. He became schoolboy champion, and then junior champion, of the Lithuanian SSR.

In 1967, when Eliezer's parents, his sister, and he applied for exit visas to go to Israel, his superiors tried to convince him to stay on. He had just qualified for his professional license as an automobile precision-mechanic. He was offered a fine promotion, giving him access to excellent training facilities, but involving moving to Moscow, away from his family. At the same time, his father's application for the visa got lost. Eliezer turned down the offers. Immediately he was demoted at work. He was not allowed to enter sporting events, even though he had come in fourth in the junior championships of the entire USSR, in freestyle, and was considered by all Soviet sports authorities as a truly promising hope.

Cairo Turns a Deaf Ear

Nearly three years went by, spent in near poverty, before they could get to Israel. He had felt a tremendous sense of relief on finally getting out of Europe.

"Most of our Olympic athletes at Munich weren't really of international caliber," Shmuel Lalkin told me. "Sports conditions in Israel are too tough, because of the absolute priority that has to be given to national defense. But from a human viewpoint, they were wonderful boys. They would not have been selected if they had not been worthy representatives of the country. Selection, to them, was a reward and an honor . . ."

Eliezer had scarcely arrived in Israel, when he was called up for military service. He took part in two raids on Palestinian fedayeen bases in Jordan, and then was transferred to a unit on the Golan Heights. During the last part of his service, Eliezer did get in some wrestling training, but that was no basis for any special military consideration. Little by little, he got back into shape. He won the Israeli championship in freestyle in the 68 kg. (149.5 lbs.) class. He reentered international competition, placing 12th in the world championships at Sofia in 1971, having just come in from a long, exhausting saboteur hunt.

In 1972, he was third at Bucharest and second in Greece in international meets. He finished his military service less than two months before the Games, and knew he had no chance for a medal at Munich. He was eliminated in the third qualifying round, August 29. He was aiming mainly at Montreal. "Technically, I'll be in top shape. I'll be twenty-eight, the ideal age for a wrestler," he said.

Eliezer Halfin was a mechanic in a big Tel Aviv garage. A bachelor, he lived with his parents in a lively little apartment in the Tel Aviv suburb of Neve Sharrett, which has a Russian accent. Jews from all over the Soviet Union have congregated there by the hundreds. Eliezer was the idol of all their kids. He had given up a quiet existence, a fine athletic career as a potential Government-subsidized competitor, to be seen often coming home in the Tsahal uniform from tough missions, which he never discussed, but which his father could not keep from occasionally boasting of. He had become champion of Israel. He was going to the Olympics . . .

You remember the silent courage, and the pride of Eliezer

Halfin when, wrists bound behind his back, he appeared along-side Andrei Spitzer in the window of Apt. 1.

His simple first name Eliezer bespoke the pious stubbornness of a virtually evaporated family.

The patient killers of the Jewish people had finally achieved their aim, insofar as the Litvak Halfins of Vilna were concerned. After his father, too old now to think of siring any more, Eliezer had been the last male of the line. The ultimate remaining name-bearer. But there was still his sister. The flame would be carried forward—albeit under different names.

XVII
STILLBORN AMBUSH

Thy dead shall live, my dead bodies shall arise—
Awake and sing, ye that dwell in the dust—
Isaiah 26:19

8:48 PM: THE IROQUOIS THAT HAD JUST MADE THE ROUND TRIP FROM the Village to Fürstenfeldbruck with Herren Schreiber, Merk, and their retinue, came down at the air base again. The *Vize* (as. his title was usually abbreviated) Georg Wolf was waiting for it, surrounded by five fellows in assorted brightly colored sweat suits. They were armed with carbines or automatic pistols, their heavy shirts swollen by hidden cartridge belts. These five were some of the fourteen certified marksmen who, since morning, had been assigned to the drama. They had gotten to the base at 7:00 PM.

Herr Wolf's bald authoritarian face betrayed the fact that he was nervous and upset. Twelve minutes ago, he had had a disagreeable call from his old friend and boss, Manfred Schreiber, complaining first about the lighting of the parking area. *"Herr Präsident,"* Dr. Wolfe had countered spiritedly, "you know as well as I no one has that kind of projectors in his pocket!"

But the Police *Präsident* had cut him off: "I sent Captain Praus' Iroquois back to the base. The layout at Fürstenfeldbruck bothers me. And that being the case, I want you to collect the five marksmen and get back to the Village with them on the double. Praus has orders to load the six of you and take right off. Don't make him wait. Every minute counts. A move to rescue the hostages while they're underground has to be our priority objective. We're locating the best possible positions for your five men. They'll be able to go right there as soon as they land."

Wolf was discipline incarnate. He merely respectfully inquired: "If for any reason the underground ambush doesn't pan out, and the fedayeen take the copter to Fürstenfeldbruck, has a way been provided to bring my five snipers and me back to the base in time for them to resume their combat posts before the terrorists land?"

"*Natürlich!* Helicopters are what we have most of. And the pilots can go slower or faster as needed, right?"

8:50 PM: Two delegation heads, elected by the Olympic representatives of ten Arab countries, arrived at G-1 and asked to see the Village Mayor, Mr. Walter Tröger, urgently. Despite the hour, he was there, and received them right away. Mr. Kamal Taha, head of the Syrian mission, then read him a written protest against the half-masting in the Village that day of the flags of the ten Arab nations that signed the document.

"We demand, in the name of the nations we represent at the Games, that our flags immediately be raised again to the tops of their masts," it went on. Herr Tröger could only agree that no one could be forced to go into mourning against his will, and assure them that their wishes would be respected.

8:55 PM: It took tough talking to get back into the Village. The Panzers, at its edges, were snorting like forges.

And now, something new!

Two troop carriers, shaped like parallelepiped boxes, having 40-mm armor and armed with 12.7 machine gun and fourteen commandos apiece—despite their rubberized caterpillar treads, they had torn up the pavement. Plus two light reconnaissance tanks, as easy to handle as jeeps, with their hollow-rimmed metal wheels: the five-man crew inside must have felt they were in an oven. And four armored cars, squealing like a flock of gulls.

All these vehicles had black markings of *Polizei* or *Grenzschultzpolizei*. They were going east, but over a very wide circle. Part of the armor was finding a niche behind the large buildings of the commercial street. The G-1 tower was totally surrounded.

The athletes either were finishing dinner or had already turned in. The fine tiered open spaces, the Plaza, the commercial street, the cement benches, all were deserted.

Scarcely a thousand stubborn gawkers were still on the surrounding elevations looking down into *Olympisches Dorf*. But around

Stillborn Ambush

the curious, lighted artificial Olympic Lake, there was the usual nightly mob. The *theatron* was jampacked, as was Spielstrasse (Games Street), that went around the serpentine shores. Strains of rock and pop wafted up toward us, and piebald boats could be seen crossing the waters that shimmered with lively reflections. Should all of that have been banned, this night?

I had not noticed there were no helicopters above. But, just to remind me, here came one, circling about, going up and down like a yo-yo.

I tried to take a stairway. Two sweat-suited men, telescopic-sighted guns in hand, pointedly motioned to me to turn back.

In side streets, or at the sides of the great avenues, policemen in leather jackets or athletes' outfits were moving through the Village, silently, as elastic and cautious as cats. It looked as if they were playing a game. But then it became apparent they feared that observers—who? how? no one knew—might alert the terrorists to their movements. There were surely more cops underground, with or without disguises. It dawned on you at last that they were circuitously laying out an ambush or protection line from around 31 Connollystrasse to the G-1 tower.

9:00 PM sharp: The head of the fedayeen and his aide known as Tony greeted Herren Merk, Schreiber, and Tröger at the entranceway, where the lights had made the light-blue door look livid. Little could be discerned from our "private" observation-posts. Binoculars only picked out light shapes that seemed part of a slow-motion ballet.

The dead fade quickly. At this same spot, in the day's first sun, there had lain the undressed body of Moshe Weinberg, with its wounds and its blood, its smashed face and spilled-out guts, the remains of a human being thrown out like the incompletely skinned game that used to be left in front of the kennels, for the dogs, after the hunt in olden days.

A hunk of moon. A few rare stars. The night was growing darker. Who would benefit most from the darkness?

The policewoman was eating a banana, watching the dialogue from behind her big slightly tinted glasses, probably intended only to hide her eyes. Perhaps she wore a wig. Once the affair was over, she was suddenly to disappear.

289

"May we get to see your Fräulein Graes, or Eichler?"

"*Wir kennen sie nicht!*" (Never heard of her!)

"What? You know, that policewoman-interpreter who was here on September 5 . . ."

"*Ach so!* That one! We have no idea what became of her . . ."

And yet, Fräulein, you were more than helpful. Two Israelis owe their lives to you, you good Samaritan.

(Before going into the details of this final discussion outside Building 31, let us repeat that this dialogue is not made up. The many press conferences held after the massacre, our personal interviews, written, spoken, or televised statements by all those involved who survive, without exception, the *Dokumentation,* what has little by little transpired of the interrogation of those fedayeen who for a while were held prisoner, and finally the criminal investigation made by the public prosecutor of Munich, Otto Heindl, all have given us, not enough but indeed too many, parts of it, often contradicting one another.)

Herr Merk started by asking once more that the deadline be moved back to eight o'clock the next morning, even though the terrorists had already refused. He promised that if they agreed, no move against them would be made during that time.

Why, one wonders, did the Germans insist, not without some success, in continually trying to put things off? Herr Merk explained after the fact: "Generally speaking, the longer this sort of thing drags out, the better chance for the terrorists to make mistakes which the law and order forces could turn to advantage. Experience has clearly demonstrated this to be the case, as the outlaws begin to tire and tense up. Consequently, the *Krisenstab's* need for more time was pivotal."

As Tony started to get sore, Merk pushed harder: "We are in constant touch with Jerusalem. The Israeli Government, at this moment, is still discussing and going over your list of political prisoners. Mrs. Golda Meir and her ministers have not made any decision yet. They are of two minds. They will not break up before giving us a definite reply. We think they will make some counterproposals."

Tony wanted to say something in Arabic, but Issa cut him brutally short, and replied: "My comrades and I don't feel that if we spend another sleepless night we can retain our full fighting strength. So we are resolved, if you go on stalling, to shoot two of the hostages before your eyes within the next half-hour. I think that West Germany in that case would be criticized sharply by international opinion for having failed to cooperate, and as a result you will accede to our desire to take off by plane with the seven remaining hostages."

The Bavarian minister coldly stressed that Germany had nothing to do with the Palestinian question, and the *Krisenstab* had merely been trying to make mutually useful suggestions. But since the commando insisted on leaving this evening, so be it! They would leave. The different steps of the trip had been set up. The two helicopters would take off about 9:30.

"I would ask you to remind the Israelis," Issa added, "that to-morrow morning at eight we will shoot all the Zionist hostages at the airport we land at, if our brothers imprisoned by Israel have not been returned to us."

Thereupon, Dr. Schreiber cut in: Why not start the departure trek right now? The two birds could take off in less than fifteen minutes. The distance from here to the takeoff area was minimal. Dr. Schreiber himself would lead the way.

He had said it well, offhandedly. Just one minute before going back to talk to the terrorists, the police head had been told the Iroquois with Wolf and the five snipers had landed. Everything now was all set.

But Issa was a bundle of nerves. His features were agitated by strains and tics, as could be sharply seen despite the white hat pulled down to his eyebrows, the big dark glasses, and the layer of charcoal. There was something overly tense, anxious, harassed, about the wiry little man. Merk watched his hands: Issa had just rubbed soot-colored paint on them; they snaked around each other; in the right he held a pistol, and the rubbing of his fingers against each other and the left palm against the gunhandle reminded one of novice gangsters, so dangerous when they panic.

The terrorist leader sourly replied, "Minister Genscher surely informed you I intend first to effect a reconnaissance."

"It was at that precise moment," the Munich police head would say the next day, "that I understood the last chance to avoid shedding the hostages' blood was going. We had hoped that the desire to get it over with and growing weariness would make the head of the fedayeen give up his plan to reconnoiter first. Everything was ready to shoot them down."

"Well, then, why not come right away?" asked Schreiber, in full control of himself.

"There and back, how long should it take?" asked Issa.

"Let's say four minutes."

Issa said he had to talk to his comrades first. The West German officials had no choice but to wait for him where they were. They thought it took quite a while for him to get back. He was jumpy, biting his lips, seemed to have been doped. In place of the pistol, he now had a cocked grenade.

"I told my brothers I would be back with them in four minutes," he said. "If they don't see me at the end of that time, they'll shoot the hostages, one per minute. Let's go!"

"Not at all!" shouted Dr. Merk. "This is sheer blackmail. How do we know how you walk, or whether there won't be reasons to make stops for security purposes?"

"Well, how much, then? You yourself mentioned four minutes."

"Better say seven or eight."

"Six. No more. How far is it anyway, from here to the helicopters?"

"Oh, say, three hundred meters, with the twists and turns."

To my mind, it was at least 350 meters, underground from the cement stairs into the lobby of Block 31 to the greensward where the long awkward Bells were set. The Bavarian operators had thought they could fool the terrorists about the distance. That was naive. The stupidest of cat burglars would take precautions before allowing his gang out on an uncharted jaunt with a potential enemy.

Issa, raising his arm and shaking the hand that held the grenade, informed his comrades of the additional two minutes, still in the same sour tone. As they were about to start, he asked who was going along. Merk said Schreiber and Tröger. Issa insisted on the inclusion of *Bundesinnenminister* Genscher, who was not scheduled to be in on it. They had to wait for the federal minister, who had gone over to the communications van to make a phone call.

9:12 PM: They finally started, Issa staying between Genscher and Tröger. About ten yards ahead walked Schreiber. The mistrust of all of the men, their carefulness, could be seen in the way they walked, the stiffness of all their movements. For all that the city police chased bystanders away, there were still some gawking at this bad dream as it went by. It had been hard to clear the underground of the athletes or coaches who waved their badges to show they were actually on their way to their own quarters. Some had still slipped through.

Before starting, Issa had set the tone: "If anyone touches me, or shoots at me, I drop this grenade. It's a reinforced antipersonnel grenade, with piercing shrapnel."

The three walked side by side on the pavement, a meter separating one's shoulders from the next. The sidewalks seemed empty. Threatening presences could be sensed on all sides. The fedayee, slim as a riding crop in his safari outfit that turned blue under the neons, kept poking his bony painted head in all directions. They were walking along the parking stalls in which the cars seemed lonely between the sharp thin partitions. But how could they have been? There were armed police officers all along the underground galleries. They watched, powerless, from behind pillars, control cabins, and doors. In this supercharged atmosphere, the enfilades rang with the sharp commanding voice of the *Polizeipräsident*. "This is a reconnaissance trip!" Schreiber was shouting. *"Achtung!* Attention! This is a . . ."

Tiny, almost funny beneath the hat that the day's activity had gotten dirty, Issa seemed at times to smile. He had two grenades in his outside pockets, hung by the pin. His vision was probably obstructed by the outsize glasses, through which, looking at him, you could scarcely see his eyes. No one ever saw the color of them, except after the final shootout, of course. Then, they turned out to be blue, a very light blue, as is common in Europe, but also among Kabyles, for example.

To the right of Issa, Herr Genscher, tall and powerful as a uhlan, towered over him. On the other side, Tröger at regular intervals shouted sharply staccatoed words at Schreiber, and they echoed in the underground.

The lights had been cut down. Between columns, and in the middle of the roadway, the white lines traced on the asphalt stood out. Near the exit, Issa looked up toward the ceiling, as if wondering whether the monstrous thickness of concrete, twisted to form caissons, joists, and beams, was not hiding aiming marksmen. They would have had a good shot down at him. Electric wires hung from there, and cables and pipes ran parallel to the ground. It was sinister and dark as the innards of a steamer.

The strange cortege came out into the open before the tower surrounded by darkness. Guttural orders could be heard, and doors slamming. Motors, brakes, soles nervously striking the pavement, created a climate both agitated and tense. All the noises were unusual, in their irregularity and spacing.

They walked first on the concrete blocks, then on the grass, maintaining the same order. Here, there were tens of people who could get a close look at them. Genscher was later to say, "You couldn't tell whether there were many people. The lights seemed dimmed everywhere. But you felt a huge swell of breath around you."

Issa slipped his left hand into the back pocket of his trousers and came out with a flat flashlight, with narrow bright beams. Everything the Black September commando used was of the latest perfection. In front of him, the outline of the three copters, their noses rounding under the cockpits like seals' muzzles. The first two were each about 30 meters away from the men. The third, over near Lerchenauerstrasse, was less clear, like a big fishing boat washed ashore.

Issa stopped short, and said, "Why are the helicopters so far from the street, and so far apart? Bring them closer."

Herr Genscher went to talk to one of the pilots, and then came back toward Issa, saying determinedly, "We're ready to make a lot of concessions to save your hostages' lives. But never, I assure you, will we consent to making our countrymen run stupid risks for an affair that really is none of our business. The regulations of the Republic's Air Ministry require helicopter pilots, during a landing or takeoff, to have a circular clearance of obstacle-free space around their planes equal to at least two diameters of their rotors by day and two and a half diameters by night. The rotor of a Bell Iroquois has a diameter of thirteen point forty-one meters, and there is at most thirty meters between the Bells, and the same space between them and the roadway."

Herr Schreiber, who had been momentarily away, returned to the trio. Issa was biting his lips in silence. Suddenly, with Genscher and Tröger beside him, he went up to the closest of the planes. His flashlight shone out. He walked around the copter. Two crewmen were at their posts. Without going into the cabin, he swept his light through it, then gave the signal he was ready to start back.

Herr Schreiber started to lead the way, but not without first putting his wristwatch under Issa's nose, and tapping the crystal with his index finger. He was saying that if they were late, it was the unscheduled inspection of the copter that was the reason. They went down the clearance ramp at a good clip, and formed the same cortege as in the other direction, in the oppressive icy-ugly underground world. Schreiber was barking: "*Achtung!* This is a reconaissance trip! This is a . . ." As he was rushing a little too much, Tröger alerted him and he slowed down.

They were back at the foot of the gray steps nine minutes after they left. The metal door to Block 31 was open. A fedayee was on the stairs, invisible, but Issa yelled to him as they approached. He stuck part of his head out, in a dark hood, holding his assault gun in both hands. The two exchanged a few words. Then Issa said to Herr Genscher: "My friends and I have to talk. Meet you up above in five minutes, on Connollystrasse."

It was then 9:20 PM. Meantime, at

9:15 PM: A representative ". . . who holds a senior position in the [Israeli] security services" arrived at Olympic Village. The time given is the one Mrs. Golda Meir indicated on September 12 in her first overall statement to the Knesset about the attack on the Israeli delegation. The Germans, in the *Dokumentation*, place this important official's arrival at 7:00 PM. After personal investigation, I stick with the time given by Mrs. Meir.

Around noon, the *Krisenstab* had asked Ambassador Ben Horin to have such a personality sent in, to act as "adviser," according to Herr Merk's terms. Mr. Ben Horin immediately notified Jerusalem. Mrs. Meir personally had her ambassador inform the West

German federal and Bavarian authorities that no Israeli personality, in an official capacity or not, could assume any share whatever of the responsibility in a matter affecting Israelis but conducted by Germans alone on German soil.

Not only was she opposed to sending such an envoy, but also were her Deputy Prime Minister Yigal Allon, General Moshe Dayan, and Messrs. Shimon Peres and Abba Eban, that is, all the members of the Cabinet directly concerned with the attack and the special services.

The *Krisenstab* kept asking for the dispatch of a high-ranking Israeli official. The Jerusalem Government answered that all it could send would be an observer who would stick strictly to that role. The Germans agreed. The Israeli Cabinet with some delay named a highly qualified observer: General Zvi Zamir, since 1968 the head of Mossad. He was seen off at Lod Airport by Ministers Dayan and Peres, whom scores of witnesses saw returning to Jerusalem at the very moment when rumors placed them in Munich. The "security specialist" was accompanied to Munich by an aide, a Mossad officer, whose identity is of no concern.

German authorities of all levels—G.F.R., Bavaria, Munich, and even the Olympic Games Organizing Committee—in full mutual agreement, as obstinately as straight-facedly, kept unofficially giving out highly famous, and presumably highly plausible, names of the "personalities of the Israeli special services" who came to Munich on the evening of September 5, 1972. Even months after the fact, they kept sending inquirers, including this writer, off on wild-goose chases, most often with the name of Shimon Peres.

I can assert without shadow of conjecture that on the one hand Mr. Shimon Peres did not set foot in West Germany during these tragic events, and on the other it was General Zamir and Captain Y who landed at Olympic Village, at 9:15 that evening.

What made the Germans cling so to these canards? Let us note that the confusion on this point is the same that occurs for practically everything connected with this affair. The tragedy of that bloody Tuesday–Wednesday, because of its victims, its scenario, its outcome, its locale, and its circumstances, is a matter of consternation and deep bothersomeness to the West Germans. The less said about it, the less researched, the better. . . .

As soon as the operations were over, the Germans did their best to discourage inquiry. One runs up against not a blank wall, but an elastic curtain, changing in aspect but never rising. There are evasions, promises for a soonest that never comes, utterly misleading tips, and unanswered letters. Yet, even the thickest curtains always have chinks in them, and there is always a chance to get around them.

As for the lid clamped on General Zamir's presence in Munich, there is another reason. The West Germans observed the strictures laid down: the Israeli army and special services have come by their reputation for secrecy honestly. The head of Mossad is never discussed: even his long-gone actions, however innocuous, remain forever unmentioned.

It was only human that quite a few dodges were used in the *Dokumentation* concocted mainly by the Bavarian Interior Ministry and Dr. Schreiber's department. It misses no chance to stress the presence both at Olympic Village and at Fürstenfeldbruck of the two special envoys from Jerusalem. It emphasizes their verbal participation in two phases of the action, and allows the inference to be drawn that they had approved the manner in which the Germans were carrying out the operations.

We will return to that "participation" of the two Israelis. When the *Dokumentation* got down to cases even it admitted that all they did was to confirm certain verifiable matters and say a few words in Arabic over the loudspeaker at German request, when Fräulein Graes was no longer there.

Quoting Golda Meir to the Knesset, September 12, 1972 (and reiterating that her second statement on October 16 would reaffirm this, with special emphasis on security measures at Munich): "The Government of Israel had no possibility to activate its forces in order to rescue the hostages." "No Israeli representative was requested to—nor did—conduct negotiations with the terrorists."

She also said, on September 12: "When [the security-services representative] arrived, the German authorities had already worked out a full plan of action. He was a witness to events from the time the hostages were transferred from the Israeli pavilion in the Olympic Village to the airport. No plan whatsoever was brought before him for his cognizance, approval, or comment. . . . He was a witness to what occurred at the airport. . . ."

During her September 12 speech, Mrs. Meir several times, heavily and energetically, stressed that the Germans alone were in charge of everything, from one end to the other: "The decision, the planning and implementation of the operation was made solely by the German security forces, without recourse to the consent of any Israeli representative whatsoever."

It is no breach of confidence to say that, had the high Israeli secret-service official been in charge, he would have acted completely differently from the Germans. Or, to quote the Prime Minister (September 12) once more: "This aim was not achieved and the outcome is indeed terrible. From the operational aspect, there is room for criticism, but nevertheless, this does not void the great value of the decision itself, taken by the German authorities to act by force against the terrorists, in the absence of any alternative, and above all, not to give in to them."

Which makes a very good postface.

9:25 PM: To the east of Block 31, the next (small) building, numbered 11, no one knows why, housed Bolivia. Its people had been evacuated, and the forward command post of the Village security forces was set up in it. The two buildings are some 15 meters apart, the space between them paved with small brick-colored rectangular blocks.

In the middle of the street there are also the thick pipes daubed in orange or gold, with short spurts of bubbling, streaming water popping up from place to place. It makes a nice murmuring, on quiet nights.

Now Issa, tic-ridden and nervous, holding his cocked grenade like a fetish in his right hand, was going toward No. 11 with Fräulein Graes. Why? Would that that were the only thing unexplained! It seems Herr Tröger alone had come to find out what the fedayeen had decided about the underground transfer to the copters, and the Black September group insisted that either Genscher or Schreiber go along with them. Tröger, having said he would ask the police commissioner about it, but pointing out that these new arrangements would kill more time, Issa, who had long since made note of what was going on at No. 11, preferred to go to the Bolivian quarters in person and hasten things along. Forewarned by the policewoman, Herren Merk and Schreiber were in the vestibule. Issa barged right in. He advised his hosts he had only one minute in which to reappear before his comrades.

"We decided," he said, "to go to the helicopters with our Israeli prisoners by bus."

"We'll have to get two vehicles."

"Why two? One will do. There are plenty of them down there. They can't all be out of commission."

The fedayee's sharp smile went unnoticed, as he specified, "The bus will have to park right in front of the underground entrance to Thirty-one. Outside limit: ten minutes from now."

"No, sir. Fifteen. We are as anxious as you to get this over with." And Merk added, before Issa could stop him, "Before we get under way, the German authorities intend to make sure the nine hostages are still alive." Issa accepted that.

With the *Krisenstab* chiefs in tow, the fedayee walked briefly over on Connollystrasse. Two minutes later, hands tied behind them, disheveled, and blinking because two white police projectors were beamed at them, the nine hostages were visible for a few seconds in the second-story window: first five of them, then the other four. They were shaved, and dressed in street clothes. All had jackets on, and displayed their habitual dignity. They could make no sound, the time being so short.

9:33 PM: The *Krisenstab* heads held a "final decision" meeting in the radio van. For one brief time yet, they had three alternatives, and examined each in turn.

1. Attack the Israeli quarters in which the hostages were sequestered.

The *Dokumentation* (p. 56) gives two reasons for rejecting this: *a)* one single terrorist might in a flash be able to kill all of the hostages Herr Genscher had seen tied up; and *b)* "The firepower of seven terrorists powerfully armed with grenades and submachine guns would have meant considerable losses in the ranks of the police." And it further stressed that the terrorists were well entrenched, whereas the assault troops' bulletproof jackets "can afford only limited protection."

Why did it mention seven terrorists? The members of the *Krisenstab* have admitted that until the fedayeen left they were convinced that there were at most only five of them. But we can skip that. Despite the dangers of an armed break-in at Apt. 1, it still had great advantages over Fürstenfeldbruck.

Yet, they unanimously rejected the idea of storming the terrorist position in Block 31.

2. Armed intervention while underground.

This would undoubtedly have been the best solution if the terrorists had not demanded motorized transport. But, with at least 350 meters to go, over a hazard-strewn course, how could anyone have been naive enough to think they would agree to walk?

Reading the *Dokumentation*, there remains a question as to whether the Bavarian authorities would have risked a rescue action for the hostages if the terrorists had walked to the takeoff point. The official report stressed the chances the fedayeen would have had to hide behind their captives; it dwells on the many shelters, the shooting problems, the poor vision.

That's too much! Snipers hidden behind, alongside, and ahead of the group, would have had plenty of chances to score bull's-eyes as they went along. The Bavarian officials, who were to contradict themselves more than once, stated many times, Dr. Schreiber more than any of the others, in my presence on September 7 and 8, that their underground setup would have worked, if only the fedayeen . . .

But, in view of the transport finally used, there would at most be 2 meters between the last cement step and the door to the vehicle. The terrorists would obviously come through in waves of two or three at a time. Even if all the windows of the bus could be lighted at once and the men at hand were champion snipers at live targets, there were too many chances of a bloodbath.

Merk and his staff were all against the attack on the bus, except for Dr. Schreiber, who stated: "We have one chance left. Let us assume there are nine hostages and five fedayeen. They say one vehicle is enough, so I'll send them one of the Village VW mini-buses. They'll be packed in like sardines. By throwing powerful light on the vehicle and shooting from all sides at once at the terrorists who will be easy to spot because of their free hands and their weapons, they can be knocked out of the fight without too much risk of their returning deadly fire. Of course, they'll kill some of the hostages, but at any rate, that can't be avoided. I think most of the Israelis would make it OK if my plan were followed."

Herr Merk felt that the ratio of risk was still too high, even this way, for both Israelis and police who could not, barring fool luck, hope to get all the terrorists on the first shot. He said so. The chief of the Munich police merely stated he might make the suggestion to the Interior Minister once more when the fedayeen had seen and accepted the minibus that was planned for use. Schreiber already had everything set up for a clear shot at them: the fourteen marksmen were all deployed around Block 31's iron door.

3. Armed action as they were getting into the two helicopters. This was quickly unanimously rejected, because of the nearness of buildings and streets, impossibility of keeping bystanders away, and the dangers to the crews.

So that left the ambush at Fürstenfeldbruck.

They all had to agree that that would be the last chance, assuming no opportunity to free the prisoners cropped up unexpectedly before that. And Herr Merk immediately advised Brandt and Goppel by phone of what had been decided.

9:35 PM: The *Pressezentrum* had tuned in to the most spectacular and hideous event of the year. Through press conferences, interviews, and tipoffs, news and rumors spread like wildfire. Herr Willi Daume had been scheduled for 9:15, and he was on time, accompanied by Herr Vogel, Vice-President of the Organizing Committee.

The headman of the Munich Games looked smart as ever, his blue eyes glistening, but his features were drawn this evening, his color subnormal, and worry showed through. The mob of journalists were like a rush-hour subway crush: over two thousand of them.

He began by retracing the events of the day: nothing new there.

301

And went on: "Only fifteen minutes ago, the terrorists had still not backed down on any of their demands. It does not seem likely Israel will agree to release all or any of the prisoners they want."

In his waterproofed tan jacket, sky-blue turtleneck sweater, and navy-blue slacks, Willi Daume paid no attention to the bunches of raised arms, waving as if greeting each other. He was perspiring. Droplets shone at the corners of his eyebrows, and then rolled down. Everybody felt hot.

He monologued on more forcefully: "The funeral ceremony in memory of the victims of terrorism to be held in the *Olympia-stadion* at ten AM will show the whole world how we feel. We have all agreed that the competitive events will be resumed tomorrow, Wednesday, afternoon.[1] The Olympic Movement cannot give in to a handful of terrorists." And then, a slight hedge, "Obviously, depending on how things turn out . . ."

He then left immediately. And Hans Klein took his place, racking his brain to try to satisfy the impossible, though purely normal, professional questions from newsmen. Bedlam.

One item spread suddenly: the helicopters parked near G-1 were about to take the fedayeen and their captives to some airfield other than Riem. This was when the name of Fürstenfeldbruck first surfaced; as did the destination: Cairo.

But, apart from Riem, there were five civilian or military airports that might be used, within a radius of at most 26 km. (16-plus mi.) from Munich.

The entire press headquarters started feverishly poring over maps of *Gross-München* and environs, picking up the names: Karlsfeld to the northwest, Oberschleissheim north, Fürstenfeldbruck west, Oberpfaffenhofen southwest, and Neubiberg southeast. All were equipped for it. The two most distant were Oberpfaffenhofen and Fürstenfeldbruck.

9:40 PM: Dark blue and glinting green in the light, a Volkswagen minibus, driven by a tough with tense features beneath the white cap of the security service of the "Happy Games," pulled up before the underground entrance to No. 31.

For some reason, the fedayeen would never use the elevator.

---

[1] At this point, the emergency meeting of the IOC, which alone could decide this, had not yet met.

Stillborn Ambush

Issa, flanked by a tall fellow masked with a blue wool stocking cap with eyeholes, appeared at the foot of the steps half a minute later. He had been called by phone, and was carrying his powerful flashlight. Quick look around, while the blue mask got down on his belly to check the underpinning of the bus. Dr. Schreiber, militarily elegant, with a storm in his eyes, mouth tight as a dagger, and teeth gnashing, stood straight as a missile, in front of the other West German officials.

Issa came to within a meter of him. They had had more than one such silent confrontation, the one radiating mute sarcasm, the other exasperation. Till the end, Issa never missed a chance to act defiant.

Schreiber was once again struck by the abnormal widening of his eyelids, the feverish shine in his eye. Was he on uppers or downers? The difference was often hard to tell.

"You will understand that this bus won't do," Issa said nonchalantly. "In case of trouble, we'd never be able to defend ourselves in it. Come, *Herr Polizeipräsident,* get us a roomier bus. You have ten minutes maximum."

"Twenty. Even in Germany you can't just press a button and get a car to order."

"Watch out. Don't try kidding with us. You're overlooking all those military vans I saw when we were walking through. If we aren't done with this by ten o'clock . . ."

With the side of his hand, Issa sliced an imaginary throat. Then he did what he had so frequently done before: he put his wristwatch against his ear to listen to it tick. And walked away.

9:45 PM: Since arriving at Olympic Village, General Zvi Zamir had gotten only a slight view of the actual state of affairs. He had been told only cursorily of the—not yet final—decision to set up the ambush at the Fürstenfeldbruck base. He asked for specifications of how the airport operation was to be carried out. The ones he got—very incomplete—left him worried. And he said so. But Merk and Schreiber evinced no reaction. Not that they looked down on or mistrusted the Israeli. But they were terribly busy, and, having their own disagreements to deal with, were not anxious to have to cope with still another view.

Looking like an unimportant little bureaucrat, General Zamir had just reconnoitered the underground path from Block 31 to G-1. He paced off the size of the takeoff pad, walked around the whirlybirds, and was now back near the hostages' building.

Herr Tröger joined him and apprised him of the Arabs' rejection of the minibus. Zamir's sharp face was as cold as the winters in his native Poland. He betrayed nothing of his feelings or presentiments. However, he did say he was sorry not to have been at the forward C.P. at 11 Connollystrasse when Issa barged in there. After Tröger left, he discussed this matter briefly with his aide-de-camp, Captain Y, and went over to No. 11 to see Herr Merk.

"Would it be possible for the officer who is with me to talk to one of the fedayeen by phone? There's one chance in ten that might lead to some kind of way out."

"Does your officer speak Arabic?"

"That is an absolute requirement in our services," Zamir replied, smiling thinly.

Merk then grasped that if Zamir did not ask to speak to the Arabs himself, it was because of that Israeli concern for secrecy: he did not want the attackers to hear his voice. Minister Genscher, who had just come over, felt the general's suggestion to be capital. He and Merk forthwith headed for Block 31 to take it up with the Black September people.

The amazing, mysterious policewoman quickly set up the contact. Issa, holding a cigarette, appeared in the doorway, swinging his frail body like a reed in the wind.

He listened attentively to Herr Genscher, whom he had deferred to from the start, both because of his title and because of his impressiveness, his unshakable self-confidence, and his Caesarian countenance.

But Issa answered without hesitation, in a tone of sincerity that the Germans could not fail to note: "I don't have to consult with my brothers to say no to this. We have understood for several hours that all the Israeli Government was trying to do was stall us off with their so-called Cabinet debates, in the hope that we would tire. We already know by the radio that they have sent representatives to Munich. You agreed to transmit a message from those people. Now, please be good enough to give them one from the Palestinian Resistance.

Stillborn Ambush

"The Israelis, as well as the German authorities, would do well to understand that Black September will brook no further delay in the takeoff of the two helicopters, and then the plane. Even if we wanted to, instructions from our superiors and our own condition at the end of this extended effort make it impossible. Consequently, I must tell you once more: If, within the next half-hour we have not taken off from the Village under the conditions agreed upon, we will start by shooting two of the hostages either here or at the helicopter pad.

"We would also like you to give the Israelis another warning. The fact that we are taking the Zionist hostages to an Arab country in no way modifies the position we have previously stated: If tomorrow morning at eight, the anti-Zionist prisoners held by Israel, of whom we gave you a list, are not safe and sound in Cairo, we will shoot down within the plane, at the country of arrival, every one of the hostages, bar none."

Thereupon, he nodded, and disappeared as he had come, a frail form in blue-gray safari outfit, a smoking American cigarette between his fingers.

General Zamir, a few moments later, impassively listened to Herr Genscher's report of this conversation.

There was Amitzur Shapira, forty, a teacher at the Wingate Institute. Married, father of four, living at Herzliya.

He was a sabra. He looked Slavic with his pink skin, blue eyes, and blond wavy hair. He was considered Israel's best track and field coach. He had the expanded chest and solid arms of an ex-decathlon competitor, and was indefatigable. He had piled up a number of titles as champion of Israel. He crisscrossed the little Promised Land as much as possible on the lookout for prospects, but never, even for the Olympics, would he have dreamed of asking the army to show the least favoritism to any athlete, male or female.

It was he who had formed Israel's young women's track star, Esther Shahamorov, who would probably have reached the finals in the 100-meter hurdles, if she had not withdrawn from the Games along with all the Israeli team's survivors, after the Connollystrasse outrage. The semifinals had been scheduled for the

305

afternoon of September 6, the day that began with the massacre at Fürstenfeldbruck.

Postponed for one day, they actually took place September 7, around 5:30 PM. The vision of radiant Esther with her mane of flaming black and her golden legs hard as apples, swam before my eyes like a screen, as the second heat of the semifinals, in which Shapira's ward was supposed to run in Lane 4, was about to start.

There was the graceful French girl, Jacqueline André, and the vaulting, fine East German Annelie Ehrhardt, with her blonde smile and insolent superiority. The huge crowd was fascinated. There was nothing more to remind them of the tragedy, were it not, atop the opposite side of the bowl-shaped stadium, the flag at half-mast, alone lowered among the 122 national banners: Israel's white flag with the two sky-blue stripes, and in the middle the *Magen David,* King David's six-pointed shield.

No, nothing. Not even a rose, one of those beautiful red Munich roses, at the start line of the empty lane. Not even an announcement to say why contestant No. 211 was not running.

The seven other semifinalists were completing their warm-ups around the black-numeraled white lane-markers. They set their feet in the metal starting blocks. The shot rang out, and the bent bodies flew forward. The legs worked like scissors across the black-and-white wood bars, set on stands of turquoise blue, Munich Olympic blue. The 80,000 spectators thrilled. But my mind was on the last great athletic satisfaction that Esther had given her coach. On September 1, she had qualified for the 100-meter dash semifinals, a feat in itself. It was the twenty-year-old girl's first big international meet, and she had never had any real competition in her own little country. The next day, Saturday, September 2, Esther missed by a breath making the finals, finishing fifth out of the eight in her heat, with the same time as the fourth, the last to qualify. Two days later, Monday the 4th, Esther Shahamorov won her place in the 100-meter hurdles semifinals, with the seventh best time of all the qualifiers, making her a probable finalist.

That was in the morning, a little before 10:00, in the sun, with a flat wind, at the height of the Games of Joy. Esther was in the first heat, in Lane 2. Amitzur Shapira was at the bottom of Stand

Stillborn Ambush

C. Coming from the warm-up field, where he had watched his girl get ready, he still had on the team's purple sweat suit. When the scoreboard flashed dark Esther's time, as she was already undoing the blue-and-white headband that held her hair in, he raised both arms. Esther was looking for him now, her evenly chiseled face reflecting her feelings like a mirror, turned toward the stands.

Thirteen point seventeen seconds: new Israeli record! "Qualification guaranteed!" he was shouting. She was waving at him, even though she was too far to hear.

Eighteen hours and twenty minutes later, Amitzur Shapira would become a hostage. Thirty-eight hours to live, and then the terrorists would kill him. Three of them at least were there, somewhere on those tiers of the *Olympiastadion,* the large but not grandiose Olympic Stadium, the sumptuous spherical ring of 80,000 seats, a crown of many colors, set in a green dale. The Black September commandos regularly got tickets for the Games; the three who worked in the Olympic Village pulled strings to get some, and then arranged with their accomplices to take turns at the pre-murder festivities.

Shapira's sweat shirt naturally had the national coat of arms: the Menorah, the seven-armed candlestick surrounded by two olive branches. Before the attack, in Munich, I often noticed long hard looks being given to this Jewish emblem, the symbol of light which had already ornamented the First Temple of Jerusalem, Solomon's Temple, three millennia ago.

That was what my thoughts were on September 7.

By then, Esther Shahamorov was already back home with all of the Israeli delegation, the dead and the quick.

Say not this universe is a useless thing, nor life absurd, or that sufferings are unjustified.

XVIII
THE REFUGEES

... now therefore arise, go over this
Jordan, thou, and all this people, unto
the land which I do give to them, even
to the children of Israel.
                              Joshua 1:2

THE FEDAYEEN, AS EVERYONE KNOWS, HAVE BUT ONE WAR AIM:
reconquest of Palestine, with as corollary the vengeful return of
the refugees, death to the State of Israel, and expulsion or extermination of all Jews. And the misfortunes of the Palestinian expatriates have become the most powerful weapon in the anti-Zionist
propaganda arsenal.

The refugee problem began brutally a quarter-century ago.
I witnessed their first flight in May 1948. *Effendis*—the VIPs, the
wealthy—went first, in their big cars, carrying as much of their
worldly goods as they could. *Fellahs*—the workers, the bulk of
city folk—were left without guides, alone and wretched. Fear took
over, nurtured by fierce propaganda which, glossing over the atrocities committed against Jews, depicted the latter as massacrers. The
report of a battle, the approach of a Jewish detachment, was
enough to sow panic. In the heat, on the smelly, dry roads, people
fled, dragging wheelbarrows, or hitching burros to their carts.
The old fell by the wayside. And every such heartbreaking clutter
on the road was accompanied by a radio blaring about the coming
Arab counterattack: "Leave your towns and villages! Give free
rein to our fliers and armored units so they can mercilessly strike
back at the Jews!" . . .

The cease-fires that followed Israel's victories did not bring
most of the estimated 550,000 Palestinian fugitives back home,

when, all things considered, that might have been rather feasible. The Israelis had done their best, from the start of the attacks by the Arab states on May 15, 1948, until the end of 1949, to give every kind of desirable appeasement to the refugee masses and assure them their return was urgently required, lest an irreversible situation be created. But, from Grand Mufti of Jerusalem to imams, military chiefs and political leaders, all those with influence in Islam and the Arab countries had urged "their brothers" in Palestine to flee before the Jewish armies, and now they called on them not to return to their homes and lands, but to await the imminent Arab counteroffensive that was about to strike Israel, kill all the Jews, and make for the greatest *rezzou* in all history.

The refugees swallowed the line and began to camp out under temporary tents, in the most awful of social and sanitary conditions, conducive to illness, epidemics, and the law of the jungle. Non-Communist world opinion quickly voiced its alarm. The Eastern bloc on the contrary took years to concern itself with the problem.

On December 8, 1949, the U.N. created a well-financed organization, UNRWA (United Nations Relief and Works Agency for Palestine Refugees in the Near East). In addition to giving each refugee minimal financial aid and grants of food supplies (admittedly inadequate), as well as a variety of other services, from 1951 to 1954 UNRWA spent over $200,000,000 to "promote constructive economic projects in the Arab countries" so they might be able properly to help the refugees work out permanent arrangements. Despite the expenditures, this aim failed completely. . . .

An April 1, 1972, UNRWA census showed 546,738 of these Palestinian refugees living in Jordan, 276,862 on the West Bank, 322,807 in the Gaza Strip, 182,941 in Lebanon, and 167,497 in Syria, for a total of 1,496,845.

With Israel now administering both the West Bank and Gaza, it had the burden of the largest number of actual Palestinian refugees, 599,669. So "that general terrified flight" of Palestinians from the Jewish hordes, the so-called "second exodus" of June 1967 so widely described in Arab and Communist propaganda, turns out to be a figment of the imagination, by UNRWA's own figures.

And that is worth mentioning, since UNRWA's heads have always been notoriously anti-Israeli.

The UNRWA budget for 1973 was to be $52,323,000. And here is how it defines the "Palestine refugee":

> . . . a person whose normal residence was Palestine for a minimum of two years immediately before the outbreak of the conflict in 1948 and who, as a result of this conflict, lost both his home and his means of livelihood. To be eligible for UNRWA assistance, he must be registered and in need, and must have taken refuge in Jordan, Lebanon, Syria or the Gaza Strip—the areas contiguous to Israel in which the Agency operates. Children and grandchildren of registered refugees who fulfill certain criteria are also eligible for UNRWA assistance.

. . . It would be shameful to deny the ordeals the true masses of these refugees suffer (and we will return to them). . . .

In August 1949, Israel offered to take back 100,000 of these refugees, but the Arab nations rejected this. In 1952, all bank accounts and deposits left in Israeli banks by Arab refugees were returned to them without any loss whatsoever. . . .

Except for Jordan, which gave most refugees on its soil Jordanian nationality, the Arab nations (Egypt, Syria, Lebanon, and Libya) refused so to reclassify refugees. But, as we saw, UNRWA's original aim was not just to help the refugees, but to restore them to normal pursuits, albeit in the countries to which they had fled. The U.N. several times undertook immediately and completely to reimburse the host nations for any efforts they made at integrating the refugees into their regular social structures. In vain. All except Jordan rejected such permanent immigration, and left the expatriates and their offspring in a restricted status. The Arab states preferred keeping masses of refugees in camps dotted along Israel's borders—like so many running sores.

Those refugees within Israeli territory have incomparably better living conditions than do the ones outside. . . . UNRWA has never voiced a criticism of Israel's handling of refugees within its borders. Over 50,000 Arabs from the administered territory work within Israel on permits, and some 20,000 more without legal permits. The rise in the standard of living since Israel took over these territories has been breathtaking: 50 percent in Judea and Samaria, 60 percent in the Gaza Strip. . . . By the spring of 1973, there were 1,150,000 souls in the Israeli-occupied regions, with continual growth, and returns from over Jordan increased apace.

Jewish policy toward the occupied territories has been characterized by pragmatism. . . . Jerusalem alone has been definitively annexed to Israel, and even this may still allow for some compromise with respect to the Holy Places. Beyond that, Israel has kept all options open for the remaining occupied lands: return to the sovereignty of the neighboring Arab nations; creation of one or more autonomous political entities; or federation with Israel. . . .

Inhabitants of the occupied zones are free to travel to Jordan, and from there wherever they wish. Their travel documents are valid for a year and renewable on demand. This has been true since December 15, 1972, although they were almost as free to move around before that.

Obviously, Israel's Arab citizens, now some 400,000, do not have all rights that Jews have. However, their civic rights have been constantly on the increase. Their prosperity outstrips that of any comparable Arab grouping anywhere in the world, and that gap, as of now, will grow even greater. But only when Israeli Arabs cease to be second-class citizens will they feel truly Israeli.

The refugees living in Jordan, while under an obligation to hew to Amman's political line, had their lives completely transformed after King Hussein liquidated or drove out the armed forces of the Palestinian resistance. No more El Fatah or PFLP dictatorship in the camps. No more obligatory financial assessments, nor conscription into Al Assifa.

Those refugees who remain in Syria or Lebanon, for their part, are held unswervingly in line. They live under the jackboot. In Syria, long since, the Government has made itself absolute master of the refugees' fate. In Lebanon, they are under the crushing dictatorship of the fedayeen. . . . Between October and December 1969, the guerrilla movements gained the upper hand in the camps, by driving out the Lebanese army, which had run them until then. . . .

Since then, UNRWA has tried in vain to get the Lebanese

Government to regain authority in these camps, where even "justice" is dispensed by the guerrillas. The Secretary-General of the U.N. has had appalling UNRWA reports on this.

The New York Times, which has tried to be even-handed in its coverage of the Middle East, has published many shocking details about these camps and reported in late June 1972 that the guerrillas had refused to give its correspondent access to the camps, even though he had been authorized to enter by the Beirut Government. After extensive efforts and pressure, he did get to visit one of the U.N. camps, but was allowed to see only the school, the dispensary, the kitchen, and the social-service center. The camp director, in an office papered with guerrilla posters, refused to let him see the rest—all of which, of course, was 100 percent paid for by the U.N. . . .

Beyond the lies and misrepresentations, a few dependable figures are worth considering: those from the U.N., UNRWA, and the Arab countries themselves.

Just how many Palestinian Arabs (Moslem and Christian) are there in all the Middle East, Palestine included? About 2,900,000. This figure is reached if we assume UNRWA's count of refugees to be correct. Of these, 470,000 Arabs live within Israel proper, including the officially annexed "Jordanian sector" of Jerusalem.

Now, how many Jews are there in Israel? At the time we are concerned with, about 2,900,000, of whom 600,000 were refugees from Arab countries. In 1948–49, 550,000 Jews had fled the unspeakable living conditions in those Islamic countries in a first wave of immigration to Israel: for them, getting there was a matter of life or death. Most of those have now died, so, despite the many later waves of immigration, the figures of living Jewish refugees from Arab states is no higher.

All of these Jewish refugees past and present, had to leave the lands of their birth empty-handed, without luggage or money, after years of persecution. They all lived through pogroms, all experienced murder, pillage, rape. They were communities rich in tradition, with roots going back to ancient times. No Arab nation offered the slightest restitution for confiscated holdings: homes, lands, bank accounts, furniture. Jewish cemeteries were desecrated, from Iran to Iraq.

The Refugees

It is hard to estimate the number of Jews murdered between the North African Arab countries and the Middle East, but 200,000 seems a plausible figure. I personally, from July 1962 to December 1963, saw how Jews were butchered in Algeria. My writings, dictated from the very sites of the horrors there, stand as evidence.

Hell is what most of Israel's Jews escaped from, they or their parents. Yet Israel is much more than just the remains of martyred communities in the Maghreb and Near East: it also means those who miraculously survived the camps and jails of Nazi-occupied Europe—and the undesirables of the postwar period in Eastern Europe—the Jews who refused to deny their identity in the USSR or Poland. . . .

Yet, world opinion seems forgetful of, or indifferent to, these refugees, these Wandering Jews by the millions, without even a beggar's bag to their names when they got to Israel. No UNRWA was set up for them!

They represent a little over half of Israel's 2,900,000 population; the other 1,400,000 are sabras, native-born Israelis.

However, all—repeat, all—of them had ancestors who were either persecuted or even murdered. The immigrant off some old tub that had somehow brought him from Baghdad or Tripoli begot children, if he was still of an age to. And the skeleton out of the Auschwitz crematories also performed a new miracle of Israel: he too had offspring.

Ever since World War II, the existence of Jewish communities in Moslem countries has been one long torture, met by the indifference or hypocrisy of the rest of the world, as the distress of Soviet Jews is comparably ignored today.

Why this silence? The answer is simple.

Next to the USSR colossus with its 250,000,000 people, what do 14,000,000 Jews matter? What kind of a market are they? What good as propaganda? And these same survivors of a genocide unique in history count for little against the 670,000,000 Moslems and the eighteen countries of the Arab League, in the political, economic, and military considerations of the great powers, or the "impartial" calculations of the rulers of the "world's business." Simple as that.

The U.S. so far has escaped this contagion, largely because its

6,000,000 Jews, 3 percent of its population, are a dynamic, hard-working, and influential group, and also because the memory of Hitler's annihilation of Jews has been kept very much alive throughout the country.

According to U.N. documents distributed during its Flushing Meadow debate on the partition of Palestine, in 1947, exclusive of Palestine there were 830,000 Jews in Arab lands. In twenty-five years, that figure fell to 58,000.

Thirty thousand of these live in Morocco, and 8,000 in Tunisia. Those 38,000, with the exception of a handful of individuals specially privileged because of their usefulness, are considered nationals rather than full citizens and are under all kinds of restrictions. Yet their existence is more or less tolerable: they are not being systematically persecuted. It is mostly the memory of past ordeals that upsets them.

Lebanon has 6,000 Jews, who are much more harshly treated. They have virtually none of the rights or privileges of citizens. It is very difficult for them to leave. Yet they do get some share of commiseration from the Christians who make up almost half the population. Nevertheless, in January 1971, at Saïda, the Biblical Sidon, El Fatah staged a pitiless pogrom, that all but exterminated the onetime large and prosperous Jewish community. Some sixty people were killed, there were countless rapes. Other, less bloody, pogroms took place at Lebanese Tripoli and Beirut. . . .

In Algeria, 1500 Jews at most remain, vegetating in terror. I saw the shadows of the Oran and Algiers communities at the end of 1969 for the last time. Most of the remaining people were very old. The few young ones I spoke to had all applied in vain for permission to leave the country. They dared not try to emigrate illicitly, for fear of being caught and given long prison terms, if not death sentences, or for fear of reprisals against their parents or grandparents if they were successful. They suffered in silence.

Elsewhere in Islam the Jews are completely cut off from the outside world; all mail to or from them is opened, and only extremely brave people dare carry messages. The best we can get is an approximate idea of their numbers: In Iraq, say, 1,000.[1] In

1 Some specialists say only 400 to 500. But, outside of Baghdad, there would seem to be, in places like Mosul and Basra, a few terrified communities, virtually prisoners, awaiting death, without synagogues or rabbis.

Syria, 4,000. In Yemen, 2,000, with 500 more in the People's Republic of Yemen; 3,000 in Egypt; 500 in Libya; some 500 in the Sudan.

These people are in fact powerless hostages. They are forbidden to emigrate. Some try nonetheless, and nine times out of ten are caught. The common punishment for this is hanging. They are all poverty-stricken, yet remain amazingly dignified. All their belongings have been confiscated. Even travel within their countries is virtually forbidden. They are not allowed to hold government jobs, nor in many cases entitled to government services. Schools are closed to them, discrimination is institutionalized, humiliations and brutalizations are everyday occurrences. Their lives are continually threatened, and every so often some are killed—like noisome animals.

Remember the worldwide TV display of January 27, 1969, on Khulmi Square, Baghdad? Fourteen men accused of spying for Israel hanged to the wild applause of a crowd, shouting "Down with the Jews!" Eleven of those victims were Jews.

Today, the remains of the Iraqi Jewish communities, which in 1939 had 260,000 souls, are penned into ghettos as closely watched as those of Warsaw or Lodz. Disappearances, soon followed by the finding of the bodies, occur periodically. . . . And in all of these countries Jews must carry a special identity card, stamped *Mussawi* (of Mosaic religion).

While there is a cruel proportion of refugees and DPs among Palestinian Arabs, yet it is infinitely lower than among Israeli Jews. This kind of misfortune, in our century, is a horribly common thing. In 1957, the Office of the High Commissioner for Refugees, set up by the U.N., estimated that Europe alone had generated 30,000,000 refugees in twenty years.

Without underestimating the travail of the Palestinian Arabs, one thing must be noted: the humanitarian concern so many nations show them smells of oil. All the Arab nations stand against Israel, and the joint oil production of those nations in 1971 was just short of a billion tonnes, or something better than 40 percent of the world total.

The best estimates for 1972 give about 14,500,000 Jews in the world (officially 14,236,420—but there may be some deliberate underreporting for the Islamic countries). The great diaspora (exile) remains, with the U.S. (6,060,000) and the USSR (2,664,000—some estimates say over 3,000,000) its main centers. With incipient emigration to Israel—44,000 in 1972—the Soviet Jewish population remains virtually constant, births being about equal to departures and deaths. After those countries come France (550,000), Argentina (500,000), Great Britain (410,000), Canada (300,000), Brazil (150,000), and so on.

This dispersed people has now regained its Promised Land and is attached to it as one is to one's own heart; and it is faced with Arab hatred—but not a generalized, ingrained, second-nature hatred. No, this is a taught hatred, made up of sundry bits of tradition, hurt pride, ignorance, intolerance, and misunderstanding. The politicos in power find it expedient to damn Israel and work for its future defeat. The masses find it a satisfying scapegoat.

All the Arab nations publicly oppose Israel's very existence, including Hussein's Jordan which, before our events, had taken part in all three anti-Israel wars, in 1948–49, 1956, and 1967. All eighteen members of the Arab League signed the Khartoum convention of August 1967: no peace with Israel; no negotiation with Israel; no recognition of Israel. None of them has backed down from these "three nos."

Of course, Jordan, were it to recover the West Bank and be given access to the Mediterranean, would be most likely to come to terms with Israel, if Amman felt it could neutralize the reactions in the other Moslem countries.

Now, there are at least 135,000,000 Arabs in the world, since there are Arab communities in virtually every country, including the People's Republic of China. But, considering only the members of the Arab League, as we noted in Chapter IX, from the Atlantic to the Gulf of Oman, they occupy land 603 times the size of Israel, with a population 42 times Israel's.

The odds being so overwhelming, Israel knows that however often it beats and crushes them, the Arabs can always fall back on their population and land reserves to come up with means for a new assault against the Jewish fortress. It is something Israel can never forget: the Arabs may suffer ten defeats, or twenty—but let Israel experience just one, and under the averted eyes of the rest of the world there will be not just the end of the Jewish State, but the pogrom of pogroms, butchery of every Jew from Dan to Eilat. No need for suitcases or caskets. So, all the El Fatahs, all the Black Septembers, and all the Soviet threats will never make Israel let the fedayeen strike with impunity, nor go back to the highly vulnerable pre-1967 borders, or return the main occupied areas without dependable guarantees.

At the time we are concerned with, 60,000 Arabs were legal residents of West Germany, and probably 25,000 more had entered illegally, to work there "on the black market." Six thousand of these are estimated to be Palestinians, about one thousand of them students. Only after the Munich tragedy did the German police take a close look at the Secretary-General for Germany of the General Union of Palestinian Students.

His name is Abdullah Hassan Yums el Frangi, and he travels a lot to Lebanon and Libya, and "on vacation" to Moscow. No one has ever known what kind of "student" he was, nor what his evidently ample means of support were. His home at Langen, a town in the industrial valley some 15 km. (9.3 mi.) from Frankfurt am Main, was finally raided by the Hessian police.

Here is how Herr Hans-Heinz Bielefeld, Minister of the Interior for the *Land* of Hesse, told what was found in this quiet gentleman's lodgings in a flower-bedecked old Tudor-type house:

> Five time-bomb fuses, made of radio parts . . . several firearms . . . documents and materials proving that the Secretary-General of the Palestinian Students in Germany had helped prepare and carry out Arab attacks against the Israeli embassy at Bonn . . .

Quite a fellow, this Abdullah Hassan whatshisname! Nor was it because of his aforementioned official position that the home of the Gaza-born Palestinian was raided: the Arab terrorists in the Munich Olympic Village had tried in vain, five or six times during the day of September 5, to get in touch with his Langen apartment by phone from 31 Connollystrasse.

Mr. El Frangi quite unabashedly represented El Fatah in Germany, calling himself its P.R. man. He also worked on a part-time basis for the Arab League delegation to Bonn. For the League is represented there, with quasi-diplomatic status accorded by the G.F.R. El Frangi was deported from Germany on September 28, 1972 [two days after Abdhel Jabber Hamad, as reported in Chapter VI].

Is it not surprising that the *Bundesrepublik* neither imprisoned nor held for trial a foreigner against whom there was such damning evidence of illegal acts? Firearms, time bombs, detailed preparation of terrorist attacks apparently do not constitute much guilt in Bonn's eyes. Its Minister of the Interior, Herr Hans-Dietrich Genscher, held a press conference on October 4, 1972, after about a hundred Arabs (no great number, really) had been expelled from the country following the Munich carnage.

He wanted to point out how generous the Government had been to Arabs living in Germany, "particularly Palestinians," to whom, he added, it has "given hundreds of scholarships since the 1967 war." For he had just announced that the West German branches of the two Palestinian organizations, El Frangi's General Union of Students (with about 850 paid-up members) and the General Union of Palestinian Workers (some 2,000 active members), were henceforth banned from federal territory. Raids at the headquarters of the two organizations, he said, had shown both to be involved in "conspiratorial actions" and to use "methods of violence."

The fate of Palestinian refugees since 1948 has been non-life. Try to picture a quarter-century in an UNRWA camp on Arab land, familiar but foreign. . . . A huge depot set down on rocky soil. With the years, gray tents have given way to "permanent" construction: reinforced concrete foundations, mud or cement walls, roofs of imitation tile (made of a kind of plastic that gets burning hot in the sun) or sheet metal.

The shanty is generally 16 to 18 sq. meters (some 19 to 22 sq. yds.), intended for a family of five. On either side of the rutted paths, endless lines of concentration-camplike hutments. Houses burn or collapse, roofs give way: patch 'em up; make more kids; now there are nine or ten to each dwelling. Ripe for illness and death. The Agency's people, always short of funds, pass out twenty-five-year-old tents, and let shacks of branches be built, sometimes with ready-made walls of old tires tied together that seem about to take off from the poverty-stricken jail cells at the first big wind or storm.

Morning to night, they queue up before the water sources: usually a thin-running faucet atop a bare pipe coming up out of the dry earth, about one per 1,000 people.

The deadly stink of the latrines, the flocks of flies, bees, wasps, and everpresent rats. Nature's calls are answered in open rooms, squatting over open holes, or on unpainted wood seats. The monthly emptying of these cesspools, with kids playing about and laughing, is something that—speaking from vast personal experience—I can vouch the worst stenches of soldiers' slit trenches never came close to.

Periodic distributions by the Agency, whether of candy or blankets, soap or teabags, means favoritism, bribes, hairpulling—and yet, over all the dissension, one deep brotherhood: hatred of the Jew. As a slogan on the peeling walls. In Hitler-like caricatures of the round-eyed, lip-smacking, fat banker with black tufts around his bald pate, nose vulturine, clutching his moneybags stuffed with dollars. As a drawing: the Crucifixion superimposed on the six-pointed star.

Regimentation: around each camp, boys and men train with wooden rifles, jump over flames, toss imitation grenades, learn to climb barbed wire. Up to sixteen as an *Ah'nal* or lioncub; after sixteen, as a fedayee. But then there is school, and, for the adults, the horrid little jobs, the weariness, the erosion of endless waiting, until even military exercises evoke small enthusiasm.

Dictatorship: along with the one obsession, a rigidly tight organization, imposed by El Fatah, PFLP, or some other group. The masses passively accepting it, their souls now collectively one.

Food: 1600 to 1800 calories a day; sufficient in quantity, but hopelessly monotonous; the kitchen personnel are part of the camps' political aristocracy.

Boredom: titanic, immense, with all those young "old people" sitting around crosslegged Turkish-style, side by side in the shade, puffing on an Agency cigarette, and letting it artfully go out, so it can be smoked again. The women keep the *khanun* (charcoal heater) or *mikkar* (oil heater) going so that every two hours there can be the ritual *Kahua,* reheated coffee, or ever-so-light tea, with lumps of sugar.

Laundry hangs from the lines: all patched, all faded. And a Palestinian flag flies, its horizontal stripes of green, black, yellow, and white, fighting each other and swallowed up by a red triangle.

Little businesses on wheels amble down the paths: slices of watermelon, single cigarettes, chewing gum, patched jeans, beauty-spots, hawked by people with rickets and dry coughs.

A small minority have energy enough to fight against getting mired down: they join the guerrillas, or slip off clandestinely, from border to border, into the countries where there is work: Saudi Arabia, the oil emirates, Western Europe, even the U.S., which scores of Palestinians enter each year from Mexico.

The rest vegetate, motionlessly. Any kind of lucrative employment spells the end to free allocations and subsidies, so most work is kept secret; idleness is king; a quarter-century of unemployment. Of waiting. In too-close quarters. Hoping, despairing.

It is a leprosy that time will not cure. And the U.N., not the people who escaped history's greatest genocide, must finally find the way for these miserable masses to be able to lead a free and decent life.

XIX
THEIR EYES

Before the silver cord is snapped asunder,
And the golden bowl is shattered,
And the pitcher is broken at the fountain,
And the wheel falleth shattered, into the pit;
And the dust returneth to the earth as it was,
And the spiri. returneth to God who gave it.
Ecclesiastes 12:6,7

9:50 PM: THE CREWS OF THE TWO HELICOPTERS LETTERED D-HAQO
and D-HADU got final instructions from the *Krisenstab* in a
ground-floor office of G-1. Each crew was made up of a flight commander and a copilot. A third machine had just taken off from the
Village.

The three copters scheduled to take part in the decisive action
were all Bell-Iroquois UH-1Ds. The German *Streitkräfte* (armed
forces) had bought several hundred of them. Iroquois have a
900-hp turbo-engine. Each can easily hold fifteen armed men.

In Vietnam, I had often ridden them. The American forces
used them there for launching rockets, six or eight to a plane,
hung outside the plane, from the two tubular struts perpendicular
to the landing skids. Some of the Iroquois, instead of skids, had
rubberized-nylon floats that allowed them to set down on the
Mekong River and board suspicious embarkations, sampans, in-
frequent junks, or motorboats loaded with strangely smiling
fishermen . . .

The two crews that met with Messrs. Merk and Schreiber belonged to the élite corps known as *Bundesgrenzschutzpolizei*, or
federal frontier guards. They were volunteers. They knew they
were running the risk of being taken hostage, and that their mission would be tough. But those were occupational hazards.

Schreiber did not tell them what the attack plan at the air base
would be, for they were in danger of falling into the fedayeen's

hands. But their specific instructions must have let them guess most of it: "As soon as you land at Fürstenfeldbruck, open all doors and get away from the planes as quickly as possible, but not in the direction of the 727."

9:55 PM: One of the Iroquois landed in front of the Fürstenfeldbruck control tower. It was the one that was bringing back *Vize* Georg Wolf and the five sharpshooters who, a little more than an hour ago, had been rushed over to the Village by Schreiber.

As soon as the commando leader advised him he would not use the minibus, the Munich police chief, judging that any ambush on the fedayeen's initial lap now seemed unfeasible, lost no time: with one copter always revved up and ready to go, Dr. Wolf had been ordered to hop it immediately with his five snipers, called back in by walkie-talkie.

Meantime, on the second floor of 11 Connollystrasse, the five *Krisenstab* members were in a last meeting, and words were flying hot and heavy.

The two real operating officers, Merk and Schreiber, were furious at having suddenly to attend this meeting when every minute was vital to overcoming the thousand obstacles in the way of their plan of action. The "nays" answered that indeed there was not a minute to waste—before changing the plan.

Federal Minister Genscher and ex-Mayor Vogel felt that the decisions they had unanimously approved a quarter-hour before were bad. They wanted the all-out effort made in the Village itself.

"I have come to the conclusion," said Genscher, "that the fedayeen made a tactical mistake in not insisting that the copters come closer to the macadamized border where the bus will have to park. They and their hostages will have to walk some thirty meters. The tied-up hostages will be slow as tortoises, so the sharpshooters will be able to bring the Arabs down ten times over."

"I agree totally," said Vogel. "We still have a quarter of an hour, and I am willing to stay with the terrorists to make them wait out that time. The triangle where this will take place has to be lighted by bright projectors; bring in the firemen's. And borrow some of the TV people's spotlights. The crime was committed in the Village, and that's where we ought to strike back. Otherwise, as soon as they are in the air, the fedayeen will turn the pilots into hostages, and force them to go to Riem or elsewhere. Then, the Arabs'll easily be able to get a plane to take them and their German and Israeli hostages wherever they say."

Merk countered, "That's fanciful. We could never get adequate lighting and all the sharpshooters back to the takeoff pad in time . . . Besides, you were in on the discussions and fully approved our plans."

"We were wrong. The lives of nine guests of Germany are at stake."

As the argument became more bitter, Dr. Schreiber cut in, "If we attack when they get out of the buses, it'll be the end of the Israelis. There are only thirty meters to go to get to the copters. The terrorists have massive weaponry. No matter how hard we try to keep people back, there will be a crowd very close by, if only of the people who have business there. The fedayeen not killed will start machine-gunning the hostages and then firing in all directions—right in the Olympic Village. The butchery will be tied to the name of Munich. But at Fürstenfeldbruck the scene has all been set up. We are holding all the good cards. There'll be no danger of killing innocent bystanders."

They decided to consult General Zvi Zamir, who was champing at the bit on the ground floor. This was the one and only time he was made privy to a possible plan and consulted, instead of being informed of a decision after the fact. He flatly came out in favor of an attack at the start or end of the bus trip, before the fedayeen could get into the helicopters. Minister Merk dismissed this by saying the Israeli envoy could not properly judge an operation on which he was far from having full details. He noted that 10:00 PM was nearing, and settled it: "I assume my responsibilities, just as the Government of Israel does in refusing to satisfy even one one-hundredth of the fedayeen's demands. Now, gentlemen, to the underground entrance to Number Thirty-one."

This was the last opinion General Zamir was to give. Would Israel, on its own territory, have allowed a foreigner's view to determine its decision? At any rate, out of politeness, Mrs. Meir on September 12 "forgot" this one time the Germans asked the general's opinion, when she stated categorically, "No plan whatsoever was brought before him, for his cognizance, approval, or comment."

9:58 PM: Georg Wolf put the phone down. The skids of the Iroquois had hardly touched ground when the *Vizepräsident* of the Munich police, having jumped out of the plane, was running toward the control tower: one of his underlings had motioned to him that Schreiber was on the wire waiting for him.

Forcing himself to keep in control, Wolf made a mental rundown. Now he had been informed by his boss that it was "absolutely certain" Fürstenfeldbruck would be selected as the site for the decisive battle to free the hostages.

A "probable" theater of operations for the past four hours, and "highly probable" for the past three, what did Fürstenfeldbruck have by way of available firepower?

• Five sharpshooters, and four "backup men," with automatic weapons; the "backup men" not to fire at the start of the action.

• A flying squad of seventeen men, wearing Lufthansa green mechanics' overalls or crew or stewards' uniforms.

• A squadron of one hundred border guards, in charge of protecting the control tower and sealing off the part of the base where the attack was to take place.

Schreiber had also just confirmed that the following elements were moving toward Fürstenfeldbruck:

• Two squads of motorized police, in six armored cars, leaving the Village as soon as the hostages and fedayeen were airborne. Schreiber anticipated they would be at the base twenty minutes later, which Wolf considered too optimistic.

• A shock commando of twenty-three men in bulletproof jackets, who would attack hand-to-hand if that was needed to rescue the hostages.

• Two squadrons of one hundred men each from the Munich police, to constitute a fallback ring around the air base.

The shock commando and two squadrons were traveling by truck, also leaving after the hostages took off. So they would arrive at the base at about the same time as the armored vehicles.

This finally added up to some 400 men at Wolf's command, when all these reinforcements arrived. Meantime, he had some 125.

The *Dokumentation* does not list any additional forces, although Schreiber often later spoke of 500 police deployed on and surrounding the air base.

To tell the truth, 400 men are not a lot, and 125 are that much less, as Wolf well knew. Remember: it was a very dark night, on a huge military base, without natural hiding places near the runways; the fedayeen, super-armed with fantastic weapons, had a wall of human flesh to hide behind.

The Munich authorities, as we know and all official documents have admitted, had at least 12,000 men specially assigned to the security of the Games. How then, eventually having almost five hours to work in (Schreiber started to set up the Fürstenfeldbruck ambush at 5:45, and the terrorists did not finally land there till 10:35), could they have failed to assign to the Luftwaffe base, say, one-sixth of these available police forces? Especially since none of the other possibilities represented any real alternative after 9:25, when the Fürstenfeldbruck solution, adopted by the *Krisenstab,* was accepted by the fedayeen?

Sending 2,000 police to the probable, and then certain, site of the action would have made the more sense since they could have been immediately replaced in their police duties by soldiers, out of the 12,000 *Bundeswehr* men the Ministry of Defense had assigned to the Organizing Committee.

Like many fellow newsmen, I spoke during and after the events to many of the soldiers stationed in Munich and assigned to the Games. They assured me that on September 5 and 6 they and their comrades had virtually nothing to do. They were restricted to idleness, so to speak.

When confronted with this, Merk and Schreiber said that in actions such as took place at Fürstenfeldbruck, numbers were not what counted, but quality. "What would we have gained," they asked, "if German units, too close together, had started shooting at each other, in the darkness and confusion?"

This is defensible. However, about numbers, one can ask: Were efforts made to get qualified volunteers among the 12,000 police assigned to the Games? Answer: No.

Were any of the thirty or so sharpshooters among the police who were not involved, ever contacted? Answer: No.

If Wolf had had enough marksmen as well as volunteers for an armed attack on the fedayeen remaining inside the helicopters, might he not have changed his tactics? That answer would seem to be: Yes.

One more question: Admitting that sending in 2,000 qualified police officers might have changed the face of things, who is to shoulder the major responsibility for the presence at the base of only 125—and then, much later, 400? Messrs. Merk and Schreiber have laid claim to this as to other responsibilities. And they have been absolved and congratulated by the highest authorities, and their popularity has increased. Would others than they have done better? At any rate, they could have done worse, if they had given way before the terrorists.

The head of Operation Rescue (as it was actually referred to) had another concern beyond the reinforcements Schreiber promised: the 727, key to the whole ambush, was not yet there. A first long-distance plane had come in at 8:45, and its crew had reported problems with one of the turbojets, and Lufthansa's technical department ordered it to be returned to Riem, and replaced by another without delay. Wolf went to see how things stood.

Walking away from the runways, he went some 15 meters south of the control tower. There was a large building there, done in the rough utilitarian tradition of military architecture: a long parallelogram, rounded out at the two ends by a kind of turret. This housed the radioelectrical and electromechanical workshops, as well as a tool warehouse. The building also had crew's lounges in which the regular 727 men would later hear the echoes of the shootout. Alongside it stood a Luftwaffe ambulance, equipped for first-aid treatments; its white-smocked personnel paced dolefully back and forth.

Herr Wolf had called into the lobby the police captain in command of the blockade of the base and protection of the tower. This officer did not hide the fact that closing off the field with the number of men he had was something like squaring the circle.

Wolf went out with him to inspect the buildings beyond the tower on either side. They were all considerably farther back from the runways, some on a level with the parallelogram in which the captain made his headquarters. These edifices, of all different kinds, constituted the installations required by any significant air-field: repair hangars, test shops, body washes, garages, electric generator, heating plant, stores and workshops, fuel pumps, ware-houses, and so on.

Schreiber's aide could see that within the larger places there were Luftwaffe people in combat dress. They were under orders to keep anyone not belonging to their arm from entering the building they guarded. Other soldiers from the base were also guarding the panoramic navigation-and-approach radar, the ground-surveillance radar, the antiaircraft pieces, etc.

But, we must make clear that, at Fürstenfeldbruck, all the Luftwaffe did was to guard those installations that held military secrets or were vitally necessary. The airmen were under the same constraint as the Bundeswehr soldiers: the Luftwaffe was not to be involved in this affair either, except on orders of the Minister of Defense. And the police, for its part, did not plan to ask the military to intervene.

Wolf turned around, hearing a loud whirr: he could see part of the taxiing area in front of the control tower.

"Well, that's good news," he told the captain. "The Lufthansa plane is finally here."

After the inspection of the so-called industrial shops of the air base, the operation head and the captain were now touring the other buildings, even farther back: messhalls, barracks, infirmary, auxiliary generator, heat-control center, refueling tanks for com-bustion-engines, kerosene for jets, and so on. Here too the key spots were guarded by Luftwaffe people, in the round federal helmet. Their appearance of motionless guards, the muffled sound of summer-night's noises, the countrified peacefulness, the distant barking of a dog, all added up to a strange sense of battle-eve waiting. The young men were nervous.

"If any of the Arabs try to beat it on out, they'll have plenty of places to hide," the captain said.

"Provided they leave the hostages alive, I don't care if some of them get away," Wolf replied, while thinking that his sub-ordinate had made a correct observation.

The two men finally came to a railroad siding where on that day there were some tank cars sitting, which we will hear more of. The air base had a small station, connected (after opening ever so many closed crossing-gates) to line S-3 of the *S-Bahn,* Munich-to-Augsburg commuter-line.

And still farther to the south was the fence, which closed the base off at that end. They certainly did not have the time to inspect any more of the huge military reservation, with its runways, its secret positions hidden by high thick fences, and its training grounds.

But the view of the fence somewhat reassured Herr Wolf. Its metallic panels, of rather tight mesh, stood some 2.10 meters (7 ft.) high, and had three layers of electrified wire across the top. Inside the fence itself was a patrolling path, and the two main black-topped exit roads went through gateways flanked by guard posts.

The two police officers hastily returned to the control tower.

10:00 PM: An olive-green Bundeswehr bus drew up before the stairway leading to the lobby of Block 31. The federal army not having many gorillas available, the driver was a career noncom who never would have dreamt of volunteering for this detail. This was to be the Bundeswehr's only part in the adventure. The noncom must have been nervous, for as he was turning his large vehicle into the underground roads, wavy as ski slopes, he ran through a freshly transplanted boxtree.

Issa and Tony, both carrying flashlights with white beams, searched the bus from tip to toe. The little leader, who had just re-blackened his face, put his light out, and said, to Herr Tröger, who was standing near the blonde policewoman, *"Sehr gut!"* (OK).

He smiled, his long, straight minishark's smile, showing overlapping upper teeth. But the jaws were painfully clenched.

The two terrorists disappeared, and at the same moment the group of *Krisenstab* members went toward the door marked 31. Worried, tense, walking carefully, they seemed to be heading for a funeral, as one of their bodyguards remarked. Their sharp disagreement of a few moments before was partly the reason. But also their feeling that they carried the real responsibilities, the die was cast, and the chances slight.

A masked fedayee came out walking backward. It was Paulo, the one with the longshoreman's build. He was pulling a hostage by the sleeve. The muzzle of his AK-47 submachine gun was against huge Yossef Gutfreund's Adam's apple. Was it because of the colossal fight he had put up to keep the door to Apt. 1 shut that the international wrestling referee was dragging his left leg? No. He was tied wrist and ankle to Zeev Friedman, who was limping out behind him. Friedman and Yacov Springer were bound together in the same way. The fedayeen had used ropes with a rough finish, very easy to handle. The three were blindfolded with Village towels.

Springer tripped on the edge of the last step. He fell heavily, pulling Friedman off balance. But Gutfreund, that Gibraltar, was already on the asphalt and kept them going. Two terrorists had come out so close behind Friedman and Springer that at first the police did not even notice them. Swathed in weaponry, their carbines shoved into the ribs and their chests pressed virtually against the backs of their human prey, the terrorists each had a cocked grenade in their free hands, as Issa had done. One, skinny and short, was hidden under a hood. The other, even flimsier, had charcoaled his face: with his septum deviated toward the right, it was unmistakably Salah.

Eliezer Halfin came out right after that behind his pal Springer, but not bound to him: he was acting as a leader and was tied to Mark Slavin and Andrei Spitzer. The ropes tied these three together at wrists and ankles, like the others, and they too were bindfolded. All were accompanied by captors who stuck the muzzles of their Kalachnikov AK-10 assault rifles into the backs of their necks or their spines. One of the fedayeen had a tan hood, the second was Issa, while the third wore large dark glasses and had his face covered with blue chalk. He was a new one. Small in body, with a thin trimmed mustache across his square face, and raven-black hair in a stiff, bushy mane that covered his ears, he was the first-aid man of the group, the one his comrades often referred to as Kader, actually named Abdelkader el Denawi.

"Six of them!" Minister Bruno Merk hissed.

Manfred Schreiber puffed his lips: yes, one more terrorist than they had thought. This would make things just a little harder at Fürstenfeldbruck. A few seconds went by; the first batch were already in the bus, getting settled. The second was starting the climb through the bus-door, which was tough on the hostages.

329

The third trio of Israeli athletes came out just as the *Krisenstab* began to wonder about them, thinking they must be waiting, bound tight, on the last steps of the stairway. The track coach, Amitzur Shapira, came first, followed by Kehat Shorr and David Berger. The latter had carefully cleaned up the wounds on his face.

The bindings and blindfolds were the same as with the first six. Schreiber and his neighbors expected that, but something totally different struck them like a punch in the mouth: a slim gandy-dancing fellow, who must have come down the steps backward, leading and pulling Shapira with his left hand while the right kept his submachine gun on him. His head was hidden in an electric-blue stocking cap with two eyeholes. With his flaring black slacks, his pulled-in gut, and his jonquil polo shirt, he looked dressed for romance. He swung his shoulders in fits and starts. He slid aside when he got to the sidewalk, and pushed Shapira in front of him. He had not been seen before either, although his manner and shape were unmistakable. He was Abdullah Mohamed Samir.

The three Israelis were carrying training duffels, which looked heavy.

The Germans had scarcely noticed the existence of the seventh fedayee, when they saw the eighth bringing up the rear of the cortege, behind David Berger. This was Tony, the tall one whom they recognized, his mouth twisted into a snarl. Schreiber was the least surprised, for he had already noted the fact that Issa's second-in-command was missing among the fedayeen who had come down. Tony shoved the barrel of his Kalachnikov sharply against the shoulder blade of Berger who seemed to be tripping; the Jewish lawyer straightened up.

"Eight! There are eight of them!" Merk kept saying, shaking his head.

"You see," the *Polizeipräsident* simply said. "We were right not to try anything during this transfer."

"I'm not so sure," came a calm voice in English, that of General Zamir, who had had a busy time of it since arriving three-quarters of an hour earlier.

He remained slightly behind the West German officials. They

had asked his opinion once, and he had given it. It had been disregarded. Never in his life had he so wished to be wrong. But he took this occasion to remind the Germans that he wanted no mistake about it: he had had no part whatever in the decision they made.

The fedayeen's arsenal had impressed even that blasé expert Manfred Schreiber by its quantity, quality, and variety.

The bus driver pulled his head down into his shoulders. Even though he had expected this . . . Issa was now standing behind his seat, and with a half-smile that the career sergeant could see in his rearview mirror was rubbing the end of his rifle against his ribs. At the rear of the vehicle, hypernervous Salah had a knee on the seat and seemed through the glass to have a bead on the *Krisenstab* with his submachine gun.

The Black September commando had gotten their captives into a tight group, and pasted themselves against them. The motor of the bus, which had been running, brayed. The overhead lights went out. The driver clutched in. The car moved. It was

10:06 PM: A few photographers, cleverly hidden along the access ramps, were able to get some shots of the bus with license plate 19-3583 during its ride. On the best ones you can see the popping eyes of Salah, the fedayee guarding the rear window: the terrorists, stooping down, legs bent, were using the backs of the seats and the hostages as shields. They eyed the parked cars, the concrete pillars, the police with weapons slung who looked back at them. Two motorcycle cops rode ahead, and two behind. It was slow going.

The bus came up into the open next to G-1, south of the parking lot, along the greenswards. Meanwhile, at

10:05 PM: Dr. Georg Wolf, getting back near the control tower, saw the medium-range airliner requested from Lufthansa. The 727 was set at exactly the spot the *Vize* had specified, that is, on the star-shaped crossroads where normally all airships are forbidden to stop, since they would obstruct all other traffic.

The plane's crew seemed to Wolf to be impatiently waiting. He noted that the Lufthansa people looked enviably radiant, marvelously real. A police lieutenant pointed out the head of Operation Rescue to them. Immediately, the skipper, copilot, navigator, mechanic, steward, and white-gloved brunette hostess rushed over to him.

"We've been here for fifteen minutes. Where is the team that's supposed to take our places? I think we have to tell them how to act and what instructions are!" said the pilot after cursory amenities.

"What do you mean? What team? You're staying in the plane. Anyway, it won't take off. Everything will be over before it reaches that point. All you have to do is act natural if the fedayeen come on to check up."

Wolf, in truth, was bluffing—and not kidding himself. The Lufthansa President, Herr Herbert Culmann, had unambiguously told Minister Merk on the phone: "It was out of the question to expose our flight personnel under orders to such serious risks in this Israeli-Arab affair. I asked for volunteers to man the ship until the fedayeen got there from Connollystrasse: there were no takers. So, naturally, the crew that lands at Fürstenfeldbruck is not intended to be in any way involved in this . . ."

And the crew as one person met Wolf's statement with tremors of indignation. They went off to the lounge reserved for crews in transit, forgetting all about any instructions to be passed on.

Herr Wolf's little trick had been one last try at saving what was one of the worst failures of the day. The fedayeen would indeed never take off from Fürstenfeldbruck: he had told the 727 crew, because they were not going to leave the base or be in touch with the outside before it was all over.

So, come what might, West Germany was going to rescue the Olympic hostages right here. But, as the one in charge of the details of action at Fürstenfeldbruck, Wolf felt urgently that the Black September gang should not be given deep reasons for suspicion. And the men who were to replace the real Boeing crew had not the slightest idea of the operation or construction of the plane. If the terrorists asked a simple question or wanted to see one thing, they would immediately catch on to the fact that they were dealing with policemen in disguise, and that the West German authorities had no intention of furnishing them a plane out.

10:08 PM: Police Lieutenant N (the members of his squad who spoke to the press having done so only on condition that they not be identified), who was to lead the not-yet-selected group who would man the 727, saw Dr. Wolf come into the room where the seventeen disguised as ground or flight personnel were waiting. From among them, in a moment, he had to choose the eight to be crew members allegedly ready to fly the plane. The lieutenant looked at his watch. He felt relieved when ten o'clock came and went—for that was the time the terrorists had been scheduled to arrive at Fürstenfeldbruck, and his men and he had not yet been called out for a detail that he considered worse than dangerous.

The room into which Wolf had come was on the ground floor of the control tower. It was the runway and information office. That was where flight plans were turned in before takeoff. It had a number of teletype machines, so the information in the flight plans could immediately be communicated to the control centers of the affected regions.

Although there had been virtually no military flights since August 22, part of the air force personnel were still there. That was why the office was being guarded by soldiers. But Riem technicians for the duration of the Games were handling all the civil flights at Fürstenfeldbruck. They had the evening off tonight, since, due to the crime, all charter and private flights scheduled to leave or come in to the air base had been rerouted after 6:00 PM. Normally, the last big transports operated till about 10:45, and light planes often even beyond midnight.

While carrying out their routine work, going from the automatic teletypes to the teletypewriters, and filing the *Notam* (urgent technical information for navigators), the air army ground men were missing nothing of the goings-on. They were chattering with the seventeen members of the assault commando, all of whom had volunteered for the attack on the fedayeen—but the latter had not anticipated so thorny an assignment as eight of them would have to carry out inside the plane. They had envisioned a classical straight-on attack.

Dressed in the fireproof overalls of Luftwaffe mechanics or the fine uniforms of Lufthansa crews, they had all just completed a second reconnaissance of the site of the coming operation, and each one hoped not to be included. Meantime, they were snacking on sausages with white radish, mustard, and good Algäu cheeses.

And assuaging their thirst, greater because of their very well-founded worries, with the strong sweetly bitter beers that had made Munich famous, Augustinerbräu, Hofbräuhaus, and Löwenbräu.

As Herr Wolf came toward them with the step he had learned in the wartime Wehrmacht, the policemen fell in, in single file, did an about-face, and came to attention before the No. 2 man of the Munich police.

A respected and psychologically adept boss such as Georg Wolf immediately senses an atmosphere. He does not waste time asking for volunteers to hide out in the Boeing, since he can feel he won't get any. Three of the men already knew they would be automatically preempted: they were wearing flight uniforms.

In a trice, Wolf had picked eight huskies, who followed him, not without some misgivings. Their nine comrades, who would take up positions near the plane in support of them, were hard put to conceal their relief. . . .

The plane was silhouetted in the night like a torpedo with backslanting wings, its three turbojets softly glinting, as the motors hummed at a slow rhythm.

Apart from the actual pilot and copilot, who were absolutely determined to stay in the lounge until this was over, there must certainly have been one or several officers on the base familiar with this type of machine. Dr. Wolf, aware he had no one to call on, sighed with rage. The next day, Minister Bruno Merk would state to the world press assembled: "In all of Germany, we were unable to find a crew of pilots willing to fly the terrorists and hostages to an Arab country. And we ourselves in the final analysis would not have wanted to face the risk of endangering under such conditions the lives of German pilots, even volunteers."

It might be said, "No such crew was needed, since the decision had been made to settle matters on the spot, whatever the cost." Wrong. A true professional might well have convinced Issa or any other of the fedayeen that the 727 was not just window dressing.

The eight of them went toward the Boeing. At its foot, their boss gathered them around him. "Remember," Wolf told them, "that if only one or two terrorists come aboard to inspect, you get out the other side as fast as you can, and get back in only when they've left. If all five of them show up, with their hostages, you'll have to make your move. You've already picked out your best protected positions. Get into them. As soon as the first Bell sets down, the order is: don't move from them except on command."

Wolf specified to the fake pilot (a brigadier acting as second to the lieutenant commanding the squad) that the motors would keep going till the end, at a low pitch like now. If before the terrorists were far enough into the passenger cabin for the hidden snipers to be able to shoot them, one of the fedayeen asked the "crew" to rev up the jets or start the plane moving, the answer was to be that only the control tower could authorize that.

"And add," Wolf went on, "that technically you can't start the plane until your fourth crew member, the navigator, is there. The latter, you may explain, will get on only after the hostages and terrorists have boarded, as an extra precaution for the helicopter pilots."

One of the policemen pointed out that he and the others had no bulletproof vests or walkie-talkies. The squad leader felt that vests would be in the way, but he obviously would have liked radio contact. Wolf replied that the plane's own radio equipment was more than enough, going on: "All lights will be on inside, and you'll be able to see excellently. You'll be able to tell the hostages by their bonds; the fedayeen are very heavily armed, so you won't be able to mistake them."

There was such silence a mosquito would have sounded like a dive-bomber. "Any questions?"

No answer. Wolf made as if not to see the expressions on their faces.

Finally, a voice was raised, the same one as previously. He was a spindly one with a Tyrolean accent: "You're right, *Herr Vizepräsident,* to say we'll see excellently. We'll have the best seats."

Wolf merely shrugged and ordered weapons inspection. The lieutenant carried it out under his supervision. The Walther retractable-stock machine pistols and KGP-70 pistols were checked. Each man was armed with both, except the three "crew members," who had no machine pistols. All in order.

Slow procession up the gangplank, Wolf at the head. It was a one-class medium-range liner, the passenger cabin looking very much like a false front.

"The three crew men, follow me!" And they went up to the pilot's cockpit. "Take your places according to the jobs your stripes indicate."

In deathly silence, the "pilot in command" and his "subalterns" sat down. Their eyes ran over the huge display of instruments, from the flight lights and controls that dotted the ceiling with sharp quadricoloration, to the levers, swingbars, joysticks, radar screen, radio aerial, gauges, and other mysteries located on the double dashboard or between the seats.

"You three, I repeat, will under no conditions go out before the Arabs get here."

Exit Herr Wolf.

The five assigned to the passenger compartment once more started looking for the least exposed, least uncomfortable, and most efficient positions. They had been told, "Two of you get behind the last seats, in front of the galleys; you can be hidden by blankets." But they quickly saw that only boa constrictors would have been able to fit into those spots.

Wolf's staff had also told them: "There are three toilets on the plane. We'll say one is out of order. To make even surer, we'll cover its nameplate. Two can lock themselves in there." The two sad sacks assigned there by the lieutenant, groaned: "The fedayeen won't think twice. One burst of fire through the lock, and the door'll swing open to show two riddled bodies." It was agreed they were right, and they were told to find other hideouts.

The lieutenant said, "The wardrobe and galley [at opposite ends of the passenger compartment] are each hidden by a curtain. We can post one man in each of them. The first terrorist who tries to look in can be shot down, and that will be the signal to start the action."

Fine. The men assigned to these booths started making tiny holes through the synthetic fibers.

The other three lifted themselves, as prearranged, up into the baggage-racks above the seats. They were closed by swingdown flaps. In many commercial planes, these flaps were made of grillwork; as luck would have it, in this one they were solid. The movable plastic partitions between the cabins had been taken out.

336

When as best they could they had all gotten into position, it was 10:26. Meanwhile, still at

10:08 PM: Issa finally jumped down on the sidewalk along the lawn behind the G-1 tower. Behind his big black glasses, he was turning his head left and right like an owl blinded by lights. The heads of the crisis staff sighed with relief: for the last two minutes, the fedayeen and their prisoners had stayed in the heavy olive-green vehicle that had drawn to a stop, and the overhead lights, on for an instant, had gone out. Moreover, the fedayeen made a screen between the windows and the hostages.

As soon as the preceding motorcop escort announced the arrival of the *Bundeswehr* bus, the crews of the three waiting helicopters shut their motors off. Their rotors had been turning for several minutes.

There was quite a crowd, as Dr. Schreiber had anticipated. But the police lines held and kept out even those with passes who were not indispensable to the takeoff. The Iroquois were just where Issa had inspected them, lined up parallel to the road. The beach-hatted leader could select whichever two he wished. Their gold-and-red parking-lights were lighted. The military bus stopped halfway between the two copters closest to the car park, which was at the north end of the lawns and fenced in.

The scene was brightly lighted. G-1 shone with all lights on, and the three tall commercial buildings of the Village were also a riot of lights. All the police vehicles had their headlights on, and it seemed as if on Lerchenauerstrasse, the lampposts of which shed a hard light anyway, projectors had been placed in the midst of the two swarms of flagpoles. . . .

It would later be learned that fifteen precision shots of the *Bundesgrenzschutzpolizei* were spread at an average of 70 meters away in all directions, with their telescopic-sighted rifles aimed at the fedayeen, muzzles swinging slowly as the two groups hopped forward. The distance between helicopters remained about 30 meters, and there was the same gap between them and the bus.

His figure narrower than ever, his safari outfit bleached white by the electric night, Issa began his walk across the sharp live grass. He was heading for the first of the two copters to the right of the

337

bus, that is, virtually in a line with the rear of that vehicle. In one hand—the left—he held his usual cocked grenade. No other weapon showed, but his waist bulged.

Once at D-HAQO, Issa walked around it. He stooped slightly to keep well under the blades of the rotor, just barely moving now. He inspected it all over, from the front headlight that sent its beam over the cockpit, to the anticoupling rotor perched atop the transmission arm at the end of the tail. He threw the violent light of his flashlight on the two crewmen seated at their posts and wearing headphones. The sliding door of the passenger cabin was open. Issa went inside, and the beam of his cylindrical flashlight could be seen moving about, stopping on something, searching away again.

He came back out and faced the bus in which the lighted overheads now showed the motionless shapes of the captives and their guards. He swung the flashlight up and down twice, at arm's length: obviously, the signal.

Then the apocalypse began to unfold.

A masked fedayee came down on to the asphalt, and behind him coach Shapira. He would have fallen, had the terrorist not caught him in the crook of an arm. Shorr and Berger followed him, off balance like acrobatic clowns. A black-sleeved forearm appeared in the doorway each time, its hand grabbing the shoulder of each emerging prisoner's jacket: obviously one of the terrorists standing inside.

The three Israelis were still bound together at their tightly tied wrists. Their ankles were hobbled. However, one change: they were no longer blindfolded. The fedayeen, realizing there would be a much larger crowd here than when they started from the underground, probably did not want the pictures to look too inhuman. That was why during these last few seconds, the time it took to hobble toward their flying coffins, the nine hostages were allowed to show their real faces, the features that were to disappear without ever seeing old age.

In view of the fact that there were two transports, the "Palestinian" commando had changed the grouping of the hostages. Here now came Slavin and Spitzer. They jumped out of the bus with feet together, the second starting even before his friend had landed on the sidewalk. Paulo (who had come down from the bus after

Issa) was close against Shorr's back, and a third terrorist now got behind Berger.

The first five captives out of the vehicle were pushed on to the lawn. There, Paulo lined them up in two ranks, facing Issa, who was 30 meters away, near the tail of D-HAQO. Behind the Israelis stood four of the fedayeen.

Each of the Black September men had at least two firearms and two grenades. During the transfer it could be seen that three of the eight had athletes' duffel bags stuffed to capacity, slung over their shoulders.

One more double up-and-down of Issa's flashlight and the parade started.

How long did they walk? Fully a minute. The light-colored ropes tautened between the feet dragging along like those of old people no longer energetic enough to raise their heels. The lawn was not level, and the tips of the shoes kicked into clumps of grass. The roaring air displacements caused by the helicopters had blown all kinds of things around that now led to stumbling. When this happened, wrists pulled apart and ropes bit into flesh.

Every one but Shapira had a guard with him drumming on his ribs or spine with the muzzle of a gun. The safari outfit, glinting with the lights, about-faced and went over to the pilots' cabin: he took out a pistol and aimed it at them.

The third Iroquois was set even farther from the back of the bus. From the minute Issa stopped in front of D-HAQO, the crew of the third machine doused its lights, and the spot that was playing on it also went out or switched its target. The copter was in the dark. Around it were the operative heads of the *Krisenstab*, along with Herr Franz-Josef Strauss, General Zamir, and Captain Y. All were silent and watching; Schreiber had his arms crossed.

There was a slight breeze, smelling slightly of flowers. An ideal time to be alive. From the Village could be heard bits of overlapping psychedelic musical pieces, a crystalline burst of laughter, and names being called out.

Five fedayeen were close-up targets, one standing still, the other four moving slowly—for at least a minute.

Even a moment later, when the four hostages still in the car were being guided to the second Iroquois by their guards, even at

Fürstenfeldbruck when the snipers went into action, there would never be another chance like this.

Captain Y was to tell me at Tel Aviv: "That was the ideal moment for liquidating the five unprotected terrorists on the spot and immediately going after the other three. The place was lighted. Our men and the Arabs were moving forward so carefully step by step, they almost seemed to be doing it on purpose."

Messrs. Genscher and Vogel, as we know, agreed. A marksman-officer of the frontier guards had suggested that two groups of the sharpshooters start firing at the same time, given the order by walkie-talkie.

The first group would have struck from the north, that is, on the one hand, from the cars in the parking lot closest to the fence, and, on the other, from the pedestrian ramp that looped up above to the northwest of the road on which the bus was standing. The other group would have shot from the southeast, that is, either from one of the windows of G-1 or from behind the curtain of silver poplars that formed a screen between Lerchenauerstrasse and the huge grassy plot on which the three copters were set. These two sighting angles would have avoided virtually any danger to the many people present nearby. Of course, the five hostages would not be protected against a slight error in aim, but the snipers would have been much closer than at Fürstenfeldbruck, in a clearly better light.

At the same time, two converging small assault squads would have broken through the side windows and windshield of the bus to finish off the last three of the fedayeen. Poor Bundeswehr driver! He would have had reasonable chances of surviving.

But, enough of these "irresponsible constructs," as Dr. Merk on September 6 was to tell "the pack of journalists."

The five hostages and their four guards reached the outside of the passenger compartment of the prairie-green Iroquois. One by one, assisted by the terrorists, the Israeli athletes climbed up the metal steps. Issa, weapon in hand, kept the pilots in his sights.

Each of the hostages, as he stooped to get into the copter held back as he was by the bonds, looked back either toward the bus or toward the edge of the grass where the heads of the staff set up to rescue them were standing and watching in the dark: they did not expect to see anything special, just a last look at the free world, and life.

Shapira with his blue eyes; Shorr, the eldest, with the glinting silvery hair; Berger, his face marked with wounds, and his shoulders rolling; Slavin, the baby, looking so robustly fresh; and Spitzer with his slim elegance and wide-rimmed glasses.

They were seated side by side on the same banquette, the one with the detached back, right behind the crew's cabin. It seated four, which meant that they had to squeeze on to it. And there were only four safety belts; so Spitzer, the last to get in, was provided with an extra attachment: his left arm was tied by a rope to the hooks in the wall that held the fire extinguisher. The guards tightened the safety belts. Issa put his pistol back in its holster and went briskly over toward the D-HADU Iroquois, on the other side of the bus.

Halfway, he stopped short. The lawn at that spot is dotted with transplanted young lindens, held up by white wood stalks. The terrorist leader stared at one of the trees, some 20 meters from him, and began to turn his outstretched left arm as if he were about to hurl the cocked grenade at the linden. But then his arm fell again and on he went. There was no one there: except perhaps a cat.

With the D-HAQO filled, its passenger door shut; contact; the rotor started up again.

Issa examined the second copter with the same care as the first, and went through the identical motions with his flashlight.

Down now came Gutfreund and Friedman, Springer and Halfin, in pairs, and they too were without blindfolds. Three fedayeen had their weapons stuck into their backs. Their leader was tall Tony, more and more stooped, his head and torso twitching almost as if he could not control them. With small steps, moving first the right leg then the left, in unison, bumping shoulders with each other, the four men in this second wave slid forward.

Officials and athletes, all of the uncaptured Israelis were standing nearby, watching the last lap of their comrades: "We were fifty meters away, and we saw all of our guys. Their faces were calm. They couldn't have made a better impression. They were resisting, you understand?"

Yes. All the nearby witnesses of the nine hostages leaving the

Olympiapark greensward agreed on their fantastic dignity, the unruffled serenity showing on their faces, and the fierce pride of all the raised foreheads and unbending figures, despite the tight ropes and the steel shoving through the fabric into their skins.

I had gone up on the terrace of a Lerchenauerstrasse building, fairly near G-1, that mainly housed BMW technicians. In the midst of a dense silent crowd, I could not make out details. There was the lighted area, so clear it looked joyful, making an isosceles triangle with the bus and the two copters at its apexes. Twice we could make out nameless, tiny human forms, small bits of life on the green grass glinting beneath the lights. . . .

The last four went up two by two, with an effort. They also looked back, just before getting into the machine.

Gutfreund with his broad face and broken nose, his tender mouth, the whole face radiating goodness; Friedman, lively and solid, in his tight-fitting royal-blue jacket; Halfin, with his thin face and his eyes that gave out a strangely sharp dark brilliance, burning with soul; and Springer, the Fighting Jew of every war, the hero of the Warsaw Ghetto, with his remarkable chiseled, kneaded, sculptured face, and that smile of his, just plain untamable, that overwhelmed all the eyewitnesses, a smile eloquent enough to bring the whole world the faith of Israel.

The turbulence of the air, making the lights shimmer, allowed us to guess the blades were beginning to whirr again.

The last four hostages were also lined up on one banquette at the front of the compartment. Issa left the doors open, and stayed at the foot of the machine until D-HADQ, yonder, had lifted off. He rubbed his eyes, barely raising his glasses. He gazed at the other Bell that was taking off and then looked back at the pilot and navigator of the machine he was going to take. Salah stayed near him, pacing on the lawn, a Tom Thumb with the neck of a crane, wildly excited, aiming his carbine sometimes at the Israelis and other times at the two crewmen.

Friedman, Gutfreund, Halfin, and Springer impassively watched the neighboring Iroquois with their five teammates, beginning to dance on its skids. While Issa, at the foot of the pilots' compartment, in front of Gutfreund, seemed to be quivering with impatience, the other machine lifted off vertically, up to a height of

5 or 6 meters, and then started moving away, climbing at an angle, until it was no more than those yellow and green lights disappearing in the darkness.

10:19 PM: Issa got into DU.

10:21 PM: In its turn, this copter lifted off, amid a few shouts of *Gott behüte euch!* (God keep you!), but the implacable silence quickly returned.

10:22 PM: One minute behind the second one, the third Iroquois lifted off, carrying passengers Genscher, Merk, Schreiber, F.-J. Strauss, General Zamir, and Captain Y.

There was Yossef Gutfreund, forty years old, a veritable mountain of a man, easily weighing in at 130 kg. (286-plus lbs.).

As the only Israeli Class A international wrestling referee, he was taking part in his fourth Olympiad. He was head coach of the Betar Club gym, married, with two daughters, ten and fourteen years old. He ran a home-electric-appliance shop in Jerusalem.

His heroism, when he held the door closed against the terrorists with his whole body despite the weapons he had seen in their hands, surprised none who knew him. His poignantly noble wife said: "His last act was typical of him. He spent his whole life helping others."

As long as her husband remained a hostage and alive, Mrs. Miriam Gutfreund prayed uninterruptedly at the Wailing Wall. Around 11:30 PM, her family came after her, shouting, "Yossef is saved! They've all been freed!"

He had left Rumania in 1950, after having gone to prison for Zionist propaganda; he was seventeen. He had fought in the Sinai in 1956. In 1967, he had been an infantry lieutenant, commanding a machine gun platoon in the attack on Khan Younis, in the Gaza Strip. During successive forward jumps under the fire of the Egyptians who fought courageously in the sector, Gutfreund himself had carried one of the platoon's three machine guns as he ran over the sandy marl, and got a mortar fragment in the shoulder.

Refusing to be evacuated that evening after Khan Younis was taken, he stayed with his unit till the cease-fire, having by then reached the edge of the Suez Canal. Meantime, he saved a score of Egyptian soldiers lost in the desert for three days, without food,

THE BLOOD OF ISRAEL

barefooted, and dying of thirst, after being abandoned by their officers. He gave them water, had their burns treated, fed them, and took them along in the trailers behind his jeeps.

He had a good full head, with a nose reflecting the wrestling and boxing he had done. And above it crinkled eyes that loved to smile. On the evening of September 3, an American friend, Mrs. Laure Lowry, and I had bumped into Gutfreund in the pretty *Neue Halle* on Siegenburgerstrasse. Between the wrestling matches which he refereed with sober authority, we swapped news of mutual friends. He was warm—an apparently indestructible tower of humanity.

The Israelis in Block 31 who were saved from death by Gutfreund's full voice, coming from the depths of his lungs, told me they could still hear it in their dreams. But it would have been unlike him to want to impinge on his living friends from beyond the grave.

There is a picture taken on the liftoff pad of the helicopters, in the besieged Olympic Park: Yossef Gutfreund is sitting, hands and feet tied, on the forward banquette of the D-HADU Bell. The door is open. Two fedayeen are aiming their weapons at the colossal referee and his three comrades. Issa is standing in front of the bubble. Gutfreund is looking over toward the other machine about to lift off, 30 meters away, and the camera caught a three-quarters view of him. His features, clear to the eye, are not tense at all. They are calm, full of serenity, with inexorable pride. It is the face of man at peace with himself, submissive to the will of God.

XX
THE FIRE AND THE WOOD

> . . . And [Isaac] said: 'Behold the
> fire and the wood; but where is the
> lamb for a burnt-offering?'
> And Abraham said: 'God will provide
> Himself the lamb for a burnt-offering,
> my son.'
>
> *Genesis* 22:7–8

10:10 PM: THE EMERGENCY MEETING OF THE IOC WAS STARTING IN a dining room of the Four Seasons Hotel. It was a very huge nondescript room, behind the main salon, and it had to be improvised into a meeting room. Tables were set out in a rectangle. No time to install a simultaneous-translation setup: the interpreters had to be packed in around a little desk set up in the middle.

Significantly, every member of the IOC at Munich was in attendance. . . . Concern and nervousness were visible on all their faces. Each felt that the Olympic idea was at stake. But, mainly, there was the horror of the events. Two murders had been committed within the Olympic precincts; nine lives hung in the balance. And they were Olympic athletes.

True, at Mexico City, there had been a larger number of dead during the previous Games. But that had to do with domestic Mexican politics, and the protagonists were in no way involved with sport.

Wherever they were from, all the members of the IOC were sorely aware of their impotence. The living (and dead) hostages had trusted the Olympic Movement. All of these officials had spent a good part of their lives in the cause of the ideal which tonight had to be preserved.

The outcome of this meeting was of the gravest importance. Using its sovereign powers, which it had seemed to have forfeited since the start of the attack, the IOC was now going to decide whether or not the Munich Games were to continue, and if so, when and how. Some observers thought there would be serious internal dissension.

Some even thought this was to be the end of the committee, that the Eastern bloc and Arab bloc would threaten to withdraw.

Several important UNESCO characters were strangely wandering about the hotel this evening. They were whispering that the time had come for the Olympics, and sport in general, to be turned over to their group, which alone could renovate the temple without bringing the pillars down.

UNESCO had been shooting barbs at Olympic amateurism for many a moon, trying to win sport into its sphere of competence. There were strong tugs in that direction, not only from UNESCO, but even from its parent U.N. Among those favoring UNESCO's control of competitive sport were two Frenchmen: its director-general René Maheu, and one of the most famous names of Davis Cup tennis, Jean Borotra. Both were at Munich, and they were said to have support within the IOC itself.

Many good people dreamt of a Supreme Council of World Sport, modeled after the General Assembly of the U.N.: one nation, one vote. Each country's representatives would be named by its Government, rather than co-opted. But would there then be a "Sports Security Council"? And, if so, who would have the veto?

However that might be, on the evening of September 5, 1972, such currents were numbly winging their way around the Connollystrasse tragedy. Could it be the detonator for an Olympic explosion? If this IOC meeting were allowed to be turned into a violent showdown, and a confrontation of ethical codes, then anything might happen.

Stiff in his dark-blue suit, secretive and rough, his square face displaying unusual pallor, President Brundage opened the meeting. On August 4, he had said good-bye to the IOC at the end of its 73rd session, at which Lord Killanin was elected to succeed him. He was not meant ever to preside over another full meeting of the group. The drama filled him with boundless contained rage.

In a broken voice that abounded in lower registers, he recounted the events of the day at the *Krisenstab*. Then he asked Mr. A.D. Touny to report his contacts with the terrorists. The Egyptian

IOC member told how he had twice gotten the fedayeen's deadline pushed back.

Then, there was the much-awaited statement of Herr Willi Daume. He also recapped the whole drama—but from the viewpoint of the emergency general staff. He spoke in total frankness, because he had confidence in his peers and also because he was one of the first to know the die had been cast: as he spoke, the two Iroquois had already lifted off with hostages and terrorists, toward Fürstenfeldbruck.

After a review that was listened to religiously, he stressed the fact that there was never any question of the German authorities or the Organizing Committee allowing the terrorists to leave federal territory with their hostages. The only reason for not attempting the rescue within the Village was the excessive danger of it.

Had it been carried out, it might have had the gravest consequences for the Olympic Movement; the Village, already the scene of two murders in the morning, would again have been turned into a bloody battlefield. This last consideration, incidentally had nothing to do with the ultimate decision, which was to get the fedayeen out where they could be attacked on terrain not of their choosing. In order to accomplish that, said the President of the Organizing Committee, they had to be made to believe their latest demand was being met, the departure by plane for Cairo with their hostages. Two helicopters, set down behind the Village administration tower, had taken the fedayeen and their prisoners aboard according to this plan and carried them to the Fürstenfeldbruck air base, 26 km. west of Munich. Operation Rescue was now under way. Special police commandos were on the spot.

It is easy to picture how the men felt: they were all haunted by the idea that at this very moment the worst tragedy of the modern Olympics was ending as it had begun, in blood.

Daume stopped. He had just been given a message. He went out.

10:20 PM: Fürstenfeldbruck was in an uproar. Georg Wolf realized that the sealing-off of the ambush area was full of holes. It would have taken a thousand men or more. The extreme darkness of the deep night created problems. Unlike most of the *Krisenstab*, the *Vize* would much have preferred for the attack to take place by daylight.

"Headquarters calling Dr. Wolf on the phone!" blared the loudspeaker. The message bounced over to him as he paced; he had them answer that he would call G-1 right away.

For Dr. Wolf had worries, even though his battle setup seemed the best possible to him. The idea was artistically simple: to start firing at the fedayeen when they were clear targets, and in sufficient number. Since they were estimated at five in all, he would wait till at least three were in view, including the leader in the beach hat. Only the marksmen—or as the Germans said, the *Hochpräzisionsschützen*, high-precision shooters—would open fire.

To quote the *Dokumentation* (p. 61), "The marksmen's positions had been set since 7:00 PM and were so good that there was no need to change them after night fell."

Three of the five marksmen were on the terraced roof of the control tower, beneath the two panoramic rotundas, and had been for 2½ hours, barring the copter-hop to the Village. They remained in position, adjusting their sights. They were hidden by a 35-cm. (something over a foot) -high concrete parapet. Each had his own field of fire, the first and third to the east, the second to the north.

The fourth marksman was some 120 meters to the northeast of the control tower, under a fire truck brought in for the purpose. In relation to the men on the tower, he was therefore on the other side of the copters and 727, but he was able to fire in any direction.

The fifth had been instructed to conceal himself 80 meters north of the tower, behind the fan marker; his field of fire was southeast.

Remember, only these five high-precision marksmen were authorized to shoot without direct command as soon as the No. 1, acting as squad leader, judged that they had the best chance to bring down the largest possible number of terrorists. As soon as his first shot was fired, the others were to fall right in behind him.

Apart from these marksmen, there were police sergeants armed with 7.62 transformable light machine guns. They were known as "accompanists"; two of them were up on the terrace, and one each with the fourth and fifth marksmen. They were not to go into action until ordered to by the marksmen they were with.

All the other armed police surrounding the fedayeen were under

348

orders not to fire until either two green flares had been fired or their officer gave a command. The eight men inside the 727, as we know, were not covered by this rule.

Instructing the police armed with automatic arms not to fire in support of the five sharpshooters right off the bat made sense. How could machine guns, submachine guns, or machine pistols be accurate enough to avoid also shooting down the hostages who at that point would necessarily be close by their captors? But, admitting that, I am far from being the only one who saw scores of cops armed with excellent precision rifles at Fürstenfeldbruck. Why were the accompanists not given arms such as that?

The most striking thing, of course, is the ridiculously small number of marksmen. Even if Schreiber and Wolf thought there were only five fedayeen, how miserly could they be?

It was painfully evident that basic conditions would be terribly tough on the ambushers. It would be dark, however good the artificial lighting, and there would be shadowy zones and uneven light beams that so often warp perspective, and the depth of vision would be very slight. There would be the motion of the silhouettes, always unpredictable down to a second when dealing with wary people. There would be the distance, impossible to judge in advance, since there was no way of knowing how the terrorists would move about, but something in the neighborhood of 60 meters.

There would be the fact that these were young men without war experience, who might be shooting for the first time at living targets, and the haunting fear of hitting one of the hostages, especially if he happened to be a German. Even before the helicopters took off, the *Krisenstab* wondered whether the fedayeen would not take the pilots hostage despite their collective promise not to. This concern for not shooting down any hostages became even more urgent as the shooting became more individual. It would be very easy indeed, after the fact, to reconstruct the trajectory of each shot fired by the marksmen.

For all these reasons, under the best conditions, that is, if indeed there had been only five terrorists, there ought to have been at least twice the number of sharpshooters authorized to shoot right from the start.

All the more reason to feel that at least twice as many snipers were absolutely indispensable from the moment—at 10:06—when the crisis staff saw there were eight Black September men and not five. It still would have been perfectly feasible to ship additional sharpshooters from the Village to Fürstenfeldbruck. But maybe no one thought of it.

And in spite of all that, there still remained one more alternative until the very second when the terrorists began off-loading from the Bells: selecting at least five men from among the policemen on duty at the field to start firing at the same time as the five certified high-precision sharpshooters. If volunteers had been called for from among those assigned to Fürstenfeldbruck, there would have been many, as we were able to ascertain. A choice could have been made among them.

I know for example that there were two ex-Foreign Legionnaires there, who had fought in Algeria. One, thirty-five, was walking his wolf-dog. And fuming about being left out "of the scrap."

What was most needed in this last-minute last-chance gamble was to shoot down at once as many terrorists as possible, once the first shot had been fired. Consequently, even if it somewhat increased the risks of hitting some of the hostages, the stakes were high enough to warrant using every card at one's disposal, meaning enough good riflemen to be sure that the terrorists aimed at would actually be put out of commission.

On September 6 and 7, Minister Genscher several times stated publicly: "There's no doubt about it: we thought there were only five terrorists, and as a result five sharpshooters were also selected to be sent to Fürstenfeldbruck. Each of the men, in whom we had the highest confidence because of their level of specialization and training, was instructed to be sure to eliminate one terrorist."

The operating heads of Operation Rescue *thought;* they had no certainty. They were up against terrorists who twice that day had committed murder, and stated they were ready to go right on doing it. Under such circumstances, would too many cooks spoil the broth?

Herr Manfred Schreiber, contradicting what the Federal Minister of the Interior had just said, stated on September 7 at the press conference in which both of them participated in conjunction with Merk and Wolf, part of which was telecast around the world:

"Five selected shooters were enough. If there had been more, they might have brought on a disaster."

What disaster? Shoot each other? Would it not have been possible to have each sharpshooter flanked by another marksman, instead of an "accompanist"? According to the calculations of the technicians who selected the fields of fire, there would have been no chance whatever of any of them hitting any of the others! And would it not also have been perfectly easy to spread the high-precision men all around the perimeter within which, whatever they did, the fedayeen would remain? This beginning perimeter, considering the positions assigned to sharpshooters Nos. 4 and 5, seems to me to have been in the neighborhood of 370 meters. All it takes is a pencil and ruler to show that scores of sharpshooters could be placed on half such a perimeter without any chance of any of them ever hitting any of the others. . . .

Now Georg Wolf went to return that call. The crisis staff wanted to inform him the terrorists and their hostages had just lifted off. The *Vize* started to ask two questions that had been bothering him: How many "Arabs" were there? And had those promised reinforcements finally left for the base, and if so when? But at the other end, one of Merk's assistants, who had been impatiently waiting for Wolf to return the call, now hung up too soon. Yet the head of Operation Rescue felt reassured by this call: as he saw it, had there not been five terrorists, that would be the most important piece of information the *Krisenstab* would rush to tell him first. The same applied to any delay in sending the reinforcements.

10:28 PM: The last starter in the sixth race counting for the Finn Class Olympic yachting category completed the course.

So the suspension of the Games had not been observed at all up north there at Kiel. The program had gone on as scheduled today, all day. It must be very difficult to change plans in waterborne events such as those.

10:29 PM: The Iroquois with the head of the Munich police and other VIPs, last to have lifted off, landed first at the military air base, well ahead of the fedayeen's two copters. The crew had covered the 22 km. (just under 14 mi.) between the Village and Fürstenfeldbruck in seven and a half minutes. At top speed.

It landed well off to the west of the tower, some 100 meters away. Its passengers started to run over to the tower, while the helicopter sank into darkness: the mobile searchlights that had illuminated its landing-pad were turned back again to where the game for human stakes was to be played out.

The *Vize*, who had been on the phone again to the base commander trying to scurry up more searchlights, ran to the tower entrance to meet his boss. Dr. Schreiber, as he saw him, blurted, "Some lousy thing to happen at the last minute, eh? We sure never expected that, did we, Georg?"

"What lousy thing, *Herr Präsident*?"

"Why, that there are eight of 'em!"

"What? Of who? You don't mean there are eight Arabs!"

The police commissioner knit his brows. His metallic look bored into Wolf's, and he slowly said, "You mean you're just finding that out from me?"

Wolf, overwhelmed, nodded. Schreiber, silently, tried to assess what stupidity could have kept the head of Operation Rescue unaware of this for the last vital twenty-four minutes, when it meant the whole prearranged plan was knocked askew.

"Verdammt!" (God damn it!), he finally raged. "Well, never mind. We can still make up for it, Wolf!"

The *Vize* moved away, to get a grip on himself. He succeeded quickly, after a few steps on the asphalt outside the tower wall. He was all concentration, physically feeling the passage of time. He was wandering in the night, looking for unattainable keys. He kept turning over the obsessive question: What would the fedayeen do, once out of the planes?

They would probably split into several groups, each with some of the hostages. Some would remain covered in the copters while the others walked through the light to the airliner.

If there were not enough fedayeen in the first targetable batch, the precision-sharpshooters would hold back for a better opportunity. But the fedayeen might also all come out in one compact group. In that case, the scenario would be: Issa, with or without a hostage, would go on his own to inspect the Boeing. While he was in the 727, all his men would come down from the Iroquois and gather between the two copters. They would have eight or nine hostages, or twelve, or thirteen, depending on whether Issa had one with him and whether he had taken the crews of the helicopters as additional hostages. The safari-outfitted leader would come back to his men, having seen the phony crew on the 727. After that, in one body, the eight fedayeen and their nine or thirteen hostages would head for the 727.

In such a case, when should the shooting start? Just as the two groups of terrorists go toward each other between the Iroquois? That would not be bad, provided the fields of fire imposed on the snipers could be canceled, and provided there were at least seven, if not reasonably a good many more, instead of only five sharpshooters. For, with Issa off toward the plane, there would be seven fedayeen to shoot down at once. Or else, to start shooting when they were all in one tight block heading for the Boeing. Issa would then be with them—all eight fedayeen together. But then, of course, to set only five snipers on the eight targets would be ridiculous, impossible, unpardonable.

Later, when all the criticism had begun about the inadequate size of the shock personnel involved, especially the number of sharpshooters at Fürstenfeldbruck, the two highest authorities involved, Bruno Merk and Manfred Schreiber, energetically defended their decision. The *Dokumentation,* on pp. 59–60, explains that they had to

> . . . take into account the need to set up means of action and direction (including the sharpshooters and armored vehicles) for each of the four combat sites considered: No. 31 Connollystrasse, the underground of the Olympic Village, the Fürstenfeldbruck air base, and the Riem airport. Each of these four locations might at any moment have been selected by the terrorists. . . .

Not very convincing. First of all, because of the sharpshooters.

Merk, in his first press conference at dawn on September 6, expounded on the "score of selected first-class riflemen" whom Schreiber and he had had sent from the Olympic Village. The judicial investigation presided over by Magistrate Otto Heindl reached the conclusion that in fact Herr Schreiber had called on only fourteen certified high-precision shots, not some twenty-odd. Which need not mean that there were not more *Hochpräzisions-schützen* available at the scene of the shootout.

Now, just among the 12,000 to 13,000 police exclusively assigned to the Olympic Games, were there no more than a score of riflemen who had qualified for the high-precision certificate? That would be unthinkable. In all developed countries of the world, no group or body more than the police keeps assiduously trained in marksmanship in all its phases. These officers have to go through rifle and pistol tests, and keep their marksmanship continually up each year. The various grades of certification mean financial raises and hierarchical advancement.

Traffic police and desk forces, in Bavaria as elsewhere, obviously may not always meet this degree of training. But they are not meant to be the experts, who are assigned to the specialized brigades; and the latter furnished more than half the officers policing the Games.

Better yet: from midmorning, September 5, we were able to see the streams of trucks bringing in *Bundesgrenzschutzpolizei* reinforcements. These men are specially trained in marksmanship, and renowned throughout Germany for their expertise in this field. On September 5, at Olympic Park, there were among them, according to several of their superiors, at least twenty-five with the highest certificate of sharpshooting.

But how were Herr Wolf's five lonely super-marksmen armed? They had G-3 carbines made in Obendorf, in the Neckar valley, by Heckler & Koch. With a Zeiss sight, this is a very up-to-date weapon, first essayed by federal experts in the fall of 1971. It has minimum recoil, its polygonal unrifled barrel provides extreme precision, and its sighting instruments are especially carefully made.

Nevertheless, Herr Franz-Josef Strauss severely criticized the selection of this gun for Fürstenfeldbruck. *Stern* quoted him as saying,

> The G-3 carbine had already proved unsatisfactory at the time of the Prinzregenstrasse bank holdup in Munich. Its barrel is only fifty centimeters [20 inches] long. The slightest motion puts the

shot off target. Precision rifles with seventy-centimeter barrels are much more dependable.

Herr Strauss speaks from his experience as head of the Federal Defense Ministry, as well as being a longtime weapons collector and passionate hunter. However, we must not overlook the fact that the decision to use the G-3 was in the province of Dr. Manfred Schreiber, a member of the opposite party, the SPD.

Apart from the marksmen, were the police at the site properly equipped in individual arms? The *Dokumentation* (p. 61) boasts of the "availability of powerful weapons [9-mm pistols were added to the submachine guns] distributed to the attack commando disguised as airport personnel." This boast would seem to suggest that the rest of the policemen were less well equipped. But this was not so: toward the end of this awful night, I saw many policemen leaving the air base carrying either one of the new KGP-70 pistols manufactured at Dachau by Erma, or a flexible-stock Walther assault-gun or 9-mm Walther machine pistol.

In his weighty worry, Herr Wolf still had one reason for satisfaction: the placement of the first three snipers. To fire down from above is always considered an advantage, especially against moving targets. Moreover, the snipers were in darkness while the terrorists they were aiming at would be powerfully lighted by the bunches of searchlights. The other two marksmen were also very well placed, and Wolf felt sure they were so well protected the fedayeen would have no real likelihood of hitting them.

Protecting the Germans! That was what the authorities were most obsessively concerned with. When Captain Y, who was with General Zamir, saw the Fürstenfeldbruck layout, he blurted: "You can't get anywhere with these static methods. You have to make a lightning attack, from all sides, come out into the open and shoot at close range!"

The Israeli survivors also said the next day, "The Germans should have gone in. You can't get bound men away from murderers by staying hidden in darkness far away, and firing at specific targets as if it were a pigeon shoot."

Now, lighting? According to Schreiber's 8:40 instructions,

355

every available extra movable light source was dug up. Unfortunately, that did not prove to be enough, and the *Vize*, in the moments just before the terrorists got in, realized this better than anyone.

Until 10:00 PM, the night had been velvety—not light, but a good light-carrier, what with all those stars winking above. Cumulus clouds, driven by a mild Alpine wind, then progressively invaded the sky throughout the Munich region. They were compact clouds, that kept dragging along. Stubborn as a lid, they were to remain overhead till the middle of the night, without raining.

Georg Wolf, having made his last analysis, came back to the tower, got into the elevator, and went up to the first of the two panoramic rotundas. He went out on the terraced platform supporting the rotundas, where he found Dr. Schreiber, rechecking the snipers' positions. The *Vize* called to his boss, "When are the two extra squadrons, the six armored cars, and the shock brigade coming in, *Herr Präsident?* We could use them right now."

"What if the terrorists at this very moment were making the crews of the helicopters go back to the Village or head for Riem? What would we do then with those units here, twenty-six kilometers from Munich? I'll give them the green light to come on when the hostages get to Fürstenfeldbruck. Not before."

So saying, Schreiber left his deputy and went back to the VIPs. They were on the third floor, which was quite high and entirely occupied by the radar room, unstintingly equipped at the time the U.S. Air Force was in control of the base.

The usual people in here were the controllers of initial and intermediate approach, and the departure controller; they worked in front of panoramic radar screens, and were officers. There were also noncoms and sentinels, normally. But tonight the colonel had left only two captains in charge, in case of unforeseen air traffic.

Directly above the officials in this huge room were the Nos. 1, 2, and 3 marksmen, kneeling or prone on the terrace.

Although Schreiber said later that he was terribly pessimistic about the upcoming events, those who saw him in the radar room felt he was quite eager. He phoned the Warner Barracks, the vital center for his police force, and grew impatient with the switchboard operator over the delay.

The police captain who answered told him the selection of Fürstenfeldbruck as "embarkation point" had spread like wildfire, the TV-radio being mainly responsible, of course. All the mass media representatives were converging on the town.

The news people, as well as curiosity seekers, came either by Highway 2, already mentioned—Munich-Puchheim-Fürstenfeldbruck—or expressway E-11, quicker to get to if coming from the Village. This motorway is the main road to the west. At the Geiselbullach interchange, the Fürstenfeldbruck-bound got off on to Highway 471. Consequently, the captain said, "We're heading for a catastrophic bottleneck on Number Two and Number Four-seventy-one; even expressway E-Eleven is beginning to clog up. There have been some accidents. And this may interfere with the progress of the armored vehicles. The earlier we start them out, the better."

"We have to wait," Schreiber cut him off, restating his earlier worry: "What if the fedayeen made the pilots . . ."

The captain suggested banning private vehicles from the only two roads leading to the base from the main highways mentioned above. These two local roads were laid out in arcs that met at the entrance to Maisach on the north edge of the base. Schreiber agreed to blocking them off, but since they were outside Munich proper, he had no authority to do so. So he asked Dr. Merk, who felt it was not possible to cut the inhabitants of Maisach off from the world. If things seemed bottled up at the base, he might reconsider.

None of the VIPs was very optimistic, either. "No one wanted to talk. Each one was wondering to himself," as Herr Franz-Josef Strauss would later recall.

Six broad double windows faced the runways to the north. The powerful air conditioner was on, but all the windows were open. Herren Genscher, Merk, Schreiber, and Strauss, and General Zamir and Captain Y, eyed the stark panorama that would doubtless soon be bloodied. The new Mayor of Munich, Herr Georg Kronawitter, was also there, having arrived by car.

Schreiber specified, with no show of nervousness, "Gentlemen, the Boeing 727 that you see lighted on our right, that is, to the east, is one hundred twenty meters from the tower. If the fedayeen

357

have not yet been brought down, they will enter it by the rear trapdoor. There is a squad of five men hidden in the passenger cabin who will then wipe them out. If they should insist on boarding at the front, they will be faced by a fake crew of three armed policemen who will be ready to go into action.

"Now please look north and northwest of the tower. You see the phosphorescent flags of the two landing-point signals. The two helicopters that set down there will each be forty meters from the tower, and thirty meters from each other. The machine that lands northwest of the tower will be exactly one hundred forty-five meters from the tail of the 727; the second, one hundred twenty meters away. These are distances for which the marksmen will be able to adjust . . ."

They were all listening, and watching, but none felt truly confident. Captain Y asked for the exact position of the snipers again.

"The first three are above our heads. Number Four is seventy-five meters northwest of the 727, under a fire truck. The helicopter setting down northwest of the tower, and thus the farthest from him, will be only one hundred and thirty meters from Number Four. And the terrorists will be going toward him, whether they head for the other Iroquois or for the Boeing. As for Number Five, he is eighty meters due north of the tower. You see two flashing lights on that axis: those are identification beacons. They are on an earthen mound with a concrete parapet around it; Number Five is behind that parapet, facing us. As soon as the first of the two copters sets down, those beacons go out."

The whirring of the approaching Iroquois became perceptible.

"It seems to me there are a great many dark spots," said Herr Genscher. "And the lighting is weak. I can understand not wanting to alert the terrorists by blinding them with lights, but I think that's been carried too far."

He spoke loudly. But no one replied.

If the sharpshooters did not have night-sights, the lighting of the field became a capital concern. That was why after the fact those responsible for Fürstenfeldbruck asserted that there was fine light on the fire zone. But many competent witnesses attested the contrary.

The Mayor of Munich, Herr Kronawitter, said, "The field was

poorly lighted. There were many places totally dark. So much so that I had trouble keeping track of what happened."

Captain Praus, pilot of D-HAQO, did, on the other hand, say, "The landing area was as light as day!" But, then, the headlights of his whirlybird helped the illumination considerably, and let us not forget that the crucial shots were aimed at targets completely outside the helicopter landing-pad.

Lieutenant Erich Konn, who just happened to be there, visiting one of his buddies, categorically stated: "There was insufficient light." Another Luftwaffe lieutenant, H. Frenkel, was equally definite: "The field was poorly lighted." Minister Bruno Merk himself, during his long predawn statement on Wednesday, September 6, clearly asserted, "At the moment the two helicopters were about to set down on the terrain prepared for the ambush, we realized that the lighting left much to be desired." And later, "Not only was the lighting much too inadequate, but the beams of the searchlights did not complement each other properly, and the helicopters created broad dark areas."

When Dr. Merk heard the severe criticism of the Federal Minister of the Interior, as they waited in the control tower for the arrival of the terrorists and their nine surviving hostages, he turned to Dr. Schreiber, who shrugged.

"You phoned them as soon as we got to G-One, didn't you? And didn't they have two hours to beef it up?" Merk asked.

"What with?" countered Schreiber.

It has been explained that, through an unfortunate congeries of circumstances, the air base on September 5 did not have its full complement of movable searchlights. But Wolf had been on the spot since 6:00 PM, and knew from the start that the action would take place at night.

"True," the spokesman for the Munich police replied to that comment, "but the air base authorities insisted the lighting left nothing to be desired, and pointed out that air traffic went on daily into the small hours and never had the slightest hitch due to darkness." Which of course meant nothing, for all that that required was for proper markers to be along the runways, certainly the case at Fürstenfeldbruck.

There seems to have been a misunderstanding: the air base

authorities took it for granted the sharpshooters' guns would be outfitted with infrared sights.

However that may be, between 8:40 and 10:30 PM, would it not have been possible to borrow (or if need be requisition) spotlights for the airfield? There were scores of film and TV crews with their own klieg lights. There was also the mobile lighting equipment of the superbly appointed international airport of Riem. And, they could have gotten some from the German Army units in the region, or other sources. Really, in 1972, in the middle of the Olympics, in a metropolis of a million and a half souls, provided with every kind of audiovisual equipment and harboring such large industrial plants, was it so hard to come by a few extra spotlights in time for Fürstenfeldbruck? Especially since the security forces covering the Munich Games had at their disposal the fastest and most diverse kind of transport. For instance, twenty-four helicopters. Why were only three used during the crucial hours? Quite a few lights can be shipped in an Iroquois or a Sikorsky S-61—to say nothing of their trucks and buses. And up to 10:10 there was no traffic jam on the roads to Fürstenfeldbruck.

10:30 PM: Capt. Reinhard Praus' hand firmly held the broomstick of D-HAQO, flying at the moderate speed of 150 km. an hour (about 94 mi.), due north. The masses of lights up ahead, the two violently lighted roadways meeting at right angles, the glittering castle on its hilltop as if in a sound-and-light show, was Dachau. The machine seemed to be climbing, but it was the ground that went down: the Amper valley. The crews of the two Iroquois preferred staying low, beneath the clouds. Any who heard them or saw their lights over the countryside understood who they were. The machine should already have set down at Fürstenfeldbruck. But Praus was meandering, quietly followed by the other copter. Dr. Schreiber had said, stall as long as possible.

On takeoff, the crew had doused the overheads. Tony immediately barked. He, too, worked in the Village (as a cook), and had no trouble expressing himself in German.

The five hostages could not see a thing. At takeoff, the hand towels removed when they got out of the bus had been put back as blindfolds.

360

The Fire and the Wood

The main job of Copilot Lt. Paul Blankenhagel was to watch Tony's four fedayeen in the rearview mirror. Tony was a bundle of nerves, subject to electrical impulses: he got up, sat back down, perhaps nauseated. Then he yelled as he shoved his watch under Blankenhagel's nose. Praus' assistant gave a hand signal indicating five more flight minutes. Issa's assistant shook his head and brandished his weapon. Why so long? What did all this mean? The copilot put his finger to the earflap of his flight helmet: sorry, but he could not hear a word. He pointed to the yellow, green, and red position lights of the other copter, following on their right, as if to say to Tony: See, you're all together, nothing to get excited about! But Tony, waving the weapon, warned him: "If we're not down in five minutes, I'm shooting one of you!"

D-HAQO pitched, as if it were afraid.

The terrorists could see an immense line against a black background, toward Augsburg, somewhere in the countryside, far below the copter. Unbroken thin white beams shone on it in the opposite direction, with red dots behind: *Autobahn* E-11.

Praus radioed to his counterpart Gunnar Ebel, piloting the other Iroquois, "They're threatening to shoot us if we keep circling. So I'm heading for Fürstenfeldbruck, full speed ahead! I'll call the tower. How goes it with you?"

"The white hat's getting real nervous. He's shown us his timepiece twice, yelling something. I was about to call you."

Captain Praus leaned heavily on the left control. The Bell swung around 90 degrees, driving Paulo's forehead violently against the big rectangular window in the door. The bull-chested fedayee had barely had time to swear and lean down to pick up his submachine gun, when the captain stepped farther down on the same bar. Paulo sprawled on his back, the only comic relief in the whole tragic event. But his comrades were yelling, and Blankenhagel felt a gun muzzle in his ribs: two of the terrorists, feline Abu Halla and his boss Tony, stood between the crew and the five hostages tied up on their seats. They steadied themselves with a hand in the steel rings in the ceiling. Blankenhagel was hoping that a miscue would not make them pull the trigger accidentally; but, no fear, they were keeping their fingers well away. The other two terrorists, Paulo and Badran who had just taken off his hood, were now sitting on the back banquette. One was aiming at the backs of the Israelis' necks, the other at the pilots', both ready to shoot in an instant.

Speed now: 270 km. per hour (171-plus mi.). QO was still slightly ahead of DU (which makes for quicker identification). The Iroquois, carrying cargoes of attackers and victims, pierced the deep black of the night with their tricolored lights. They were shaking. They seemed to be sliding down along two parallel invisible steel cables, like the nacelles of a lift. In three minutes, having flown over the Maisach River, whose waters shone slightly with the reflection of the headlights, they were over the Luftwaffe base; Maisach town, which they flew around, was unusually lighted up: its people already knew . . .

Issa, in DU, was sparing in his movements, in contrast to his sidekick. But his excitement could be felt by a kind of current he radiated. It was dangerous. Flight Sgt. Klaus Bechler kept a wary eye on the four fedayeen. The pilot, Capt. Gunnar Ebel, aged thirty-three, in turn radioed his squad leader: "I'm landing right after you. Over, Reinhard."

Perhaps there was some foreknowledge that came through the tone of Ebel's voice, to alarm his leader, who answered, "Gunnar, remind Bechler to keep cool with those guys, whatever they do. As soon as our motors are off, we all four get out, and make it quietly over to the tower."

With lips scraping the mouthpieces, their barely-more-than-whispered dialogue could not be heard by the fedayeen. Blond Samir, up front with Issa in Ebel's DU, went through an eloquent dumbshow to tell the German pilots to speak louder. Issa felt how ridiculous the idea was and quieted him down by bawling Samir out.

At the same time, in the 727, 120 meters northeast of the Fürstenfeldbruck control tower, a cough. Someone swore as something fell. Grumbling. Sighs mixed with outcries. The three cops up in the baggage-racks had the uncomfortable feeling that their plastic supports were beginning to give way under their weight. They too had pierced holes in the lids to be able to see, and each one had made a larger opening where the lid met the partition, so as to be able to insert the tip of his weapon's muzzle.

The lieutenant was walking back and forth in the center aisle of the long tunnel-shaped passenger compartment. Noises could be heard from the cockpit.

Such was the situation when a resounding voice gave off with a string of exclamations: "This is completely nuts! *Sie wollen uns wohl hochnehmen!*" (They're really putting us on!)

The lid of one of the baggage-bins dropped loudly open. Some-one jumped down, and started to pace the floor. It was the Algäu character, complaining, "We'll all get it in the neck! What the fuck are we doing here anyway?"

The onetime volunteers saw their lieutenant, who had been up front with the fake crew, run back; there were words between that officer and the patrolman. The flaps of the other two baggage-bins also opened, and now it was a four-way barking argument. Soon, in spite of himself, the lieutenant had all seven of his men around him in the middle of the passenger compartment. The curses and complaints from all their throats were enough to set the fuselage to shaking.

"Two or three of the Arabs may get killed, but the others'll throw their grenades, and bye-bye, baby! We'll be goners!"

It should be pointed out that the wing-tanks were full of kero-sene: the Lufthansa services had been told too late not to load the triple-jet with any more fuel than needed to get it from the Riem hangar to Fürstenfeldbruck. Those in charge of the operation had worried that such an order might leak out, with catastrophic re-sults, so it had not been given. Consequently, the 727 that was to be within firing range was loaded with some 35,000 liters (app. 9,240 gallons) of fuel. What was more, the eight "volunteers" were well aware of it.

10:32 PM: The terrorists being about to land, rebellion was growing inside the 727. The eight men were between twenty-one and thirty. Two of them, in particular, were probationary recruits, fresh from their military service. Police, all through Germany, are very conscious of their rights, and organized into a branch of the West German labor federation, DGB *(Deutscher Gewerkschafts-bund)*. . . . As such, they don't often let themselves be exploited.

The lieutenant would have liked to report to Wolf before it was too late. But how could he leave the 727? It had been strictly

363

forbidden. Use one of the pilots' radios? He had tried unsuccessfully as soon as Wolf left them, and this failure was the first thing
to start the revolt brewing up front.

The disguised cops were saying, "The only thing is to decide
whether we have to croak like rats here, or whether we oughtn't
get out of this flying coffin and meet the terrorists on even terms.
Put it to a vote!"

Seven shouted, Yea! The lieutenant demurred. Seven to one in
favor of desertion!

"We had had no close-combat training, and I for one had not
had a marksmanship test in over six months!" one of the eight
two days later told an assembled press; he, like several of his
buddies, was trying to win over public opinion, since it had been
rumored the police authorities were planning "serious sanctions"
against the B-727 rebels.

The lieutenant tried in vain one last time to keep them in line:
one of them was announcing the appearance of helicopter lights
in the sky.

Only one door was available this evening: the rear trapdoor
under the jets. The front door was closed, and there was no gangway outside it. Two of the non-volunteers made for the trapdoor.
From there, the low whirr of their own engines did not keep them
from hearing: the star-studded sky was full of wild sputtering of
a copter sliding down diagonally without moving off its axis.

They were yelling, "Here they all are! One of the copters is
down already!"

The machine in question had been down for over five minutes,
but on the 727 only the fake crew had seen it, and noted that it
brought in Dr. Schreiber and the "wheels."

Apple-green overalls and fine rank-striped Luftwaffe uniforms
ran for their weapons and quickly forsook the 727 with its yellow
stork insignia. They were barely down the ramp, when QO, with
the five and Issa, stopped in midair above the concrete slabs, 120
meters away.

The detail these police had been ordered to undertake, it must
be admitted, had little chance of succeeding: it was pretty much
an out-and-out sacrifice.

The revolt of the young policemen was fairly well known
already by late afternoon on September 6, when Manfred Schreiber

reappeared in the lobby of G-1. The newsmen pelted him with questions about it. The *Polizeipräsident* was livid, his eyes hidden behind metal-rimmed sunglasses, his hands nervous and his voice hoarse. But for all of that, he still had his elegant torso, lordly cuffs, clean-shaven cheeks, his air of self-confidence, and that dimpled chin that jutted out like a fist.

"What you say is generally true, but there are two errors. There were not twelve men, but eight, including the fake crew. They did not abandon ship, but sent a delegation to see their superiors. The latter saw that they were right and agreed to allow them to leave the plane. There will be no sanctions whatever."

The statements of two of the young cops jibe too well with those of other participants in the last act of the tragedy to allow for Herr Schreiber taking us in. This was not the first time the Munich Police Commissioner stood up for his men in the face of overwhelming evidence—with actual settlement later to be made within the family.

To call it mutiny would be absurd, since these were not soldiers and at worst might be punished by dismissal. But the departure of the 727 "volunteers" left a huge gap in the Schreiber-Wolf plan for the final operations.

There should be no great surprise that the five men in the passenger cabin decided not to play the kamikazes, especially in view of the *Krisenstab*'s obsessive concern for sparing German lives. But what about the three disguised as flight crew?

They might have felt warranted in getting rid of their fine KGP-70 pistols, once their backup men had left. But they still should have stayed on. They had indeed volunteered, knowing it would be a risky business. The helicopter crews, and the drivers of the minibus and the military van, had accepted going on equally dangerous details.

Subject to further change of mind and giving in to their fears, the three fake crewmen might more justifiably have rid themselves earlier of their disguises, instead of deserting the 727 at the last minute, when it was much too late to try to find replacements for them.

In a little while, when the fedayeen came to inspect the plane, they would see it had no one on it at all. That alone should have been enough to tip them off.

XXI
THE BIG FIZZLE

Lift up your eyes, and behold
Them that come from the north . . .
Jeremiah 13:20

10:34 PM: IROQUOIS D-HAQO, CARRYING HOSTAGES BERGER, SHAPIRA, Shorr, Slavin, and Spitzer, and four terrorists, Tony, Abu Halla, Paulo, and Badran, was to land first at Fürstenfeldbruck. Capt. Reinhard Praus exchanged the habitual formulas with the control tower in an impersonal voice. A handsome, well-built fellow, with an impassive expression, he would say a few hours later, "I felt right from the start that this was not working out, either for the Israelis or us. The first thing the terrorists did was aim their weapons at my navigator and me. I said to myself: they had nine hostages, now they have thirteen."

In the last stage of the gently slanting descent, the speed decreased; the green and red position lights were blinking as if they were carrying on a coded conversation with the base guide lights. Praus brought his copter to a halt a meter up from the prefabbed concrete blocks, in a deafening roar of turbines. A signalman in green overalls crossed his little phosphorescent flags in front of him. He was a border-police guard, as were the Iroquois crews.

QO landed. The rotors were still turning full blast and the skids had hardly touched ground, when the right passenger door slid open, under the eye of the copilot, Lt. Paul Blankenhagel. A fedayee jumped down, submachine gun to the fore, aimed at the tower: Paulo, recognizable by his build.

10:35 PM: The cop-signalman turned around unconcernedly. The terrorists who now saw his back could make out on the fire-

366

proofed material the large-size torpedo-nosed emblem of Lufthansa, the dark-blue stork on yellow ground.

Praus and Blankenhagel took off their headphones, straightened out some levers. They opened the doors of their cockpit, and stepped down toward the concrete field.

Less than twenty seconds behind them, down came D-HADU, bringing hostages Friedman, Gutfreund, Halfin, and Springer, and four terrorists, Issa, Denawi, Salah, and Samir. Its crew—Capt. Gunnar Ebel and Sgt. Klaus Bechler—in turn made it hover briefly just off the ground. Issa, like a true star, did not wait for full landing before jumping out.

Ebel and Bechler did the final operations, undid their safety belts, and started out in the same calm tempo as their counterparts.

Forty meters away, Dr. Schreiber was phoning his command post at *Olympiapark* and ordering the waiting reinforcements, the two squadrons of Munich police, the shock brigade of twenty-three border-police volunteers, and the six armored cars, to "proceed full speed ahead" to the air base.

Dr. Wolf's Aryan features and smooth skull were turning purple with rage: before him, on the terrace where three of the five marksmen were on the lookout, a young pilot in shimmering gold braid stood at attention. This was actually the *Feldwebel* who had acted as aide to the lieutenant in charge of the unwilling kamikazes on the 727. The noncom had just finished reporting: the lieutenant and four "mechanics" armed with submachine guns had remained near the plane, behind a metal-grille anti-blast barrier, in a dark patch. The two other members of the fake crew, having only pistols, had come back to the tower with the noncom.

"You'll be hearing from me when this is all over!" was all Wolf replied. The nine men who were supposed to come to the help of their eight comrades in the 727, as needed, and had been hidden near the place, now got the order to return to the control tower.

The *Vize* called Schreiber on the intercom, and reported to him. The Chief went to whisper the disastrous piece of news to Minister Merk, who was just watching Paulo jump down from QO. The

Bavarian minister shook his head silently, without taking his eyes off the scene.

It was all a chessboard . . . Now, you had the two helicopters and the control tower forming an isosceles triangle, 40 meters to the side, its base the 30-meter line between the two Iroquois. Captain Ebel's DU was northwest of the tower, while Praus' QO was almost due north, just slightly off to the northeast.

On that tarmac in front of the control tower, almost all of the action was to take place. This huge area was much broader than the air base's main runway: an average of 130 meters (about 143 yds.) wide at the spot we are concerned with.

At its start, the Fürstenfeldbruck drama took place in a pentagon. The control tower, pivotal element, was the first of its five angles; the second was the 727 to the east, at the end of the longest side; the plane, in fact, was a few degrees northeast. Then, next angle, Marksman No. 4 at his fire truck, due northeast; No. 5 and his group of beacons, due north; and finally, helicopter DU, northwest.

The surface of this pentagon was about 9,000 sq. meters (some 10,800 sq. yds.).

Two shouts of "Halt!" like one snap of a whip brought the crew of QO to a stop the second they began to leave the ship. Tony had a bead on Lieutenant Blankenhagel; big Badran had the same on Captain Praus. From outside, Paulo was also aiming at the two officers. The fourth terrorist, Abu Halla, with his fake-sleepy look because of his open mouth, was sweeping the narrow space with his submachine gun, aiming successively at the napes of the five Israelis jutting above the seatback.

Tony jumped to the ground. He called on Blankenhagel to follow suit, which the lieutenant did. Tony had him put his hands up, stuck the muzzle of his weapon at the nape of his neck, and told him to walk around the nose of the copter. The two men stooped as they walked, on account of the rotor blades that kept turning of their own momentum and were displacing great swaths of air. They brought Blankenhagel to a stop just as the pilot had gotten beyond the small noncoupled rotor which was also still turning, at the back of the plane.

The Big Fizzle

Abu Halla jumped down to the tarmac, too. He now guided Captain Praus through a similar course, as Tony went back into QO to keep watch on the tied-up Israelis with Badran.

Young Mark Slavin no longer had his two fellow Russian-born friends beside him, Friedman and Halfin. But Kehat Shorr got along all right in Russian: it had been so useful in Communist Rumania! So that Slavin was not isolated from his comrades. But Tony reacted to some whispering by roars that could clearly be heard even over in the tower.

No, the five Israelis were not holding still for this—as the Germans would be able to see, when it was all over.

Paulo and Abu Halla were both out of QO, but Abu Halla was guarding the crew alone. Paulo walked away.

Praus was tired of keeping his hands up and put them down on top of his head. Abu Halla screamed in his falsetto voice. Praus answered that he was tired, and stayed as he was. The terrorist let him.

Similar scenes were taking place with the DU crew, 30 meters away. Captain Ebel and Sergeant Bechler were taken by Issa and Salah to the tail of the copter. Then Issa went on to the runway, Salah staying behind to keep the two German pilots in his sights. Blond Samir with the girlish features, and little Denawi, highly typed by his teased mane and his narrow mustache, remained in the DU keeping the four hostages covered.

The latter were not taking it lying down either, despite being tied, blindfolded, and watched. Huge Gutfreund, Friedman the vest-pocket Apollo, raging Halfin, and Springer who had gotten out of so many desperate scrapes, were exchanging quickly repressed whispers. Their two pilots, Ebel and Bechler, stood with hands crossed at the backs of their necks, under the eye of Salah, skinnier and crustier than ever, with his bowed legs. "Moving my eyes all the way over to the corner, I could just catch sight of Praus over there, elbows pointing," Captain Ebel said.

Four German hostages! In the radar room, there were suppressed exclamations, oppressive worry. And everyone noticed: now none of the eight fedayeen bothered to hide his face any more.

Issa and Paulo, keeping the same space between them as there

369

was between their copters, stood out in the Iroquois headlights. Backs to their hostages and their accomplices, they headed for the lighted 727.

Whereupon, Captain Y made a loud remark in English that all those present understood and recognized inwardly to be correct: "Not only is the lighting bad, but those moving headlights will probably throw the aim completely off!"

True: headlights of vehicles in a nearby road sent reflections over the tarmac, just slight reflections, to be sure, but the kind that moved, trembled, disappeared, and then reappeared like signals. And, however slightly, they did warp all perspective. This was the local road already mentioned, the only one leading to the main gate of the military base. It came from the town of Fürstenfeldbruck, ran along the northeast and northern edges of the base, crossed the townlet of Maisach, then going off due north through the countryside crossed the Maisach River and went on into one of those thick, romantic, royal Bavarian forests, combining firs and yoke-elms, willows and birches. From then on, it was of no further concern to us.

When the special correspondents and reporters of all kinds became convinced the final act would be played out at Fürstenfeldbruck, they finally, after more or less roundabout efforts, all got on to this one road leading to the base. But so did the rubbernecks, the neighboring inhabitants, the police reinforcements, and officials who were sure they could be of assistance. It quickly became a real bottleneck. And it took roadblocks, detours, and traffic control until finally—so very late—it was cleared up again.

Georg Wolf, fifty-two years old, born in Munich and proud of it, had a fine Renaissance *Reiter*'s face—high in color, with hard even features, a voice made to command in a body perfectly preserved for physical exertion. Baldness lent a kind of nostalgic touch to the character, who seemed all of one piece, whereas he had skill and finesse to spare.

After fighting well in the Wehrmacht, Wolf studied law at the University of Munich, and formed his friendship with Schreiber there. Getting his doctor's degree in 1952, he devoted himself until 1960 to the rebuilding of Munich, became a magistrate, and then in 1963 replaced Herr Schreiber as chief of Bavaria's tactical police. In October 1966, Schreiber made him his assistant, with the title of Chief of Police of Munich.

All other solutions having been rejected, the question at Fürstenfeldbruck was now strictly a military one. Were Wolf, and over him Schreiber, who supervised the ambush, technically up to the task? Should not the Minister-President of Bavaria have put a soldier in charge?

10:36 PM: Issa and Paulo, 30 meters apart, walked carefully forward on the concrete surface. The latter was no longer disguised: going through a really light zone, he could be seen to have sideburns, long hair down into his neck and behind his ears, and a square face with thick lips and the floured complexion of Pierrot by Moonlight. Of medium build, all width and muscles, he mainly held the interest this evening because of a wound that must have infuriated him. After having shot Weinberg from the balcony of Apt. 1, Paulo was in turn wounded by Romano, who gave him a deep knifecut on the septum. His nose, big to begin with, with its spreading and curving tip, now seemed bruised and swollen.

This time, Issa was carrying a Kalachnikov with a round ammoclip, but no cocked grenade, and Paulo had a Tokarev carbine. They knew they were being watched by thousands of pairs of eyes. The two Iroquois were not at the same distance from the 727: Paulo's QO was 120 meters (133 yds.) away, and Issa's DU was 145 meters (160 yds.) The big international TV star, Issa, whom over a billion viewers had seen since morning, was therefore closer to the tower and the VIPs.

"There are four of them! For now," said Wolf.

He was kneeling against the terrace parapet, next to the *Oberfeldwebel* (sergeant-major) who was Sniper No. 1, and thus the leader of the *Hochpräzisionsschützen*. The latter was authorized to open fire on his own, but the sub-commissioner of Munich police was his feared and respected superior: Dr. Wolf's orders retained absolute primacy.

"*Ja wohl*" (Sure enough), replied the noncom. "But there are four more Arabs in the copters."

"We'll never get a better chance."

"Do you want me to open fire, *Herr Vizepräsident?* The one in

371

the safari outfit is coming into my field of fire. The tough in the jacket will be coming into it, too."

Dr. Wolf did not answer.

Fedayee Ibrahim Messaud Badran, through his mouthpiece, the distinguished Algiers lawyer Ben Toumi, who saw him on September 26, 1972, and then in later declarations, tried to say that it was Tony who was with Issa. But that is wrong. Tony, as we know, was with Badran, guarding the five Israelis on QO, and in command of the five terrorists who stayed back at the helicopters with him. With Issa indeed there was Paulo, with his strong, heavy, and brutal features, which like very black eyes with white eyeballs suggest the racial admixtures of Upper Egypt. Perhaps Paulo, like Tony, was a Christian Arab. Egypt has many Copts.

Issa and he were silent, their fingers on the triggers, glancing left and right to try to see into the darkness beyond the hard surface, poorly lighted, but still too much so for their taste. A three-phased nervous cough sounded dry and strident, coming from the tower. Who had lost control? The two fedayeen did not care. At a sign from Issa, half-lifting his left arm, they started to converge some 10 meters from the tail of the 727. They met at the foot of the ramp, and exchanged a few whispered words. Issa went up, Paulo in tow. They went in through the trapdoor.

10:38 PM: Each of the five snipers in turn had Issa and his comrade in his sights.

The only witnesses who could get a look at the terrorists when the latter came to inspect the 727 were the five ex-kamikazes. Three times, a head was framed in a porthole, its eyes peering at the naked runway and the buildings, minimally lighted on the orders of the base commander. One time, it was clearly Issa, recognizable by his glasses. The two went into the cockpit. Paulo's athletic silhouette, in the tight black pants, suddenly appeared facing down toward the five carefully hidden policemen: he had opened the main passenger door, and then closed it again. The devolunteers watched as the two figures, lighted by the overheads, went by window after window, heading rearward.

The two terrorists reappeared, coming down the ramp steps without haste, like two technicians who might just have installed some new gadgets; their weapons almost like tools in their hands.

They looked around, as if surprised to be out in the open again, in the heavy silence, in this falsely deserted unknown place, where the ground-level signal-lights shone beyond the lighted part of the concrete tarmac.

10:40 PM: They seemed to hesitate. They talked to each other. Paulo nodded yes to something. They started out again, leaving a space between them, but less than before: some 20 meters (22 yds.).

Over on the helipad, Tony was turning the two crews and their guards 90 degrees.

Forty meters north of the two helicopters, the nine volunteers dressed as mechanics, recalled by Wolf from support of the 727 when their comrades abandoned their posts, had taken up positions, replacing less-trained fellow policemen. They had quickly found the best spots, hidden by four trucks. They could hear Tony's very high-pitched commands coming from the Iroquois to their left, for he often stuck his nose out the door.

Dr. Wolf, looking over the parapet above, said in a stage whisper: "We can't let the leader and the other one go back near our pilots."

The question remains whether the sharpshooters, on their own, might not have waited. Munich police, tomorrow as yesterday under Schreiber-Wolf authority, they refused to emit any opinion. Very qualified Israeli personalities have made no secret of the fact they thought the moment very poorly chosen, and that, at any rate, if the attack took place then, the four fedayeen left in the copters had to be hit at the same time.

The next day at noon I visited the scene of the ambush. I was able to get close to D-HADU, the one that had had Gutfreund, Captain Ebel, and Issa. The cockpit windshield was pockmarked with impact-points, circled in white chalk with numbers written next to them. The pane was very dirty. However, through the Plexiglas a border-police officer in white epauletted shirt and a civilian, probably a police inspector, could be clearly seen. They were stretching varicolored threads that came in through the windshield holes, the other ends held by people outside, on the tarmac. The point was to see whether the shots came from inside the machine or the various floors of the tower.

The two men I could see through the windshield were perfectly outlined. Wolf's trained police could equally well have seen other human figures in the machine that night. As against the holding area as a whole, the two copters and their pad were brightly lighted. And inside each one, the two fedayeen had their backs to the windshield.

On September 7, late afternoon, I heard Dr. Wolf tell a United Press correspondent, "Yes, the fact that the four German pilots had been taken hostage seriously changed the whole setup. The last thing we felt we had a right to do was cause the shedding of German blood."

After which, taut and solid, vigilance and distrust written all over his intelligent authoritarian face, the *Polizeidirektor* took a tangent. He explained that as the fight developed the fact of Germans being in danger in the final analysis in no way changed things.

The qualified Israelis say, "Mr. Wolf called for the shooting exclusively in terms of the two German crews. He was afraid they might be put back aboard the helicopters, and he wanted to give them a chance to get away."

Issa and Paulo were walking faster than they had come, over the runway on which all the Games of Joy charters had landed. They must have reached a conclusion: the 727 with its three turbojets softly purring, but no crew aboard, was a bluff. A booby trap. Why had none of the VIPs who had so often been alongside them at Block 31 felt they ought to be at the foot of the 727 at least to give the two terrorists some explanation?

In this context, Wolf's orders may find justification: the two fedayeen were heading back to their accomplices, to begin the fight—or so it would seem. And would be dragging the four *Grenzschutzpolizei* pilots down with them.

But what if, even though it proved empty, Issa had led his men and their thirteen hostages toward the 727? Would Dr. Wolf have been able, or dared, to attack the terrorists as they made their way across the tarmac, closely mixed with their prisoners? No, he would not have chanced it. And if the Black September commando got into the plane with its Israeli and German prisoners, it would be 31 Connollystrasse all over again. With 35,000 liters of kerosene ready to go up in a fantastic explosion if a real firefight broke out.

The Big Fizzle

Roughly every 15 meters, Issa and Paulo craned their necks to look at each other. The sharpshooters kept breathing deeply and regularly, their knuckles relaxed around the trigger guards. Their muzzles swung imperceptibly, magnetized by their targets. The two fedayeen were now less than 20 meters from the halfway mark.

Dr. Wolf, as hunter or hunted, had often been under fire in the worst circumstances. He knew they were not ideal conditions.

The searchlight beams did not meet properly; the helicopter shadows spread too far; the car headlights created flutterings; and the light was sparse.

Yet the *Vize* felt there was no more time to waste before getting the killers who had already struck twice and now had four Germans a breath away from death. He turned to No. 1:

"OK. Whenever you're ready!"

"At your command."

The head marksman told the other two alongside him, "Fire at will beginning in ten seconds!"

He knew that, once past the halfway mark, the athletic fedayee with the bloodied nose, walking on the outside, would be beyond his range, although Issa, closer in, would still be in his sights for another 20 meters or so.

He made the right choice: since later he would be unable to hit Paulo, he aimed at him first, planning, once he was out of the way, to turn back to Issa, if the others had not gotten him.

Over there, No. 5, hidden to the north in the midst of unlighted signals, behind the small roundtopped concrete parapet, was in a similar situation: one of the two fedayeen walking on the runway and coming closer to him was about to get out of his range. For No. 5, placed due opposite No. 1, that was Issa, if he were not brought down right off. When the shooting started, Issa was 90 meters (100 yds.) from Sniper No. 5, and Paulo was 75 meters (83 yds.) away.

So the ideal spot for shooting down Issa and Paulo was when they were about 75 meters from the 727. They would never again both be any closer to their hunters.

At that moment, give or take two or three meters, both were the same 55 meters from the control tower. Sniper No. 1 being up on the terrace, about 30 meters high, he was a little farther from Issa and Paulo than if he had been on the ground: 65 meters instead of 55. But this additional distance was more than made up for by the fact that he was shooting down at them.

As for Nos. 2 and 3, their field of fire was north. So their targets were Abu Halla and Salah, who were guarding the four helicopter pilots.

And No. 4? Well—under his fire truck, excellently placed to the northeast, he was empowered to fire in any direction. No. 1 could unfortunately not communicate with him, but he felt sure that, since Paulo and Issa were a double moving target less well lighted than Abu Halla and Salah, therefore harder to hit, No. 4 would first shoot at them as they came back from the 727; not at Abu Halla and Salah, covered by Nos. 2 and 3.

No. 1 set his gun and rested his arm against his body to relax it. He lowered his eyelids, then raised them again. He took a deep breath, as in a great legato motion he lowered his gun toward Paulo.

For two seconds, he followed his human prey with his eyes as he softly exhaled. His trigger finger as if by itself got into position. He held his breath with half-filled lungs—and the finger pressed evenly down. . . .

No. 1's first shot just resulted in Paulo giving a start, as he hunched down and turned toward the tower.

No. 1 repeated the shot, a quarter of a second later, since the fedayee was standing still: this time, Paulo took a step forward, but did not seem to be hit.

At any rate, No. 1 shot a third time immediately. Paulo jerked violently up, throwing his face back as if he were looking for a star in the inky sky. He fell to his knees, back stooped, then slid over sideways without straightening out, and started to roll like a barrel that had been kicked downhill—but without letting go of his Tokarev.

No. 5, from his end, had logically aimed at Issa. Could he not have opened fire more quickly on hearing his leader's first shot? There are several recordings of the battle noises. The one I heard several times (now in the German TV files) shows a pause of two tenths to three tenths of a second between the first and second

376

shots. Another two tenths till the third, then two tenths more, and some eight shots can be made out bunched into a second and a half.

These certainly came from the sharpshooters, for the difference in sound volume is noticeable, and the shots are clearly detached from each other. It is impossible to count the shots exactly, for at times several coincide. Then after a half-second's stop, the automatic fire begins.

At any rate, they missed Issa. He bent down, steadied himself with his left hand on the tarmac, got back up and started to run as fast as he could with slight zigzags—toward the closer of the Iroquois, QO.

No. 5 repeated his shot, but in vain. On either side of No. 1, Nos. 2 and 3 aimed at the terrorists guarding the copter crews. Each had his own target; distance down: 45 to 48 meters. The one at the west, fragile Salah with his thin chest, pitched forward, head against the back of Captain Ebel, who tottered. The other fedayee, elastic Abu Halla, whose eye Weinberg had closed in opening a cut above it, fell backward.

Both of the downed terrorists were motionless, one in a heap, the other on his back, arms outstretched. A puddle of blood could clearly be seen forming around each; they were dead. After Tony made them switch positions with their prisoners, they had had their faces to the tower, instead of their backs as before.

No. 4, under his fire truck, chose his own target. Instead of aiming at one of the two terrorists on the tarmac, he fired at Abu Halla, guarding Praus and Blankenhagel. But Abu Halla was 100 meters from him, and besides, his prisoners were hidden from No. 4 by the tail of QO. Paulo and Issa, respectively 65 and 85 meters from the fire truck, would have been much more sensible targets. No. 4 was mainly bent on trying to save his imperiled compatriots. The autopsy was to show that he aimed well: feisty Abu Halla, that black cat, had been twice fatally hit.

But—in the time that it took No. 4, once his first prey was down, to get a bead on Issa and fire again, the serenade had begun: all possibility of surprise was gone.

Paulo suddenly stopped rolling. He half-raised himself. One knee on the ground, without putting the gun to his shoulder, he sent a salvo of some fifteen shots at a searchlight-stand in front of a maintenance hangar, on the edge of the runway, some 40 meters from the tower.

No. 1 turned his aim toward Issa as soon as Paulo was outside his field of fire. But the terrorist leader had slanted off toward the northwest, in zigzags; shots now were coming from everywhere. And No. 5, hidden on the mound among the unlighted beacons, had turned toward Paulo when he lost Issa. The sideburned fedayee had just stopped his roll, to shoot at the searchlight, and in the explosion of flying glass, the sharpshooter's two shots missed him.

Among the four fedayeen on guard in the helicopters, Tony was the first to react, yelling to his men for all of them to return the fire.

"We could see him jumping right out in the light, like a tiger coming down from a tree. His mouth was wide open and he was yelling things we could not hear," said a pilot-captain from the base, who had watched from behind the panes of the highest of the panoramic rotundas.

Tony squatted as he jumped down on the concrete, holding in both hands his Soviet assault-gun with its banana-shaped clip, and blocking its stock in his armpit as he aimed at the tower. He still had his tropical hat and wore colored glasses, but not round ones like Issa's. Long and slim, a packet of raw nerves, stooped, and his long legs slightly arched, he was an unforgettable vision of aggressiveness unchained. It was he who immediately knocked out the whole radio-contact system situated on the terrace of the upper rotunda: the two fixed yellow lights, in front of the radio installation, were blown to bits, the big searchlight knicked, and several bullets went through the see-through walls of both rotundas.

The other three terrorists on the Iroquois immediately followed Tony, for a moment leaving their hostages unguarded.

The Israelis, however, were stuck to their seats, eyes blindfolded, wrists and ankles tied, bound to each other by the arms, and held tight by the safety belts. They heard everything, from the very first shot—and understood. Except for Mark Slavin and David Berger, they were all military veterans, familiar with firearms. They surely recognized the kind of weapons in use, could tell the distances of the firing, and felt the blast and smelled the sulfured scent of the salvos fired close to them. They could identify the noise of the lamps being shot up and conclude that the ambush had at least partially failed, that the Germans dared not attack head-on, and that this would now turn into a duel to the death, no quarter shown, but a duel in which the cards were stacked—and they knew they were in the hands of terrorists who had already killed two of them. Yet they stood up to them right until the end.

The four doors of each of the Iroquois remained open through the whole affair. Exasperated salvos of shots belched from them, first of all to cover Issa's and Paulo's retreat. But Tony's order was clear: smash all the lights.

One fedayee at least, in the beginning, was not obeying him: that was big olive-colored Badran, who jumped to the foot of the copter and started spraying bullets on the two crews. Tony, inside, was framed in a door, one knee on the floor.

In fifteen seconds or so, all the major lights on the area, without exception, were smashed. The three groups of double searchlights on stands, the most powerful, which had run along the edge of the concrete area from the tower to the 727; the two cupolas installed on the two rotundas; the rotary searchlight on the permanent base placed in front of a repair shop some 40 meters west of the tower: all these beams were so many easy targets. Any group so surrounded would first attack the lights.

Paulo's broad shoulders were rolling as on a heavy sea. He was teetering, and observers could see a trail of blood behind him on the tarmac, still warm from the day's heat. And in the fiery crescendo of bursts, as the lights exploded, Paulo kept coming on toward the helicopters like a drunken man.

He was now out of the fields of fire of Nos. 1 and 5. Sniper 4, northeast under his big green truck, might have nipped him, but he had his eyes on Issa, whom he took as his second target because he recognized the slim figure as that of the angry chief of the fedayeen who had been seen all over on world TV.

No. 3, up on the terrace to the right of No. 1, knew he had already gotten one terrorist, as had No. 2. He had Paulo within range from the last 30 meters, but he too kept his sights on Issa, whose wispy silhouette seemed impervious to the bullets.

No. 2's field of fire, as he lay to the left of the squad leader, swept north as did No. 3's, but circled off slightly to the west. He pointed his gun at Paulo: without infrared glasses, he could barely see the huge fedayee. Tony and his men were completing the noisy triumph of darkness.

Paulo, although his body was wracked with twitches, still found the strength to direct one more burst at Blankenhagel, who fell flat. Then the powerful fedayee started to run again, knelt, shot a burst at the sniper to the northeast without even hitting the big fire truck, and took off again. When everything became dark, Paulo was 25 meters from the closest helicopter, QO, which he had left three and a half minutes before. No. 1 sniper's third shot—the only one that got him—went through his stomach and then his right lung. He made a furious leap as soon as he felt safe in the shadows.

Issa had just thrown himself down between the skids of QO, which held Tony, Badran, and five of the hostages. The commando leader had come from the other copter, DU. But, the better to mislead the Germans, he had shifted, by fits and starts, toward QO, thus crossing some 110 meters, with his zigzags, in the fields of fire of the successive snipers. And he was all in one piece! During most of his run, he was a highly visible target, for the last of the lights were not knocked out until just when he reached his goal.

As soon as he got under QO, Issa pushed down the trigger of his AK-47. The flashes of the shots going off could be seen. The terrorists' furious reply was growing in the darkness, and they had no lack of ammo. Now Paulo, painfully, dragged himself beneath the belly of the ship. In order to have a freer field, Issa moved up under the nose cone.

For the four *Grenzschutzpolizei*, it was hell. The two crews were prisoners, 25 meters apart, when the first sniper started to fire. They saw at once that their guards had been picked off. Each of the four took out separately, bent on escape. They had something under two seconds' respite before the fedayeen started sprinkling their escape routes with metal.

But the German pilots exhibited as much sangfroid as reflexes. Captain Praus headed straight for the tower; his copilot Blankenhagel toward the 727; Capt. Gunnar Ebel toward the trucks that hid the shock commando; and Flight Sergeant Bechler toward the signal block where No. 5 was posted. They thus went simultaneously to the four cardinal points.

Moreover, the fact that Tony ordered his men to get the lights first unexpectedly helped the two crews. But there was also the reaction of Badran, sure of himself and hard to handle as he had been since dawn, who first concentrated his fire on Ebel and Bechler because, facing north, they were the only ones he could see. Praus and Blankenhagel were going the other way. Knees bent and features taut, at the foot of the nose cone, he was holding the submachine gun in both hands, and swinging its muzzle in a wide arc.

"It did not hurt right away," Captain Ebel was to recall. "I knew I had been hit in the chest. It felt very hot. Blood came up to my mouth. I said to myself: This is it. I felt calm. I found I could move all right. The automatic fire was bouncing off the concrete around me, and I thought: There may be a chance of pulling through. I got hold of myself, tensed my muscles. I was weakening quickly, and blood was running down my hands, but I thought I would still be able to run . . ."

The 9-mm bullet came in on a diagonal, going through one lung and scraping the other, tore through his pleura. Captain Ebel, a remarkable specimen as are most of the members of his corps, is a dry, nervous type, trained to toughness, with sharp features. He could feel a weight on his chest, and each time he exhaled a small pastiness bubbled up in his mouth. He went down. As he tried to start off again, he noticed that, in all this noise, one after another the lights were bursting. Even the hardtop he lay on, which machine-gun bullets were peppering, was turning completely dark.

Badran, who kept shooting his way, to try to finish him off, was fortunately some 30 meters away. But now another one was aiming at the captain: taciturn Denawi who, seeing the German hostages of his ship run away right before his eyes, started firing. He was barely 8 meters from Ebel.

That the latter was not hit again was some kind of miracle. The next day, the emplacement of his body on the tarmac was marked by little puddles turned bloodred in the sun; the outline of several fingers could be seen to the side, probably from when he pushed off. And all around the lozenge in which the wounded man had huddled, there were scores and scores of black notches in the light-gray pavement.

Ebel took off, with a violent bound. His legs carried him, but the pain was spreading, twisting and burning his organs, eating at his back. He had some 50 meters to run till he got to the trucks. He could not catch his breath. He was feeling dizzy. Still, he made it as far as the big vehicles, from which the shock brigade was watching him. There, he collapsed in front of one of the hoods.

The base's emergency equipment was first-rate, and Wolf had had everything laid on. An ambulance came for Ebel, took him to the infirmary, where first aid saved his life. He was to be off the base, unconscious, a little before midnight. Restored to health today, he has been awarded the Red Cross Medal of Honor, an extremely rare distinction.

His copilot, Flight Sergeant Bechler, got to the signal-block, near Sniper No. 5, without so much as a scratch. "I never ran so fast in my life!" he exclaimed. He had run through bright light, and the bullets had burst around him mainly at the end, while No. 5 and his backup man were hiding out behind the little concrete parapet.

Captain Praus had covered about 12 meters when an endless burst of fire whistled about his ears, coming not from his Iroquois but from DU, the one Ebel had piloted. It was surely elegant Samir who was shooting at the convoy captain. Indeed, several witnesses later identified him as the fedayee who had suddenly appeared at the south door of DU. Samir was far from his target, some 30 meters, yet he almost got him nonetheless.

Praus, at the shots, hit the dirt, on his side, knees drawn up, a maneuver that saved his life, for the spot just ahead of him was being raked by fire. He was so motionless that Samir and friends thought they had killed him. The last working lights illuminated the place where he was. Now Samir set about knocking them out.

Lt. Paul Blankenhagel had taken off right opposite Paulo, who had just shot out a light and was probably not yet feeling his wound too badly. The fedayee recognized his flight fatigues and belched a burst at the pilot, who jumped sideways and fell flat on his stomach. Paulo thought he had scored a bull's-eye, or he would have fired at him again. Blankenhagel got a bit farther out of Paulo's axis, dragging on elbows and knees, while the terrorist turned his weapon toward the northeast. After a bit, the lieutenant lay completely still, face to the ground, and that was how he was when all the light was gone.

Der Münchner Polizeiobermeister (City of Munich Police Brigadier) Anton Fliegerbauer, thirty-two, commanded a group of the protection squadron; he was sturdily built, dark of hair, and had narrow side whiskers coming down to his jaws. His troubled face was reminiscent of Jean-Paul Belmondo's.

His squad originally was to cover the VIPs as well as the whole north facade of the tower, on the runway and eventual battle site. As the two helicopters bringing the hostages had appeared in the sky over Fürstenfeldbruck, Fliegerbauer had answered Dr. Wolf's order to come up to the terrace. The *Vize* had a high opinion of him, for several difficult raids he had handled so well against narcotics dealers.

"There are eight terrorists instead of five," he told him. "So, bring your men who are guarding the officials back on to the ground floor here. You have to be numerous enough to ward off any attack by the Arabs. Your orders remain the same: absolutely no interference in the fight, unless the terrorists try to come into the tower."

The brigadier saluted and started right off for the big radar room where the VIPs were. He picked up three of his men there. As he finished telling them to get their comrades on the second floor, and bring them below, there was new action on the landing area: the four Iroquois pilots had been taken hostages, and Issa and Paulo were heading for the 727.

Fliegerbauer, his Walther 9-mm machine pistol slung, tore down the stairs: better that than to wait for the overworked elevator. Right now, he had to redeploy his people, against the fedayeen. Someone tearing down behind him called to him imperatively. The *Obermeister* came to a halt, despite the emergency: he had recognized the voice of Mr. Big, Schreiber.

"Fliegerbauer! Go and back up the sharpshooters! At the first shot, start machine-gunning the two Arabs who'll be coming back from the airliner. And keep under cover, for sure!"

He replied with the ritual *"Ja wohl, Herr Präsident,"* but took it on himself to point out that the head of Operation Rescue had just given him totally different orders.

Schreiber cut him short; disregard that, and get to work.

The brigadier complied. Even though it meant leaving his squad without instructions, and the ground floor unprepared to stand off a first assault. As for the Big Boss' "keep under cover, for sure," that was eyewash. Fliegerbauer would barely have time to make it to a spot he could properly fire from. How in so short a time could he find cover, too?

Still running, Fliegerbauer got to the main door of the tower. As he was going through, there was his assistant, to whom without explanation he turned over command of the team, and went on out. He was looking for a firing position that was not out in the open; nothing, close by. He could see the two terrorists heading back toward the copters, walking in their even step over the tarmac.

Fliegerbauer made for the east corner of the tower and, one knee on the ground, his side to the wall, he swung the barrel of his submachine gun toward Issa, who was closest. The first shot was fired, then other single shots. He could see Issa running west, toward the tower. Actually, the zigzagging fedayeen leader was veering off, gradually going northeast, but it was hard to tell that yet, because he made so many detours.

The *Obermeister* took aim at him. He had to edge out beyond the corner of the wall a bit. Forty meters away, Tony saw the brigadier's profile, and guessed at the muzzle of the gun. The big fedayee, from the doorway of QO, let fly a burst that tore away the top of Anton Fliegerbauer's head. One bullet went in through a ground-floor tower window, and just missed hitting another policeman in the temple.

While this was going on, at 10:40, a spokesman for the Munich police informed those at the *Pressezentrum:* After the helicopters left for Fürstenfeldbruck, three of the terrorists were found in the Israelis' building, dead or very seriously stabbed. The West German news agency S.I.D. checked out this fantasy and released it, and it was picked up by other wire services, so that it reached all five continents, and died hard.

10:44 PM: The shots multiplied, came closer together. Only the fedayeen were shooting in full bursts. There was an absurd feeling that they were carrying the day. Where was the response of all the police who surrounded the six survivors from Black September?

There had been four mad minutes.

Hundreds of people present, witnesses or participants, were shaken by what they felt was the scandal of the inaction by the head of Operation Rescue. And he himself, perhaps, was more shaken with rage than anybody, in his impotence.

"What the hell are we waiting for to reply? Are they the only ones with machine guns?" yelled one member of the *Krisenstab*.

"What for? To blow up the two helicopters and the Israelis in them?" Dr. Schreiber screamed back through the bedlam.

It was absurd and unbeatable. The hail of automatic firebursts from the fedayeen was being met by the ridiculous counterpoint of single shots from the marksmen.

Issa and Paulo were under the righthand helicopter, QO, with Tony and Badran inside, the latter having climbed back up after half a minute. Denawi and Samir were in the lefthand one, DU. And inside both, the nine tied-up hostages. And, lying on the tarmac near the terrorists, Praus and Blankenhagel; and Flieger-bauer, flat on his belly at the corner of the building.

Herky-jerky shapes could be seen throwing things down to the tarmac, at their feet, from the doors of QO: things that could be guessed to be full ammo-clips, or weapons. A small figure jumped down from DU, slid along the ship's belly, threw a grenade that burst not far from Praus but without hurting him, and started raining fire on the tower. Like a fury.

The machine-gun fire nicked the walls, plowed into the pavement, broke windows on the lower floors of the tower and especially in the small annex that abutted it to the west. The windshields of two of the four trucks off to the north of the copters were shattered. At times, a few seconds of letup. Then, bang! bang! the individual shots from the marksmen.

Paulo came out from under QO. He got up. He was staggering.

He took a few steps forward, in the open, facing the tower, and fired without a stop, and without aim, his Tokarev on his hip. Even in the dark, the silhouette of the biggest of the fedayeen stood out in charcoal tones.

By now, the five sharpshooters of course no longer had any fields of fire. Sniper No. 1, who had previously wounded Paulo, now finished him off with a shot to the heart. One of the surviving terrorists would say of him, probably truthfully for once, Paulo was suffering tremendously from his wound; he was losing a lot of blood. His accomplices had what it took to bandage him and stop the hemorrhage. But he must have thought he was through, that he was dying. He was merely close to passing out.

Then suddenly everything stopped, after a last burst of fire from DU. No sharpshooter answered. Everyone expected it to start again. But no. Nothing more. Unreal silence, such as occurs on every battlefield of the world, when all there is to do is wait for the apocalypse to start in again.

10:45 PM: The Organizing Committee, on the say-so of Schreiber's office, announced: "The Palestinian commandos opened fire at Fürstenfeldbruck air base. The police replied. The battle is now in progress."

10:46 PM: On the big arrival runway of the military air base, the shards of glass and pools of blood were delicately luminous in the darkness, but no one was moving. Only slight sounds of crinkling, steps that were being hushed up, a car starting up somewhere in the area. The fedayeen must have heard all those things; but they stayed put.

Still, the powerless *Krisenstab* observers were wondering whether maybe the fedayeen weren't shooting still, with silencers. All those noises, sometimes muffled. And there seemed to be a trembling in the blue lights that marked the north edge of the tarmac. The ground lights were indeed moving, for they are set on little stems, so as to remain above the snow, which can be heavy in the winter around here. And in order for the blasts of the jets not to shatter the glass casings and the bulbs behind them, the stems had to be made of metal springs, that would give slightly with the winds. The exhaust gases of the armored vehicles were making them quiver.

386

The Big Fizzle

A red light went on before one of the two-way radios in the radar room. The soldier in charge motioned to Schreiber that it was for him. He had been out only long enough to give his orders to Fliegerbauer on the stairs.

Schreiber put on the headphones. When the conversation was over, he had to make an effort to look self-assured again. In a strong, serious voice, he informed the VIPs without comment of the death of Anton Fliegerbauer. To a question from Herr Strauss, he forthrightly replied there was no one in the 727.

"The commando that had been in it left without permission," Herr Merk chimed in. The two pieces of news dumbfounded them all.

Schreiber went out to find Wolf. The two men had a discussion that witnesses called stormy in the first rotunda, on the elevator landing. Nothing transpired of it. The two heads of the Munich police worked in perfect harmony the rest of this bloody night, and since then their understanding and the *Vize*'s loyalty have never faltered.

Pending the arrival of the shock commando of border guards, a group of Munich police had moved into line, on their stomachs on the tarmac, some 50 meters west of the tower. They were ahead of the base's internal rail line. And straight back of the feet of these men aiming their submachine guns at the two Iroquois, on the rails, were four huge tank cars, visible in fuzzy outline.

"What if they're full of fuel?" asked the brigadier in charge of the group.

XXII

THE HOLOCAUST

. . . Surely the people is grass.
The grass withereth, the flower fadeth;
But the word of our God shall stand for ever.'
                    Isaiah 40:7, 8

10:50 PM: STILL NOTHING. ANOTHER WAIT.

The Schreiber-Wolf sharpshooters' surprise attack added up to three terrorists killed out of the four who had been exposed targets; the fourth, their leader, untouched. The nine Israeli hostages remained in the terrorists' grip. As for the four new German hostages, two were motionless on the tarmac very near the fedayeen, while the other two had gotten away, one of them severely wounded. Including the two Israelis massacred at dawn, the Black September crew already had three corpses to boast of.

It was a terrible result. A chapter could be filled with testimony to show that two factors would have been enough to change Fürstenfeldbruck around completely, despite all the mistakes the authorities made: 1. At least three more marksmen; 2. Infrared sights on the G-3 Heckler & Koch guns they used.

. . . According to the best French and Israeli experts, there should have been at least two sharpshooters for each human target; my own combat experiences confirm this. In the Djebel Amur in July 1957, I was alongside a French military pistol champion, who had several times qualified for international competition; at 50 meters, from above with a machine pistol, he shot at half-a-dozen fellagha coming out of the rose laurels and heading across a wide *oued*, and missed. About ten of us were firing, and not one of the fellagha was hit.

The Holocaust

Moreover, the normal strength of the Munich police in the summer of 1972 was about 5200 men: 80 percent of them had passed the "advanced shooting technique" examination, meaning they qualified to use all current weapons in all circumstances. At least 180 of these had certificates as "specialized shots." And some 30 of the best were in the top category, classed as *Hochpräzisionsschützen*. Besides which, the Organizing Committee had other police corps at its disposal: those of Bavaria, and the border guards, which also had scores of specialized marksmen.

The fact that, at the Fürstenfeldbruck air base, not one officer, whether a marksman, part of the shock brigade, or a member of one of the security groups, had an infrared sight, is absolutely beyond comprehension.

Every army, every police force in the world have long since been equipped with infrared sights. What armored car is without such equipment for night driving? The French counterpart of the Heckler & Koch G-3, our FRF-1 repeater, has excellent night-sights, plus six peepholes for use according to the amount of available light.

Infrared sights are based on a simple principle: the radiation of warm bodies. The most modern of such sights for portable weapons magnifies from 30,000 to 60,000 times any sources of light. At Fürstenfeldbruck that would have meant that even after all the main illumination was shot out, it would still have been possible for the marksmen to see the terrorists with adequate clarity. The dark overcast sky allowed some light, however slight, to come through. There were the ground lights, and the 727 was totally lighted. During the second half of the shootout, several trucks and all six of the armored vehicles turned their bright lights on the battlefield.

The *Dokumentation* (p. 63) asserts, "Infrared sights could not have been used because of the three banks of searchlights. Indeed, such sights are good only in darkness." That last is untrue, but the important thing is this:

As long as the searchlights and other main sources of light played on the field involved, the sharpshooters would merely not have used the infrared sights on their guns, if the guns had had such sights. But, almost from the start, the three banks of power

389

lights and all the rest were irretrievably blown. That was when night-sights would have become priceless!

The chance was great: for four full minutes, the six surviving fedayeen acted with utmost carelessness, showing themselves framed in doorways, moving out in the open, and even standing up full-length to machine-gun invisible Germans.

But—the snipers had no infrared sights—beneath the overcast sky, in the sudden lightlessness, facing an ideally exposed adversary . . .

The fact that only the five sharpshooters took part in the earliest affray was something else that exasperated observers. Only in the closing moments did other elements of the Germans get involved. Scores of the police present remained outside the fight quite beyond their will.

Many of us heard them say, later, "We did not have a single walkie-talkie! We were spread out in the dark, around a field unfamiliar to us, not knowing where our own men were, and out of touch with the heads of the operation . . ."

Every security guard at Olympic Village had his walkie-talkie, but none appeared at Fürstenfeldbruck. Where was the Munich police's ultramodern equipment that Herr Schreiber is so proud of? As far as I could find out, some of the outfits sent to the air base (e.g., the two armored patrols) had radio intercommunication, but Dr. Wolf could not reach them because the senders on the control tower had been destroyed.

The truth is, the lack of walkie-talkies was most disastrous right at the start. If Snipers 4 and 5 had been in radiocommunication with their squad leader, they might have opened fire at the same fraction of a second, as well as checking out the targets to go after. However, Dr. Wolf would probably not even then have authorized going after them with repeated bursts of automatic fire. He had told each detachment leader what flare would be his signal to go into action—and no flares were ever fired! Wolf was too afraid of having the forces surrounding the fedayeen wound each other with their automatic fire. And even more afraid that such bursts might hit Praus and his copilot, who remained motionless on the concrete.

There was one other enormous deterrent to Wolf's recourse to the automatics: the tanks of the two helicopters, as well as the 727, were brimming with fuel. Yet, when the two Iroquois left *Olympiapark* for their last trip, their crews (to say nothing of the *Krisenstab*) full well knew they had to fly only some 40 km. (25 mi.). They also knew what was to happen at Fürstenfeldbruck. Even on the lawns behind G-1, there would have been ample time and opportunity to relieve the Bells of their dangerous superfluous fuel. Why was it not done?

Of course, until the landing at the Luftwaffe base, the terrorists might have been able to force the crews to change destinations. In that case, had the tanks been properly unloaded all the pilots would have had to do was point to the fuel gauges.

Wolf, perplexed and pained, stood exposed in front of the tower entrance, eyeing the field, his rounded forehead dotted with perspiration. His first concern—because they were Germans and public opinion, as well as his bosses, would hold him responsible if he disregarded this "sacred" priority—was to save Praus and Blankenhagel. No mistaking them, even in this lack of lighting. Their green flight outfits, zippered with black metal, showed in dark shades different from those of the ground. For four minutes, they were thought to be dead, or very critically wounded. Shortly before the end of the affray, it seemed Blankenhagel was moving. "He ought not to move, good God!" Schreiber mumbled in powerless prayer. Whereupon the QO copilot reverted to such immobility that they wondered whether he had ever moved his arm at all. Praus was stiff as a corpse.

Now, at 10:50, Blankenhagel started to crawl, unnoticeably at first. He was heading for the 727, 120 meters from his copter. Why in that direction, three times longer than heading for the tower, the trucks, or the signal-blocks to the north? Because by instinct the four pilots had split off in four directions, and seeing Praus head south Blankenhagel had gone east. Whatever the direction, the idea was not so much to reach any one point as to get away from the terrorists.

Seeing how well-coordinated Lieutenant Blankenhagel's movements were, his superiors quickly became sure he was not wounded. At each centimeter, he was darkly harder for the fedayeen to see. Watching his progress was full of terrible suspense: had the terrorists been watching him for a moment, or just noted one reference point, they would have understood he was getting away. He was still so close—only 15 meters or so from them when he began to crawl—that an almost random automatic burst would have chopped him up.

Was Captain Praus still alive? Face down, one leg up, one arm out palm up, he was in so uncomfortable a position as to make his motionlessness even more worrisome, but Wolf thought that if Praus were alive he would have had to see that, by mischance, only a dozen meters from the fedayeen bent on killing him, he was in a tiny zone less dark than the others. To the northwest of the holding area where planes stand before takeoff or on arrival, there was a curtain of trees with bright lights on a beltway beyond. Reflections from them came through the leafy branches. One such beam was right on Praus, which was probably why he did not move a hair.

And what about the Israeli hostages? At 10:50 a flashlight was briefly put on inside QO, the Iroquois farthest to the east. In its light, the faces of the five hostages tied up and blindfolded inside could be seen. None of the faces was dropped to the chest: all looked calm and attentive. No, they were not dead, yet. As for the four on DU, from the area of the trucks that copilot Bechler had reached, four forms could vaguely be seen through the bubble's Plexiglas. They seemed to move their heads from time to time. It was likely the four hostages had been allowed still to live: Who knew whether they might not come in handy as a medium of exchange?

The fedayeen hoped that their resistance would finally wear the Germans out, that the latter would ask to negotiate again, see that the hostages were alive, and decide to let them fly out with the Israelis. However naive it seems, this, according to the survivors, was really what the Black September men thought they could get.

10:55 PM: The wire services reported, *"Olympisches Dorf* is no longer in a state of siege. All the Panzers have been withdrawn. The last detachments of border police are getting into their buses." Yes, the Village was liberated, except for the Munich police cordon around Block 31.

More than that: the Village was having fun!

Ping-Pong, pop and blues, Mozart and Visconti, flirtations and parties: the "Amusement Center," in the surrealistic building housing it, was going full blast. Its dance palace, Bavaria Club, was the A-1 attraction.

People in sweat suits. Young couples slid across the floor, rubbing against each other like fish in the aquarium of a mass-production restaurant.

"Love, love me again, Jane my love!" the Sextett Jochen Bauer played and shouted.

The décor was topical; on the deep seats shaped like Waldi, kisses were many and interracial. No hard liquor, *natürlich!* But tea, milk, fruit juices, and whatever, were enough to keep them going. Yet many slipped out from time to time to catch a glance at the TV. The name of Fürstenfeldbruck ran like a cold wind among them.

And as the cease-fire continued and kept fraying nerves, there was no harmony in the big radar room.

The first firings had fascinated the VIPs. All windows had been open on the heavy night. The lights in the big room had been put out just as the thunder made by the rotors of the Iroquois with Praus and Tony aboard stopped in final position on the tarmac.

Strauss, baby face and beer belly, was as usual the first to swear in disappointment when he saw that the two fedayeen returning from the 727 were still standing on the runway after the first sharpshooters' shots. Then the automatic fire started. They left the windows, the wise thing, for it really seemed as if bullets were coming into the room.

Capt. Gerd Scharnhorst, a pilot attached to the base, was one of the officers who had stayed in the radar room.

"Half of the VIPs fell to the floor," he related. "Others tried to hide behind pieces of furniture. Dr. Schreiber until the end stayed just where he was at the start of the attack: framed in the window. Herr Strauss got up calmly when the shooting stopped, and said, 'We're in a state of war, and had better realize it.' "

Neither Captain Scharnhorst nor anyone else reacted to this. They were appalled; they had seen the puddles of Ebel's blood, and were sure Praus and Blankenhagel were dead, and the Israeli hostages even more so. General Zamir and Captain Y did not say a word. Then Schreiber announced the death of Brigadier Flieger-bauer. The Police Commissioner, back from talking to Herr Wolf, was shouting into the intercom, but no one listened, as if nothing more he might do could be of any importance.

Once again, it was Franz-Josef Strauss who broke the ghostly silence, when Schreiber had hung up, damning to hell those marksmen.

"And did you, *Herr Präsident,* get a bull's-eye the first time you shot at an enemy?" the Police Commissioner inquired, politely but stiffly.

The head of the CSU, with what is called a distinguished war record, waved the question away and started in on the "ridiculous" number of marksmen. Schreiber answered as Wolf would to the September 7 press conference,

"We never hoped to have more than four Arabs at once under fire. We had noted since morning that they stuck to working by shifts. So, five sharpshooters were enough."

Herren Strauss and Schreiber could not agree on much. Their political views were as different as their characters. Indeed, in principle Herr Strauss did not belong here. He had asked to be taken in the VIP Iroquois. Merk and the Commissioner had been eager to do as "King Franz-Josef" asked.

And now, what? All kinds of opinions: "Let's get a truly important Arab personality to act as go-between . . ." "Tell them we shot only because they reneged on their agreement not to take the pilots hostage, and say we'll let them go in the 727 if Praus and Blankenhagel can be got out safe . . ." "We have to send an attack group against the two helicopters right now, with assault guns and submachine guns. There may be some losses among the hostages, but some'll surely be saved. If we use armor, all the hostages and both pilots will be massacred."

The final opinion was that of Captain Y, spoken privately to Captain Scharnhorst, and devoid of illusions: "If the two planes were stormed, the terrorists would not blow everything up; they're not kamikazes. They try to get out with their skins; when they throw a grenade, they take cover. In case of assault, they'd hit the floor. But the *Krisenstab* is too worried about any more German dead, and they'll make it a very careful attack, nullifying any surprise effect."

After the rain of suggestions, there was heavy silence. No, the *Krisenstab* leaders did not agree with any of this. What, then, did they think? "I have an idea," said Herr Genscher. "It may be no use at all, but . . ."

11:00 PM: Still the oppressive silence, and the darkness niggardly of light, under clouds that seemed to threaten rain. Suddenly a rough voice roared out from a dark window of the control tower. Dr. Georg Wolf was shouting in German through a megaphone, and 40 meters away fedayeen and hostages heard: *"Left eure Waffen nieder und ergebt euch!"* (Throw your weapons away and give yourself up!) "In the name of the German Federal Republic, we promise your lives will be spared. Give us your answer vocally."

The call was repeated in English, and Captain Y, at Herr Genscher's request, agreed to repeat it in Arabic.

Dr. Wolf thereupon asked the VIPs to go down to the reception room on the ground floor. There were bulletholes all over the facade around the radar-room windows. They would be in much less danger downstairs. Moreover, now that the battlefield had shrunk, the sharpshooters on the tower would want to get as close as possible to the fedayeen, without losing the advantage of height.

At the same time, I was taking a taxi to "Fürstenfeldbruck." The sexagenarian driver with phenomenally bushy eyebrows wondered whether I did not mean the "Luftwaffe air base." *Sicherlich!* He warned he would try to get me there in good time, but I had better let him choose how to go. We agreed on it.

11:03 PM: Radio and TV had a news flash "of utmost importance":

> An officer of the Munich police states that all the hostages have been freed and four of the terrorists captured. From authoritative sources at the air base of Fürstenfeldbruck, it is learned that one Palestinian has gotten away and several persons have been injured, among them perhaps some of the hostages.

This was, of course, unofficial, and only very vague. Nevertheless, its being flashed around the globe gave rise to a considerable amount of joy. A happy consummation was so devoutly wished for that people were ready to believe any reassuring word. My taxi driver was one of the skeptics. "I've heard plenty of those reports in my life," he was saying. "Why, as late as April 30, 1945, in Berlin . . ."

11:15 PM: Paulo's corpse seemed inordinately broad, sprawled with limbs in all directions, some 5 meters from the skids of QO, toward the tower. His assault gun was a shiny bar near his hand with its contracted palm.

The sniper leader thought he was dreaming: Paulo was reviving. He was moving! But no, it was not he, but the bar, that is, his gun, slipping on its own, sliding silently down toward the easternmost of the helicopters as if pulled by a string. The sergeant whispered to his buddies. Yes, the Tokarev was disappearing completely under Bell QO: Issa had crawled out as far as Paulo's feet and, with the tip of his gun, pulled the carbine in by its sling.

The surface the five Black Septembrists now controlled was a rectangle with a base of about 90 meters (100 yds.). In addition to the 30-meter gap between the copters, there was their length (26 meters in all), and the "territory"—some 15 meters either way—that the fedayeen had under point-blank cover with acceptable visibility even in this darkness. The rectangle was about 35 meters wide, in terms of the zones under direct cover of the automatic weapons. So, it was still a pretty good-sized area: some 3,300 sq. meters (close to 4,000 sq. yds.).

But Dr. Wolf rather quickly concluded that all the terrorists remained in the combat posts they were in when their wild firing stopped. Two of them, including Issa, were still down under QO. A third was under the west copter, DU. And one fedayee guarded the prisoners inside each bird. The flashes of shots going off had clearly shown this layout.

After the fact, other things came out: some of the terrorists had moved around during the last instants of the firefight. Issa remained under the righthand Bell, QO, with its five hostages. Inside, Badran was still pushing the Jewish prisoners around, with the wild gestures of his long arms and the twitches of his blackened face.

Blond Samir, dropping out of the lefthand copter, DU, had come over to Issa, on orders of Tony, with whom he was changing places, and Tony, now under DU, was being assisted by little Denawi, of the hippie mane. Now and then, one or the other climbed up into the whirlybird, so as not to leave the hostages unattended. But they were no longer moving between the copters, as they were sure they could be picked off in the uncovered zone between.

11:30 PM: On the carefully flat surface of the tarmac nothing was clearly visible, but the two corpses and the two border-patrol pilots could be made out. "The Arabs'll be taking potshots at them, and they can't miss," Herr Schreiber had been doomsaying a quarter of an hour earlier. But no, they had not fired at them, just remained quiet under their two helicopters.

Now Blankenhagel was half-saved! Centimeter by centimeter, he had covered about 50 meters in three-quarters of an hour. Since he had been about 15 meters away from QO when he had to drop, now he was so far that they would have to have a very careful aim to hit him in the darkness from the copters. Impossible for the fedayeen not to have noticed his tortoise progress: but that too remained a mystery.

In the reception room, the atmosphere was suffocating. Schreiber and Wolf burst in separately. The latter had just looked over the new attack setup, and was appalled: "Where are the armored cars? And the shock commando?" he demanded of the Commissioner.

Schreiber shrugged impotently: "They've been on their way fifty minutes. We can't get radio contact with them or anyone else. The fedayeen shot up the works."

"Will you really set the armor on them?" asked Genscher.

"What else can we do, *Herr Minister?*" said Schreiber. "The armor won't fire as it moves up, of course, but it can get in very close behind its protective shield."

"One grenade in the turret, and they're done for!"

"We'll protect them. When they see them, let us hope the fedayeen realize their choice is between death and surrender."

11:31 PM: Reuters, almost simultaneously with the rest of the services, flashed a bulletin that caused immense relief:

> The police and the Bavarian Ministry of the Interior announce that the forcible action taken at the Fürstenfeldbruck air base has been successful. All the hostages have been safely freed. Three Palestinians were killed; the others fled and are being pursued.

Where did the word come from? "Not from us!" Merk and Schreiber said. "In fact, we were hardly able to phone any more."

The central installation of Fürstenfeldbruck's telecommunications system was on the second panoramic rotunda, around the big beacon. Naturally, as a former NATO base, it was more than adequately equipped, telephonically speaking. There were lines aplenty and to spare. Perhaps the military switchboardman was at times swamped by the flood of calls from all over the world. But all he had to be told was to keep one line free. The colonel, his second-in-command, the fire brigade, and others had their direct lines. Are we really to believe it was not possible to phone anyone from the military air base of Fürstenfeldbruck on the night of September 5–6?

11:35 PM: An insistent voice kept coming in on my set, authoritarian but almost happy:

> A spokesman for the police of the *Land* of Bavaria confirms that shots have been exchanged. The hostages, taking advantage of the battle, were all able to escape. Some of the terrorists have still not been taken by the authorities. The police ask us to warn motorists against stopping for any hitchhikers they might see in the neighborhood of the air base at Fürstenfeldbruck. *Achtung!* Attention! The fleeing fedayeen are heavily armed.

This bulletin was repeated many times during the night by every station in the German Federal Republic.

The mass media spread word of the rescue of the hostages to every corner of the globe. By 11:40, details would be added to the effect that all the terrorists had been either killed or wounded during the shooting, such as: " 'The six Arabs have all been caught!' shouted the driver of a *Bundeswehr* ambulance carrying one of the seriously wounded to Munich."

And so, until the very end, the West German authorities abstained from ever giving the correct number of fedayeen as it had been known since 11:06. Strange! But what would have been done about that elsewhere?

At the Hotel Vierjahreszeiten, the special meeting of the IOC was still going on. Herr Willi Daume had come back in, twenty minutes before, saying that the shooting had been fierce at the air base, but had now completely stopped, and news was still unavailable. Called back to the phone, he now told his colleagues that his highly qualified informants "had very good hopes." But he specified he was only passing on what official authorities were telling him.

There was a general sigh of mixed impatience and half-relief. Arguments began about the manner of the attack and the victims. President Brundage reminded the body that they had several other points to handle, particularly the proposals of the Executive Board.

One member spoke up to say he was surprised to hear the President-elect had been detained for hours at Kiel, where he had gone the day before as First Vice-President. Lord Killanin took the floor to answer him.

With purely Olympian calm, the powerful Irishman said that, indeed, when the tragedy started, Jonkheer van Karnebeek, Prince Takeda, and he, all representing the Executive Board, had been in Kiel where they quickly heard of the attack by radio. They had then tried to get back to Munich as soon as possible. But, Lord Killanin added, the arrangements they had made for their immediate return had been canceled by President Brundage.

Nevertheless, they did get back to the Olympic city by 5:15 PM, and learned that President Brundage had not himself remained at the Vierjahreszeiten Hotel as he had requested all IOC members to do, but since morning had been meeting with the *Krisenstab* set up by the German authorities. Now, in the Executive Board's view, the IOC should never in any manner have been involved in problems which were totally out of its realm, and on which it could have no effect. That was why the Board had expressed regrets at seeing the IOC represented on the crisis staff by its President.

Marble-faced Mr. Brundage evinced no reaction to this. The whole assemblage was silent, obviously endorsing the Board's stand. Yet, it was not ready, and certainly Lord Killanin was not, to condemn the conduct of a man who had brilliantly presided over it for twenty years and was now irrevocably leaving.

Having made that point, Lord Killanin gallantly went directly on to tell the meeting that the Board unanimously felt the Olympic Games must be carried to their proper conclusion, at whatever cost. They broke into applause. Lord Killanin then turned to Mr. Brundage, so the latter might inform the meeting of the Board's other proposals (memorial service for the two Israelis killed at dawn, and so on).

Herr Daume was called out again. They waited, breath held between whispers.

11:40 PM: Lieutenant Blankenhagel, having veered off to the southeast, was only about 40 meters from the 727. For a moment, he had stopped crawling. He pulled himself up in a sudden motion and dashed ahead, his body bent forward. All eyes shifted to the two Iroquois. The terrorists paid no attention to this last lap of his flight. The lieutenant who had been the restive commando leader on the plane jumped out of the shadows, ran toward the pilot, and got behind him, to shield him with his own body. Two other members of the late "volunteer" group also came out toward Blankenhagel and surrounded him until he could collapse in safety behind the metal antiblast barrier. That left Captain Praus . . .

11:45 PM: Herr Daume returned to the meeting room with a bursting smile. All faces turned toward him as, raising his arms in a V-sign, he shouted in English, "We have won!"

He then quoted exactly what Conrad Ahlers had told him on the phone: all the terrorists were either dead or captured. The nine Israeli hostages were all alive, but there was no word as to whether any of them had been hurt.

The room exploded with joy. They voted by acclamation to congratulate Presidents Brundage and Daume, as well as the West German Government.

When calm was more or less restored, Lord Killanin asked to speak again so he could impress on all IOC members that they should make no statements to the press. Only President Brundage should speak in the name of their committee.

With all the anxiety, followed by confident joy, what happened to the threats of internal cracking? There never was any offensive by the "Arab bloc" or the "Eastern bloc." There was not the least attempt to argue politics. The IOC had been instinctively and fully put together again.

"Leipzig! That's where I was born. You ever been there?" the taxi driver was saying, without awaiting my answer. He was the kind who talk to hear themselves talk. Large-bellied, cigarillo-smoking, with white hair and rounded face, keeping the radio on and switching the dial all the time to get as much news as possible, he was a sharp one. He drove his Mercedes 200 as if in a slalom, and at Puchheim, while we were inching along since coming out of the suburb of Pasing, he was smart enough to get off the main road to Fürstenfeldbruck and go to the right via a smaller road through the largish town of Olching.

It was like billiards. We got through Olching without bottle-neck, and crossed the Amper River, but could not avoid meeting Highway 471, so fantastically crowded. That was some 5 to 6 km. (3 mi. plus a little) by car from the north edge of the base, but it meant going through Maisach. The driver swore a good rush-hour curse as we became awash in the tide.

The noise was unbearable, with horns tooting and whistles blowing; old Beethoven must have turned over in his grave. Four motorcops in black helmets cut through the masses of cars to clear the middle of the roadway, making us get along as best we could on the shoulder, while other drivers, less adept than my old pro, went hurtling off into the bumps of the nearby fields. Behind the motorcycles came police Volkswagens, their red lights twirling on the top, and sirens going. Behind them a column of six armored cars, with headlights as blinding as lightning, and then six more big Mercedes police buses with mesh-grilled windows.

"If it was all over, you think they'd be bringing in such rein-forcements?" my driver asked. "Want my opinion? It don't look good."

We were just about stopped still by the wild mishmash.

"I think, if I'm going to see anything, I better walk . . ."

He answered with an understanding *"Wahrlich!"* (Sure thing!). "Cutting across the fields, you can make it in half the distance. *Glückauf!"* (Good luck!).

Over pathways, fields, bosks, the edge of a frogpond, I made a beeline for the base. Lord! I was not alone. How many locals were there heading for the still-invisible base? Thousands. We bumped into each other without seeing who we were. It was our rendez-vous with the martyrdom of others. O Jesus! You were walking in the heart of these shadows, that is certain. You were here with the crowd on this night of horror, to sustain the martyrs with Your prayers, and then to receive them, these fallen victims from among Your People.

11:50 PM: A slight rise with a breeze at the top, and the airfield only half a kilometer away, in the plain, at the foot of this gentle slope from the east. It pierced the heavy darkness with a network of weak varicolored lights. Silent columns, hesitating in the dark hollows, carried me this far, at the end of a detour toward the south. As up on the Panoramic Hill of Olympic Park during the evil day, here we were elbow to elbow, turned toward the airfield, of which for the moment we could not make out one exact detail. It seemed nothing was moving there; nothing was happening.

I was listening to my pocket radio quietly but others had theirs blaring out. There was a round dovecote on the grass, behind me. Some photographers had taken up their positions on it, with zoom lenses as big as bazookas. The airfield was outlined by concrete electric pylons with cables between them, set with luminous red balls.

"The hostages have been freed . . . The Palestinians in the commando group killed, taken captive, or surrounded . . . ," the European stations kept repeating, half believed. The commentators themselves sounded impatient to get details, and irked at their correspondents for not being able to get closer to the base. You could tell nothing was over, seeing the roadblocks, the crowds of police closing off the air base, the whole tense atmosphere.

Near me, a still-young man was saying his rosary. The district road to Maisach and Eisenach ran behind us, circling the hillock. Motors and car horns sounded continuously.

And over there, on the off-limits air base, a strange absence of any strong lights. Yet the luminous colors of the ground lights provided a pacifying note as if, after all, things were coming back to normal. The control tower could have shut those lights off, but had not done so.

Blue-paned lights along the tarmac, hard-white fluorescent tubes on the axes of the two converging runways, green-and-white zebras marking off the landing spots, all shone discreetly in the overcast night. There were also a variety of red lights, indicating the edges of grassy or pebbly stretches, areas under repair, or raised mounds.

All eyes were riveted on the military air base. It was decorated with flags adorned with spirals on a background of turquoise blue or pale green, the flags of the Games of Joy. Dogs were barking around it, and no wonder: on the way, in the tohu-bohu of the road, I had seen two police buses full of quiet dogs at the ready, held in check by their uniformed masters; German shepherds, the best police dogs in the world. The farm dogs could smell their presence and voiced alarm at their total silence.

The woods that belt the base to the west were suddenly lighted by white beams: the armor! The panting roar and metallic grinding were unmistakable. The lights hit one group of firs after another.

We stopped listening to radios. We were waiting for the first shots of the renewed fight, marking time, in a crushed silence.

"You know what the Arabs are going to do, if things keep dragging out?" Herr Schreiber finally said, in the face of the contradictory opinions. "They'll announce: We are going to kill a hostage. They'll fling a corpse violently out on the concrete. Then they'll ask for a bus to take them to the airliner with the surviving Israelis, warning: This time there better be a crew and the plane better be ready to take off immediately for such-and-such Arab country, or else, in five minutes, two more hostages . . ."

11:55 PM: The long-awaited reinforcements were finally there! Here were the twenty-three shock-brigade volunteers from the border patrol, the two squadrons of *Münchner Stadtpolizei* assigned to seal off the base, and the six armored cars!

All the VIPs knew that the six pieces of armor were what the heads of Operation Rescue were counting on to try the last throw of the dice. Dr. Wolf was walking like a caged tiger along the rail track when someone came to tell him of their arrival, at the very second he heard the rumble of the six armored vehicles that stopped at the edge of the airfield, to the east, some 800 meters (half a mile) away.

The head of the convoy, a police lieutenant, jumped out of his command car. In a second, a very simple plan was agreed on, and okayed by Dr. Schreiber, who had come over. In a word: frontal attack supported by a pincers movement.

"Are my vehicles to fire? Under what conditions?" the lieutenant asked.

That was the tough question, the drama of the drama. If one of the copters got a machine-gun burst and it hit the tanks, chances were it would turn into a torch. As for the hostages, how could they possibly not be hit? And especially—for the Germans— would that not mean Praus was as good as dead?

Dr. Schreiber settled it: "Your mission is to rescue Captain Praus and wipe out the resisting Arabs. The shock brigade will try, during your action, to save the hostages. Your crews will therefore be free to use their machine guns, with one exception: absolutely no bursts aimed at the helicopters!"

"But the Arabs will be hiding around them."

"Not necessarily. And the closer you get, the better you'll be able to aim at them, without too much danger of hitting the Israelis."

"As you go forward," Dr. Wolf added, "the snipers will have a bead on any of them who stick their noses out."

The three *Hochpräzisionsschützen* on the tower were now at the windows of the radar room. The other two were still in their original spots: No. 4 under the fire engine, No. 5 near the signal-block.

11:58 PM: The lieutenant stated his march order to Dr. Wolf: Light Armored Cars 1, 2, 3, and 4 would go straight to the helicopters, in "stair formation," that is, following one another in such spacing as to cover the entire area. If the terrorists tried to turn their backs on the armor, they would be facing twelve frontier guards from the shock brigade, ambushed behind the trucks. These twelve had just replaced the nine policemen who were disguised as mechanics.

L.A.C.s 5 and 6 would lock in the fedayeen on the two flanks. Car 5 would go over near Sniper No. 5 on the mound with the signal-blocks, while No. 6 followed the base's motor roads to come out on the concrete tarmac some 40 meters west of the tower, in front of the rail line, near the eleven other members of the border-guard shock brigade just detrucked.

So the five Black September survivors would find themselves surrounded on all sides by virtually invulnerable steel mastodons that would close in on them more and more. . . . Well, that was the way it was supposed to be, anyway.

The lieutenant had parked his command-car alongside the control tower, just where Fliegerbauer had been killed. Radio contact was perfect between the armored commander and his vehicles.

"There was nothing more we could prepare for!" energetic Dr. Schreiber would shout next day. The newly established battle order was to leave no escape for the guerrillas, as the German radio so often proclaimed. For, apart from the five sharpshooters, the twenty-three-man shock brigade, and the six pieces of armor, there was "all the rest"!

First, at the front (if we may euphemize), there were the seventeen policemen known as the "disguised" squad. Five of eight reluctant kamikazes from the 727 were still hidden at the foot of the antiblast barrier right near the plane; nine others, lying on the pavement, were spaced between Snipers 4 and 5. Moreover, three squadrons of a hundred men each had the field closed off, and ten police dogs were patrolling between the metal enclosures and the guard-paths.

Despite all that, there was still no radio contact between the commander of the operation and these various units. And sight signals were out of the question, in darkness like this.

The lieutenant gave his order: "Contact!"

The six L.A.C.s revved up: they were now lined up abreast about 500 meters (550 yds.) from the tower. Between them and the two invisible helicopters, the Boeing 727 stood at the crossroads, still looking ready for takeoff, with its lighted windows and the stubborn soft hum of its three turbojets.

The armored cars began to rumble in the deep darkness, the flat air of which seemed to deaden all sounds.

How quiet they seemed, those four Israelis in Iroquois D-HADU! They had two tough warders: Denawi, the little Palestinian student with the blooming mane and long thin mustache, and hypernervous Tony. The latter could not keep from smoking, even under the belly of the Bell, despite the warnings from Denawi, who was afraid that the red dot, however well hidden beneath Tony's hand, might be a target for the German shooters. Each in turn, they popped in to keep an eye on the prisoners.

You may remember the picture taken on the morning of September 6, showing Yossef Gutfreund dead in his seat on DU. He was not blindfolded: the first thing the Bavarian police did when the affair was over, was to take off his bonds. They felt it made just too abominable a picture.

The four Israelis did not even bother to ask any questions or make any requests, although within the parching atmosphere of the machine they must have been very thirsty and heard their captors drink. The Germans had intended the canned refreshments left in the helicopters to be for everyone.

Before leaving Block 31, the fedayeen had apparently let their hostages, without getting out of gunsight, go to the toilet, shower, shave, and change clothes. Otherwise, Issa and his accomplices would not have been able to deny they had been inhumane to their prisoners. The terrorists themselves had taken full advantage all day long of the facilities in Apt. 1, and on leaving had helped themselves to shirts, sweaters, and underwear from the Israelis' wardrobe.

Despite the hard, close watching of their guards, the nine hostages without exception must have taken that opportunity to grab some object that might come in handy: Springer had a Waldi key chain with a very pointed-nosed dachshund, Halfin a small nail file, Gutfreund half-a-dozen Japanese matches, and Friedman a heavy closet key. Three of them had bits of matches in their pockets.

The Holocaust

The fedayeen had obviously kept away from them all such things as razor blades, knives, and so on. The surviving fedayeen claimed that before going into the underground they had searched all the hostages, running their hands over their clothes—but without undressing them or putting their hands in their pockets.

The Israelis were seated left to right in the helicopter: banty Friedman, fiery Halfin, old soldier Springer, and Hercules Gutfreund. They scarcely moved except for an occasional shift of the head or chest to break the tension.

Their wrists and ankles in the semidarkness were working at the ropes holding them, twisting in every direction, turning, rubbing the bonds against shoes or trouser legs. Sometimes, they loosened. Teethmarks were also found on the four ropes that had been around their wrists.

Unbelievable as it may seem, Halfin's fiery eyes could see, and Springer was not blind either. They were side by side. One of them had gotten hold of a burnt-out match and used it to make two virtually invisible peepholes in the towel blindfolding him. Then, he had given it to his neighbor. From then on, by some agreed signal—a cough or a clearing of the throat—Springer or Halfin could alert their friends to an opportunity or a danger. When the fedayee on guard in the DU stood at the open door and peered out, each Israeli immediately brought his crossed hands up to his mouth.

By bite and pressure, they had all succeeded in loosening at least one of their bonds. They had also undone the buckles of their safety belts.

By midnight, the two "seers," Halfin and Springer, would have freed their hands, hiding in the cuffs of their jackets the pieces of undone rope. Their next step would be to free their ankles. By little fast jerks, while one kept watch, the other would work on the knot. Springer had by now almost undone his.

Then, there would be only the most dangerous, though not the most difficult, part of the whole operation.

A smooth rope, as we know, circled the chests of all four Jews and tied them to the back of the seat. Tight at the start, it was by now somewhat looser thanks to their efforts, and had slipped down to the safety belts. It would be easy to raise it and shove it back in the same movement that would bring them to their feet.

If they coordinated well and worked fast, they could do this with overwhelming speed, so that the fedayee on guard in the machine, Tony or Denawi, would logically not have time to react before they jumped him. There were good chances they could knock him out, grab his weapons, and immediately shoot his sidekick hidden at the foot of DU . . .

11:59 PM: The lieutenant commanding the armor gave the order: *"Vorwärts!"* (Forward!).

They were not to shoot first, and were to travel at 16 km.ph (10 mph) as far as the 727. That meant one minute to cover the 250 meters from their start to the plane and to maneuver around it. Then, until the lead Panzer was about 50 meters from the helicopters, cut their speed to 6 km.ph, a snail's pace. So the second part of their course would take the L.A.C.s another full minute. After that, L.A.C. 4, which had been bringing up the rear, would take off suddenly.

The armored vehicles immediately staggered themselves into a diagonal at 45 degrees from the edge of the area. No. 1, the leader, was farthest from the edge, with No. 4, at the rear, hugging the fence.

The forward action of the high-slung armored cars on the prestressed concrete slabs took on a grinding sound that turned into a charging drumbeat as they approached. The five terrorists must have been crouching like surrounded jackals. With L.A.C.s 5 and 6 off on separate courses, the sounds reaching the helicopters and the tower seemed to emanate from all around, to be stereophonic. Up to now, the frightened barking of dogs at nearby farms or houses had been heard. Now only these motors filled the air with their warning roar: and they had not yet turned on their headlights.

The four vehicles heading so crushingly toward the fedayeen calmly split into two groups to go around the 727 on either side, and then slowed down.

"Full lights!" the lieutenant ordered, as he lighted his own and brought his command-car to a stop on the tarmac facing the helicopters.

At the tail of the 727, the four L.A.C.s turned on their three headlights and the moving searchlight in the turret. The other two vehicles, just now completing their encircling maneuver, did likewise. The bright lights of the armor were joined by all the additional illumination they had been able to lay hands on for the second round of the tragic fight to the finish: trucks, cars, and especially two movable searchlights with narrow beams, just brought up from near the tank cars.

One of these searchlights was halfway between the tower and the 727, at the edge of the tarmac, the other in front of the rail line, some 20 meters west of the tower. But they had to be moved so as not to become targets, and their beams came from too far away from the copters really to show what was going on.

In fuzzy, sporadic flashes, the pathetic figures tied to their banquettes could be seen through the open doors. As for the fedayeen, they could not be spotted clearly enough to pick them off: they kept moving, finding hidden corners, and the shelter of the aircraft.

When a concatenation of auto headlights picked up the backs of three of them, they immediately sensed this and scampered up into the copters. Once there, of course, even the world's best torches . . .

A disjointed body, in greenish coverall, lay motionless some 10 meters from QO: Capt. Reinhard Praus.

L.A.C. 4, riding last, against the south edge of the tarmac, suddenly raced its motor and shot forward. Its big livid lights came on like balls of fire. It really seemed to be going into a head-on attack. In a wink, it had overtaken the other three L.A.C.s on its right flank, and cut northwest toward the trucks with their twelve border guards. The first three L.A.C.s lumbered on at their 6 km.ph, hoping the fedayeen's nerves would crack and they would run away from their craft, or surrender.

The terrorists in the two helicopters might well believe the armored car catapulting forward was coming at them like a battering ram. Its steel shell, outlined by the other lights, made it seem explosively powerful, immanently threatening. Its sparkling headlights shone straight on the two Iroquois.

12:01 AM, September 6, 1972: Automatic fire burst at the same second from both QO and DU, in exasperated continuity. The flashes from the muzzles danced madly outside their fuselages. Yet, Issa and Tony had not been able to speak to each other. How had they so coordinated? By some signal?

The Black September men's weapons were practically against the hostages' legs, and their bodies were almost rubbing together as well, so that firing from any distance at the fedayeen up in the copters would have been madness.

The firing, full-blast from the start, echoed throughout the surrounding hills. We had first seen a sudden renewal of lights, the progressive invasion of the headlights, the sweep of the sharp, narrow beams of the AA searchlights. The roar of the L.A.C.s was increasing. Then suddenly there was this mad outburst as the five of Black September let go all together. It was a petrifying song of death.

It was also a mad waste of ammo. The bullets bounced off the armor, period. But the terrorists were peppering all of the darkness at random with a sweep that quickly forced the policemen, out in the open between Snipers 4 and 5, and then the eleven border guards in front of the rail track, to scamper for shelter. The lieutenant's command-car was hit in a front tire.

L.A.C. 1, the farthest on to the tarmac, was only some 50 meters from QO, when the wild firing began; L.A.C. 4, in its dash, was already within 30 meters of each of the copters, and still going full-speed ahead. The other three, moving forward in a line at a snail's pace, went on until No. 1, at their head, was some 20 meters from QO. Then the lieutenant ordered a halt. . . .

Up to now, bullets had been hitting all around without the Germans uncorking a single shot, so everything was going according to plan. L.A.C. 4 was about to pass between the two helicopters and head for the trucks. It would then swing sideways, followed by twelve border guards, protected by its steel mass. The other eleven men of the *Bundesgrenzschutzpolizei* commando would come out in front of the rail line to take shelter behind L.A.C. 5, which would escort them into a line abreast of the first three L.A.C.s right near the copters. The fedayeen would be caught in the net . . . Except that the unexpected always happens, as André Maurois used to say.

410

The Holocaust

12:04 AM: Suddenly, five or six amazing seconds of absolute cease-fire. This time, the two groups of fedayeen had not been able to communicate either. Did they make a signal from one Iroquois to the other, in all this noise and tension?

The Bavarian police were not talking, after the fight, but it seems almost certain that the Black September group—for its part —must have had at least one walkie-talkie.

The motor noises seemed less loud in the sudden absence of automatic fire. One clear, slight silhouette jumped from QO: in his safari outfit, it was Issa, for the first time without his beach hat. He had long hair, and the light-brown strands curled at the back of his neck. His face appeared in its square truth: the look in the eyes behind the big round black glasses must have been properly unspeakable.

At the same instant as he, through the opposite door, the other two QO fedayeen, Badran and Samir, jumped out. The weight of their equipment became apparent: Samir and Badran had assault guns, Issa a submachine gun, each had a pistol, and a beltful of grenades. Beside that, two sports bags undoubtedly brimming with ammunition.

Issa had just as much weaponry, but no bag. He held his AK-47 by the breech, and in the other hand—what else?—a grenade. But this time it was not cocked.

He bent over, and pulled the pin. And then, not in the classic movement but as if he were competing in the shot put, he stood up and sent the grenade square into the center of the fuselage, at the feet of the hostages. His throw was so carefully precise as to forbid any speed.

The explosion was terrific.

It was a double-bodied grenade, shattering into antipersonnel fragmentation. In addition, inside, it must have had some very active compressed incendiary material, perhaps thermate. In a hundredth of a second, the fuel tanks exploded and the kerosene went up in a strident hiss. Blinding light, a horrible artificial sun, shone in the night. The fuselage was shattered, the cockpit was no more.

Would that the God of Mercy allowed the five Israelis sudden death, and no burning alive! The explosion, the flashing heat, the shrapnel must have killed them all on the spot—Berger, Shorr, Shapira, Slavin, and Spitzer.

"The bodies were completely incinerated. Identification was possible only by where they were sitting and personal objects belonging to the victims, described by their friends and families," said a Bavarian police statement on September 7.

Just as Issa's grenade landed in the copter with the five hostages, Tony and Denawi, 30 meters away, began to fire again. Their fingers never left the triggers while the bright light spread with such prodigious violence all over the helipad. They were aiming at the searchlights on wheels, but these were continually moved from a distance by pulling on their cables.

Tony's slouched back and Denawi's almost childlike body with the slightly raised shoulders were briefly framed in the same doorway facing the tower, as if in closeup, lighted by the searchlights and headlights. The first three snipers, up in the radar room, fired at the same time, but were bothered by the shadow of a rotor blade. They were probably also afraid of hitting the hostages behind the fedayeen. The latter disappeared.

The three L.A.C.s stood stock-still on the tarmac, as if nonplussed. The blinding beams of their headlights became very narrow, as the car commanders closed the protective flaps. They waited, in proper spacing, watching the terrible pyre. In each of them, there were three men with the wherewithal immediately to wipe out all those responsible for the crime.

But there was Captain Praus, still nailed to the tarmac in the same uncomfortable position for the past hour and a half, in front of the machine he flew in, bits of which were beginning to fall on him. And, in the other Iroquois, there were still four hostages presumably alive. So the three L.A.C.s stood there, lumpish and paralyzed. So far, they had not fired a shot.

The proximate cause of Issa's throwing the grenade would seem to have been the sudden appearance, in the flare of its white lights, of L.A.C. 4, which had rushed away from the edge of the tarmac, bypassed the other Panzers, and made a beeline between the two Iroquois. Tony as well as Issa might have thought the huge battlewagon, with its 12.7 machine gun and its rocket-launching tube reconverted to accommodate various anti-mass demonstration projectiles, was coming straight at him.

Why did Tony not do as his leader did? Did he disobey? Rather, the Black September men had reached a point where chain of command and logic were suspended; all that was left was fear and hate.

D-HAQO was sucking in huge amounts of air as it burned. A rain of sparks, a gold, white, garnet, and black fireworks, with infinitesimal bits of human being mixed in, broke like a living constellation above the enormous burst of flame. The three fed-ayeen, in the moments immediately after the awful explosion, were invisible. Many thought they had been wounded or killed. But then there they were again, hopping, bent over, busying themselves at the edge of the pit of fire, shooting at random again.

Thirty meters away, in DU, Tony and Denawi did not stop their salvos in all directions. One was in the cockpit, with its flaps open; the other, in the passenger compartment in which the four Israeli hostages must be taking in everything that was going on, hunched down in a corner of the doorway, having pushed the big door three-quarters shut.

Suddenly, they changed positions. And they no longer aimed their exasperated fire at some attackers somewhere out there.

The flaming light bathing the whole helipad gave a clear view inside the DU fuselage of Tony's skeletal stooped carcass and Denawi's fragile short skinniness beneath his raven-black mane that waved to every gust of air. Side by side, standing with their backs to the pilot's cabin, they were aiming their assault guns at the four Israelis.

12:05 AM: The terrible whistling and crackling noise of the QO fire drowned out any other sound. But some believed they heard Issa's mysterious second-in-command and the little Palestinian student start to empty their clips, as the weapons bounced up and down. Yes, Friedman, Gutfreund, Halfin, and Springer must have been massacred just at that moment. Before, when the midnight machine-gunning was at its height, they were undoubtedly alive: their two jailers too carefully kept popping back into the machine, and their weapons could be seen pointed at the prisoners. In the following minutes, on the other hand, Tony and his assistant seemed no longer to worry about the hostages. They fought, moved, and went out, without a single further move to guard them.

The four Israelis were hit on an average by four shots apiece. They must have died instantly.

XXIII
THE BLOOD CRAZIES

For there is hope of a tree,
If it be cut down, that it will sprout again,
And that the tender branch thereof will not cease.
            Job 14:7

12:05 AM (CONTINUED): THE BRANDS AND ASHES SLIGHTLY SCORCHED Reinhard Praus, but saved his life, for they brought the first sheets of smoke, light at first, cottony and whitish, that kept Issa, Badran, and Samir from properly aiming at the prone man, whom they were peppering once again with bullets.

Why had they spared him until now? They must have considered him still a hostage, even though he was no longer completely in their hands: he was indeed at their mercy. So why suddenly try to kill him? Because he had started to move, and so might be able to get away. And, for these commandos conditioned to and fed on hate, the satiation of their long yen for a big killing had come. Once the liquidation was over, each of the fedayeen planned to try to make his own getaway.

The gesture by which Issa, having duly informed his accomplices in the other copter, massacred the five hostages in QO, was dictated neither by despair nor by the faith of the Jihad fighter that his actions and sacrifice would take him to Allah's heaven, but by the coldest of calculations. First, liquidate the insolent Zionists. Then, try to get away, which was not really so impossible, considering the dark night, the imperfection of the cordon around the base, the nearness of Greater Munich, and the thousands of Arabs in the area.

If the escape attempt failed, well, it would mean capture or surrender, and the fedayeen were sure the Germans would never dare do away with their prisoners: such things were not done in the West, with the whole world watching. So the survivors of their commando would become political prisoners under the protective jealous watchfulness of the brother countries: the Arab states, and a few others, would noisily make the most of the German trial of the Olympic Village fedayeen, and it would end in very light sentences. Or else, one of the Palestinian movements would organize a "forced exchange," which in the final analysis would make everybody happier. So, whether escaping or caught, Issa, Tony, and the other three survivors of the bloody attack were sure of being heroes in the eyes of their people, and being treated as such.

Captain Praus got to his knees, rose from the ground, and ran off upright, zigzagging, with fists clenched and elbows tight; his head was thrown back as if the helmet held him back.

The irony of it was that he was picked up by the headlights of the L.A.C.s like klieg lights follow a movie dolly shot. Issa, Badran, and Samir, more and more protected by the waves of smoke enveloping the helicopter zone and assuming the color of the raging flames, concentrated their fire on Praus, but with their eyes beginning to tear all their shots went astray; Issa, incidentally, was very nearsighted, and his black glasses were no help. The five sharpshooters reacted reflexively to all this, and their rapid-fire shots, coming very close to the three fedayeen, drove them back into the volcano QO had become. The "accompanist" of Sniper No. 5 swung his machine gun upward and let go a sustained burst that convinced the two jailers of DU not to expose themselves to try to get a bead on the pilot.

QO was still burning. The thick globs of smoke were getting darker, thicker, and heavier, and seemed to come from a boiler under compression.

This was one of the very few comforting things in the death trap: all the VIPs amazedly watched the emergence of a man they had feared had been seriously hit. He was all right; he was running toward life; it would be too stupid, if . . .

Five seconds more, and Dr. Wolf himself was rushing out on to the runway to meet the border-guard captain and protect him with his body. They got to the entrance to the technical building, the annex to the tower, together. Praus was hale and hearty.

12:06 AM: The light placed in front of the rails was blown up. None of the five fedayeen had been hit yet, and they kept machine-gunning the area, some from the edge of the conflagration in which the flames were fighting the black rolls of smoke, the others from the fuselage of DU.

The driver-commander of the fire engine, 100 meters from the fire, had one of his four crewmen get off. Best to be as few as possible for what they were about to do. He turned the ignition on: this was a huge 30-ton vehicle that was part of the base's regular fire brigade. Its crew were in radio contact with their superiors, and the latter had consulted the colonel before ordering so hazardous a mission.

How did it happen that this Luftwaffe supertruck was available at the site, when the Bavarian police had taken exclusive charge of the action? The commanding colonel had first of all to think of keeping his air base in good working order. He could not risk the potential harm of a serious fire breaking out. So it was imperative to send the firemen into action. Yet, outside of this one fine 30-ton truck, there was not another piece of firefighting equipment on hand at the ambush. Why?

Herr Schreiber's office replied: Although Munich's firefighting facilities were worthy of the greatest of cities, they had been taxed to the limit since the start of the Games. The Connollystrasse events had of course multiplied the demands on the Munich firemen (huge concentration of firearms and inflammable materials; fire engines required at every spot the fedayeen or hostages might potentially get to).

The fire truck moved off, with its inner tank of 14,000 liters of water (some 3700 gallons), its loud siren topping all the other noises. Bright blue lights whirled on its roof.

With Praus safe, the L.A.C.s could start their slow move forward again. They were now on a line parallel to the one between the two copters. L.A.C.s 1 and 2 were about 20 meters from QO, and No. 3 the same distance from DU. The Panzers had put out their lights. The terrorists' bullets bounced off their 100 mm(4-inch)-thick plate. Then they stopped again. The fire truck pulled up some 20 meters northeast of the crematorium-helicopter: the front of QO was now merely a bed of fire. The firemen jumped down on the tarmac. Two of them, hose in hand, went as close as they could to the fire. Sizzling flashes burst through the tides of black smoke.

12:08 AM: The huge bright red of the Luftwaffe stood alone, some 30 meters from L.A.C. 1, which was closest. Its siren was turned off, but the signal lights kept revolving. The two firemen had bulletproof vests under their fire-resistant uniforms—but were still very vulnerable.

"Two more possible hostages!" said some of the VIPs, as they watched the new developments with horror. But how else to act? The fire could not be left on its own. Besides, the powerful streams of water the firemen were shooting at QO were some protection for them against the fedayeen.

Issa and his two accomplices had disappeared again. But they were still operating: their shots kept coming from somewhere near the edge of the suffocating hearth. But they were clearly not shooting at the fire truck or the two men in chinstrapped copper helmets.

The firemen were dousing the flames with chemical foam, which swelled whitely. Light as air, these masses seemed like airborne octopuses running their tentacles around fire, soot, sparks, flying debris, and dense vapors. The formation of the light shroud with its soft contours, swallowing up the metal-plastic-and-kerosene pyre in which the five Israelis had been cremated, was like the appearance of a mirage.

Tony and Denawi kept sending out salvos of shots, in fits and starts; Issa and his men were spacing their shots further and further apart. None of the terrorists was aiming at the firemen. The sharpshooters were now absolutely not firing back at all: the thing was to expose the firemen to the least danger possible. The mountain of foam kept growing by the minute, in both size and thickness. Soon the fire would be so cut off from oxygen that it would have to go out. The three fedayeen might also run the risk of asphyxiating.

12:10 AM: Complete stop to the firing! What if the battle were over? Were the terrorists finally surrendering? Perhaps over in DU, plowed with bullets but still apparently quite intact, the last four hostages had been spared, some of the VIPs thought out loud, as in prayer. The two Israeli envoys shook their heads. "The longer it lasted, the more we wanted to hope," Herr Genscher would later say.

The flaky white foam had swallowed the cockpit, the passenger compartment, and was now well above the rotor. But half the tail stuck out of the death-and-fire-stuffed mound, and displayed gay tones for such a tragic moment, the basic green of the fuselage with the large yellow ring near the stabilizers. But the flames were beginning to flake off the white capital letters BUNDESGRENZSCHUTZ, too close to the hearth. Soon all the paint on the tail, except at the very tip, began to split and come off in slabs. The steel was twisting with creaking bursts, as if it too were in pain.

Tony and his sidekick, like the other three hidden 30 meters away, around what had been QO, must have been taking advantage of all this to reload.

12:11 AM: Issa, Badran, and Samir, momentary visions, twisted out of shape by the waving of the flames and the sheets of smoke, appeared at the far north end of the phantasmagorical white hump that was streaked with fiery bands the color of a terrible yellow sun.

L.A.C. 4 had not moved since getting up to the trucks under cover of which the twelve border guards ripe for action waited impatiently. Now it started to turn, doused its lights, and very slowly advanced due south, getting close to the three fedayeen on QO. As planned, the twelve border guards, in a column by threes, moved forward too, hard behind the vehicle.

But where were the three fedayeen? The outsize bubble that the firemen's hoses kept feeding was still growing bigger, enclosing the fire in a bed of goo as sticky as a leech, and somewhere in that syrupy mass, its ghastly white broken by flashes of flame, Issa and his two companions disappeared, as if drowned. They were breathing nosefuls of carbon oxide. The foam was locking them in to the hellish heat, and they seemed annihilated.

L.A.C. 4 and its twelve border guards had to pull up some 12 meters away from the heart of the fire, which little by little was declining in convulsions like showers of shooting stars. The three crewmen, running with sweat, were suffocating inside their oven.

We could see that from our grassy knoll. The moving carapace of foam took on moderating shades that were suddenly burst by geysers of flame. But we thought the bursts of fire were now continuous. From all the roads came concerts of horns, shrill sirens, sputtering motors, and it seemed as though the nerve-boggling bedlam was only a background for an uninterrupted succession of shots. This was because the explosive noises of the burning helicopter kept coming on after the fantastic blast of the first combustion. Scores of little things kept cracking, bursting, in sorry imitation of gunshots.

What was to be done? Keep firing at the flaming machine? How would the other two fedayeen in DU react to that? As for imagining even one of the hostages had been able to survive the burning of QO, no one dreamt of it.

At the Village Press Center, as the first signs of dawn broke over Oberwiesenfeld, Herr Bruno Merk would be saying about those five Israelis: ". . . Perhaps some of them were lucky enough to escape. We have no way of knowing. Only after the bodies are examined will we be able to tell."

No one among the thousands of newspeople took any hope from these strange words by the Bavarian Interior Minister. From a strictly legalistic viewpoint, he could of course rightly say they had no real proof the five Israelis in QO were dead, since their ashes and few remaining bones were horribly unrecognizable. But the awful truth could not be doubted for one second, after Issa's grenade exploded.

12:12 AM: The two Luftwaffe firemen had been fighting the fire for four minutes.

"They popped out like devils. They were running sweat, their clothes were stuck to their skin, holy mackerel! And their popguns were going like mad . . . ," one of them was to say.

Issa looking like a clown suddenly thrown into the pot, tall Badran, blond Samir with soapy coal-dusted hair, emerged together from the hearth of foam and fire. And, still unable to see, two of them started to fire at random, at arm's length, reaching up over the flaky foamescence.

420

It was pure luck that neither of the firemen was hit. Both their hoses were pierced, and there were bulletmarks on the heavy sheetiron of the engine.

Badran was not firing; he seemed dizzy, unsteady, fell to his knees, dropped his Kalachnikov without anyone touching him. Was he drunk? Beyond his limits?

At that moment—no more than three seconds after the mad reappearance of Issa and fragile Samir—the armored lieutenant ordered L.A.C.s 1 and 2 to fire on them.

When the firemen were first attacked, the lieutenant had his driver get out. Taking the wheel of the command-car himself, he went forward in strange little flea-jumps over the reinforced concrete, until he was right near the two L.A.C.s stationed in front of what remained of QO. He bumped along because of the blown-out tire. As Tony and Denawi fired at him, he cut his lights and moved into an area covered by the shadows of his armored vehicles.

For the first time, Germans other than the sharpshooters would be firing at the Black Septembrists. It was a tough decision: the 12.7s, running at 400 shots per minute, would be riddling the burning QO fuselage. That meant admitting beyond doubt that the five hostages inside were dead—but how could they not be? The bursts also might revive the fire. Nevertheless, the lieutenant was right: fire from the L.A.C.s was the only real way to protect the firemen. And since the three fedayeen from QO were now caught between the fire and open terrain, this was the time to finish them off.

The bursts now came from the turrets, in a sharper and more sustained crackling than that of the portable automatics. This was crushing fire, a carpet of bullets burning up the blue-black air. The thick short barrels of the 12.7s swung up and down, left and right, and by the pattern of the firing flashes one could see the slight but methodical pressures of the machine gunners on the handles. In this way they covered all of the truncated cone made by the compact foam that shone like snow wherever it was not already sullied. In the space covered and smothered by it, there were no more darting bursts of fire, but just tonguelets of flame, less and less brilliant.

From the minute the police machine guns went into action,

Issa and his two men were lost in that monstrousness of snowy, creamy, swelling froth. The bursts of fire went into it at a mad pace. By all odds, the fedayeen by now were either smothering to death, or shot through and through.

The chauffeur had jumped to the tarmac at the first shots. The firemen, a miracle of calm, collected their apparatus and climbed back on the truck with unbeatable alacrity. The fire engine was now rapidly backing away.

Sharpshooter No. 5 had joined his No. 4 fellow in front of the signal-block to the north.

The helipad, from our height, seemed plunged back in darkness. . . . But now, little by little, the car headlights, the AA searchlights, the endlessly moving beams that the L.A.C. commanders were sending out of their turrets, all of these lights aimed at the two helicopters began to make sense again, and became appreciable targets.

In DU, Tony and his companion seemed to have an inexhaustible arsenal. To tell the truth, their bursts followed each other, rather than coinciding. They were shooting up lights again; two cars were hit. But they wasted too much effort in aiming at the searchlights of the armored vehicles, which themselves were moving about, colossal and invulnerable.

From time to time, a glimpse could be gotten of the four figures immobile on the banquette of DU: nothing more.

None of the three fedayeen from the burning copter had given a sign of life since the 12.7s started their terrible onslaught.

12:13 AM: "This time, we really raked 'em . . . ," the lieutenant thought aloud. Yet he wanted to continue firing for another minute. Without realizing it, he had talked into his radio transmitter.

The leader of L.A.C. 2 returned: "I see an Arab under the nose of the burning Iroquois. He's either dead or playing dead."

That was Badran. He had fainted. A biting pain in the thigh brought him to again. The bullet did not hit any artery or bone but tore away a good hunk of flesh. The youngest of the fedayeen dragged himself to the edge of the monstrous foam bubble. There, he lay motionless on his back.

422

The Blood Crazies

The leader of Armor 2 had barely spoken when a silhouette leapt out of the nightmare stack that the fire was still convulsing. This was Issa, landing on both feet, knees up, submachine gun cradled in his elbows, and hands flat against his chest.

"Concerted fire on the safari outfit!" the lieutenant cried.

On the tarmac, the slugs could be heard bouncing.

The fedayeen chief fell, rolled over, got up again as if on a spring, and ran in short fast strides toward DU. He had 30 meters to go, in exposed terrain . . .

He was miniaturized instead of magnified by the thick white flakes of foam that stuck to him all over, on his soot-covered skin, and his blue-gray playboy outfit. The soaked synthetic fabric stuck to his skinny little body, canceling any thickness: he was a light-clad skeleton barreling along. How could he see through his his black foam-encrusted glasses?

Sharpshooters and machine gunners from the first two armored vehicles had at him: no result. He defied the bullets, as he had done when before he ran 100 meters or so with a hare's artful zigzags. This time he was running straight, his head pulled in— a carnival figure with hair full of white cotton and blackened face. The bullet-bursts surrounded him.

He got to about 8 meters from DU, from which Tony and Denawi kept determinedly shooting full clips, keeping the leaders of the border-guard commandos off balance and unable to attack. The lieutenant, in a rage, ordered the L.A.C.s to stop firing at Issa: if the four Israelis were still alive, he could not risk hitting them. The fuselage that was their prison remained an inviolable sanctuary. During this time, Tony and Denawi were getting their salvos off only by grazing, rubbing, and shoving against the corpses that guaranteed their immunity.

The lieutenant bawled out his machine gunners. Why? Four seconds to pin down a fugitive who had not been expected, to get a bead on him from the turrets, in such lousy light, was no snap.

The sharpshooters could still keep after him until he got right up to the copter, and all five furiously did.

Issa lost his balance just as he was getting to the tip of DU. He seemed to slip on a fuel puddle, and fell on his side. Was he going to get up and take the few steps between him and the fuselage? He remained prone, shaking his head. As if startled, he slipped beneath the nose of the Bell by rolling from shoulder to shoulder, face to the ground, He seemed wounded, perhaps no longer able to use his legs. But he was one to watch out for.

Tony's rough, rutted face showed in the open door, at floor level. Issa's second was probably lying on his belly. He dropped a rope to his chief. A salvo of bullets made him dart back into the fuselage. The end of the rope reached Issa's leg, and he grabbed it.

12:14 AM: The lieutenant told L.A.C. 1 commander to keep an eye on the moving, smoking, dying fire. There was still a third Arab inside: Samir. He seemed swallowed up by the floating waves of foam. But what if he too now came out?

The two fedayeen still in the DU fuselage began their bursts of automatic bullets again, one to the north, the other through the opposite door, toward the tower.

Issa was moving under the copter, hugging the edge. He dragged along by holding with one arm to the rope that Tony was pulling at the other end, as Denawi continued firing. He got to the curved front end of the right skid, directly below the cockpit door. He clung to the tubular steel.

A mobile searchlight began sweeping rapidly across the tarmac, now under the DU's belly. It was the one from L.A.C. 3, which had come within 15 meters of the machine, ignoring the risk of a direct hit on the globe of its turret. Salvos kept bouncing off the armorplate, missing the light.

The first three sharpshooters on the tower's third floor took advantage of this light. Their sharp, detached shots could be clearly heard on the tapes. Issa had not gotten far enough in: only his head and shoulders were protected by the skid. He was shot three times, once at the bottom of the spine. He shook as if electrocuted, each time a bullet hit him.

Tony and Denawi were still trying to get the light on L.A.C. 3. They were about 2 meters from Issa, and could not see him, but surely must have been able to talk to him.

Issa still had strength enough to take a grenade from his belt, pull the pin, and throw it toward the open door of the Iroquois. At the exact same second, Tony and Denawi jumped out the other door, but Issa's looping throw this time had no power behind it.

The grenade fell back on the concrete, rolled slowly away, and exploded without doing any harm. The head of the Black September commando dropped his arm. His forehead bumped against the ground. Issa was dead.

12:15 AM: Denawi hunched up, but then fell flat the second he hit the tarmac. Had he gone 10 centimeters farther, the converging fire of the twelve border guards positioned 20 meters to the north around L.A.C. 4 would have made a mash of him. He seemed to have been killed. Rolled up fetus-like, he was no longer moving. His stiff mane, blacker than the darkest darkness around, spread on his knees.

Tony, jumping facing the south, was in the lights of two L.A.C.s, Nos. 3 and 5, which had gradually inched very close to DU. Behind 5 was the second team of border-guard commandos. Tony's jacket and pants, both black, faded into the night. Without aim, he fired several bursts toward the west.

Only the sharpshooters on the tower were still trying to bring down the last remaining fighting fedayee. Neither the L.A.C. crewmen nor the border guards could use their automatic weapons with hostages still possibly alive inside the machine.

Tony's long stooped silhouette bounded up from the concrete, agile as a roebuck. He sped due west, then switched and returned southward: beyond the buildings at the edge of the tarmac in that direction, there were the rail line and the fence. He bounced, rolled, jumped, turned somersaults, ran a broken field, hunched up like a monkey, and on and on . . .

All the German weapons in the area plowed the ground around him with their fire, but Tony's course was not slowed. The officers ordered the firing stopped when he was some 30 meters from the rails, on which stood the four big cyclindrical tank cars. After that, there was too much chance of Germans being in the way of the bullets.

The rails were being patrolled by police. They knew nothing of the fate of the hostages. It seemed to them the automatic fire was heading their way. They took cover, and prepared to fire. They did see a single man running, holding a weapon and followed by shots. But there were over thirty disguised cops on the base. Suppose it were one of them. Later, of course, that did not hold water.

But, at the time, anything seemed possible. Sure, there were 9 chances out of 10 it was an "Arab." But, still . . .

Visibility was very poor. For the fifteen seconds of Tony's broken field running, the lights kept looking for him, finding him, and losing him. The headlights did nothing but create reflections on the tarmac of the penultimate scene.

The burning of QO was ending; the foam collapsed, spread, disappeared. The hot dark night enveloped the debris of the helicopter and the ashes of the dead.

Tony, reaching the rail line, dove under a fine tank car with the yellow-and-green BP shield. He had run 80 meters from DU, and not one bullet had scratched him.

The German shepherd dogs barked voraciously. Tony could see enough in the dark to know his only possible salvation lay south. Beyond the rails, there, there were buildings with inanimate facades. Lightless side roads ran along them.

From the spot he was hiding in, Tony could make out, at the end of walkways perpendicular to the railroad, the metal fence of the base, repeatedly briefly lighted by the headlights of cars on the road to Maisach. He could imagine the patrols, and hear the police dogs. He waited. He was sure (and right) that the tank car was full of kerosene: enough to set off one monumental fire. Certainly, the coating of the tank was thick: 18 mm (¾ inch), I've been told. So it would resist even the fire of the 12.7s. Nor is it so clear that a bullet going into the tank would ignite the fuel. But the Germans were in no mood to put that to a test this night. Tony caught his breath in his precarious shelter.

He was still running when Dr. Wolf started out toward DU. The *Polizeidirektor*, pistol in hand, ran over to Denawi, leaned over him, and shook him. The fedayee did not react. Eyes closed, mouth open, he was stiff and motionless.

"He's playing dead!" Wolf said, and grabbed him roughly by the hair. The pain brought Denawi groaning back to life. The iron grip got him to his feet. A knee in the ribs made him realize he had to hold his hands up. He did not have a scratch. In a moment, he had been handcuffed.

12:16 AM: Schreiber ran up and jumped into the fuselage.

He was to say: "The four Israelis seemed to be asleep, peace-

fully. Their heads were bent and they leaned against each other."
Piously, the blindfolds were immediately taken from their eyes.

Wolf was splitting Panzers and police into two main groups,
one in front of the rail line, the other around QO.

In the rubble of the Bell were the remains of five Israelis, and
also two terrorists, perhaps still dangerous, although one seemed
out and the other had disappeared.

The Panzer lieutenant, pistol in hand, went near the awful mess
that had been Bell-Iroquois D-HAQO. The headlights of the three
L.A.C.s cut through the flakes of smoke and dying foam that still
came from the conflagration. They seemed like strips of fog.

Slim Samir lay on his back, arms and legs spread, under the tail
stabilizers. Like Denawi's, his mouth was wide open, his eyelids
closed. The officer grabbed him by the collar of his polo shirt,
raised him like a puppet, and with the other hand applied the
muzzle of his pistol to his temple. The eyes opened, the jaws half-
closed, and the mouth twisted: Samir was screaming. His arm was
jerked violently behind him. He screamed again. He had a very
minor gash in one arm.

A border guard, meantime, had jumped on Badran who, like
his two friends, was deliberately playing dead. He shoved a pistol
under his nose and tried to drag him to his feet. The young terrorist roared with pain. The policemen could see the wound in his
thigh, and the blood. An ambulance came whiningly up.

12:17 AM: Herren Schreiber and Wolf were looking at the unspeakable mix of the five cremated Olympic athletes.

Hidden beneath his steel tub, Issa's next-in-command was the
only one of the eight Black Septembrists still free. There is no
question that he took out a white handkerchief—stolen from the
Israelis—and unfolded it. Was he trying to give up? We have no
way of knowing.

He could obviously not be left under the tank car full of aviation
fuel. So the teargas the police had brought along was the only
reasonable recourse. It was a classical solution, with a benzyl
bromide base, but including specially irritating ingredients. It had
violent immediate effects, with suffering that lasted for a long
time and, if not treated, could cause serious lesions. Tony should
be groggy in a moment, his eyes blinded, tearing, and burning,

his mouth and nose very swollen, as the gas was murder on the mucous membranes.

All the effectives around the railroad track donned their gas masks. A Volkswagen with a blue light-bubble on the roof pulled up near the kerosene tank. Two policemen carefully opened the doors, their faces looking like pig snouts in the masks. They aimed their launchers under the tank car, without ever getting out of the armored "ladybug."

12:30 AM: Conrad Ahlers, state secretary and spokesman for the Federal Republican Government, appeared live on German TV. In a vibrant tone, he announced the total success of the rescue operation carried out at Fürstenfeldbruck air base.

> All the hostages are free and unhurt! All the terrorists have been knocked out of the fight! There was never any question of Germany allowing Israel's Olympic athletes to be taken out of our country as hostages.

Herr Ahlers' declaration went out on all German wavelengths. It was picked up everywhere in the world.

The next evening, Ahlers was to explain as follows his fantistically phony official announcement:

Having phoned in the name of the Federal Government to the Bavarian *Land* police, this was the information the captain had given him. He had immediately called Chancellor Brandt. The latter had just heard the same news, probably emanating from the same captain. Brandt then asked Ahlers immediately to broadcast the magnificent outcome.

In a flash, all the Israelis had known of the official confirmation by the West German Government spokesman of the freeing of the nine hostages. Mrs. Golda Meir and most of her ministers had been sitting up together, waiting for the end of the ordeal. They burst into delirious joy. They drank a champagne toast to the survivors. Mrs. Meir went to bed at 1:00 AM, totally unaware of the truth. *Kol Israel* (Voice of Israel, the official Israeli radio) kept paying tribute to German skill, as it repeated over and over, "Our nine Olympic athletes are hale and hearty!" and relaying the congratulatory messages arriving in Jerusalem from all five continents. It would go on like this until the end of the night broadcasts. In the homes of the nine hostages there were crowds, enthusiasm, tears of joy.

A Reuters bulletin announced that after midnight shots were still being exchanged at the Fürstenfeldbruck air base. The battle seemed hot and heavy; one helicopter was burning.

We went down in bunches toward the fences of the base as soon as the shooting really seemed to be ended, about 12:20. By dirt paths and then the road from town, we got to the base's fence.

Not far from a gateway flanked by guard-huts, the mass media were Johnny-on-the-tragic-spot, whether with big-nosed cameras, telescopic lenses, or just pencil and pad. Climbing the approximately 2.30-meter(7½ ft.)-fence was no problem, since all reporters worthy of the name traditionally give each other a leg up. But there were those German shepherds, leashed, it was true, but still patrolling the guard paths inside. Their muscles rippled beneath their clipped tan-and-black hides. Their shining eyes ferreted us out. Dryly beautiful, but deadly silent, those attack dogs! On either side of the metal mesh, there were border guards on patrol, holding their Walther automatic pistols by the breechblock, and Munich police who over their light-colored raincoats had buckled on the belts that held the KGP-70 with the clip in the grip.

No use trying to get through. There were buildings between us and the landing strip. We could see the tower against the dark. Occasional meager lights, coming from the field, cut through the sky up to the heavy clouds.

We heard the gunbursts resume. When they stopped, the clip-clap of individual shots rang out. Flashes of fire made striations in the sky. Broad accumulations of smoke still hovered outside the windowed rotundas of the tower, and swung ever so slightly, uninclined to move away, their thickness and sooty blackness standing out against the less sharp tones of the cumulus.

Nothing could be clearly made out. Spot-news reporters were right to stay here in order to catch any movements of people or vehicles through the gate; but for the rest of us the overall view was much more revealing from atop the dovecoted hill.

I went back up there. Several TV teams, including ABC and

DOZ, had set up there; you could not move without bumping into their cables and tripods.

Every radio station in Europe was bursting with enthusiasm. We listened to them all—as sporadically the reports of automatic weapons broke through the false calm of the air base. Between the huge vertical rolls of smoke, the quarter-moon reappeared from time to time. The gaseous offshoot of the conflagration, cinders, ashes suspended in air, partially hid the field. The four-colored ground lights looked like some kind of hashmarks, and we were disturbed by the thin beam of the AA searchlight. On the pathways, there were blue or red globes revolving in the roofs of the only vehicles allowed inside.

Tony was reacting furiously. The reddening tongues that flashed with each shot showed he was turning in a complete circle as he fired from his prone position. He did not have to worry about running out of ammo: he got out of DU with a bag slung from his shoulder holding some 100 clips and three grenades. The police were forbidden to fire back.

The fedayee's firing stopped. Logically, he must have been groaning in pain.

The BP tank car was the last car of the train toward the west. No cops had been put under the other three because they would have been trapped like rats if Tony shot his machine-gun bursts between the rails. Wolf decided to give him five minutes more. The pain from the gas by then would be intolerable.

No more sign of Tony. Armored personnel and police had the tank cars surrounded.

12:35 PM: Cautious as Red Indians, watchful against an interdiction blast, Wolf's men inspected the belly of the BP tank by flashlight: Tony was gone.

The gas is almost odorless, but Issa's assistant must have detected it from the first gusts with the instinct of a hunted animal. Perhaps he saw one of the launchers. He had on the dark glasses which had been part of his special image at Connollystrasse and had covered his face with a scarf of pretty Carmel silk that had belonged to elegant Moshe Weinberg. The gas hardly got to him. It was as he was crawling out of the contaminated zone that he let go

The Blood Crazies

that haphazard blast, at arm's length, without looking, so as to protect his face.

One by one, the other three tank cars were inspected. It was inconceivable that Tony should have been able to get away from the siding. They got to the head tanker, the empty one, thinking perhaps he was under it.

The police dogs until then had been kept away from the rail line because of the gas. Now one was brought in. As soon as he was near the lead tank car, he began to pull on his leash. He pointed under the steel cylinder. And a burst answered. The fedayee was there all right. The animal saved his head, but he had a wounded paw. He was crying in almost human tones. His master jumped forward and, hugging the macadam, emptied his machine pistol under the tank car. He was dragged back and given hell, while Tony riposted with bullets against the armored wheels of the L.A.C.s.

12:50 AM: The policemen, protected by their cars, peppered the tracks beneath the tank car. It was rolling fire, exasperated and sustained. The men, hurt at not having been able to stop the massacre, knew that the one before them was that arrogant Tony from Connollystrasse. While the fedayee's shelter was crisscrossed with bullets, flashlights played on it, but no one was close enough to see under the tank. Dr. Wolf risked getting closer. At the end of his inspection, he swore as he got up: to their stupefaction, the long fedayee with the rounded back had flown the coop once more. They rechecked every square centimeter, and then back under the other tank cars. No one there.

1:00 AM: Yes, on this ground around the track, where virtually every meter had a cop on it, Tony had succeeded in getting through their net. The dark night, the black, airless night that the *Krisenstab* had been so hard put to reach in its obsessive desire to buy more time was now the surest helper to the last of the Connollystrasse fedayeen. How did he do it? Certainly, the Munich police would never tell—and it is doubtful whether they know.

Ahead of this train of tank cars, maybe three meters away, was a small tipcart with a few sacks of cement in it. It had been considered too close to the fuel tanks to have men hide behind it, but now two border guards were against it, on the side opposite from

431

the last empty tank under which Tony had wounded the dog. The rails were fairly well lighted between the tanks and the tipcart, but the latter threw a rhomboid shadow southward. The only explanation seems to be that Tony got up against the side of the movable tank and jumped goatlike into that dark rhomboid, where there were no cops. They were busy covering the tank car. If they saw him, did they think him one of them? I for one could not fault them if they did. Several times, in combat, I lived through similar situations—and I am not exactly inconspicuous.

Some 10 meters due south of the tipcart, there was a small car park of about 200 square meters. Perhaps eight cars were parked there, with a group of cops standing guard. Tony slipped between them. "The light was lousy!" as a Munich police lieutenant who was involved in it told me six months later.

Dr. Wolf was sure Tony had to be in that parking lot. The reactions of German shepherds confirmed it. They had to be restrained from rushing in toward their deaths.

It was hermetically sealed off. The park was much too crowded for the six L.A.C.s to be able to maneuver in it. They stayed at its corners, aiming their lights on to it.

The commando of twenty-three border guards started through it in a tight wave, covering it centimeter by centimeter, supported by thirty-odd Munich police. Six dogs were spread among this troop that moved forward virtually on its knees.

1:17 AM: Three minutes later, the rapid fire broke out again. Fortunately, the bullets got lost among the cars. A guard had thought he saw Tony crawling between two cars: it was one of his buddies. They changed the arrangements. It seemed the lights from the L.A.C.s were lighting up too much territory at once. They were put out. Flashlights were set up on ground level, creating worrisome reflections, halos, cryptlike lightings.

Then they closed in in silence, in the most dangerous way. The concentric raid reduced the free area for the fedayee's potential retreat to the space covered by four cars.

1:30 AM: Tony was flushed out, lying under a Mercedes 200.

He had left the white kerchief under the BP tank car. But he might still have yelled that he was surrendering, since he knew German. But—having set up so many traps, gone back on his solemn pledge by trying to kill the helicopter crews, with his accomplices murdered eleven Israeli athletes—the last of the fedayeen by now must have felt it was too late, cornered as he was; no one would believe him. Or maybe he did not want to surrender at all.

From where he was, there were still some 30 meters to cross to get to the fence. He must have known that darkness was teeming with enemies.

Tony shot first, a volley of five or six shots. The guard he aimed at was crawling toward him around the back of the vehicle standing just in front of the Mercedes 200. There was a long cry of pain. Germans jumped out on all sides. Tony started firing haphazardly. At the tarmac, at tires, chassis, the legs he thought he saw, twisted and moving too rapidly.

The border guard he had hit (who was never identified) was seriously wounded by two bullets, one entering at the base of his neck, the other in the side. He got out of it, but only after several months in the hospital. He had had the strength to take refuge immediately under the car he was pressed against, so that Tony lost sight of him.

The flashlights quickly picked out Issa's second-in-command now. Some saw him from the side, others from the back, with his long legs constantly moving in their shaky rhythm. He was less than 2 meters away, putting his next to the last clip into the Tokarev, when two border guards riddled him with their machine pistols, puncturing his ribs, his spine, and the back of his neck. It was

1:32 AM: And Tony's nose finally slumped to the crook of his elbow.

XXIV
ZION

Ho, thy plagues, O death!
Ho, thy destruction, O nether-world!
Hosea 13:8

2:00 AM: CHARLES BIETRY, SPORTS REPORTER FOR AFP (AGENCE France-Presse), keeping a watch at the main entrance to the Fürstenfeldbruck air base, saw an overwhelmed man come out: Herr Georg Kronawitter, *Bürgermeister* of Munich.

To all his questions, the Mayor could answer only, "It is terrible. All the hostages are dead. Four Palestinians were killed."

2:16 AM: From a public phone booth, Bietry dictated the story to his agency's Munich office, scooping the world. Paris did not think of questioning its special correspondent's flash and beat all the other services by over an hour. But the facts seemed too awful to believe: most of AFP's subscribers were leery, and decided to await a confirmation, rereading (and hearing in their minds) the victory proclamation smilingly put forth by Conrad Ahlers in the name of the German Federal Republic. Nowhere on the radio wavelengths carrying or relaying the German radio's news was there the slightest confirmation of the AFP bulletin.

Yet, all observers felt increasingly ill at ease. The fallout from Fürstenfeldbruck sounded too ominous.

3:17 AM: Reuters carried the wire-story: "All the Israeli hostages were killed during the shootout at the air base, according to an announcement made tonight by a West German military spokesman."

The unbelievable truth was forcing its way through.

At the *Pressezentrum*, Herren Genscher, Merk, and Schreiber, along with Willi Daume, held the fateful press conference already referred to. Only after half an hour did the Bavarian Minister of the Interior, finishing an endless recap of the day's events, finally announce the massacre. Three of his words alone told the whole story, and awakened not only all Germany, but the whole world: *Alle Geiseln getötet!* (All the hostages are dead!).

8:15 AM: The Executive Board of the IOC met in the blue room of the Vierjahreszeiten, under the presidency of Avery Brundage. A member of the Organizing Committee was also there, representing Willi Daume, unable to attend.

From 3:30 AM on, the top authorities of the Olympic Movement had been awakened one after the other by news of the disaster. It was feared that the white flag with its five rings might forever disappear from the world's stadia—though it would not really be forever, since, contrary to the false saying, history always repeats itself.

The main floor of the large hotel was full of a nervous mob made up of IOC members not on the Executive Board, heads of federations, newspeople, cops in mufti. Everyone was repeating Willi Daume's statement at the predawn press conference: "I'll never have the courage to suggest to the IOC that the Games should go on." His waxen color had been accentuated by his sky-blue sweater.

The sun was beating down already; a beautiful day.

9:25 AM: Mr. Brundage came out of the Blue Room, followed by Lord Killanin and the seven other Board members. No statement was made. Yet the results of the meeting, to be sure, were quickly known: The Munich Games would run their course.

They had been officially suspended since 4:00 PM yesterday, with extensions rather liberally granted, as we have seen, for those events already under way. Today, Wednesday, September 6, at 4:00 PM, after a mourning period of twenty-four hours, the schedule would resume where it was interrupted yesterday. Tomorrow, every event would be held, simply one day late. Thus, the Games of the XXth Olympiad would end Monday, September 11, instead of the day before. The closing ceremony would be curtailed and adapted to fit the circumstances.

The pressmen rushed toward the phones. All that mattered was the flash, "The Games are going on!" Although some pointed out that the President of the Organizing Committee was not there, and that the West German Government had not been heard from. Who could be sure?

10:00 AM: In the fine stadium where the eleven victims had been part of the opening parade eleven days ago, the Olympic Movement foregathered for the memorial ceremony in honor of the Israelis. The doors were open to one and all. A silent, troubled, crowd filled the stands. The delegations taking part in the Games had their places facing the official reviewing stand, on the field, where 3,000 seats had been set up. At ten o'clock, the Munich Philharmonic, dressed in black, began the funeral march from Beethoven's *Eroica*. The slow lamento of the strings, in its breathtaking beauty, filled the temple of bodily triumph as in a nightmare.

All was not only emotion and sadness. There was also the question: What would Messrs. Brandt and Daume say? The public was still not aware of the IOC Executive's decision of a few hours before. Even the newsmen still questioned it. The Israeli Government had again called on Chancellor Brandt to cancel the Games. The former Labour Prime Minister Harold Wilson had voiced the same sentiment. There was also the most violent kind of statement from François Mitterrand, head of the French Socialist Party, condemning the very principle of these Games now as a "capitalist fair"—a statement that this morning was drawing bitter reports from Soviet officials. The USSR, since the start of what had been this fine Olympic celebration, had made great propaganda efforts to have the 1980 Games awarded to Moscow. On the competitive level, it had spared nothing to win the largest possible number of medals, and was well on its way to do so.[1]

Herr Brandt was also a Socialist, as was Herr Heinemann. Add to that the fact that the team from the Philippines, as well as four members from Holland and thirteen from Norway, withdrew from the Games in protest against the crime. The Egyptians and Algerians were leaving, too.

A shiver ran through the crowd. No announcement, but all at once 80,000 heads turned toward the Marathon Gate.

---

[1] In the unofficial overall results, the USSR would win the Munich Olympics, with 99 medals (50 gold, 27 silver, 22 bronze) to 94 for the U.S. (33 gold, 31 silver, 30 bronze), and 66 for East Germany (20 gold, 23 silver, 23 bronze). West Germany was fourth, with 40 medals, so the two Germanys united would have topped the USSR. The latter was adamant about having the Games continue.

The Israeli team, or what was left of it, seventeen out of twenty-eight, appeared. During World War II, out of 15,000,000 Jews in the world, 6,000,000, or 40 percent, were slaughtered by the Nazis. Eleven dead out of twenty-eight also came to virtually the same 40 percent.

The Jewish athletes displayed such grief, and such dignity, that in silent spontaneous homage the whole stadium rose to its feet. The stigmata of the ordeal could be seen on the faces of all the survivors. None had slept for the past twenty-nine hours. Today, they were oblivious of the crowd. They were at one with their martyrs. The men must also have been musing on the special luck that spared each one of them.

They were wearing what was at hand. Those who were housed in Block 31 had not been back there since yesterday's dawn. The Organizing Committee had relocated them elsewhere—in the Village, at their own request—and their effects had only just been brought on to them, pell-mell, after the usual police examinations. The fedayeen, in fact, had gone through everything, and messed up quite a lot of it. Those Israelis who could had donned their parade uniforms, with the Menorah resplendent on the blue blazer. Others had to make do with borrowed shirts or shoes.

Coach Tuvia Sokolovsky, who had escaped from Apt. 1 under fire, wore a new sweat suit, that he would never wear again. Overwhelmed, he kept going over the tragedy and reliving the moment when he heard Gutfreund's heroic shouts of warning. He was not religious at all; but now he prayed incessantly.

The Olympic delegations were allowed to sit anywhere: only Israel's was placed right in front of the stand of honor. As they sat down, the Hebrew survivors left eleven empty seats in the front row. These fascinated all eyes.

The West German athletes were there in full complement, with black crepe on their jacket lapels. The very numerous French wore their parade outfits, as did many other delegations, such as Nigeria and Kenya in their nobly draped lines. The Swedes came in yellow-and-blue sweat suits: they were not the only ones who chose to show solidarity through informality. But most wore the traditional kind of funereal garb.

There was loud whispering on the official stand: Moshe Weinberg's mother was arriving with her husband, the stepfather of the young official who had knowingly sacrificed his life to save some of his athletes. The photographers all wanted shots of this fine-looking woman, greeted by Herr Willi Daume. How moving she was! Beneath her light hair covered by a net, shivers went through the pure sculpture of her long face, as Herr Uwe von Hassel, President of the Bundestag, and his wife came up to present their condolences to the lady in black who this very evening was to have had dinner with her late son.

The stadium, set in its bend of landscape like a ring in its case, was now filled to cracking. It gave a breathtaking feeling of vibrant life and happiness, a gigantic multicolored palette beneath a resplendent sky. A soft breeze kept the heat from being oppressive. It was record-breaking weather.

On all the Israeli heads there was the *yarmulke,* or ritual skull-cap. Other athletes, American, British, one French, had also put on the head covering of their Jewishness.

Some one hundred policemen in blue dress uniforms, unarmed, entered the field and took their places alongside the Olympic delegations. They were there in homage to their fellow, *Polizeiober-meister* Anton Fliegerbauer. At this point, it occurred to some that the Germans had taken a loss, too, and that this ceremony was as much for him as for the eleven Jewish martyrs.

The wonderful music ended powerfully. Silence lay heavy on the heavy air. Herr Willi Daume, President of the Organizing Committee for the Games of the XXth Olympiad, got up.

He gave a sober speech, poignant in its sincerity. This man had been the soul of the superb and grandiose accomplishment the Munich Games were until yesterday. In a life full of successes, this one, begun in 1966, was perhaps the crowning glory, certainly the most spectacular. And now it had come down in blood.

> For us [he said] who had planned these Games of the Twentieth Olympiad with confidence in the good will of all men, today is a day of immense mourning. Even in the world of crime, there are still some taboos, a final limit of dehumanization beyond which one dares not go. This limit was crossed by those guilty of the attack in the Olympic Village.
>
> They brought murder into this great and fine celebration of the peoples of the world, this celebration that had been dedicated to peace.

Zion

When Herr Daume left the microphone-smothered lectern, the newspeople noted he had not said a word about the future of the Munich Games. He left that announcement to the IOC President.

Shmuel Lalkin, head of the Israeli Olympic delegation, followed the master planner of the 1972 Games. Why stress how moved we were by his rugged voice? He spoke in Hebrew. He had excellent English, but he was right to do this. He was wearing a blue-and-white yarmulke, the same colors as the prayer *tallith* and the Israeli flag.

> They were good Israelis, true comrades, faithful sports companions, and now they are dea   cut down in the flower of life: David Marc Berger, Zeev Friedman, Yossef Gutfreund, Eliezer Halfin, Yossef Romano, Kehat Shorr, Amitzur Shapira, Mark Slavin, Andrei Spitzer, Yacov Springer, Moshe Weinberg.

The sound-system, usually excellent in the *Olympiastadion,* was not working well this morning. . . . His words could not be fully heard. The crowd progressively sensed that these syllables so forcibly thrown out against the blazing sun, in a trembling tone, were the names of the eleven murdered athletes. And then it got up all in a body; its sadness, its contemplativeness, were tangible things.

Speeches here were successively repeated in three languages: German, English, and French. So this one was heard four times. Despite the defects of the sound-system, each time the eleven names were read off, the crowd got to its feet, with a spontaneity that was all heart.

All the Israeli athletes had the same mournful look. Many could not hold back the tears that rolled gleaming down their cheeks. The shiver of Esther Shahamorov, the first time she heard the name of her coach, Amitzur Shapira . . . All eyes were on the survivors, and the terrible empty chairs in front of them.

Lalkin concluded: "The abominable crime notwithstanding, we have decided to participate in future Olympic Games in a spirit of brotherhood and honesty."

Whether or not because of the poor sound, the various translations of this sentence—as Lalkin would explain to the press in the afternoon—were not quite faithful. Hearing them, one might have inferred that the Israelis meant to stay on in these Munich Games, which was of course inconceivable. However, in all three versions, the sentence was met with the first applause of the ceremony—warm and relieved. I bowed my head.

A large part of the IOC was on the stand of honor, with its outgoing President Avery Brundage and his successor Lord Killanin. The highest authorities in West Germany had come, headed by President Dr. Gustav Heinemann. Then *Bundeskanzler* Willy Brandt, Minister of Foreign Affairs Walter Scheel, opposition leader Rainer Barzel, among others. Prince Rainier III of Monaco and his beautiful wife, Princess Grace, were there. Immortal athletes, such as Jesse Owens and Emil Zapotek, were weeping, without false shame. And then there were those who were absent—deliberately . . .

Not one athlete, not one official from any Arab country was present in the stadium. Nor was there anyone from the USSR or East Germany. Apparently, the Yugoslavs and Poles had not come, either. The Olympic flag, in its nacreous whiteness with the five overlapping wheels, waved softly at half-mast, and like it the flags of the 122 nations participating in the Munich Games were also lowered. Before the ceremony ended, there would be wild protests from Arab officials, because of that. Their governments supported them, with cables which in some cases were terrifying. For this respectful ceremony, without any prayer service, was being seen on world television, so that hundreds of millions of people could see the colors of Egypt, Syria, Algeria, and the others, lowered to the mourning position . . .

There was ostentatious security around the Israelis. In civvies or turquoise training outfits, Schreiber's men were all around. At the top of the opposite stand, the Olympic flame shone in a golden geyser. A bouquet of yellow and red roses had been placed at the foot of the deep bowl in which the flame bubbled. They seemed like flowers at the foot of a burial monument. As if eight terrorists were all it took to kill off an institution with traditions going back 3,000 years.

The ambassador of Israel to Bonn, H. E. Eliashiv Ben Horin, now spoke in his turn, his round face showing gray patches as a result of the night of ordeal. He spoke of the bitterness of the Jewish people, and its determination.

Then, *Bundespräsident* Gustav Heinemann, a universal man, of noble soul, and often against-the-grain frankness, inspired by his Protestant faith. He calmly took his place before the metal lectern. At seventy-three, he was not going to put on kid gloves to say what was on his mind. As ever, he looked like a retired professor, white hair neatly combed, dark-shell-rimmed glasses, round and serious features, with slightly soft and pale cheeks. His hard-headed softness . . .

"Eleven days ago, in this enclosure," he began, "I declared the Munich Games of 1972 to be open . . ." And he went on to denounce the "abominable" attack. Then, in his unemphatic tone, contagious because of its deep conviction, he said:

> Who bears the responsibility for this crime? First of all a terrorist organization that thinks hatred and murder can be methods of political struggle. But, in addition, there are the countries which do not stop these men from perpetrating such acts.

His voice was growing louder and stronger. The President of the German Federal Republic stressed each sentence separately:

> The Olympic Idea lives on. Our commitment to it is more powerful than ever. In the events that we have just lived through, there is no line dividing North from South, East from West. Where the break comes is between the brotherhood of all men who wish for peace and the hatred of those who expose to the worst of dangers all the values that make life worth living. Life demands reconciliation, not that we fall victim to terror. In the name of the German Federal Republic, I address this appeal to all the peoples of this world: Help us to overcome hatred. Help us to pave the way for reconciliation.

All right, they may be nothing but words. But how he would have liked to imbue them with power! He spoke the way people pray. God heard him. Men did not.

I have several times been close to President Heinemann. I could never see any mask on him. He may be clever, may have passions, may switch directions at times. But he has immense honesty. He is a man. What he said in the *Olympiastadion* ought to have been listened to.

The IOC President, Avery Brundage, was to give the last speech.

> . . . Sadly in this imperfect world, the greater and the more important the Olympic Games become, the more they are open to commercial, political, and now criminal pressures. The games of the Twentieth Olympiad were subjected to two savage attacks. We lost the Rhodesian battle against naked political blackmail. . . .

One's blood froze at hearing this coupling of an argument over the biracial representation of a racist country and one of the most atrocious massacres since the War! All the Black African countries were outraged by this sentence of Brundage's. The next day, September 7, facing these counterattacks, the outgoing President of the IOC issued a statement that said, among other things: "There was not the slightest intention of linking the Rhodesian question, which was purely a matter of sport, with an act of terrorism universally condemned . . ."

But, to get back to Mr. Brundage's final speech in his thencapacity, he went on:

> We have only the strength of a great ideal. I am sure the public will agree that we cannot allow a handful of terrorists to destroy the nucleus of international cooperation and good will we had in the Olympic movement. The Games must go on! . . .

Then the old outgoing President was interrupted by a long, echoing ovation, that gave me the shivers. Any crowd in the world would have had the same satisfied reaction.

But, watch out: the IOC was right to stand its ground. The symbol of a cancellation of the remaining Olympic events would have been horrible, in this Munich where, twenty-four years before, the Western Powers had thrown Czechoslovakia to the wolves.

At the top of the official stand, off to the side, a tall young woman, her face hidden by outsize dark glasses, kept her composure. Her head was covered by a black scarf. This was Mrs. Andrei Spitzer. In her silk glove, she had a handkerchief. Beside her was a man looking utterly undone, with a skullcap on his white crown. From time to time, the two of them whispered to each other.

The organizers announced that the memorial ceremony was

over. The VIPs said good-bye and left. Below, on the green, the delegations were getting up, too. Only the seventeen Israelis remained seated, their faces reflecting an exhaustion and desolation that would not yet yield to pity. They were not expecting anything. They just wanted to be the last out of the Olympic Stadium.

The orchestra was playing Beethoven again: *The Egmont Overture.* The slow cadences of the beginning, its nostalgic modulations, were more in keeping with the mourning tone than the victorious chords that finally broke forth beneath the blue sky.

Over the feedbacking loudspeakers, an official was detailing the schedule which was to resume at the end of the afternoon with exactly one day's delay: distribution of weight-lifting medals, in the crowning superheavyweight category, and individual épée; two matches in the elimination round of handball; boxing quarterfinals in six categories; and, here in the now-emptying Olympic Stadium, at 8:00 PM, a semifinal soccer match between West Germany and Hungary. There would also be the resumption of the eliminations in Greco-Roman wrestling, in four categories, but competitor No. 184, the Israeli Mark Slavin, would not be available for his scheduled match in the 74 kilos (163 lbs.) category: he, who had still been alive when this day began, was to have appeared at 6:00 PM on the circular yellow carpet.

At the end of the opposite line, halfway up the tiers of seats, a group of spectators seemed to be meeting: they were the last batch still in the Stadium. Several of them were wearing yarmulkes. They were standing. On closer inspection, it was obvious they were overcome.

A little while back, during Shmuel Lalkin's speech, as the Israeli delegation head was calling the roll of the dead, one among these people had quietly collapsed to the side, against his neighbor's arm. The latter, looking at him in surprise, understood from the livid face and the large wide-open vitreous eyes. He called for help. A hostess ran up. The unconscious man was given room to lie down. He was about forty, wearing a skullcap on his black hair. He was well built, slim, and had a thin mustache. The hostess put a cover over him, and sent for a doctor, who arrived quickly, gave him injections, heart massage, and artificial respiration. But all in vain. He was already dead. There is a terrifying picture of him, showing him with his head thrown back, his mouth open beyond belief.

His name was Carmel Eliash. He had no cardiac history. Had always been in excellent health. He was one of a group of Israeli tourists who had come to Munich for the Games. He was a cousin of Moshe Weinberg's.

Noon: In Jerusalem, an official communiqué was released, following the Cabinet meeting. Prime Minister Golda Meir had cabled Chancellor Willy Brandt her personal appreciation of his Government's decision to "take action for the liberation of the Israeli hostages and to employ force to that end."

The Israeli Government ordered a national funeral for the murdered athletes, and a seven-day period of official mourning.

Grand Rabbi Mordechai Piron, chaplain-general of Tsahal, the Israeli army, left for Munich to bless the victims and accompany their remains on the trip home.

An explosion of rage had been stirring the Holy Land since yesterday morning: bitter criticisms were leveled at the Government for having spared the life of the Japanese Kozo Okamoto, sole survivor of the murderers responsible for the butchery of the previous May 30 at Lod Airport. All important personalities, including even the moderate Foreign Minister Abba Eban, were against the continuation of the Games. Israel, that thin slab of land squeezed between the sea and the Arab immensities, had to swallow its bitterness and pull together its energies.

6:45 AM, *Thursday, September 7:* The four-engined El Al jet carrying the remains and the survivors flew out of Munich-Riem.

The afternoon before, after administrative formalities and autopsies, the bodies of the eleven victims had been provisionally coffined. The Israeli Olympic officials took charge of their dead and moved them to the Munich synagogue. Grand Rabbi Mordechai Piron had thereupon arrived, with national flags for the draping of the biers. Each body was made ready, with a bag of Jerusalem earth beneath the head, dressed in a white shroud, and the ritual tallith, from which one of the four corners had been cut away.

At dawn, today, in the presence of the survivors from the Israeli delegation, the coffins had been put into hearses and moved from the synagogue to Riem Airport.

One of them, that of the weight lifter David Marc Berger, had been turned over to a platoon from the U.S. Army, the parents of the young Jewish lawyer having asked that he be returned to them for burial. This afternoon, a plane from the U.S. Air Force would take off and fly him back to the States. Until he finished his Israeli military service, David M. Berger still had dual American/Israeli nationality. He was a bachelor. Might he not have preferred to await resurrection in the Promised Land, since he had chosen to go to Israel for the rest of his life?

David Berger, whose fiancée remained in Israel, was to be buried at Shaker Heights, Ohio, Friday, September 8, in impressive and pious ceremonies.

But at Riem, early on the morning of September 7, the special El Al plane was waiting at the end of the runway, protected by an army of police.

Some sixty Israeli tourists had gotten permission to return home on the El Al 707. Many of them were from the International Youth Camp: forty children in tears, immaculate in their outfits identical to those of the team, except for the blazers being brown.

The Grand Rabbi entrusted the victims to the mercy of God. Prayers were offered. The ten coffins one after another were put on the moving carpet to be hoisted into the baggage hold. The body of Carmel Eliash would follow them the next day.

Chancellor Willy Brandt had suggested flying to Israel with the victims. He was dissuaded from it. Jerusalem argued that his arrival in Israel would create security and protocol problems; that this was a purely national ceremony; and that, besides, Prime Minister Meir had lost her sister Sheina during the night of September 6–7 . . .

In truth, it did not seem opportune for the first visit by a head of the German Government to be on the occasion of the Munich massacre. There was fear of unfair popular reactions, further inflamed by the fact that the resumed Olympics would be in full swing at the time of the burials. Word had indeed been sent to the West German authorities, late in the afternoon, that it would be better if no member of the Federal Cabinet attended the funeral.

However, the Chancellor had delegated the Minister of Foreign

Affairs, Herr Walter Scheel, to go to Riem Airport and present Germany's official condolences in a last farewell to the coffins. Willi Daume was also there, with Hans-Jochen Vogel. The latter, representing the Organizing Committee, was going along with the victims.

By now, all of the survivors had been able to dress in proper parade uniforms. They were wearing the white straw hats that on August 26 they had doffed before President Heinemann's box. Their farewells to the helpless German officials were cursory. Their springlike costumes in no way diminished their sadness. Each member of the Israeli Olympic delegation had a black triangle pinned to his/her chest; the girls in double-breasted blue blazers and pearl-gray miniskirts were hard put to control their tears.

A young woman in a tailored black suit, square in the shoulders, stood off to one side near the ramp. Herr Vogel came over to say hello to her, and her pretty young round face began to tremble, and the lids fluttered over her eyes that could for the first time be seen to be sky-blue, wide and warm. A large scarf with a dark-green background, tied under her chin, covered her hair.

The Israelis from time to time looked briefly over at the aloof, solitary woman, wondering who she might be. Perhaps some organizer from the International Youth Camp? But she recognized all the Connollystrasse survivors, among them Drs. Kranz and Weigel who, were it not for her, would have finished up at the Fürstenfeldbruck air base. They would have run to thank her, had they but known. But she preferred to remain anonymous while coming to pay tribute to the victims of the tragedy she had so valiantly participated in.

For, yes, this was Fräulein Graes, the policewoman-interpreter. A few of us observed her from afar. She hid her face in her hands when the last of the coffins went in the trapdoor.

The Jewish athletes walked up the ramp without looking back. The heavy door was locked. The plane flew out and soon was only a bright arrow in the limpid sky.

7:00 AM: In several large German cities, attacks on Jewish monuments had occurred during the night. The police department of Frankfurt am Main reported that about fifty tombstones had been knocked over and vandalized in the city's old Jewish cemetery.

Zion

11:45 AM: The plain of Shefela, between the mountains of Judea and the sea, bathed in the sun and heat. At the international airport of Lod, 19 km. southeast of Tel Aviv, flags hung limp at half-mast. Four thousand people massed behind the metal barriers biting into the concrete landing strip on which the special El Al plane would come down with its mournful load.

There was strict order around the arrival point. This event was for Jews only; the presence of members of diplomatic missions and foreign newsmen was merely tolerated. But no stiff solemnity, no soldiers at attention, no music. The rough simplicity of Israel.

Now came the plane with the two-toned fuselage. In front of the barriers, chairs had been set up for the families of the dead. But there were so many relatives! Many had to stand. All eyes were on the huge four-engined machine coming down, coming in, finally coming to a halt.

Tsahal rabbis, identifiable by discreet insignia on their khaki shirts, but mainly by their beards and sidelocks, supervised the transfer of the bodies. Each of the coffins in turn, covered with a national flag displaying the Shield of David, was put on to a sand-colored military truck, open but armored. Armfuls of flowers had come from all directions to Riem. It had seemed they were haphazardly piled in, but now on off-loading they were carefully arranged over the remains: roses, lilies, carnations, against the white and azure of Israel, created striking waves of color with white and snow dominants, and red and yellow.

The Olympic survivors stood in a bunch at the foot of the accommodation ladder, unmoving in thoughtful sorrow. Hard but furtive wrinkles marked the sunburned faces of the girls. After all, they were now back home, the living and the dead.

There were sobs, buried in hankies. Noises wet with sorrow. But mostly silence. During the slow transfer of the dead, pious people prayed, bent over their Torah, the tallith around their shoulders, and the *tfillin*—the phylacteries, with the little black leather boxes holding verses from Deuteronomy and Exodus—attached by straps to the forehead and left arm.

There were only two more coffins to set in place when several of the relatives exploded: fists shaken at the murderers, screaming moans, and repeated names of the departed. Widows, mothers, then bunches of afflicted kin crushed toward the coffins. On the side of each truck, a plaque indicated the name of the victim.

A time was allowed for the suffering to spend itself, and then the honor guard took over, six soldiers per vehicle. The vehicles moved out, to line up a bit farther on, facing the microphones and the place where the VIPs were. All the heads of the country were there, except for Mrs. Golda Meir, who had gone into personal mourning, because of the death of the sister who was closest to her, Mrs. Sheina Korngold. A dry, weak wind was blowing like a heating vent.

The President of Israel, Mr. Zalman Shazar, stood, impassive and sweet, from one end of the ceremony to the other. In a month, he would be eighty-three, and he had been President for nine years, holding office but not governing, greatly beloved.[1]

Near him, the informality and determination of Israel was symbolized by the short-shirtsleeved Gen. Moshe Dayan, looking like a kibbutznik. His square face with the mouth twisted to the side by his war wound was implacable. The khaki linen cap, darkened with sweat at the temples, underlined the blackness of his eyepatch. Dayan stood motionless during the entire service, solidly set on his wide hips, muscular arms crossed, gut in. The other Cabinet ministers displayed the same informality of attire. Abba Eban's Bond Street suit stood out among the light-colored shirts.

Chaplain General Piron, his superb voice rolling and resounding with the depth of brass, recited Psalm 83:

> O God, keep not Thou silence;
> Hold not Thy peace, and be not still, O God.
> For, lo, Thine enemies are in an uproar;
> And they that hate Thee have lifted up the head.

The imperious accent swelled from stanza to stanza. The tone finally became thunderous in the concluding verses:

[1] Presidents of Israel are eligible only for two successive terms of five years each. So, the next year, Mr. Shazar was to be succeeded by a Russian-born physicist, Prof. Ephraim Katchalski, who, because of the rule that those in the Government must have Hebrew names, became henceforth Katzir. It is relevant to our story that his brother, also a scientist, Prof. Aharon Katzir, had been killed May 30, 1972, by the Japanese terrorists at Lod Airport.

Zion

> Let them be ashamed and affrighted for ever;
> Yea, let them be abashed and perish;
> That they may know it is Thou alone whose name
>   is the LORD,
> The Most High over all the earth.

Then Mr. Yigal Allon, Deputy Prime Minister and Minister of Education and Culture, spoke. He was stocky and solid, with the haughty face of a proconsul. A sabra and kibbutznik like Dayan, he was one of the great rivals of the one-eyed hero. He too had long since held the rank of general. He had a fantastic military past: he had enlisted in the Haganah at thirteen, in 1931, and commanded the prestigious Palmach, the spearhead of the clandestine Jewish army.

After having recalled some of the fedayeen's bloody past attacks, he cried out in his biting tone:

> The Arab countries—though not all of them—lend support and assistance to these terrorists. Their responsibility is no less than that of the murderers. They will suffer the consequences. . . . Unable to meet Israelis with arms in hand, unable to get any support from the Arab populations of Israel or the West Bank, the terrorists have no other recourse but to keep attacking in the free countries of the West, to sow blackmail and murder. . . .
>
> We have understood and appreciated the resolution of the German Government to use force for the liberation of the hostages, though we deeply regret the inadequacy of the security measures taken for the protection of our athletes.

Fainting and groans of despair punctuated his speech. In front of the barriers, the khaki troops marked off the concrete rectangle reserved for the ceremony. They were soldiers in the image of their small besieged nation, tough fellows, trained in the rough, born of 2,000 years of surviving persecution. In flat berets, broad light belts, baggy trousers over their soft boots, legs spread, they held their rifles by the barrel and listened to Mr. Allon like wild animals ready to spring to revenge.

The red-hot sun created a fire, far over to the east, on the first swells of the fawn-and-green Judea foothills.

The military vehicles carrying the draped and flowered coffins moved out one by one. The Grand Rabbi chanted: "O Eternal, full of Mercy, Who dwelleth upon high, find a safe resting place for Zeev Friedman . . . Yossef Gutfreund . . ."

As each body went by, it was thus greeted by name.

The families followed in Army jeeps. The seventeen Olympic survivors rode along in a truck pulling up the rear. The convoy exited the airport, escorted by command-cars carrying President Shazar and members of the Government.

At the crossroads of the Petah Tikva–Ramla road, the tragic Munich team was separated for the last time, after a final stop, an ultimate farewell. Ministers and athletes broke up into the ten funeral processions, and went off toward the various burial grounds, spread throughout the land of Israel.

The cities they crossed all held their arms out to the victims of the Munich Games. The people massed on the sidewalks. That day, the entire country joined in a communion of pain and anger. No shop, no office was open. Every population center seemed strangely paralyzed. All the armed forces were on call.

In ten cemeteries in Israel, and also beyond the oceans, in Ohio on Lake Erie, an honor guard folded back the flags covering the coffins and handed them to the next of kin. The bodies were lowered into the graves. Each person threw three handfuls of earth on to the top of the coffin, and the Kaddish, the prayer of obedience and peace, composed in Aramaean, was heard: *Yisgadal v'yiskadash sh'me rabbo, b'olmo deevro chiruseh v'yamlich malchuseh . . .*

Everywhere the funerals were over before the end of the afternoon, under the same brilliant sky. Then the People of the Book went home and closed their doors.

The next day, Friday, was Rosh Hashanah, the Jewish New Year, the year 5732, according to the Hebrew calendar.

It was a day darkened by national mourning. But, in picture and in word, all of Israel, in these hours, bent over the children of those who were the Olympic dead, with wildly determined affection.

This was the triumph over death, the perennation of the Jewish people—of the blood of Israel.

AFTERWORD

THE BODIES OF THE FIVE DEAD TERRORISTS CAUSED A GREAT DEAL more talk than those of the eleven murdered Jews.

On September 6, the day the massacre ended, the Bonn Ministry of Foreign Affairs got tens of official messages from Moslem capitals demanding the "return of the remains of the fedayeen to the Arab people." At the moment, the bodies were in the Munich morgue, awaiting autopsy.

As "doyen of the Arab diplomatic corps," the ambassador of Tunisia at Bonn, H. E. Mahmoud Mestiri, already familiar to us, in turn made a démarche, informing Herr Scheel that Tunisia wished to give "worthy burial to the *Chouhada"* (martyrs, those fallen in the struggle).

The *Aussenminister* answered that he had just had a similar request from the Libyan Government. M. Mestiri bowed to that: on Monday, September 11, at 8:00 PM, the bodies of Issa, Tony, Abu Halla, Paulo, and Salah arrived at the Tripoli airport.

It is interesting to note that neither Egypt nor Syria, to mention only those two Arab neighbors of Israel, came forward to claim the bodies and hold the funerals. As if it were understood that the moment Libya expressed its interest, it had to have its desire satisfied.

The five dead commandos from Connollystrasse were buried on the afternoon of September 12, at Tripoli. Colonel Khaddafi was not present at the funeral. But two of his ministers represented him. Present were all the ambassadors of the Arab countries accredited to Tripoli, as well as a large Tunisian delegation headed by M. Chedli Klibi, Minister of Cultural Affairs and Information. The funeral service was held in the Bourguiba Mosque. Then the cortege, swollen by tens of thousands of mourners, assembled in Martyrs Square, which rang to vengeful speeches as well as prayers. The five coffins, accompanied by an excited throng, went off to the Sidi Munaidess Cemetery.

How about the three surviving fedayeen?

Here is what happened, the following month.

Sunday, October 29, to be exact, at 6:00 AM, its yellow stork on blue background shining happily in the matutinal Lebanese sun, a Lufthansa 727, on the regular Damascus-Frankfort run, with stops at Beirut, Ankara, and Munich, landed at the Beirut-Khalde airport. It had left Damascus empty, except for its crew of seven.

It picked up thirteen passengers, of whom eight were nationals of Arab countries. Not much of a load, and no women or children aboard. At any rate, so it seemed, not much chance of an unpleasant surprise, in these days of skyjackings: the Khalde police had, as usual, carefully searched all passengers and baggage.

It took off. The first half-hour was a perfect flight. The Mediterranean danced in a sparkling blue gown below.

It was 7:30: two gentlemen came forward to visit the pilot's cabin. The steward who saw them asked them not to go up there. But then, seeing the looks on their faces and what they were beginning to take out of the wardrobe compartment, he desisted. The visitors spoke to the pilots in English, telling them it was in their best interest to skip Ankara and head straight for Munich. They underlined their words with several handguns that seemed to be in good working order.

The skipper, Capt. Walter Claussen, thinking mainly of the remaining seventeen presumably innocent people who were his responsibility, did not have to be told twice. He merely pointed out that the 727, a medium-range liner, did not carry too much kerosene (as shown by the fuel indicator), and recommended a refueling stop at, say, Nicosia. They agreed.

At 7:50 AM, the plane's radio transmitted, to be given to the

Afterword

Government of the German Federal Republic, the desiderata of the two terrorists: namely, the immediate freeing of the three fedayeen who had survived the crimes they committed at the Olympic Games and who, pending something better, had been using their Bavarian prisons to give lengthy interviews through the interposition of their attorneys. "If our demands are not met, the plane will be blown up, and all of us with it," the two air-pirates finally announced.

At 12:15 noon, the plane was at last over Munich-Riem. Dr. Manfred Schreiber, the well-known Police Commissioner, sent word to the Beirut terrorists that of course their demands were accepted, but that it would take another hour and a half to get the three September 5 fedayeen to the airport. The fact was, these killers were being kept in three separate prisons rather far from one another. "We have sent three helicopters to comply as quickly as possible," Schreiber specified.

The pirates consulted with each other, then ordered the pilot to gain altitude.

"Head for Zagreb," they said. "But we won't land there until our comrades have been delivered to the field!"

"What if they are delayed? We only have fuel for less than five hours."

A fatalistic shrug was, apparently, the only reply.

Why did the skyjackers refuse to land at Munich-Riem, as planned? It is said that the Arabs were disagreeably impressed by the display of police vans, ambulances, and uniformed people awaiting them on the ground. But others find it hard to believe that the Bavarian police would on this occasion have come out into the open so accommodatingly.

According to Lufthansa and the federal authorities, the fuel tanks of the B-727 so easily taken over were getting down to near zero when it reached the Croatian sky.

During this time, the three Connollystrasse survivors, although indicted for any number of offenses, including eleven counts of premeditated murder, had been put aboard a two-motored Lufthansa Condor. They were guarded by three policemen, in turn escorted by two high officials. The chairman of the board of Lufthansa, Herr Herbert Culmann in person, was also aboard.

According to Herr Culmann's statements, it was he who, at 3:45 PM, instructed the Condor pilot to take off for Zagreb immediately: "I figured that Captain Claussen's Boeing, in the air since eleven AM, would run out of fuel at about five thirty PM. I could not stand the idea of letting the crew and the eleven passengers who had put themselves in Lufthansa's hands run such a risk."

The Free State of Bavaria not being the Beggars' Kingdom, it seems unbelievable that the Condor carrying three surviving terrorists guilty of a recent murderous attack now forever famous could have taken off from Munich without official approval. Yet, that is Herr Culmann's version, corroborated by both the Bavarian government and Bonn.

The 727 and the Condor met in the airspace over Marshal Tito's federated republic.

Above the Zagreb-Pleso airport a courteous dialogue took place between the two hijackers and the German officials escorting the three indicted criminals.

"We ask for your solemn word that you will free the eleven passengers immediately, as soon as your three colleagues are on the 727 with you," the Germans asked. "You will still have the seven crew members who will take you to the destination of your selection."

The two terrorists from Beirut agreed to the deal.

At 4:50 PM, the Condor landed first just opposite the control tower, in a pouring rain. Low clouds and the winter climate made it dark already.

The 727 landed at 5:07, at the very end of the single runway. The three who had been freed were taken aboard the liner in a Volkswagen minibus. This must have reminded them of another bus of the same make in which, fifty-four days earlier, with their five Black September buddies and the nine hostages still alive, they had gone from Connollystrasse to the helicopters set down at the edge of the *Olympisches Dorf.*

There were great embracings among the fedayeen, after which the 727 crew said it was time to free the eleven uninvolved passengers aboard since Beirut. The plane was being refueled.

The hijackers now announced that all aboard would be kept aboard until they had reached their destination.

Afterword

"But . . . what about the agreement you just made with the West German authorities?"

The two pirates, reinforced with their three experienced fellows, smirked and shoved their persuaders under the noses of the crew, already familiar with them.

At 6:50 PM, on this wet autumn Sunday, the plane took off again for a predictable destination. The airport authorities, on instructions from Belgrade, had been as cooperative as can be.

Tripoli was reached at 9:15 PM. The ambassador of the German Federal Republic, H. E. Gunther Bruner, was at the foot of the gangplank to greet not the five terrorists, but the eleven hostage-passengers to whom he presented Lufthansa's most profound excuses. He also greeted the crew, whom he congratulated.

Had the Germans done it on purpose?

Supporting the idea of a put-up job, there are several oddities. For instance, a Boeing deadheading from Damascus to Beirut and then leaving the Lebanese capital with the skimpy fateful number of thirteen paying passengers, two of whom are terrorists! "If the Lufthansa planes carry so few passengers, the company must be in trouble!" was a general comment. To which Lufthansa replied that it was not so unusual for companies to operate some of their scheduled runs at a loss: that subjection to implacable schedules, which was their burden, was also their advantage as against the freedom of movement and undependability of charters.

That may well be. But a look at the names of the eleven "innocent" male passengers who boarded at Beirut shows that among them were four Palestinian exiles traveling on varied passports (which is something they can hardly help), and two Lebanese Sunnite Moslems, notoriously prone to links with El Fatah. These six were in support of the air-pirates all along the way. There were also five "non-Arabs," whose family names indicate nothing either in terms of Lebanon or elsewhere. To which Lufthansa replies, "To us a customer is a customer. We are not expected to be police."

Where were the pistols and grenades brought on board? The only possibility was Damascus. By the cleanup crew? There are other means during a layover. Here is what qualified circles in Israel told me at the time:

"The truth is Black September had warned the Germans that,

if this skyjacking failed, the movement would undertake a wide-scale offensive against Lufthansa: plastic bombing, threats, shootings, and kidnappings. It would have been enough to ruin business. A week before the hijacking, the Mossad had warned the West German Government and Lufthansa that it knew from a dependable source that a Black September commando was very shortly planning an operation aboard one of the company's craft in the Middle East. The normal effect should have been for security measures to be taken on every flight. None was."

Also, how can one overlook the interview published on September 26, 1972, in the Munich weekly *Quick*? A Black September spokesman, in Beirut, had told the publication: "We have anti-Zionist friends all over the world, and can strike any time we want. The sky is full of German planes." After the hijacking, Federal Interior Minister Genscher stated, "We put sixty security specialists at Lufthansa's disposal. Its president, Herr Culmann, hesitated. He was afraid of discouraging business."

The trial of the three Olympic Village survivors promised to give off some sparks. The whole sorry mess would have had to be dragged out into the open. All kinds of responsibilities would have been exposed—all kinds of mistakes! In that connection, if a recording had been made of the sighs of relief uttered by West German VIPs when the three killers were turned over to the sky-pirates on October 29, 1972, the decibels would have hit a record high.

Following this incident, Mr. Ben Horin, the Israeli ambassador to Bonn, was called home "for consultation." Relations between Jerusalem and Bonn turned icy. But things soon got straightened out.

The delighted satisfaction of the six "innocent" Arab passengers at Tripoli that night was something to see! On that occasion, television was truly educational. Of course, one is always relieved at ceasing to be a hostage, and exuberance is likely to follow. But such defiance, and those V's for Victory, and the mimicking gestures . . .

The five terrorists, for their part, preferred the poetry of mystery, hiding their faces behind white veils. The five "non-Arabs" seemed relieved, but mainly eager not to be photographed. As for the crew, it was visibly upset and irate.

Afterword

Giving in to terrorism never pays off, and splatters a government with mud. I absolutely do not believe that a head of government such as Willy Brandt could be involved in covering up a fake skyjacking. Apart from his revulsion against such things, there is also the memory of the 6,000,000 Jews murdered by the Third Reich. In November 1969, the *Bundeskanzler* told this writer: "A German of my generation who was an enemy of Israel could be nothing but a criminal." His later official visit to Israel (June 6–10, 1973), was, moreover, enough to prove the Jewish state's esteem for the head of the G.F.R. regime. . . .

His trip, the first of its kind, was a huge success. Of course, there were some adverse reactions, but the discreet empathy of the masses for the *Bundeskanzler* with the frank blue-eyed openness surprised foreign observers. Stranger still, apparently: even those who protested did not mention the September 5, 1972, outrage. It was not forgotten, by any means. For this people never forgets. But it would not dream of holding the Germans responsible for Arab terrorism, and it was grateful to the Chancellor for not having made a deal with the killers.

All of that being so, did anything occur at the lower levels of German government, or within Lufthansa, insofar as the three captured fedayeen were concerned? I mean: Were there any dealings with El Fatah? . . . *Chi lo sa?*

Around 11:00 AM, on Sunday, October 29, 1972, a handwritten paper, adorned with a seal showing an undernourished eagle, was put into the mailbox of Agence France-Presse at Beirut. It claimed credit for the hijacking of the Lufthansa 727 for the "Organization of Arab National Youth for the Liberation of Palestine."

The two air-pirates apparently had not been let in on that secret, for according to Dr. Bruno Merk—still the Interior Minister of the *Land* of Bavaria—they indicated on several occasions that they belonged to Black September. Informed circles at Tripoli appear to have confirmed that.

And yet, they were the most grandiose, finest, happiest, most exciting Olympic Games in all history.

One hundred and twenty-two nations participating; 7,147 actual

457

competitors, including 1,070 women; 3,028 officials; 1,109 medals; 313 national records and 37 world records broken.

Das Deutschland des Friedens! (The Germany of Peace!)

Then—4:00 AM, September 5, 1972.

Out, damned spot! Out, I say!

Go to Munich. It's a very beautiful city—unforgettable.

APPENDIX I

Cast of Characters

Israelis in Olympic Village

Don Alon—fencer
David Marc Berger—American-born weight lifter
Zeev Friedman—weight lifter
Yossef Gutfreund—wrestling judge
Eliezer Halfin—wrestler
Henry Hershkowitz—rifle shot
Dr. Mattityahu Kranz—medical officer
Shaul Ladani—walker
Shmuel Lalkin—delegation head; President, Israel Sports Federation
Yossef Romano—weight lifter
Amitzur Shapira—track coach
Kehat Shorr—rifle coach
Zelig Shtroch—rifle shot
Mark Slavin—wrestler
Tuvia Sokolovsky (Sokolsky)—weight-lifting coach
Andrei Spitzer—fencing master
Yacov Springer—weight-lifting judge
Gad Tsobari—wrestler
Dr. Kurt Weigel—medical officer
Moshe Weinberger (Weinberg)—wrestling coach
Moshe Yehuda Weisenstein (Weinstain)—fencer

Arab Guerrillas

Tony (Guevara)—their leader
Abu Halla—also known as Abu Laban

459

Ibrahim Messaud Badran
Issa—Mohamed Mahmud Essafadi
Kader—Abdelkader el Denawi
Paulo—Saïd
Salah—Atif
Samir—Abdullah Mohamed Talifik

Other Israelis

Premier Golda Meir
Avigdor Bartle—member of investigation committee
Eliashiv Ben Horin—ambassador to Bonn
Elie Friedlander—yachting official
Chaim Glovinsky—Secretary-General, Israel Olympic Committee
Josef Inbar—President, Israel Olympic Committee
Moshe Kashti—member of investigation committee
Pinhas Koppel—head of investigation committee
Aaron Lahan—newspaperman
Yaïr Michaeli—yachting competitor
Shlomit Nir—woman swimmer
Yitzhak Nir—yachting competitor
Dan Schillon—head of TV sports
Esther Shahamorov—woman hurdler
Amiel Slavik—newspaperman
Gen. Zvi Zamir—head of Mossad; observer at Fürstenfeldbruck

Germans

Chancellor Willy Brandt
Klaus Bechler—helicopter copilot
Berthold Beitz—IOC head at Kiel; chief operating officer, Frederich
    Krupp enterprises
Lt. Paul Blankenhagel—helicopter pilot
Sigismund von Braun—State Secretary for foreign affairs
Capt. Walter Claussen—Lufthansa pilot
Herbert Culmann—chairman of the board of Lufthansa
Willi Daume—head of Organizing Committee; President, German
    Olympic Committee
Gunnar Ebel—helicopter copilot
Fräulein Echler—(or Fräulein Graes), policewoman-interpreter
Manfred Ewald—head of East German Olympic delegation; Minister
    of Sports, German Democratic Republic

Appendix I

Anton Fliegerbauer—Munich police brigadier
Paul Frank—Undersecretary of State
Hans-Dietrich Genscher—Minister of Interior, German Federal Republic
Dr. Alfons Goppel—Minister-President, State of Bavaria
Judge Otto Heindl—investigator for Munich prosecutor's office
Gustav Heinemann—President, German Federal Republic
Hans Klein—public-relations head for Organizing Committee
Georg Kronawitter—Mayor of Munich
Dr. Bruno Merk—Minister of Interior, State of Bavaria
Konrad Müller—border guard
Werner Nachmann—President, Central Council of German Jews; preliminary Olympic attaché for Israel
Capt. Reinhard Praus—helicopter pilot
Leni Riefenstahl—photographer; onetime official Hitler film maker
Capt. Gerd Scharnhorst—pilot attached to Fürstenfeldbruck air base
Walter Scheel—Foreign Minister, German Federal Republic
Dr. Manfred Schreiber—Police Commissioner, City of Munich
Hans-Georg Steltzer—German ambassador to Cairo
Franz-Josef Strauss—head of CSU party in Bavaria
Walter Tröger—Mayor of Olympic Village; Secretary-General, German Olympic Committee
Hans-Jochen Vogel—Vice-President, Organizing Committee; former Mayor of Munich
Georg Wolf—head of Munich security police

Others

Yasir Arafat—head of El Fatah
Daoud Barakat—Yemeni diplomat, involved with Black September
Comte Jean de Beaumont—Vice-President, IOC; French
Avery Brundage—President, IOC; American
Fuad Chemali—late Black Septembrist
Abdelaziz Elshafei—Egyptian delegate to Olympic Games
Luis Wolfgang Friedmann—Uruguayan delegation official
George Haines—Mark Spitz' ex-coach
Mohammed Khadif—head of Arab League in Bonn
Salah Khalaf—Yasir Arafat's second in command (alias Abu Ayad)
Lord Killanin (Michael Morris)—President-Elect, IOC; Irish
Mahmoud Mestiri—Tunisian ambassador to Bonn
Gamal Abdel Nasser—late President of Egypt
A. de Oliveira Sales—head of International Swimming Federation

THE BLOOD OF ISRAEL

Fakhry al Omari—an El Fatah leader
Daniel Rocher—head of sports service for Agence France-Presse
Elissa Saadé—widow of Faud Chemali
Anwar el-Sadat—President of Egypt
Juan Antonio Samaranch—Spanish member of IOC Executive Board
Aziz Sedki—Prime Minister of Egypt
Alexandru Siperco—Rumanian member of IOC
Mark Spitz—Jewish-American swimmer; winner of seven Olympic gold medals, an all-time record
A. D. Touny—Egyptian member of IOC
Ramon Young—head of Hong Kong delegation to the Games

APPENDIX II

The Housing of the Teams

CONNOLLYSTRASSE: 4-6, Rumania; 8-12, Italy; 12, Puerto Rico; 14-16, Hungary; 18, Burma, Luxembourg; 20-24, German Democratic Republic; 26, Togo, Tunisia, Libya; 28, Argentina; 5, Gabon, Vietnam; 7, Sudan, Liberia, Saudi Arabia; 9, New Zealand; 11, Bolivia; 15, Republic of Korea; 17, Mali; 19 & 29, Bahamas; 25 & 29, Canada; 27, Trinidad & Tobago, Sri Lanka (Ceylon), Cambodia, Swaziland; 31, Israel, Hong Kong, Uruguay; 33, Zambia, Dahomey.

HELENE-MAYER-RING: 10, Portugal, Rhodesia; 14, Ghana, Guatemala, Panama, British Honduras, Netherlands Antilles, Dominican Republic, Lesotho, Sierra Leone, Congo, Philippines, Ecuador, Madagascar, Malaysia, Pakistan, Albania, Jamaica, Fiji Islands, Ivory Coast, Malta, Peru, Virgin Islands, Paraguay.

NADISTRASSE: 4 & 6, Sweden; 6, Chile; 8, Iran; 10, Turkey; 12-16, U.S.; 16 & 18, Yugoslavia; 18, Colombia; 20 & 22, Spain; 22, Haiti, Upper Volta, Liechtenstein; 24, Belgium; 26-32, USSR; 7-15, Thailand; 17-25, Lebanon; 27-29, Monaco; 31-33, Afghanistan; 35 & 47, Switzerland; 37, Niger; 47-53, Senegal; 55-67, India; 93 & 127, Morocco; 113-117, San Marino; 129, Mongolia; 131-137, France.

STRASSEBERGER STRASSE: 2-6, German Federal Republic; 8, Nigeria; 8 & 10, Great Britain; 10, Guyana; 12, Republic of China (Taiwan); 12 & 14, Australia; 16-18, Czechoslovakia; 20, Brazil, Nicaragua, Malawi; 22 & 24, Denmark; 24, Chad; 24 & 26, Norway; 26,

Uganda; 28 & 30, Finland; 30, Iceland; 32 & 34, Japan; 34, Indonesia; 34 & 42, Poland; 42, Kenya; 9, Austria, Kuwait, Venezuela, Nepal; 9 & 25, Greece; 11-13, Algeria; 15-17, Cameroon; 23, Tanzania; 25, Costa Rica, El Salvador; 27-29, Singapore; 31-35, Ireland; 47, Netherlands; 57 & 85, Barbados; 73 & 93, Ethiopia; 95 & 137, Cuba; 97 & 99, Egypt; 99, Syria; 101, Bermuda, Somalia; 101 & 129, Mexico; 125, People's Democratic Republic of Korea; 139, Bulgaria.